# BUILDING THE STRATEGICALLY-RESPONSIVE ORGANIZATION

# THE STRATEGIC MANAGEMENT SERIES

Series Editor
HOWARD THOMAS

---

STRATEGIC THINKING
Leadership and the Management of Change
Edited by
JOHN HENDRY AND GERRY JOHNSON
WITH JULIA NEWTON

COMPETENCE-BASED COMPETITION
Edited by
GARY HAMEL AND AIMÉ HEENE

BUILDING THE STRATEGICALLY-RESPONSIVE ORGANIZATION
Edited by
HOWARD THOMAS, DON O'NEAL, ROD WHITE AND DAVID HURST

Further titles in preparation

THE STRATEGIC MANAGEMENT SERIES

# BUILDING THE STRATEGICALLY-RESPONSIVE ORGANIZATION

Edited by

HOWARD THOMAS, DON O'NEAL, ROD WHITE
AND
DAVID HURST

JOHN WILEY & SONS
Chichester · New York · Brisbane · Toronto · Singapore

Published 1994 by John Wiley & Sons Ltd,
Baffins Lane, Chichester,
West Sussex PO19 1UD, England

Telephone (+44) 243 779777

*Other Wiley Editorial Offices*

John Wiley & Sons, Inc., 605 Third Avenue,
New York, NY 10158-0012, USA

Jacaranda Wiley Ltd, 33 Park Road, Milton,
Queensland, 4064, Australia

John Wiley & Sons (Canada) Ltd, 22 Worcester Road,
Rexdale, Ontario M9W 1L1, Canada

John Wiley & Sons (SEA) Pte Ltd, 37 Jalan Pemimpin #05-04,
Block B, Union Industrial Building, Singapore 2057

*Library of Congress Cataloging-in-Publication Data*

Building the strategically-responsive organization / edited by Howard
Thomas . . . [et al.].
    p.   cm. — (Strategic management series)
    "An outgrowth of the 11th Annual International Strategic
Management Society Conference, titled 'The Greening of Strategy-
-Sustaining Performance,' . . . held in Toronto, Canada, in October,
1991"—Pref.
    Includes bibliographical references and index.
    ISBN 0-471-94399-1
    1. Industrial management—Congresses.   2. Industry—Environmental
aspects—Congresses.   3. Strategic planning—Congresses.
I. Thomas, Howard, 1943–  .   II. International Strategic Management
Society Conference (11th : 1991 : Toronto, Ont.)   III. Series.
HD29.B85   1994
658.4′012—dc20                                                    93–50782
                                                                      CIP

*British Library Cataloguing in Publication Data*

A catalogue record for this book is available from the British Library

ISBN 0-471-94399-1

Typeset in 10.5/12 pt Palatino by Acorn Bookwork, Salisbury, Wiltshire
Printed and bound in Great Britain by Bookcraft (Bath) Ltd.

# Contents

# Contributors

JOHN B. ALVORD
*Procter & Gamble, P.O. Box 599, Cincinnati, OH 45201, USA.*

PROFESSOR GEORGE BAIN
*London Business School, Sussex Place, Regent's Park, London, NW1 4SA, UK.*

JANE A. BARNETT
*The Andrew Jurgens Co., 2535 Spring Grove Avenue, Cincinnati, OH 45214, USA.*

ANDREW CAMPBELL
*Ashridge Strategic Management Centre, 17 Portland Place, London, W1N 3AF, UK.*

BALA CHAKRAVARTHY
*INSEAD, Boulevard de Constance, Fontainebleau Cedex, F-77305, France.*

DR JON A. CHILINGERIAN
*Brandeis University, Florence Heller Graduate School for Advanced Studies in Social Welfare, P.O. Box 9110, Waltham, MA 02254-9110, USA.*

ARNOLD C. COOPER
*Purdue University, Krannert Graduate School of Management, West Lafayette, IN 47907, USA.*

DR ROLAND DEISER
*CAST Management Consultants, Eckpergasse 31, A-1180, Vienna.*

Yves Doz
*INSEAD, Boulevard de Constance, Fontainebleau Cedex, F-77305, France.*

Carolyn P. Egri
*Faculty of Business Administration, Simon Fraser University, Burnaby, British Columbia, Canada, VSA 156.*

Dr Avi Fiegenbaum
*Faculty of Industrial Engineering and Management, Technion Israel Institute of Technology, Technion City, Haifa 3200, Israel.*

Dr Peter J. Frost
*Faculty of Commerce, University of British Columbia, 2053 Main Mall, Vancouver, British Columbia, Canada, U6T 132.*

Michael Goold
*Ashridge Strategic Management Centre, 17 Portland Place, London, W1N 3AF, UK.*

Professor Vijay Govindarajan
*Professor of International Business, The Tuck School, Dartmouth College, Hanover, NH 03755-1798, Germany.*

Dr Anil K. Gupta
*University of Maryland, College of Business and Management, College Park, MD 20742, USA.*

Jan Hall
*64 Courtney Street, London, SE11 5PQ, UK.*

Dr Gary Hamel
*London Business School, Sussex Place, Regent's Park, London, NW1 4SA, UK.*

Dr Sam Hariharan
*Department of Management and Organization, Graduate School of Business Administration, University of Southern California, Los Angeles, CA 90089-1421, USA.*

Stuart Hart
*Department of Corporate Strategy and Organizational Behavior, School*

*of Business Administration, University of Michigan, Ann Arbor, MI 48109, USA.*

BO HELLGREN
*Department of Management and Economics, Linkoping University, S-58183 Linkoping, Sweden.*

RIKARD LARSSON
*Department of Business Administration, School of Economics and Management, Lund University, P.O. Box 7080, S-22007, Lund, Sweden.*

R. IAN LENNOX
*President and Chief Executive Officer, Monsanto Canada Inc., 2330 Argentia Road, P.O. Box 787, Streetsville, Mississauga, Ontario, Canada, L5M 2G4.*

MARTIN LINDELL
*Swedish School of Economics and Business Administration, Arkadiagatan 22, SF 00100 Helsinki, Finland.*

PETER LORANGE
*Norwegian School of Management, P.O. Box 580, N-1301 Sandvika, Norway.*

DR JOHN MCARTHUR
*Harvard Business School, Soldiers Field, Morgan Hall 125, Boston, MA 02163, USA.*

DR LEIF MELIN
*Department of Management and Economics, Linkoping University, S-58183 Linkoping, Sweden.*

PROFESSOR HENRY MINTZBERG
*Faculty of Management, McGill University, 1001 Sherbrooke Street West, Montreal, Canada, H3A 1G5.*

TOSHIKAZU MITSUDA
*Sharp Corporation, Sonninstrasse 3, 2000 Hamburg 1, Germany.*

SUSANNE ÖSTLUND
*Stockholm School of Economics, Department of Marketing Distribution and Industrial Dynamics, P.O. Box 6501, S-113 83 Stockholm, Sweden.*

Dr C.K. Prahalad
*Graduate School of Business Administration, University of Michigan, Ann Arbor, MI 48109, USA*

Dan Schendel
*Krannert Graduate School of Management, Purdue University, West Lafayette, IN 47907, USA.*

Professor Françoise L. Simon
*Columbia Business School, Uris Hall, 116th Broadway, New York, NY 10027, USA.*

Dr Clayton G. Smith
*Oklahoma City University, Heinders School of Business, Oklahoma City, OK 73106, USA.*

Dr Michael Spence
*Graduate School of Business, Stanford University, Stanford, CA 94305-5015, USA.*

Paul J. Verdin
*INSEAD, Boulevard de Constance, Fontainebleau Cedex, F-77305, France.*

Kim Warren
*London Business School, Sussex Place, Regent's Park, London NW1 4SA, UK.*

Professor Peter J. Williamson
*London Business School, Sussex Place, Regent's Park, London, NW1 4SA, UK.*

Timothy C. Woods
*Director of Technical Services, Nestlé Enterprises Ltd, 1185 Eglinton Avenue, Don Mills, Ontario, Canada, M3C 3C7.*

# Series Preface

The purpose of the Strategic Management Society is to bring together, on a worldwide basis, academics, business practitioners and consultants, for the development and dissemination of information.

Recognizing that the membership of the Society is a relatively small, albeit important and representative, sample of the total population of academics, business people and consultants, the Strategic Management Series of publications is intended to play a key role in bringing information and ideas on strategic issues that are being discussed in the Society to the attention of the broader interested audience. To that end, the purpose of the series is to illustrate 'The Best of Strategic Management' by publishing three types of books:

1. an annual volume based on a selection of papers from the annual Strategic Management Society conference. Selection may be based on either a particular theme or on a collection of 'best' papers from the conference, whichever seems to the editors to best exemplify that particular conference.
2. volumes based on selected papers. Each volume is selected from mini-conferences on topical issues in strategy.
3. short monographs on current research or novel conceptual frameworks identified, chosen and periodically reviewed by an editorial committee.

This volume is the first in the series representing Strategic Management Society annual conferences. Papers presented at these conferences tend to address not just the conference theme but, more importantly, to discuss 'live' issues—those that are currently confronting the Society and its members. In this context presenters feel more freedom to step outside the boilerplate-type issues and formats that sometimes tend to constrain discussion, and utilize these conferences as an opportunity to take chances—to address issues that are more 'interesting', though perhaps less conventional.

This gives the editors a broader range of ideas, thoughts and themes from which to select papers, and the opportunity to make available an interesting and intriguing selection of conversations to anyone interested in joining the conversations or in just reading about them.

Attending a conference at which a number of presentations are occurring simultaneously requires attendees to make choices and, in the process, inevitably miss some sessions that they may have found interesting. This results in most conference presentations playing to audiences of only a few or, at most, a few dozen of those who might be interested. The volumes of this series will offer the opportunity for hundreds of interested individuals to, in effect, attend several of the most interesting presentations from any given conference, while giving much wider exposure to those papers deemed most likely to be of interest to a broader audience.

This particular volume is an outgrowth of the 11th Annual International Strategic Management Society Conference, entitled 'The Greening of Strategy—Sustaining Performance', which was held in Toronto, Canada, in October 1991.

The theme of the conference was meant to focus participants' energies on the questions of managing for sustainable performance. The greening theme can be interpreted in different ways, at different levels. At one level it deals with the strategic challenges presented by environmental and ecological concerns. At a second level, greening deals with the shifts in strategic thinking required as organizations strive for sustainable performance in turbulent environments. At yet another level it encompasses our changing views about strategy and the strategy process; the greening of the managerial mind.

So many fine papers were presented that a decision was made, early on, not to attempt to select a set of 'best' papers from the conference. Judging which papers are best is highly subjective and is, moreover, unlikely to provide the balance of content that will make the volume interesting and useful to a broad range of members.

With that in mind, a theme was selected that is not only consistent with the thrust of the conference but also strikes at the heart of the Society's *raison d'etre*—'Building the Strategically-Responsive Organization'. Papers were then selected that seemed representative of some of the most significant issues currently facing business strategists. These included education, strategic intent, competitive dynamics, industry evolution, strategic change, value chains, and globalization. Balancing theoretical and practical perspectives was an equally important consideration.

The result is, we feel, an interesting and effective integration of strategic perspectives that exemplifies many of the most important issues facing strategic management, both now and in the immediate future.

An eclectic ensemble of contributors, including academics, business executives, consultants, and business school administrators, addresses one of the Society's primary concerns—building and maintaining bridges between management theory and business practice.

Editorial commentary provides integration among the papers included, and references some of the more appropriate previous research in each subject area, for the reader's convenience in supplementary reading. The result is not just a volume of currently relevant papers, to be read once and set aside, but a reference manual that explores currently-relevant issues and links them with previous research streams.

HOWARD THOMAS
*Series Editor*

# Introduction

# Changing Business Environments

A primary concern of the Strategic Management Society is building and maintaining bridges between theory and practice. This involves, on the research side, generating and testing theories related to business and management and, on the practitioner side, learning about, understanding and applying tested theories to practice. No organization is more central to this integration of theory and practice than the business school.

In their plenary session 'The Greening of Business Schools', moderated by Henry Mintzberg, Deans George Bain of the London Business School, John McArthur of Harvard and Michael Spence of Stanford set an appropriate tone for the conference as they addressed the issues facing business schools, both currently and in the future. The challenges they foresee for business schools—including globalization, increased emphasis on learning (as opposed to teaching), academic/business partnerships, accelerating change and technological advancement—are remarkably similar to the strategic issues facing the primary consumers of their outputs—business practitioners and consultants.

The edited transcript of their session, which constitutes Chapter 1, is, then, a fitting and proper lead-in to this collection of papers and presentations which, the editors feel, exemplifies not only the spirit of the 1991 Strategic Management Society Conference, but also the purpose of the Society itself: to bring together, on a worldwide basis, academics, business practitioners and consultants, for the development and dissemination of information.

Discussions and presentations from all three perspectives are represented, and it quickly becomes apparent that their messages are equally germane to all three membership groups.

| Chapter 1 | The Greening of Business Schools<br>*George Bain, John McArthur, Michael Spence, Henry Mintzberg* |
|---|---|

Business education is undeniably undergoing substantial transformation or, in a sense, maturation. This maturation is occurring in all facets of business education—from undergraduate programs, to masters and executive education, to research, and to the training of new generations of teachers and researchers.

The reasons for the maturation of business education are manifold, but centre on the increasingly rapid pace of change within the business world itself. Technological, social and political change are speeding the evolution of economic activity. In response to these environmental pressures, the form and practice of business are changing. In turn, firms make clear that traditional approaches to management education have not kept pace. In response, in addition to developing their own education systems, businesses are asking schools to provide graduates with international understanding, modern perspectives on operational and functional areas, and an ethic of cooperation and the skills to support it. Firms are asking for new forms of education, such as extended on-site programs; new approaches, such as coordinated team teaching; and new topics, such as the strategic implications of continuous improvement.

Perhaps the most important request from business is for education that provides a truly integrated understanding of business. Disjointed curricula based on historically disjointed functional perspectives have received tremendous criticism. Management education has begun to respond, but there is a long way to go. To provide an integrative, interdisciplinary education, schools themselves are pursuing the removal of internal barriers, both practical and cultural, which hinder integration of teaching, research and understanding.

Business schools feel a degree of pressure unfamiliar and often uncomfortable to them. Viewed in a positive light, however, that pressure offers management education a wonderful evolutionary challenge, from which it may emerge a better partner for business.

# 1

# The Greening of Business Schools

GEORGE BAIN, JOHN MCARTHUR, MICHAEL SPENCE, HENRY MINTZBERG

*Henry:* The session is officially billed 'The Greening of Management Education', but it is really the Canadian Deans' Panel that you are watching. The deans of Harvard, Stanford, and London Business Schools are all Canadians, and in fact INSEAD nearly had a Canadian dean at one point, too, recently. [From the audience: 'They were saved!'] We have brought them all together in Toronto, of all places, to discuss management education.

I would like to express the difference between an American and a Canadian: an American, as somebody told me recently, says, 'Hey, get off my car,' and a Canadian says, 'Get off my car . . . eh?' And, in some ways, I think that characterizes the difference and may explain why all of these prestigious business schools have Canadian deans. All were raised in Canada, in one way or another, and all left for education abroad, in one way or another, and didn't come back except for visits. But I think all retained, as we will find out, Canadian character, in some respects.

Mike Spence, from Stanford, was actually born in the States, but of half-Canadian parents, came up to Canada, to Ontario, at quite a young age, spent his youth there and went off to do his undergraduate degree in the States at Princeton. And, in fact, there's a note in his CV that says that he played varsity hockey at Princeton. This is an important point (the principal of McGill Uni-

*Building the Strategically-Responsive Organization.*
Edited by H. Thomas, D. O'Neal, R. White and D. Hurst.
Copyright © 1994 the Strategic Management Society. Published 1994 by John Wiley & Sons Ltd.

versity played varsity hockey at Yale and he was Eric Segal's roommate, and if you put that together in terms of a book called *Love Story*, you might come to an interesting conclusion). John McArthur from Harvard did his bachelor's degree at UBC and then went off to Harvard to do his MBA and DBA. And George Bain did his undergraduate degree at Manitoba, was raised in Manitoba, in Winnipeg, and then did his PhD at Oxford. (I have a suspicion that somewhere in Beijing there is a great big room that has a big map of the world around it, and there is a little pin in every village of more than 3000 people that doesn't have a Chinese restaurant, so they keep track of where they should put the next one. Well, in Montreal there is a similar kind of room with a similar map and we have got a little pin for every business school that doesn't yet have a Canadian dean. There are some Canadian business schools on that map too. We're off to conquer the dean market.)

Well, let me tell you, if any industry has a dominant design, to use Abernathy and Utterback's expression, my suspicion is that it is management education. Even though there are different approaches—and I think Harvard and Stanford represent the poles in some respects—in terms of the kinds of core courses that are offered and so on, there is a dominant design. And I think that it has come under a fair amount of criticism recently. And so we would like to address that here.

The format is as follows: I will ask each dean, in alphabetical order, to talk for about ten minutes on the greening of management education, in terms of how they view it in general, and particularly what they are thinking about in terms of change in management education within their own schools. Then I have got one nasty question for each of them. I have already warned them what it will be. After that, we want to address, briefly, assuming a sample of three is enough to draw conclusions (for me it's more than enough), why Canadian deans are taking over the prestigious business schools. What is it about being Canadian? And then we will open it up to questions from the audience.

*George:* The only Canadian dean besides myself that I knew until this morning was John McArthur, and I had assumed the reason why there are so many Canadian deans was that besides having to have the wisdom of Solomon, the courage of a lion, and the cunning of Machiavelli, you needed the stomach of a goat. And I am well equipped in that respect, and indeed have spent the last two years growing into my job. But, when I looked at

Mike this morning, I wondered if he was really doing his job. Mind you, he has only been in post a year.

I understand the Society is composed of thoughtful practitioners and insightful scholars. I have been looking for an audience like that for over 20 years and I am glad to have found it here. We have been asked to speak, as Henry said, on the greening of business schools. Rod White and David Hurst, in the conference brochure, said that greening has several levels of meaning, and I was glad to discover the second level which they mentioned: that it deals with shifts of strategic thinking required as organizations strive for sustainable performance in turbulent environments. Business schools have been in turbulent environments for the last decade, and also during the current decade. The reason is simple. Business schools, like most organizations, are products of their environment—in our case, the world of business—and the business environment has also been extremely turbulent over that period. It has forced business schools to look at three basic questions: How do we more effectively internationalize ourselves? How do we develop curricula that are not only rigorous but also relevant? and, finally, How do we develop more effective learning partnerships with business? It is these three themes that I want to touch on. And, in spite of retaining a strong Canadian accent, I will probably approach these more from a European than a North American perspective.

First, internationalization: the one thing I have never met, in the last four or five years, is a dean who says he is *not* trying to internationalize his school. Everyone, whether they come from the smallest place in the Midwest or a large international center, is into the business of internationalizing. I personally believe that there is more rhetoric than reality, and I also believe that there are limits to which most schools *can* internationalize. The reason is that there are two basic requirements for internationalizing a school: one is structure, and the other is curriculum. The structural aspects are more difficult for some schools to achieve than others. If you want a truly international school, then you need to have a student body in which no one nationality dominates. The same applies to faculties and their research, and to governing bodies and advisory committees. Some business schools, depending on where they are located—London is fortunate in this respect, being in a major international city—can achieve this structural aspect more easily than others. The second aspect of internationalization is curriculum. Almost every school can achieve internationalism, to a greater or lesser extent, through international materials, teaching foreign languages, and international exchanges and internships.

The second theme also concerns the curriculum. Managers increasingly need to have corporate vision and imagination, to be generalists rather than specialists, to possess process skills and a flexibility to manage change, and to be sensitive and adaptable to different cultures. The traditional business school curriculum, which came out of the Foundation reports in North America in the late 1950s and early 1960s, is ill suited to producing managers with these qualities. To begin with, it is too functionally fragmented. Too much teaching and learning is compartmentalized into distinct disciplines. Students leave business schools thinking that there are accounting problems, finance problems, marketing problems, production problems, and so on. What they find, however, are business problems which involve several of these functional areas and which require managers to manage the interfaces between them.

The curriculum is also characterized by process fragmentation. Harold Leavitt has argued that the management process consists of three steps: pathbreaking—creating a vision and setting objectives; problem solving—finding solutions to the problems that obstruct the path; and implementation—working through people to translate the solution from analysis into action. Business schools have concentrated mainly on problem solving. They have done so because it lends itself, to a greater extent than pathbreaking or implementation, to quantification and rigorous analysis.

What is now needed is more interdisciplinary, issue-based, and project-based teaching, a greater stress on learning and less on teaching, and more emphasis on pathbreaking and implementation, including such process skills as negotiation and team building. In short, business schools need to develop a more balanced relationship between analysis and the more subjective aspects of management. And since the extent to which some of these aspects of management can be learned in an academic setting is limited, business schools need to look more explicitly and systematically for the requisite personal qualities in selecting students and participants to their programs.

The final theme concerns the business schools' partnerships with business. No matter how good the general education of managers or how much they learn in business schools, a large part of what they need to know can be acquired only by *working* as a manager. Hence, companies have a key role to play in management education. They need to foster an attitude and an environment of lifelong learning, both on and off the job. They also need to emphasize the role of the manager as a mentor, a trainer and a developer of human resources. In short, they need to become 'learning companies,' because increasingly their only sustainable competitive advantage is their ability to learn faster than their competitors. Business schools and companies are increasingly appreciating the significance of this point. Many are attempting to develop learning partnerships—partnerships that emphasize learning for groups as well as for individuals—by developing company-specific and other learning programs.

To conclude, when I look around business schools in Europe and North America, I see them trying to re-balance the two basic ideologies, the two basic models, that are inherent in any professional school: firstly, what might be called the academic—where the objective is the generation of new knowledge and the reference group is other academics—and, secondly, the vocational—where the objective is the passing on of current best practice and the reference group is practitioners. In the past, business schools have tended to emphasize one or the other. In North America it has largely been the academic, whereas in Europe it has primarily been the vocational. Increasingly, however, the major schools are now trying to achieve a better balance between these two models.

*John:* Well, last spring one of my colleagues, an editor, was leaving the school after four or five years and came to see me on the way out. So I asked him if he had any good stories or if anything interesting had happened to him while he was there and he told me the following story, which I think is sort of illustrative of what all of us have to deal with. When he arrived in the summer of 1987, he was given an office in what used to be the attic of the building. After a few hours in this room he found that it was very noisy and he called the maintenance staff, who came over and said, 'No, that is fine, that is what it is, it has always been there and don't worry about it.' And the next summer the noise came on again, and he said that by then he had enough self-confidence to really raise hell about it, and so he made it a project for the early summer. Eventually the carpenters and electricians came over and they opened a hole in the wall and behind this wall, he said, they all crawled through. What had happened, in 1955, was that the school had moved the faculty club from the room below this attic to another building, and up in the attic had been a ventilation system for sucking cigarette smoke out and blowing it out through the roof. Well, sometime along the way we must have been short of space and so this attic was recovered for offices, and they boarded up the sides of the roof, and this machine was in there and they had forgotten to unhook it. So, for 32 years it ran. He said, 'When we went in there with a flashlight, hanging on a string on a 2 × 4, on a stud, was the thing that the maintenance guy had checked off every year, signed his initials that he had greased the bearings and everything was OK, and that went on from 1937 until 1955, and then there were no more signatures because the club had moved and in the meantime the roof had been redone and the ceiling had been plastered over, so there was this damned machine in there and the only thing was that no one had ever unplugged it, and it ran on and on and on.'

Basically, that is what deans do: they listen for these machines—usually they're called tenured, sometimes they're programs or research programs or courses—but in any case, we are all surrounded, every organization here today, with these machines that got plastered up and people forgot about them and nobody unplugged them. And as long as the economy is booming or it is easy to raise funds for universities or you can increase tuitions twice as fast as inflation, and so forth, you can leave these machines alone. But that is not how things work in the decade of the 90s. So I want to identify four or five of the machines that I think I can hear and I think that all of us, to some degree, need to deal with, although, like George, I recognize that there is a tremendous range of institutions here serving very different needs and having quite different circumstances.

Let me start with what I think, in the United States, at least, is going to be a really big deal over the next few years, and that is particularly important for universities of the kind that Mike and I are now at: the attack on universities. I think the public has had it with people like us in places like ours. If you follow the popular press at all, or if you pay attention to what several parts of Congress are actually spending their time on and looking at, I think you'll agree that the kinds of questions that are in the minds of parents, taxpayers, employers and everybody who has a stake in this enterprise certainly have to do with cost. And our costs— the costs of running the place, and consequently the prices we charge for things—have raced ahead of most other institutions and what is going on in most other markets. I think there is a great concern, in particular in large research institutions like

Stanford and many others, about access. You can hardly find anybody whose kid can get into one of these places, even though they are, I think, among the most open institutions in the world. I mean, all you have to do is get admitted and you get financed and the rest of it, but nevertheless the imbalance between the demand to get in and the supply is enormous, so most people feel that there is no payoff in it for them. Their families, their kids cannot get in. The challenge is about the balance between research and teaching. I think many people feel that we are not interested in teaching their kids; we are interested in doing research and in spending time at conferences like this and with each other— almost anything but working with young kids in the classroom. There is a challenge to faculty workloads and indeed, I think, in these particular kinds of institutions, faculty workloads are very different than they were 20 or 30 years ago. There is a challenge around the theme of conflict of interest and conflict of commitment. There is growing concern about the difficulty that the universities, the schools, and we as faculty members have in balancing the work we are doing for the institution and for our students with the work we are doing for ourselves, and between the financing of our research and the subjects we are studying: these things are sometimes hopelessly conflicted. There is a challenge to standards of behavior. As far as cheating is concerned, there have been some notorious cases in the United States around the research venture, which have created a lot of questioning about our capacity in these large collegial universities, with this tradition of academic freedom, and of being undermanaged or not managed at all, to manage this domain of cheating. In the past few weeks in America, but I think it has been going on for quite a few years now, is the challenge around harassment, whether it is sexual or by race or by other things, but in any case, a sense that we are not yet leading the pack in how we deal with many of the people that work and study in these institutions. We are basically white, male and middle-aged and that is not very much like what the student body is or the group of people—professionals and support staff—that work in these institutions.

And, finally, I would mention at least my sense—and I get hammered, I would say, daily—about the relevance of our work, not just to business, but also to society's needs. The concern in the United States is about the public education system, health care, the aging, the communities—all of these things. I think, basically, the universities—in any case, our kind of university—have stayed out of it. I think the business schools are going to have to, in these areas I am thinking of, become involved in working out a new period of stability with the rest of society, that pays our bills. I don't think they are going to support us unless we are seen to be a real player in trying to get at some of these really profound problems that are almost the cancer of our society. So, the first main thing that I think is going to become very important, 10 years from now looking back, is this that I am calling the attack on the universities.

Secondly, I want to mention faculty. From the resource side there has been a profound change over the past couple of decades in where we are getting people for the faculties of the two thousand or so business schools in North America. In our own case, if you look at where we have recruited most of our entry level faculty, assistant professors, over the last 25 years, 80% of those PhDs are from overseas. This is a tremendous thing from some points of view. And it certainly reflects no more than that they're the strongest applicants applying to the pools. But the other side of the coin is that our kids have figured out that this is a lousy profession and they are not interested, so are not in PhD programs and we are not getting them. In our case, we had an increase in applications for the three doctoral programs we were involved with at the school this past year, we think largely relating to the economic conditions in the United States. But even if it is beginning to move in the other direction, which I doubt myself, it is going to take years before it begins to change. So, we have had to try—and we are all going to have to try—very hard to go where the outstanding people are, whether or not they have gone through these PhD programs, to try to attract some of them into our faculties. We are going to have to deal with the imbalance between the diversity of our students and the communities we are in, and these white male faculties we have now. Increasingly, they are going to have to come from other pools—women and minorities—and I think also from overseas.

In addition, I think the tenure system has to go in the schools that all four of us sitting here come from. There is no way that it is going to be possible to make it through the kind of changes that George suggests, and I am sure Mike will suggest. The change that has to take place is profound. And there is no way we can do it unless we can find some way to manage the tenure system. In the United States in just two more years there will be no mandatory retirement age for professors. This is a death knell for universities like ours that try to live at the cutting edge. It is the death knell because it means you have lifetime employment, and in a way that the Japanese never dreamed of. It is until you die. I'll have a contract until the day I drop as long as I can make it to January 1994, because the federal law says you cannot be pushed out because of age. Retirement has to be on the basis of assessments of your work, which I think is the right principle. But tenure says you can never be assessed once you get over the barrier. So, the two things don't fit and we just have to find a way around that for these kinds of universities.

I also want to mention the growing diversity. You read regularly the statistics about what the work-force is going to look like in 2000 or 2010. In the *Economist*, coming up in the plane last night, I was reading a couple of statistics in relationship to the United States saying that 15% of the entering work-force in 2005 would be white males. I think this is an important consideration for our institutions as we change them. But, I think our capacity to manage that diversity and to be able to successfully pull off the kind of changes that George, for example, outlined around the curriculum and the research and the teaching is a real challenge.

Thirdly, I want to mention technology. In our case, if you take software, video, computers, networks, telecommunications, the cost in our budget is about $20 million out of $115 million. Three or four years ago, it was $5 million. And if you just let go of the reins, and let it happen, it would double in two more years. There will be a revolution before us as we all try to figure out how to relate to all of that. I have this vision—no, it is not a vision, it is a nightmare—of faculty that are teaching all around the world via satellite and via all of these other things, while we make tremendous investments year after year in research and in the development of the people that are doing our version of this global networking. We have basically lost control of a faculty, and we have lost control of our expenses, yet when you see the material—when I look at what my colleagues are doing with some of these—it is breathtaking. The days when students sit around and read cases on paper, or read whatever they read on paper, are gone. They start out with Nintendo when they are two, and they are working with all of these things for 20 years before they get near our place. I think the kind of materials that I can see my colleagues and many of yours developing is where we are heading.

For example, in the middle management program—one of our

programs where we have centered our main development activity around teaching materials—we are spending a million dollars a class session. Now, I am quite sure that as we learn how to do it, the cost will come down by half or by two-thirds (or it may even double!). But it may well come down. The investment is enormous, and, yet, it is going to happen. The kids aren't going to work with this stuff, our technologies that we are all using, now. We have had it. And this is the last decade for it. So, I think this whole technology thing that a lot of the companies here are dealing with, we have got to deal with it too. And I don't think we are prepared. I actually don't think we are going to have a very important part in it when it finally settles because we can't generate the resources in these kind of institutions to pay for it. So I think in order to lay off the cost there will be some kind of intermediary organizations that are able to reach global markets that do it.

In the curriculum, I would underscore what George said. I would add that there is pressure on at least these kind of schools to get involved with what is wrong with society. I think they are going to push us, and are pushing us, and that we are going to have to be successful in dealing with things like the environment, the work-force, moral and ethical standards of behavior, community service, and international aspects none of which fits into any of the existing compartments that we have all inherited from the past. Neither the disciplines nor the traditional functional breakdowns in business schools of marketing, production, accounting, and so forth relate to any of that. And I think we have to find some way to do it without simply adding onto our organizations, making them bigger in order to have the people to do this and have these damned machines, these old fields and old disciplines, pumping away in the back room doing nothing that anyone knows about. We cannot afford to do it. And we cannot manage the conflict inside the organization if we leave those machines sitting there. We have got to deal with them in order to get into these other areas.

The last thing I will mention is funding. Maybe the market will take off this afternoon and bail us out one more time. But I think if you look around in the United States and certainly in Canada, in my mind, the resources that have been lavished on our kind of institutions over the last 20 or 30 years have come to an end. And as I have said earlier, unless this society feels that we are making a different kind of contribution than we have been, we are going to find it very hard in this competition for scarce public resources. And looking at our universities—I don't think it matters whether one looks in Canada and the United States at either the large private universities or the ones that aren't private—how they are funded isn't very different. Harvard is a private university, and it gets hundreds and hundreds of millions of dollars a year from the federal government and from other government bodies as well. So, our business schools are going to be sitting in the middle of this nexus where everybody is really pressured for funds, and our capacity to do what we need to do is going to be going on in a decade where there is less to do it with. Therefore, in my mind, these other kind of issues that I have tried to underscore become so important. We can't afford to carry all of this any more and do what we have to do. So, I think it is going to be a real challenge for our generation to get out of the way, let the young people come along and let these places change. And I think that has got to be the same perspective that all of you—from industry, and from some of the other professions serving industry—must have from now on.

*Mike:* I don't agree with anything George said, but I agree with everything John said because I used to work for him. That is not true. Mark Twain was never a fan of scholarly attitudes or works and he once, in holding a book written by a faculty-type that had been handed to him, said, 'This book fills a much-needed gap.' I am afraid, having been flying for two nights in a row, trying to internationalize our school, George, that I may do the same thing. But I would like to focus on an aspect of the challenge that John and George have adverted to, one that falls more in the area of the development of science and technology in the substantive areas of product development, manufacturing, and so on. Let me try to put this in a frame of reference.

We are in a service industry and we try to serve our students, the participants in our programs, and the business community on a worldwide basis. The issues that confront us are really, I think, issues that represent challenges faced by our principal customers and clients. Now, I should tell you that I spent six years as the Dean of Faculty of Arts and Sciences at Harvard. This is the part of Harvard that includes much of science and engineering; it is Harvard College in the Academic Graduate Schools. So, that means two things. Firstly, I was away from watching and participating to some extent in business matters outside the university for a period of time. Secondly, I learned a great deal about those disciplines and how they are funded. I dropped out, in a sense, in 1984 and came back last year to see what had happened. What is so striking is the acceleration in the rate of change of the structure of both business organizations and markets. Though I am no economic or business historian, in the sense of Al Chandler, I think it is probably true that you have to go back to the turn of the century to find a period of change like this. Evidence is everywhere. There is a growing collection of industries in which the product cycle is measured in months rather than years: changes of a factor of ten. The organization structures are flattening out. The relationships of people who work in the organizations—to the organization itself, and to each other—are changing. The level of interest in—serious interest—in human resources management and the perceived centrality of that is really quite different from what I remember when I, in a sense, dropped out. Now, I don't pretend, nor do I know many thoughtful people who do pretend, to understand all the forces that are at work here. And I don't think it is worthwhile, short of taking a big aside, to try to get at them, but I do think there have been important innovations on a worldwide basis in management, generally, and in the management of particular functions and the interfaces between them. I am sure that one of the powerful forces let loose in the world is the one John discussed, the information technologies. And there is a tremendous acceleration in the production of scientific knowledge upstream from the private sector. So let me talk a bit about that general area for a moment, just to make a couple of points.

First, let me focus on manufacturing and operations, product development and the management of technology, and on information systems as issues that confront businesses. Two points: first of all, there is enormous variance across businesses, corporations, and industries in performance of these dimensions. That by itself is a sure sign of change—enormous variation, from best practice to having barely noticed that something is happening. The diffusion process is very imperfectly worked out, and may not be working very well. I, personally, believe that the product development area construed broadly (maybe it is better to think of it as the product cycle) is a dimension of competition that is rising in importance in a large number of industries, and is a dimension of competition in which one is going to have to achieve some mastery if one is to be relatively safe in a multi-national competitive environment. The issue is time: it's time-based management, it's time to market, it's time to break down. And it's a set of things that relate to time. If I had to take a wild swing at it to provoke some discussion, what has been learned is that you can't run things serially and get the job done fast enough. And if you can't run them serially, you have to run them in parallel.

It is natural therefore to turn to parallel processing in computer science, to see what can be found. If you line up 400 very powerful microprocessors and then give the machine in which they are embedded a problem, and ask them to do it faster because they can do the bits and pieces simultaneously, you'll find that the software engineers don't yet know how to write the software to make that happen very effectively: that is, to break the problem down. It isn't surprising that they don't yet know how to do it; it is an incredibly complicated problem. So I think one of the challenges, and I would like this to be a kind of minor theme of what I say, is that we have a great opportunity in the academic world to try to bring some conceptually useful frameworks to this problem, to try to understand in an organisational setting how you deal with parallel processing and increased speed. Now, one solution you can adopt if you are running a computer is you can just waste resources. You can give each of these processors something to do and if a few of them run into a roadblock because you gave them the wrong problem and a piece of data is missing, then they can just stop. It is hard to do that with human beings because of the negative effects on motivations. So the most natural, dumb solution for the computer software engineer is not a solution for the human system.

The second subject I wanted to mention is standards. I think that in an astonishing number of industries, the process by which product and technology standards are set, is, if not *the* central, certainly *one* of the central dimensions of competition. And we don't know much about that either. It is set by a complex process involving competition, some cooperation and alliance formation, much of which looks very chaotic, and a considerable amount of public sector activity. These issues arise in all kinds of places; certainly, in all aspects of electronics, food and drugs, securities, banking, and other financial services. In the construction industry, my colleague Jim Gibbons, who is the dean of Engineering at Stanford, and his colleagues, have estimated that perhaps 15% of the cost in construction firms worldwide is essentially waste associated with issues of reworking and incompatibility. The stylized version of that would be that you have two major companies working on a project and they are not using the same underlying databases. So every time you have to move something from one to the other, you print the blueprints and then re-enter the data in someone else's system. The total is on the order of $100 billion dollars a year worldwide. I think there is a great challenge and opportunity here.

The third area I wanted to mention has more to do with science and technology policy. I want to argue that it is an area that needs to be mastered better. What I would like you to focus on is the vertical structure of the value-added chain in a country like the United States that generates a lot of science and technology and then applies it, very productively, to creating new products. The fairly basic research part is done largely in universities, financed by public sector investment, at least 85%. And it is almost entirely non-proprietary. Then there is an intermediate zone that is increasingly controversial, by which that science and technology is handed over (in a sense the baton is passed to the world of corporations), and below that you have applied research and development oriented towards products. That part is largely private sector investment, and except problems in patents and intellectual property, it is largely proprietary. That intermediate zone is associated with a thing that is hotly debated now in the United States. It has to do with the question of whether there is an area that is being underinvested in, called the precompetitive area. That is, it is in some sense downstream from where the public sector investment stops and upstream from where the proprietariness of the returns is such that you can justify it, in terms of private investment. Now, if you imagine yourself in the 1960s, you don't have to think about this very much if you are a participant in the system. If you are in the upstream part, you don't have to worry too much about what the businesses are doing. And if you are downstream, as long as the government keeps investing, you don't have to know much about it. The technology will keep coming. There are some important intermediaries, venture capitalists, who do have to worry about it. What is interesting is how much more complicated this gets in a multinational setting, and how much more you have to know about the institutional structure. So, if you consider another country the line that separates the upstream and downstream parts is in a different place and the magnitudes of the investment are different. Now the reason that is important, from a competitive and a policy point of view, is that the upstream part is open and generates a great deal of the technology flow. There are a number of policy questions here: investments go back up from the corporate sector into the basic research sector; there are transnational technology flows. The technology transfer out of the open, upstream end is accomplished mainly through the foreign students that John McArthur was talking about. There is some talk of trying to cut off the investment flows that cross the national boundaries.

The challenge in creating a multinational corporation might be summarized with three points. Firstly, you have to be firmly rooted, not just in your domestic market but in all the national markets where you participate. Secondly, you have to be fully integrated and coordinated across all the functions where there are scale economies that are not exhausted within national markets. And thirdly (and this is more controversial), in fifteen years, if you do not have a fully integrated, senior management team and perhaps board, with respect to nationality, you will be at a competitive disadvantage. The reason is that, without that kind of sharing of leadership, the multinational will not be able to recruit successfully the greatest talent in the various national markets in which it operates. I wish I had a little more time to develop that area. It suggests that if you think of the schools following the route that businesses are going to have to follow themselves, in some sense mirroring them, then our schools are going to become, not quickly, but on a steady pace over about two decades, fully multinational institutions. They will, in some sense, belong less to the country in which they reside than they do now.

*Henry:* Listening to our three speakers, I am reminded of a comment Jimmy Carter once made when he was running for election and speaking to southern audiences. He said, 'If you elect me, finally we can have someone in the White House who doesn't speak with an accent.' Finally, we have deans of business schools who don't speak with an accent: 'Aboot' and all that.

I promised some nasty questions, which I will ask not individually but together. These will bring our discussion more to the running of business schools than what the business schools are doing to serve the market. I have one general question and one that pertains to each, but in a sense, they are comments on management education in general.

The general comment is that we keep talking about the need for parallel processing and much more interaction, breaking down the chimneys, and yet I find that the chimneys are stronger in the business schools than anywhere else that I know of. So we have people in marketing saying, 'We have to have more teamwork,' and we have people in strategy saying, 'You know, we have got to have more teamwork,' and we have people in operations saying, 'We have to have more teamwork,' but they never say it together! I think this is true of every business school I know, and it discourages a lot of innovation, because it is hard to cut across the chimneys. As far as internationalization is concerned, I hear a lot from business schools about internationalization, but I don't know how international the faculties are. And my question to George is: How do you internationalize when I walk up and down the corridors of the London Business School and hear mostly a wide variety of English accents, of British accents, with an occasional American or Canadian one? I think the problem is much more severe in North America, where everybody talks about internationalization, but few people live it in the sense of internalizing foreign cultures and foreign languages. My nasty question to John has to do with the nature of management education and the fact that we detach people from their context and make their education thin in a lot of regards. I think particularly of the case study method, where the object of the exercise is to read twenty pages on an organization the night before and come in and pronounce on that organization the next morning. And if you say to the professor, 'I refuse to pronounce, I have never been in their factories, I have never met the people, I refuse to comment on this organization, because all I read was a twenty page case,' you fail the course. Because the assumption is that good managers are decisive, MBA students therefore have to make decisions in the classroom. And the question is: What kind of attitude does that engender when these people end up in the executive suite? And my question, finally, to Mike, but again really common to all business schools, is my concern about the disciplines taking over the business schools. I want to tell an anecdote about Dan Schendel being approached by a well-known professor of sociology, in the sociology department of Columbia, saying, 'I would like to get the back issues of the *Strategic Management Journal*.' And Dan said, 'Sure, but why do you want that?' And the fellow said, 'Well I want to find out what strategy is.' And Dan said, 'Why would you want to know that?' And he said, 'Well, I have been approached concerning a chair in strategy at Stanford.' So my concern is, what are the roles of the disciplines in the business schools? I will throw it open to you now.

*Mike:* I think on the question of disciplines I would make the following observations. It is true, that a majority of the business schools in the general segment of the market that we are in are still recruiting their faculty at a young age from a combination of disciplines in functional areas, or, to put it differently, social science disciplines in functional areas and increasingly people from engineering backgrounds. I would say, as well, that if you think people never change, or if the forces at work are so powerful that they would never change, it isn't relevant that they are in a business school teaching executives and having to respond to their interests and ultimately letting that be a prominent influence in the setting of their research agenda, then you would say that this will never really connect with management. And I would say, about Stanford, but I think it is true on a much broader front, that that proposition is not true, and historical evidence bears it out, and there is a noticeable evolution. So, in some sense, the answer to this is faculty development, and business schools tend, among academic institutions, to pay a lot of attention to their version of human resources management, which is structuring in a careful way, over time, the experiences of people from when they first start, after they get their PhD, until they are in their 50s, to give them an opportunity at the right pace. And you don't ask somebody who has just graduated with a PhD to teach the advanced management program at Harvard. You have to start in the MBA classroom and you probably need a fair amount of help to start with, and our various schools do that in different ways. But, what I am trying to say is that it probably isn't useful to think of this in terms of what disciplines people came from, because business schools by and large have had only limited success in generating internally the full array of intellectual talent that is required. The second point I want to make is this. I am very sympathetic to the proposition that there are important issues out there that people with a great feel for leadership and management are wrestling with. And they are a challenge for us, in the sense of getting into the curriculum, and they don't fit naturally into the disciplines that we currently configure ourselves around. But I think that it is very easy to go over what I regard as a boundary line and say that those disciplines or those problems don't lend themselves to conceptual organization. Take the way a business organization is put together now. There are lots of really important innovations. There is a lot of experimentation and there are lots of academics who have bits and pieces of insight into it. We lack, both as practitioners and as teachers and scholars, a sort of integrating conceptual framework. But I haven't run into anybody who has tried to do this job who says that it wouldn't be nice to have it. The state of the art is very much like the state of the art in competitive strategy. That is, the external market oriented 30 years ago. A lot of people knew a lot of things, and the knowledge resided among people who called themselves strategists and people who called themselves industrial organization economists. And then some very smart people, including some of the people in this room, got together and said, 'Let's see if we can put this together in relatively simple frameworks that help people who have to assess strategy against the competitive environment do that job well.' The frameworks aren't perfect, but they are very powerful. That's what we need in the area of organizations, now, so what I wanted to issue a mild plea for, is not a sort of operating as if this set of issues is somehow so totally different that very thoughtful, imaginative scholars interacting with business can't, in what they do best when they are being creative, come up with a similar kind of organizing set of principles that will help people manage change in the organization as well.

*George:* I mean to make two points, and to build on what Mike said. I think that before you can integrate disciplines, you need to know the disciplines. And although I was arguing for greater integration, this is not synonymous with saying 'let's get rid of the disciplines'. I also think that the way in which you bring it about is not so much having multidisciplinary scholars coming in, particularly, as Mike says, at the beginning of their career, as beginning to change the curriculum and using it as a way of actually integrating the scholars. I think, for example, of a course that colleagues run on mergers and acquisitions at London, which is taught by somebody from OB, somebody from strategy, and somebody from finance. You can begin with a very loose form of integration, with each person making a contribution, and ultimately go into a much stronger form. So, in some ways, rather than thinking we are going to find multipurpose scholars, it seems to me you can actually drive it the other way, by using the curriculum to bring about a greater degree of integration, not just of the curriculum, but of scholarship. As far as internationalization goes—and I had better be careful because a lot of my colleagues are here today—I sometimes think (and I have an Irish mother) that my job is rather similar to the IRA. I am getting the

Brits out in London Business School. In terms of the student body, we are down to about 35% now that are British. The vast majority—there are not very many Irish, by the way—are from other parts of the world. On Henry's nasty question, a quarter of the faculty are non-British and about half of that speaks English as a foreign language. But, frankly again, there is no way of doing it by exhortation. You have to keep working at it, and in our case we have actually discovered—and it is quite a revelation—that economics actually works. That is, you try to get people to work for British academic salaries: some of the Brits, including expatriate Canadians, have been stupid enough over the years to do that, but most of the world's population is not. And, hence, what we did two years ago was break with British academic salaries and are now pushing up salaries quite dramatically. We have also become a privatized institution with a view to getting foreign scholars from a wide variety of backgrounds into the school. I also think that nationality just isn't enough. If I take myself—I don't know about John and Mike, but I sit here very much as a Canadian, very proud to be a Canadian, very much a Canadian passport holder—my hunch is that any, if not most, of my operating assumptions after almost three decades, are British. And I have a hunch that this is a problem for all of us, no matter what our nationalities originally were.

*John:* I think it is too early in the morning for me to get worked up about the case method. I don't think I would argue that it is the panacea to anything. For some people, though, it is easier for them to learn this way than for other people. In any case, it is part of the tradition of our school and I think everybody—every individual, and every organization—has to be what they are. It is what we are. Further, in the cluttered market-place that has become management education, with literally thousands of schools, if you taught this as a marketing case I am sure the school solution would be to do what we are doing. Because it even gets Henry stirred up, that we are doing something that doesn't seem right somehow. So, in this cacophony of thousands of people clamouring for students and money and faculty, I am rather pleased that we hang out there as somehow—I don't know quite how—but somehow, a little different. I don't think it is a very important part of the explanation of what is going on. I think much more important is that each teacher, certainly, and each school, has a commitment to really outstanding teaching. And a commitment to the learning of their students. And in the cases where we do it poorly, whether it is teaching strategy or something else, I would say it has to do with our effectiveness or not, in bringing along young faculty who don't work with their students and with ideas and material they are using in the way that concerns Henry and concerns me. And I think there are other forces that seem to me to account for—in practice, not just in the classroom—the ineffective thinking and implementation of strategy, things that we have had to deal with in the last decade, and still are: for example, the changing composition of our applicant pool. We have, for the class that entered just a few weeks ago, I think about 1900 applicants in the MBA pool from 15 investment banking firms in the world. And they, in turn, have swept the colleges of very many outstanding kids, but from a relatively small number of colleges and offer high salaries and exciting places, cities to live in around the world in the middle of the action, and all that kind of stuff. And we had another 800 or 900 from ten consulting firms. Well, you can imagine if we actually admitted a class that looked like that, it would be a monoculture of people who had gone to Williams College and then spent two years in London working for Goldman Sachs, traveling first-class with partners that only travel first-class. The power of that would be pretty awful. Then on leaving the school, if we have these firms that would offer 50 to 100 jobs—one firm—to our class, for $100 000 or $125 000 a year, people go into those kind of positions and spend their formative years, in the laboratory, as it was referred to earlier, the real laboratory. I think that is where these habits of mind and ways of dealing with the strategic problems that people often have when they get into leadership roles are formed. So there are so many other things besides whether the case is twenty pages or ten pages, whether we use cases or we don't, that shape whether or not people end up at the point where they are able to be in a leadership role, whether they can be effective. In short, I am sure we are not going to throw out the case method, but it has problems and we certainly understand them.

*Henry:* Just one last quick issue and question for our panelists. Is there a Canadian style of management, and is it coincidental that three major business schools end up with Canadian deans? I have my own suspicion that we are good at managing professionals in Canada because we are a tolerant, low-key kind of people. We can't run trucking companies worth a damn according to the head of Canadian Pacific, but maybe there is a Canadian style of management that has to do with a low-key kind of style and maybe that has something to do with the news items last night about Mike Porter suggesting we get more competitive. Maybe that is not to our comparative advantage. Does anybody want to pick up on why we have so many Canadian deans around?

*John:* I think it is just a fluke, myself. In any case, I have to confess, of course—I grew up in Bernardine and went to school in Vancouver—that I couldn't have gone on, at that time, to graduate school in business in Vancouver. So I had to leave and I ended up in Boston and until this day nobody has offered me a job and so I am still there. And if you want to test Henry's proposition, someone offer me a job today and then we will find out what I would really do. And then, I think, if it is just, Canadian Pacific trucking, even I would be happy to do that. And then again, I am not sure how to interpret having been made dean, because I think in all my life as a faculty member I rather thought if you ever ended up being a dean you had slid downhill. So, whether I have made any progress since I left Bernardine, in short, I don't know. But I think it is not related to whether I am Canadian or not.

*George:* Well, I would accept that. As you said, Henry, three is only large in your methodology. I don't want a job with Canadian Pacific trucking. My father only had one ambition for me—he had worked for the Canadian Pacific, my grandfather worked for the Canadian Pacific—and his ambition for me was that I would not work for Canadian Pacific. And in that sense, I think I am a success. The more interesting question, perhaps, is why do Canadians seem to leave Canada. And like John, I couldn't have done a doctorate in Winnipeg when I was a young man. I went to Oxford to do mine. And then you perhaps find that there are bigger operations out there and you become rather excited by them. There has been a lot of work in Europe recently, as to what makes a Euro manager. And funny enough, after you get away from things you can't control, like having multi-cultural parents, and things of that kind, you find the people from small countries—and I think, in this sense, Canada is a small country— often are disproportionately represented as international managers, and particularly the Canadians, the Irish, and even more so, those who have a language that no one in their right mind other than a native would learn. The Dutch and the Scandinavians tend to be disproportionately represented. And maybe that is a more important factor than being Canadian. Some of us look abroad or go abroad and never come back.

*Mike:* You know, there is a fairly long tradition—one of the great presidents at Stanford was a man named Sterling, who came from the Canadian west—but I guess the only thing that I would say is that (and this is an exaggeration) it does strike me that if you ask what is academic administration most like, it has to be, as Henry intimated, like organizations with a lot of people who are sure they know what they are doing and want to be left alone to do it, i.e. partnerships in a number of fields, yeah, law firms, and investment management, and I have found, in talking with those people—the ones who get dragooned into supposedly organizing everybody else—that we have a lot in common. But I think, more interestingly, there is a less big difference now in the way business, the management of more traditional corporations, is thought about than was true in academic institutions at the height of the command and control era. The idea of command and control, of course, in the academic environment is so absurd that it doesn't even enter your mind. But I actually think there is a slight convergence going on here. As to how you end up getting conned into doing this, I am not really sure.

# Section I

# Strategy, Strategic Intent, and Competitive Advantage

Discussions of strategy frequently characterize important issues as being related to either content (formulation) or process (implementation). This distinction is increasingly viewed as a false dichotomy, recognizing that it is impractical, and often counterproductive, to attempt to examine or manage either in isolation from the other. Although the chapters in this section focus on subject matter more concerned with strategy formulation (content), they are presented in a context that either provides clear linkages to implementation or gives ample evidence of the importance of such integration.

Several different perspectives on formulation are offered, very much in line with the implications of the plenary session, of the importance of being responsive to the idea of ongoing change.

Hall emphasizes the importance of top management understanding the firm's core identity and recognizing how differently it may be visualized by different stakeholders of the same firm. In so doing, she addresses the first key element of a strategy formulation, the firm's mission/purpose—the need for a firm to ask 'who are we?', 'what business(es) are we in?'.

Hamel addresses the next logical step in the formulation

process—discussing firms as resource 'bundles,' but in an interestingly different context. He suggests viewing strategy as 'stretch'—deliberately leaving a gap between ambition and resources—and *resource leverage*—focusing on creative approaches to multiplying a firm's resource base as key foci of a resource leveraging process rather than a resource allocation process. Although more concise versions may ultimately be published elsewhere, we feel this perspective of strategy is sufficiently thought-provoking to justify sharing it here in its entirety.

Fiegenbaum, Hart and Schendel describe how strategic behavior and performance can be directly influenced by a firm's choice of reference points. They define a strategic reference point by three dimensions: the firm's internal capability, external conditions, and time. Thus, they not only address the issue of *distinctive competence*, or factors endogenous to the firm, but also *exogenous* forces—those a firm's management can not necessarily influence—and *time*—quickness of response—as key strategic drivers.

Goold and Campbell hold that the fundamental question for corporate strategy is whether and how the corporate center (parent) adds value to the individual businesses in the company. This perspective tends to integrate the firm's mission, or scope, with its distinctive competences, in a manner that should help illustrate to managers the importance and utility of constantly examining where the firm is, in a strategic sense.

Seeking competitive advantage is arguably the most important objective of strategic management. From this perspective, the chapter by Warren offers not only an appropriate conclusion to this section, on formulation, but also an effective lead-in to the next section, on implementation. Warren posits that a producer can gain competitive advantage by eliminating the retailer as an intermediary and dealing directly with the consumer. Although seldom discussed as a strategic issue, this may be an effective way of shifting the balance of power from the retailer to the producer.

| | |
|---|---|
| Chapter 4 | Strategic Reference Point Theory<br>*Avi Fiegenbaum, Stuart Hart, Dan Schendel* |
| Chapter 5 | Corporate Strategy and Parenting Maps<br>*Michael Goold, Andrew Campbell* |
| Chapter 6 | Removing Intermediaries from Distribution Channels<br>*Kim Warren* |

These chapters extend and expand on significant current trends in strategy formulation. The following readings are recommended for those who require additional background information on these important concepts.

Gary Hamel and C. K. Prahalad have been among the primary proponents of the importance of *core competences*—those things a firm is capable of doing better than its competitors—and *strategic intent*—creating, throughout an organization, an obsession with winning, through individual contributions and teamwork. (The core competence of the corporation, *Harvard Business Review*, May–June, 1990; Strategic intent, *Harvard Business Review*, May–June, 1989.)

Michael Porter is considered one of the leading authorities on *competitive strategy*. His 1980 book *Competitive Strategy: Techniques for Analyzing Industries and Competitors*, introduced what has become known as the 'five forces model,' for analyzing the primary forces driving competition in an industry, and three 'generic strategies' for coping with the five forces. Porter's subsequent books on competitive advantage include *Competitive Advantage: Creating and Sustaining Superior Performance* (1985), *Competition in Global Industries* (1986), and *The Competitive Advantage of Nations* (1990).

In 'Strategic groups: Theory, research and taxonomy' (*Strategic Management Journal*, 7, 1986), John McGee and Howard Thomas expand on Porter's concept that companies within an industry may be grouped based on their strategic behavior. They suggest that differences between groups may be due to *mobility barriers*, which can be categorized by market-related strategies, industry supply characteristics, and individual firm characteristics.

Birger Wernerfelt, in 'A resource-based view of the firm' (*Strategic Management Journal*, 5, 1984), views a firm's resources as those tangible and intangible assets that are semi-permanently tied to the firm. He suggests that firms' resources can be thought of as strengths or weaknesses, and proposes the concept of *resource position barriers* to describe the relative positions of different competitors. In this perspective the optimal growth of a firm involves balancing exploitation of existing resources with development of new ones.

Ingemar Dierickx and Karel Cool emphasize that the sustainability of a firm's competitive position is a function of how easily its assets can be replicated. (Asset stock accumulation and sustainability of competitive advantage, *Management Science*, December, 1989). In this view, *strategic resources* are those that are 'nontradeable, nonimitable and nonsubstitutable,' and must be accumulated over time, rather than acquired in the 'strategic factor markets' described by Jay Barney (Strategic factor markets: Expectations, luck, and business strategy', *Management Science*, October, 1986).

# 2

# WYSIWYG: Perception, Reality and Organizational Focus: Core Identity as a Holistic Framework for the Management of Change

JAN HALL

The theme of this conference can be interpreted at several different levels. This chapter addresses the greening of strategy in the deeper sense: it takes a holistic view of the organization as defined by its values as well as its competencies, and considers the question of core identity and its relation to strategy. Implicit in this approach is the relationship between perception and reality, which is essentially an issue of organizational integrity.

Perception is as powerful as reality in shaping and changing behaviour. Perception is reality, in that what is believed to be the case is what determines people's responses in any situation. And it is certainly true that perceptions, if carefully managed, can

*Building the Strategically-Responsive Organization.*
Edited by H. Thomas, D. O'Neal, R. White and D. Hurst.
Copyright © 1994 the Strategic Management Society. Published 1994 by John Wiley & Sons Ltd.

change reality itself. This is the guiding principle behind the concept of core identity as a framework for creating and managing organizational change.

## THE NEED FOR A HOLISTIC APPROACH TO CHANGE MANAGEMENT

The concept of core identity is a holistic one. Because it embraces every aspect of a company's activities, it is an immensely powerful force for change. Furthermore, holistic tools are the only ones that will work effectively in a rapidly changing world. So rapid is the pace of technological and social change today that many organizations find themselves in a constant state of reaction as they attempt to reflect the values and demands of the external environment. But reaction is no route to organizational renewal: true responsiveness—rather than reactiveness—demands that organizations understand and manage their own identity. 'Know thyself' is a precept as fundamental to the success of the organization as it is to the individual. The chameleon organization— white hot with technology one moment, glowing greenly the next—generates cynicism about its products, confusion about its role as an employer and concern about its genuine commitment to the values of the society in which it operates.

A holistic approach to all management, not simply the management of change, will become increasingly the norm during the next decade. The leaders of the 1990s will find that the technical skills of line management will be prerequisite, a necessary but not a sufficient condition for both individual and organizational success as companies increasingly realize that they have a wide variety of audiences, not customers alone. The achievement of the Green movement is that in increasing awareness of the impact of the activities of business concerns on our physical environment it has called into question much wider and more profound issues of values and culture, issues that lie at the heart of core identity.

## WHAT IS CORE IDENTITY

An identity is not something an organization can choose to have or not to have. Greyness, blandness and anonymity are as much identity characteristics as innovativeness, social responsibility, efficiency or ruthlessness, although companies that match any of the latter category of adjectives tend to be much more aware of the values and principles by which they govern their operations than those in the former. A clearly defined identity is, more often than not, the signal of a dynamic and energetic organization. Identity derives from everything the organization says and does. It is manifest in its tangible components—in its structure, systems, appearance, products and promotion, and people (FIGURE 2.1). These are the skeleton, the body and the clothing of identity, its physical expression—what the company is and does.

But, like people, a company also has a soul, a spirit, a heart—

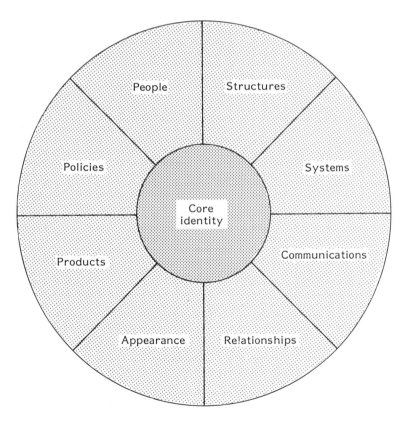

FIGURE 2.1   The core identity of an organization: tangible components

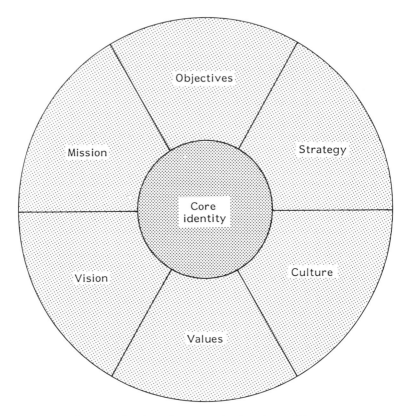

FIGURE 2.2   The core identity of an organization: intangibles

the real essence of what it *is* and what it believes it is *for*. Mission, objectives and strategy are relatively easily articulated and changed, but culture, values and vision, which shape the way in which the organization goes about its entire activities, are less easily susceptible to definition and infinitely more difficult to change. But here is where the essence of any change programme lies (FIGURE 2.2).

If a sense of 'this is what we stand for, this is who we are, this is how we do things' is shared by everyone within an organization, its day to day operations become smoother and simpler. Decisions can be taken quickly and confidently, because everyone understands the principles that lie behind the company's actions.

There is less need to pass things up the line for approval, less need for formal chains of command to slow the decision making process. Knowing the 'right' course of action in any circumstances becomes intuitive, in the sense of being a learned skill. Yet many organizations reduce their effectiveness by failing to examine and codify their own identity, forcing themselves to react when change is needed in a piecemeal, fragmented and inconsistent fashion.

## CORE IDENTITY AS A TOOL FOR ORGANIZATIONAL RENEWAL

Using core identity as a tool for renewal forces the organization to define what it now is and stands for, to decide what it wishes to be and stand for, and to determine the structural, procedural and attitudinal modifications that will bring the necessary changes about.

The process of defining a core identity demands a deep understanding of both the *hard* and the *soft qualities* that combine to create it. On the hard side are those aspects that lend themselves to easy measurement—profitability, return on investment (ROI), market share, production output and efficiency, manpower policies, labour costs, product formulation and performance, promotional activity, the way the company is structured— whether control is exerted from the centre, if it is a cohesive organism or a series of fragmentary outposts. These tend to be characteristics that lend themselves to easy measurement—and, more often than not, to easy imitation. It is now widely accepted that the tangible, functional aspects of an organization are very rarely a long-term source of competitive advantage.

On the soft side are the less tangible, less measurable aspects of company culture—the emotional relationships, the way in which people address, respond to, and consult each other, the way in which decisions are made and implemented, morale and loyalty, vision, culture and values. The two are inextricably linked: what the company does determines what it stands for; what it stands for determines what it does.

So, the process of defining a core identity is holistic, involving not only describing the facts and figures of the organization but also the feeling and signals within it.

## DEFINING CORE IDENTITY

Many organizations conduct 'image' and 'attitude' research among their customers, potential customers and employees, and it is often this kind of research as much as the hard facts of sales, share and profit figures that brings about the impetus for change. But all too often the attempt is made from the wrong direction: product reformulation, a price cut, a new advertising campaign, additional incentives for the sales force—changes that look outside rather than inside the company, that are reactive rather than proactive, piecemeal rather than holistic and, above all, that address surface manifestations rather than tackle the heart of a problem.

If a company is perceived as a desirable place to work, a supplier of high quality goods and services, as environmentally responsible, as a good *corporate citizen*, no one has a problem about perception and reality: people believe we're good because we are good. The converse is a different matter. Companies with a poor reputation tend to believe that the perception is flawed, that reality is different – but this is very rarely the case. In both instances it is the company as a whole that is judged; and if we are judged holistically we must respond holistically. It is the entire identity of the company that determines its reputation and, ultimately, its success.

Identity is composed of what the company does and what it believes in—its competencies and its values. What is it good at in functional terms? What are the essential qualities and attributes it has acquired to compete in its chosen markets? What unique skills and characteristics set it apart from its competitors? These are the essence of its competence; they are relatively easy to define. What the company believes in and acts according to—its values—are less easy to articulate (FIGURE 2.3).

Those who work in an organization are usually those who understand it best; they often know what has to change to revitalize and renew their organization. Most people are capable of articulating what they know about what their company does and the structures and procedures through which things get done. But describing the culture and values that determine the ethos of the company is more difficult. When people are questioned, there are inhibitions imposed by inarticulacy when faced

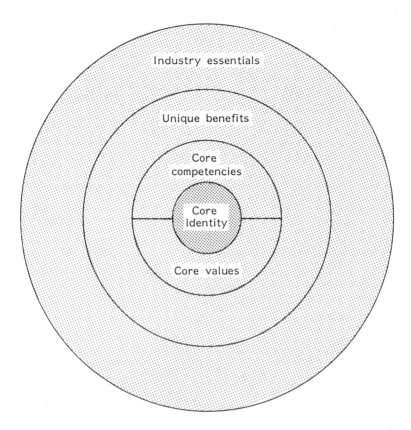

FIGURE 2.3   The identity of a company

with abstract concepts, by apprehension about the results of frankness, by fear of appearing foolish or speaking out of turn. Normal interviewing techniques tend to produce conventional and acceptable responses, which can miss the richness of information that actually exists. The danger is that they reflect the shared perception, the received view of the organization, rather than the reality.

What is needed is a *new language* to allow people to express their understanding and experience of the 'soft' side of their organization. Words are often inadequate. But pictures—'something between a thing and a thought'—can speak where words cannot. By encouraging people to express themselves through visual stimuli, a deeper, richer and more authentic understanding of organizational identity can be reached. Several different techniques can be employed to this end.

A key one is the *visualization technique*, a series of team exercises carried out by people within the organization. The teams are provided with large quantities of visual stimuli—scrap art which can be used to illustrate either directly or by analogy their perceptions of the company and the way in which it operates. At the practical level the technique is fast, efficient and enjoyable. It can be done in an hour, very productively, and has the great advantages of shared participation and enjoyability. The process of selecting and discussing suitable illustrations encourages laughter, relaxation and the release of inhibitions. The shy or inarticulate can participate as fully as the confident and loquacious. By encouraging the use of visual stimuli and symbols, the visualization technique helps people to arrive at a new language for describing the essence of their organization and gives permission to explore areas normally perceived as 'no go'; the emphases on the team and the lack of formal discipline encourage speed of involvement, understanding, interaction and, in time, assist the final adoption and integration of both problem definition and solution.

Other visual approaches facilitate the accurate definition of perceptions: people can draw their impressions of the organization—as a car, a house, an animal. Or they can take a camera and do a visual 'journey through the company', recording features, the events and the situations that seem to them to symbolize what the company is all about—the out-of-date notices on the notice board, the queue for the photocopier, the informal meetings around the coffee machine. Such evidence is often astonishing to managers, for it forces them to recognize what they would generally prefer not to acknowledge: the gap between what the company says and what it does.

Equally effectively, visual techniques can help to specify the new identity for the organization. The same methods that enable people to describe what *is* can be used to define what *should be*. Words such as 'caring' or 'efficient' can be pinned down and given real meaning by using illustrations of different interpretations of them to fine-tune definitions. Caring like a doctor in a high-tech surgery, like a mother with a baby, like a social worker with a deprived family? Suddenly the platitude, the generality, the blandness is given focus and precision.

## CASE HISTORIES/EXAMPLES

A series of case histories were presented in visual format during the conference. Copies of these may be obtained from the author. An example of the visualization technique was given in the case history for the Ahlstrom Corporation; an example of visual journeys was provided by the Leeds City Council case history; drawings were shown from a research study by Coley Porter Bell/BMRB; and an example of visual clarification was shown through the Bloomsbury and Islington Health Authority case study. Finally, the Taylor Group case history demonstrated the visual implementation of their core identity.

## EXPRESSING THE CORE IDENTITY

Importantly, the definition of the desired core identity is simply the beginning of the process. The identity itself becomes the defining principle behind the strategies necessary to reshape and revitalize the organization. The strengths of the policies and practices that went to make up the historic identity have to be built upon to help ensure that the newly developed identity is thoroughly expressed in every aspect of the organization's activities. The end towards which all the effort is directed is that perception and reality become identical and indivisible in the regenerated organization: *What You See Is What You Get*.

The visual expression of the company identity is hugely symbolic. It is not simply the expression of how the company wishes to be seen, but the visible, manifest declaration of change and commitment to renewal. A new visual identity can be a powerful symbol for the core identity and, ideally, it must be apparent in every aspect of the company, internally as well as externally. The process of defining the core identity is one of reducing the complexity of the entire company into a single, simple and easily expressed set of values which lies at the heart of its identity. Then the process broadens out again into complexity as the new identity is expressed throughout the organization, through its systems, structures, products, people and appearance, communications, and so on (FIGURE 2.4).

The focus on the core identity will have highlighted policies

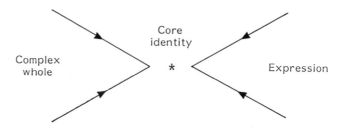

FIGURE 2.4   The process of defining the core identity

and practices that must change. Structure and systems will be modified for consonance with the organization's declared values. The renewed company may need new objectives: it will certainly need new strategies in most areas of its operations. This is why core identity is such a powerful tool for regeneration: it demands the examination of the company's soul, which in turn affects every aspect of its operations.

## IDENTITY, VALUES AND THE ORGANIZATION IN SOCIETY

Defining and reshaping company identity means looking both into and beyond the organization. A core identity must, above all, give the company a competitive advantage; it must discriminate itself from the competition in a way that its publics—all of its publics, from shareholders to customers, from employees to the government—find relevant and attractive. This is not done by navel gazing, but by examining the outside world with the assiduousness and sensitivity that is given to the world inside the organization. This work enables the core identity to be translated appropriately to all of an organization's different audiences (FIGURE 2.5). A company has to be familiar to, be understood by and influence people who:

- buy its brands
- use its brands
- work for it
- might work for it
- represent the people who work for it

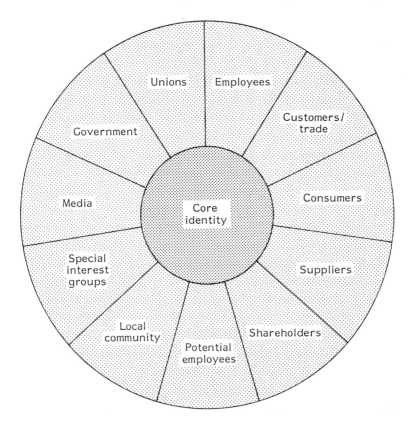

FIGURE 2.5   The organization's audiences

- sell its products
- supply it with the materials to conduct its business
- consider its request for a loan
- might buy shares in it
- advise others about investing in it
- write or talk about it for public consumption
- live near it
- have a special interest in it

and the better known, understood and respected a company is, the greater its chance of influencing all of these audiences in its favour.

Increasingly, people are demanding real values from the organizations they deal with. They are demanding that companies act with social and environmental responsibility, that they are open and honest in their behaviour to everyone inside and outside the organization, and that what they say is what they are and do. The definition of core identity in terms of company values as well as the core competencies and product performance ensures that these values are built into the objectives and strategies that will drive the organization in future.

## CORE IDENTITY AS BRAND ASSET

As people begin to take the quality of what they buy for granted, they become more interested in who they are buying it from. The *reputation of the company* behind the product or service is assuming more and more importance in people's brand choice and in all their other dealings with it, whether as employees, shareholders, suppliers, stockists, members of special interest groups or neighbours. This links closely to the increasing desire for knowledge about the companies behind the products, who they are, what they stand for, and what they do.

There is now a growing trend for companies to give real thought to their own identities in relation to their product or service brands. *Identity structure*—the way in which a company manages all the different identities in its portfolio in relation to each other and itself—is set to become a key issue for the 1990s.

Many years ago in the United States, McGraw-Hill ran an advertisement whose copy read:

> *I don't know your company*
> *I don't know your company's product*
> *I don't know what your company stands for*
> *I don't know your company's record*
> *I don't know your company's reputation*
> *Now, what was it you wanted to sell me?*

People want to buy from, work for, invest in and do business with people they know, like and admire. Familiarity has been demonstrated time and time again to be closely correlated with favourable attitudes.

It simply makes it all the more important that companies should have a planned and considered strategy for identity structure, deciding which audiences should understand what about the company, its brand and their relationship to each other. It may be important that non-consumer audiences should be aware of a company's ownership of important brands: stationery and litera- ture can make the relationship clear without affecting consumer perceptions. It may be that the company stands to gain from pro- claiming its ownership of famous brands to all of its audiences. Recruitment, for instance, will be a key issue for all companies in the 1990s. The young, and those with skills of all kinds, will be able to pick and choose their employers once we have emerged from this recession. The invisible and anonymous have rarely had the pick of the bunch—and the bunch to be picked from will be much smaller than it has been in the past.

Planning an identity structure forces the company to examine and evaluate all of its reputational assets in terms of its brands, its divisions, every name that it uses to identify itself and its products or services. In large, complex organizations it isn't always easy to decide where core identity truly lies and how it can most effectively be used (FIGURE 2.6). Is it at, or should it be at, headquarters level and/or at divisional level? Does one company brand sum up the essence of the company better than its current name?

Asking these questions serves to highlight issues rather than to provide solutions, for there is no single 'correct' approach and no

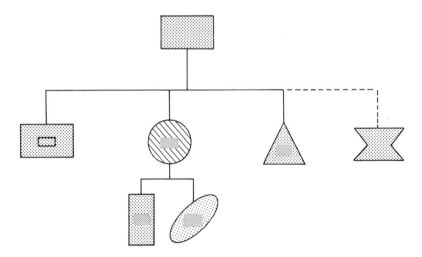

FIGURE 2.6   Planning an identity structure

need to adapt a single model for a whole organization. Some divisions may be better off free-standing in identity terms; some brands may lose a great deal more than the company could gain by association with them. What matters is that the questions should be asked, so that an appropriate solution for each organization can be developed and that difference audiences of a company are addressed appropriately.

The search is for patterns and templates rather than for rules and structures, and the outcome is coherence rather than rigid conformity of identity throughout the organization—a managed identity architecture whose expression is thoughtfully planned, developed and executed. However, without a clearly defined and well-understood core identity there is no basis upon which to build.

## THE VIRTUOUS CIRCLES

The effect of a clear understanding and communication of the company's identity spills over into all of its activities. The reputation of the company can enhance that of its brands—or vice versa. Lever, a division of Unilever, took the decision a few years ago to identify itself as the parent of some of the UK's leading household care brands. A recent research study by CPB/BMRB showed 78% of British adults are familiar with Lever and that the company is very highly rated as an employer, a dynamic organization and a good investment prospect. Its sister company, Elida Gibbs, has been reticent about its brand ownership and the research indicates that it does not benefit in the same way from its association with familiar and respected brands such as Timotei and Denim.

If employees understand the company's vision and values, and how to play their individual roles in it, they feel more confident about decision making, and can act more efficiently and decisively. This in turn increases motivation and loyalty, with benefits to both employee and employer. Equally, if employees are proud of the products they produce a greater commitment is seen. This, of course, will also be enhanced, or not, by public attitudes to the company and its products, which employees are likely to be well aware of.

Companies rarely define their values in negative terms—at least

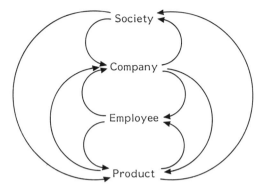

FIGURE 2.7    Virtuous circles

not overtly! The very act of an organization describing what it believes its role in society should be makes it aware of its social responsibilities, its position as a corporate citizen—and it is forced to act upon that articulated awareness. The motives may be cynical—a desire to be *seen* to be doing good rather to do good for its own sake—but the ends are the same in any event. Doing the right thing for the wrong reason often leads to an appreciation of the right thing for its own sake.

Society needs business to be successful. Successful business means economic success for everyone. 'What's good for General Motors is good for America' may not be a fashionable dictum, but there's still a grain of truth in it. More and more companies are learning the advantages of doing well by doing good.

All of these benefits are self-reinforcing: success breeds success. Whatever the motives behind good employee relationships, corporate responsibility in the community, openness about ownership, in the end, the results 'have to be' positive. Each interaction influences the others and one virtuous circle leads to the next (FIGURE 2.7).

## CONCLUSION

We live in a world where almost anything that can be made today can be imitated tomorrow (or sooner!). Functionally and physically, it is harder and harder to maintain differentiation, and 'quality' in its physical and functional senses is increasingly becoming a given as far as consumers are concerned. The reputation of the company behind the product or service is assuming more and more importance in people's choices, whether as customers, employees, shareholders, suppliers, stockists, members of special interest groups or neighbours. Increasingly, people are demanding that the companies they deal with are honest, responsible, responsive and—above all—open about who they are and what they do.

Core identity as a concept provides a framework for clarifying and providing a holistic definition for who and what a company is, enabling this to be expressed in how the company behaves and what it does, so that WYSIWYG results.

In the very short term, the implementation of a core identity programme may result in a bottom line less laden with zeros than if the company had continued as before. In the medium and long term, however, the value of values becomes self-evident. If the world knows and approves of what the organization stands for, it rewards that organization with loyalty through thick and thin: ask IBM, Marks & Spencer, Johnson & Johnson, Mercedes–Benz.

# 3

# Breaking the Frame: Strategy as Stretch and Leverage

GARY HAMEL

---

## UNDERSTANDING COMPETITIVENESS

### BEYOND THE INDUSTRY STRUCTURE PARADIGM

The goal of strategy research is first to explain and then to predict competitive outcomes. Like peeling an onion, the search for the determinants of competitive outcomes is a multi-layered task. How far have we got? Early attempts to explain outcomes led to simple universalities such as 'fit' (Andrews, 1980) and the oft-observed correlation between market share and profitability (Buzzell, Gale and Salton, 1975). More recently, the literature of industry economics has been enriched to provide a detailed understanding of the ways in which competitive position (i.e. the inherent *potential* for profits; Porter, 1980) and competitive advantage (i.e. the ability actually to *realize* above average profits; Porter, 1985) conspire to determine profitability. Yet the inevitably *post hoc*, usually static, and often deterministic nature of strategy conceptualization and prescription suggests that additional layers remain. Strategy researchers still have far more good questions than they have good answers.

For example, why do some firms, more than others, seem to

*Building the Strategically-Responsive Organization.*
Edited by H. Thomas, D. O'Neal, R. White and D. Hurst.
Copyright © 1994 the Strategic Management Society. Published 1994 by John Wiley & Sons Ltd.

possess an autonomous capability to create fundamentally new sources of competitive advantage and to radically extend existing sources of competitive advantage? Examples of such advantage creation include Toyota's highly developed supplier relationships, Canon's capacity for value engineering, Honda's fast pace of product development and Fujitsu's success in exploiting a web of strategic alliances. It is interesting to note that while General Motors and Ford are seeking to close the gap with Japanese rivals on a score or more competitiveness parameters, Japanese automakers don't seem to be emulating their American counterparts in any dimension of competitive advantage. It's not just that Toyota is ahead in some areas and GM in others, but that Toyota seems to have a capacity for advantage creation that GM lacks. A careful exposition of the elements of Toyota's lean manufacturing system (Womack, Jones and Roos, 1990), although worthwhile, provides little insight into *why* it was Toyota, rather than General Motors, that developed this complex array of advantages.

There is a need not only to keep score of existing advantages—what they are and who has them—but to discover the 'engine' that propels the process of advantage creation. The tools of industry and competitor analysis are much better suited to the first task than the second. Relying only on these tools, business educators and consultants can be little more than conduits for the transfer of best practice from these firms that are net advantage creators to those that are net advantage imitators. This leaves many firms in a perpetual catch-up trap, doing little more than observing, decoding, reinterpreting and attempting to emulate the already visible advantages of out-in-front competitors. It is little wonder that many managers feel as frustrated as a would-be investor trying to make money from yesterday's stock price quotations.

Other questions also elude the considerable explanatory power of traditional industry structure analysis. Why, for example, do some firms seem to take industry structure or less as a given, while others work proactively to harness the forces of globalization, deregulation, technology and demographics in order to transform industry structure to their own advantage? Almost single-handedly, IBM determined and dominated the structure of the worldwide computer industry during the 1960s and 1970s. IBM's dominant market share was the product of the firm's success in shaping the evolution of the industry. Yet by the end of the 1980s it was apparent that IBM was no longer the sole, or even the most influential, architect of computer industry structure. That mantle had passed, at least in part, to a group of firms intent on undermining IBM by orchestrating a move towards 'open,' rather than proprietary, operating systems. This example, and many others, demonstrates that while market share growth typically testifies to a firm's success in shaping its industry, market share leadership, once achieved, may be more of an impediment than a spur to rethinking and remaking industry structure.

Industries don't 'evolve': firms with little respect for industry conventions circumvent barriers to entry, redraw segment boundaries, and establish new patterns of competitive interaction. As Canon demonstrated in its battle with Xerox, and as Dell Computer has shown in its rivalry with Compaq and other PC makers, seemingly insurmountable barriers to entry may become, for the incumbent, barriers to retaliation and repositioning when rivals successfully alter the topography of an industry.

In industries such as telecommunications, financial services, computing and biotechnology, industry structure seems to be almost permanently 'under-determined.' Here, restructuring is less an occasional upheaval than a permanent state of ferment. Any careful rendering of industry segments, strategic groups and so on would be of no more lasting value than a map in the middle of an earthquake zone. As with the search for the essence of competitive advantage, we must search for a deeper dynamic that helps to explain why some firms demonstrate a greater capability than others to systematically reshape industry boundaries, undermine the competitive position of rivals, and create 'new competitive space.' Again, *ex post facto* explanations and pre-existing capabilities are different things. A capacity for industry structure analysis is related to a capacity to proactively reshape industries in the same way that biblical exegesis is related to sainthood.

Of course, if there were no systematic differences between firms in their ability to build competitive advantages or reshape industries, there would be no need to delve any deeper into the issue of 'competitiveness.' One would be content with an ability to accurately portray industry structure, calculate industry and segment attractiveness and measure relative competitive advantage at each stage of the value chain. But I believe there is evidence of systematic differences between firms in terms of an underlying 'competitiveness dynamic.' Although the evidence is by no means incontestable, it nevertheless compels strategy researchers and concerned managers to move beyond the industry structure paradigm in their search for the wellspring of competitive vitality.

---

## DIAGNOSING JAPANESE SUCCESS

The success of Japanese multinational enterprise, across a dozen or so industries, is a body of evidence that demands an explanation. Yet the account of this phenomenon offered by traditional industry structure analysis is partial and unsatisfactory. During the 1960s, Western firms in industries such as textiles, cameras and toys came under intense pressure from non-traditional competitors. The simple explanation, offered by industrial economists, was that with their lower wage rates, Japanese and other 'foreign' firms possessed an inherent advantage in labor-intensive industries. With this orthodox, and narrow, explanation of Japanese competitive success, it was not surprising that few managers in the steel, car or shipbuilding industries felt they had much to learn from their less fortunate compatriots. Hadn't Western firms erected significant barriers to entry in these more capital-intensive industries? Didn't one need a large domestic market to amortize investment? 'Surely,' thought managers in heavy industry, 'what happened in labor-intensive industries won't happen to *us*.'

But during the 1970s the pattern of attack, belated defense and sometimes surrender that had been observed in labor-intensive industries repeated itself in the supposedly less vulnerable capital-intensive industries. New explanations for Japanese victories were therefore needed, and were found. Japanese firms possessed a cost of capital advantage, benefited from an undervalued exchange rate, and were lucky enough to have patient and undemanding shareholders, so the argument went. And, of course, Japanese firms were merely imitators. It wasn't difficult to catch up when one had success models of the likes of US Steel, General Motors and the British shipbuilding industry.

As the 1980s dawned, managers in technology-intensive industries such as semiconductors, telecommunications and biotechnology could not fail to notice the significant encroachment of Japanese firms in 'mature,' 'smokestack' industries. Of course, a cost of capital advantage might give Japanese producers an edge in commodity products like dynamic RAM chips, yet without the Western advantages of individual creativity, great research universities and massive R&D spending, Japanese firms would surely not be able to occupy the high ground of 'high tech,' would they?

Yet by the close of the decade it was widely acknowledged that American companies were either behind, or no more than neck and neck with Japanese rivals in fields as diverse as materials science, electronic imaging, supercomputing and high definition video. Again, new explanations were needed and found. Many managers seemed to believe that the Japanese government had pumped billions of yen into research. Japanese companies were accused of 'stealing' Western technology, with little distinction made between industrial espionage and diligent exploitation of the increasingly global market for technology. And it was admitted that whilst US companies had been content with one defect per hundred or thousand, Japanese companies measured quality in parts per million.

Perhaps, thought some managers and policy makers, it would be in service-intensive industries that Western companies would uncontestedly prevail. After all, in service industries the advantages of global scale manufacturing disappeared. While the market for the Walkman or Yamaha digital piano might be global, markets for services were decidedly local—weren't they? Proximity to customers and flexibility in offering were deemed the keys to success. Blue collar automatons were of no use here. While it is too early to tell whether Japanese success in manufacturing industries will be matched by similar success in service industries, the rate at which these firms are acquiring fashion retailers, financial institutions, ski resorts, hotels, movie studios and software houses suggests that they will, at the least, be formidable competitors in these last few bastions of Western leadership. The already formidable productivity advantages of some Japanese companies in producing systems software are described in Consumano (1991).

As competition progressed from labor-intensive to capital-intensive to technology-intensive industries and beyond, managers not yet confronting the so-called 'Japanese challenge' were tempted to think, 'my industry is different, it won't happen here.' In one sense they were right. Each industry was different; advantages that were critical in one industry context were tangential in another or took a radically different form. Yet in many cases these managers were misled by the inherent superficiality of industry structure analysis, with its focus on the *what*, rather than the *why*, of competitive advantage. All that these managers could safely assume was that it wouldn't happen in their industries *in the same way*.

For example, although by the early 1990s Philips no doubt possessed a quite precise understanding of Sony's specific advantages in audio or video products (e.g miniaturization, quasi-integration with suppliers, short product development cycle times, and elegant design), such insights were of potentially limited value in preparing Philips for Sony's entry into the very different competitive arena of pre-recorded media. For Philips, the critical question was less, 'How did Sony succeed in the TV or hi-fi business?' than 'What constitutes the wellspring of Sony's competitiveness across a broad spectrum of consumer and industrial businesses?'

Not surprisingly, a partial and superficial diagnosis of competitive 'decline' has yielded partial and superficial policy solutions, for the firm and the nation. For example, in the recent past, many managers in Europe and America went to bed every night with a simple prayer on their lips: 'Please, God, force our Japanese rivals to come and manufacture locally, using the same bloody-minded workers we have to use, at continental, rather than global scale, and with the same input cost penalties.' 'And by the way, God, if you could make the yen appreciate by 100% that would help too.' Well, no one can claim that God doesn't answer prayers. Managers got the 'level playing field' they asked for. Yet, oddly enough, this does not seem to have taken the pressure off managers in Western car companies (where Japanese companies are now winning the 'excitement sweepstakes' among the next generation of buyers), nor has it bought much breathing space for managers in consumer electronics companies (who have watched Japanese firms increase their global market share with each additional product generation), nor has it reversed earlier Japanese share gains in the semiconductor business (where the pressure to localize production corresponded neatly with the trend toward design-intensive specialist chip production).

Thus, despite converging quality standards, the 'de-integration' of Japan's export-oriented domestic manufacturing base, the 'opening' of the Japanese home market, the narrowing of differences in the cost of capital around the world, and successive rounds of down-sizing, delayering and re-focusing, few Western managers feel that they have regained the offensive in industries targeted by Japanese competitors.

By now it is evident that what Western managers and policy makers have seen as the 'competitiveness problem' is both transcendent with respect to industries and persistent with respect to time. Thus, we must seek explanations and managerial approaches that are equally transcendent and temporally robust. Once it is obvious that a series of competitive engagements, each conducted in a substantially different industry venue, has produced, more often than not, a similar outcome, it must be admitted that there is little more to be gained from yet another well-documented, industry-specific case study. Our vantage point must shift from the battlefield (the purview of industry structure analysis) to the minds of the opposing generals.

## DEEPENING OUR ANALYSIS

A useful metaphor can be borrowed from the world of medicine. Describing competitive outcomes can be likened to the taking of vital signs (heart rate, blood pressure, blood chemistry, etc.): one can say whether the patient appears to be well or ill, but little more. To diagnose a specific disease, the physician must dig deeper. What are the specific symptoms? In what combination do they appear? How persistent have they been and how severe? The act of making a medical diagnosis (e.g. 'You have Parkinson's disease') can be compared to the identification of position-related handicaps and deficits in particular areas of competitive advantage (e.g. 'You're in an inherently unattractive segment with a relative cost disadvantage').

In the search for a cure or palliative, it is the medical researcher who seeks to unravel the working of specific disease mechanisms, although the diagnostician must also have a good understanding of how disease mechanisms manifest themselves. Biochemistry, pharmacology and physiopathology are the realms of the medical researcher. The corollary for one seeking to understand competitive outcomes is the realm of organizational structure and process. For example, what are the specific process attributes of rapid product development or continuous improvement programs? Or, conversely, what are the organizational pathologies that frustrate functional coordination or the pursuit of zero defects? Only with such a fine-grained understanding of the processual attributes of specific forms of competitive advantage can one move from diagnosis to therapy.

Yet just as the diagnostic power of industry structure analysis is of little value unless accompanied by the therapeutic power of deep insight into process and structure, so the usefulness of process understanding is extremely limited unless it ultimately speaks to the issue of competitiveness. Medical research that does not ultimately make a contribution to wellness is likely to be poorly regarded. Any student of process and structure must be just as concerned about competitive outcomes as the industrial economist. But, ultimately, the process researcher arrives at the same impasse as the industrial economist. *Why* is it that patterns of lateral communication and mechanisms for employee involvement are often more developed in Japanese companies than in American companies, at least when one looks at paired comparisons of firms in the same industry? *Why* is it that total quality management and value engineering had their full flowering in Japan, rather than in the United States? Another layer must be peeled back.

Lifestyle and genetic predisposition are the twin roots of disease. The impact of diet, occupation and exercise habits on wellness are akin to the impact of institutional context on competitive outcomes. Monetary and fiscal policy, trade and industrial policy, the structure of financial markets and corporate ownership, the existence of uniquely national industry 'clusters' or skill sets, and the social norms that predominate in a particular country all have an impact on competitiveness (Porter, 1990; Prestowitz, 1988). Yet researchers who offer an account of the ways in which institutional context has, in the past, contributed to the competitiveness of some selected firms and undermined the competitiveness of others must be aware of two risks.

First is the risk that managers will 'externalize' the causes of competitive decline as 'beyond their control.' While some aspects of lifestyle-related causes of disease may be largely beyond the control of the individual—the level of air pollution in the city where one lives might be an example—there are many lifestyle factors that are controllable, with eating and exercising habits the most obvious. Likewise, there are many institutionally-related determinants of competitiveness that are at least partially within the control of managers. Examples include the collective bargaining environment (whose fault is it if Western managers often regard, and treat, workers as variable costs when they are seen in Japanese companies as a strategic resource?), the nature of buyer–supplier relationships (whose fault is it if Western managers take an adversarial stance with respect to suppliers when Japanese companies view suppliers as partners?), the degree of shareholder patience (whose fault is it if Western managers in large industrial companies do not have a track record of ambitious, profitable growth that commands the respect of shareholders?), and the degree of commitment that workers demonstrate towards the firm (whose fault is it if the yawning compensation gap between CEOs and blue collar workers in American companies undermines a sense of common purpose?). Researchers must be careful to distinguish between institutional factors that are inviolable givens (e.g. a separation of executive and legislative roles in government), those that can be altered through consistent coordinated action (e.g. anti-trust legislation), and those that are simply the product of uncritical allegiance to industry convention (e.g. adversarial supplier relationships).

A tendency to externalize institutional causes of competitive decline may also blind managers to opportunities to exploit national differences in institutional environments. In a world of nation states, institutional and cultural contexts remain more local than global. Yet in a world of transnational firms, asymmetries in access to institutionally-derived advantages need not persist indefinitely. Nor must institutionally-imposed disadvantages be simply tolerated.

Take some examples: companies like IBM and Philips are increasingly able to tap into what has long been regarded as a unique source of advantage for major electronics companies in Japan—the broad base of medium-sized, highly efficient, components producers. Firms like Nissan and Honda, which are as good at exporting their manufacturing competencies as their products, can jump trade barriers, establish local manufacturing and benefit from the relatively high price levels in Europe's tightly protected car markets. Motorola is increasingly able to compete on an equal footing with its Japanese rivals in hiring the best graduates of Tokyo University; and Japanese car companies can and do take their share of new graduates from California's leading auto design schools. Kodak can form a mini-keiretsu in Japan, and Fujitsu can take venture capital stakes in Silicon Valley firms. If Ford is unhappy with the nature of trade unionism in Britain, it can locate a new factory in Germany or Spain. If a firm feels it has unsympathetic shareholders, it can issue shares in a foreign equity market.

Thus the risk of overstating the impact of institutional context on firm competitiveness grows apace with the spread and success of transnational enterprise. For researchers interested in the problem of competitiveness, this suggests that the question of *why* different institutional contexts and national skill sets exist may ultimately be of less importance than the question of what companies can do to *exploit* institutionally-derived advantages, wherever they exist. Managers must be encouraged to develop strategies for institutional and cultural arbitrage.

A second hazard facing researchers eager to document the impact of institutional factors on firm competitiveness, and one much more of their own making than the externalization hazard, is the risk of unwarranted generalization. While institutional context undoubtedly impacts on competitiveness, conclusions about the competitiveness impact of institutional factors need to be drawn industry-by-industry, advantage-by-advantage. There seems to be an implicit belief on the part of many managers that Japan's institutional context is, in almost all respects, more conducive to the pursuit of global leadership than the institutional context of any other country. Yet one would be surprised indeed to find within any industrialized country a set of institutional arrangements and cultural traditions that worked systematically to the benefit of all of the firms in that country all of the time. Nor is one likely to find an industrialized nation whose institutions and structures work systematically to the detriment of all or most firms there domiciled. The institutional context and cultural milieu of any particular country are likely to benefit some firms at some times in some industries, and penalize other firms at other times in other industries.

Just as industry is not destiny—one can find profitable firms in supposedly 'unattractive' industries (Rumelt, 1991)—so institutional context is not destiny. If variability in firm performance within a particular institutional and cultural context is as great as variability in firm performance across institutional settings (and that 'if' points to an interesting research question), it becomes difficult to make any encompassing statement about the relative merits or demerits of different institutional settings. While managers in the car industry regularly style themselves as victims of a particularly hostile institutional environment, few complaints are heard from managers at Corning Glass, 3M, Cargill or EDS. Certainly the institutional context of American-based industry is not uniformly hostile to the pursuit of global leadership.

Likewise, not all Japanese-born firms grow up to be global giants; it's not something in the tea. In fact, there is no evidence, to date, that Japan has produced a higher proportion of global winners, given the size of its industrial base, than has Germany, Sweden, Switzerland or the United States. Neither is it clear that all of the globally successful firms that have emerged from Japan received identical sized helpings of clever advice, government largess and protectionism. Some firms, like Toyota and NEC, have long been government favorites; others, like Honda and Sony, were initially regarded as strong-headed interlopers, more likely to circumvent government advice than to take it.

Generalizations about the role of institutional context in determining competitiveness thus tend to obscure the fact that differences in competitive performance between firms can and do exist independently of any difference in institutional context; just as differences exist between individuals in their propensity to contract specific diseases independently of differences in lifestyle. Medical researchers must account for the committed couch potato who is still happily glued to the television at the age of 95, the fanatical young jogger who expires in mid-stride, the non-smoker who contracts lung cancer, and the strict vegetarian with arteriosclerosis.

In practice, we regularly observe firms that escape the inherent disadvantages of their institutional context and others that fail to benefit from the inherent advantages of their institutional context. Why is it that a Japanese firm, Yamaha, should become the world's largest producer of quality grand pianos—a product not well suited to the homes or traditional musical preferences of Japanese customers? Why should Shimano, another Japanese firm, beat European competitors like Campagnollo to dominate the world market for bicycle dérailleurs, gear changers, pedal sets and brakes, when Europe is the traditional home of sophisticated multi-gear bicycles? For Yamaha and Shimano, institutional context appears to have been as much a burden as a blessing.

Conversely, what prevented Ampex, the first firm to produce a video tape recorder, from ultimately dominating the video tape recorder business in the same way that Intel came to dominate the microprocessor industry? (In 1960 Ampex and Sony were approximately the same size, and Intel had not yet been founded.) And if protectionism, favoritism and the lavish attention of bureaucrats could propel a firm to global success, Japan's banks and brokerages would have given a much better account of themselves in international markets than they have thus far.

It is in these outlying cases that researchers reach the limit of institutionally-based explanations for global competitive success. It is here also where researchers can expect to uncover the deeper dynamics of competitive success and failure. For one must still answer the question of why a particular group of Japanese companies successfully challenged much larger Western rivals, why leaders become laggards, and why past industry leadership was, and is, such a poor predictor of future leadership. These are questions that often seem to elude industrial economists, process researchers and public policy makers. It is here that the student of competitiveness, like the medical researcher, must finally confront genetics.

The simple fact is that for many, if not most, diseases, the population of individuals who are genetically predisposed to contract a certain disease is not the same population as those who are disease-prone as a result of lifestyle. The population distributions of some maladies—sickle cell anemia, muscular dystrophy, Down's syndrome and male pattern baldness, to name a few—are determined almost exclusively by genetics. Diseases like breast cancer, colon cancer, hypertension and Alzheimer's are now known to have both genetic and lifestyle components. It is the task of disentangling the two that presents the medical researcher with his or her greatest challenge. The student of competitiveness faces a similar challenge.

---

## MANAGERIAL FRAMES

If genetic heritage manifests itself as a pre-programmed susceptibility to particular diseases, what is the managerial analog? I believe it is the foundational premises, beliefs and values that managers possess and that bound or 'frame' their perspectives on what it means to be 'strategic,' the available repertoire of competitive stratagems, the nature of senior management's value-added, the weighting of the various interests that senior management serves, the most effective tools for policy deployment, ideal organizational types, and so on. Acquired via business schools and other educational experiences, from consultants and management gurus, absorbed from peers and extracted from career experiences, managerial frames establish the range and likelihood of managerial responses in particular situations. Managerial frames may, more than anything else, determine a firm's strategic degrees of freedom.

Given two firms with identical resources, competing in the same industry, within the same institutional environment, one might nevertheless predict asymmetries in competitive performance, armed solely with the knowledge of a systematic difference between the two firms in the dominant mental frames possessed by their managers. Thus, the proposition arises, that the conceptual context of managerial action may be as important an explanation of competitive success and failure as the institutional or cultural context. If this is even potentially true, it suggests a radical reorientation in research efforts: strategy researchers should give as much attention to the relative merits of competing managerial philosophies as to the conduct and outcome of specific competitive engagements.

To date, strategy scholars have seldom addressed themselves to the issue of competing managerial frames.* Failure to do so was entirely forgivable as long as competition took place within a 'closed system,' i.e. among firms whose managers operated within a similar strategy frame. As long as competition took place between firms whose managers graduated from the same universities, hired the same consultants, subscribed to the same trade journals, and job-hopped among the same few companies, there was little to be gained from delving deeply into mindsets and mental models. After all, it wasn't Ford that challenged General Motors' long-held managerial precepts; it wasn't Texas Instruments that forced Motorola managers to reassess basic principles and practices; nor was it Thomson that compelled Philips to discard once-sacrosanct organizational tenets.

New patterns of global rivalry have made it obvious that com-

---

*Two notable exceptions are: Ouchi (1991) and Pascale and Athos (1981). These authors stress the sociological and institutional antecedents of so-called 'Japanese management.' Unfortunately, this focus on cultural imperatives tends to leave practitioners in the cul-de-sac of national 'culture,' from which there is no easy escape. The proposition put forward in this chapter is that while the systematic success of Japanese firms in the automobile, electronics and heavy equipment industries cannot be denied, it is unsafe to assume that this success is the product of a uniquely Japanese sociocultural context, in the same way as it would be unsafe to assume that the success of American multinational enterprise following World War II was attributable to particularly American cultural attributes. *Managerial* context and *cultural* context are not the same thing. While cultural context undoubtedly shapes managerial frames, the two can be disentangled. Just what it was that globally successful Japanese firms *did* possess in common, apart from their Japanese-ness, is the subject of this chapter.

petition takes place not only between firms, but between competing managerial frames. Strategy consultants and academics can no more avoid a fundamental reassessment of the managerial frames they have helped to create, than can managers escape the challenges of global competition. To often, strategy professionals have been content to document the processes and structures of successful Japanese firms, and then commend them to Western managers, without going to the trouble of understanding the managerial context that spawned and supports those processes. But organizational processes, stripped of their philosophical roots, are unlikely to take root, as the abundance of abortive attempts to impose quality circles, automate plants, and achieve cross-functional integration richly illustrates. As any first year medical student knows, an organ transplant is unlikely to be successful unless the donor and recipient are genetically compatible. This is why the best donor is an identical twin. Again, this suggests that the most appropriate starting point for competitive revitalization is an understanding of the managerial frames possessed by competitors, and of how they interact.

## GETTING OUTSIDE THE FRAME

To challenge the dominant frame, one must step outside it. For the most part, strategy researchers have been imbued with the same genetic coding as the managers they study. As a group, strategy researchers are the architects of the managerial frames that predominate among Western managers. If it is true that the culture hardest to know is your own, strategy researchers, like managers, cannot easily escape the constraints of deeply etched patterns of cognition, interpretation and action.

To step outside the frame one must first be dissatisfied with it. Strategy professionals have reason to be uneasy with the frames they have invented, employed and sold; for as the strategy industry has waxed, the international competitiveness of much of Western industry has waned. The 1970s and 1980s saw the blossoming of the strategy industry: up went the revenues of consulting companies, up went the number of pages of strategic plans cranked out within companies, up went the number of best-selling management books, and up went the number of business school graduates armed with the tools of strategic analysis. But as the strategy industry flourished, the world market share of Western firms declined, and the process of retrenchment accelerated.

The negative correlation between the growth of the strategy industry and the international competitiveness of Western industry may or may not be spurious. Perhaps the growth of the strategy industry has been driven by managers' ever more desperate search for the keys to revitalization. In any case, it is reasonable to expect a time lag between the publication of research, the giving of advice, the development of more sophisticated strategies, the onset of competitive renewal and the achievement of leadership. A less kind reading of the data leads one to enquire whether the growth of the strategy industry has in some way abetted the process of competitive decline. In any case, strategy consultants and academics might reflect on how lucky they are to have thus far escaped the ever widening net of product liability prosecution.

Practically, strategy academics and consultants must address tough questions: Why hasn't the question of the culpability of the strategy industry for competitive decline been more widely debated? Why isn't 'contribution to competitiveness' used more often as the yardstick by which to measure the value of strategy research? Why hasn't the competitiveness problem, which was brought upon Western companies by competitors who did not, for the most part, have the benefit of the Harvard Business School, McKinsey, *et al.* provoked a fundamental reassessment of the assumption base of the strategy profession? Strategy researchers are unlikely to pursue the quest for alternate paradigms with vigor unless they first confront the potential shortcomings, if not toxicities, of the dominant strategy frame.

Stepping outside the dominant frame also requires an unwillingness to submit to what Henry Mintzberg once called 'theoretical imperialism' (Mintzberg, 1979). Within business schools, PhD students and young faculty members are perhaps too prone to take the professionally safe route of testing and annotating theories handed down to them by their elders, rather than embarking on the more risky path of theory development. Given the pressing challenge of accounting for dramatic shifts in patterns of global competitiveness, do notions like strategic groups, generic strategies, barriers to entry and competitive signalling really deserve the attention lavished upon them by young researchers?

In accounting for shifting patterns of global competitiveness, the central challenge may be neither better description nor better theory testing. It is entirely possible to have rich description at the front end of the research process, thorough testing at the back end, and still end up with results whose only significance is statistical, if, between description and testing, there is a theoretical lens ill-suited to the phenomenon under study.

The assumption sometimes seems to be that only after a young researcher has paid his or her dues among the legion of theory testers can he or she join the ranks of the theory proposers. Only with enough gray hairs is one deemed capable of challenging existing theory. Such a system of implicit apprenticeship almost ensures that by the time a researcher has earned the right to question orthodoxy, he or she has become a hostage to that orthodoxy. The more inadequate we find existing theory, the more tolerance we must have for contrarians.

Finally, strategy researchers need the gravitational pull of an alternative managerial frame in order to break free from the existing frames. The goal is not to abandon one frame for another, but to become capable of critiquing each in the light of the other. Truth emerges through dialectic; yet there can be no dialectic without an intimate acquaintance with alternative, or at least different, frames. For the strategy researcher the implication is clear: the limitations of the existing frame only become visible as one becomes familiar with alternatives. To be intellectually honest, strategy researchers must exercise their curiosity and endeavor to fully understand alternate managerial frames.

At a minimum, theories developed and tested in a single industry context or in a single national context must be suspect, not because they may lack generalizability, but because they may represent a very small part of the whole truth. Imagine a study of the patterns of control and influence between head office and operating subsidiaries of diversified British companies. Given a sufficiently large sample, one will be able to draw defensible conclusions about which governance processes appear to work better or less well, or seem to be more or less suitable in particular contexts. Yet with such a narrowly drawn sample, however statistically significant, what assurance does the researcher have that the practices observed cover some reasonable spectrum of the total distribution of better and worse governance behaviors of firms around the world? How confident can the researcher be that he or she has observed anything approaching the maximum feasible repertoire of head office/business unit governance mechanisms? Research that fails to include firms whose managers possess widely varying mental frames may have little prescriptive validity, whatever its statistical validity.

---

## THE MEANING OF STRATEGY

### BEYOND 'STRATEGY'

Central to the managerial frame is a conceptualization of what 'strategy' is. In strategy theory and practice, three themes recur regularly. The first is the notion of 'fit' between the firm and its competitive environment. Fit entails the *positioning* of the firm *vis-à-vis* competitors, customers, channels, the regulatory framework and other external factors, and the *balancing* of opportunities with resources. SWOT analysis (strengths–weaknesses–opportunities–threats), market segmentation, five forces analysis and strategic group analysis are just some of the tools that have been suggested as means for considering and testing fit.

The second strategy notion is 'selectivity' in resource allocation: given a limited pool of funds and resources, the firm must decide which investments are truly *strategic* and which are not.* The techniques of strategic planning and business portfolio analysis address the allocational problem in strategy. In particular, the concept of corporate strategy centers on the problem of allocating resources, financial and otherwise, among competing investment alternatives.

The idea that strategy is concerned more with the long term than with the short term constitutes the third notion of strategy. For many managers, 'being strategic' implies a willingness to take the 'long view,' which is equated with a willingness to forgo immediate returns in hopes of a bonanza sometime in the future. Being strategic and maximizing short-term profitability are seen as antithetical. A 'strategic' investment is one that has a distant pay-out, demands patient money and, because of the uncertainty of the future, is inherently risky. The recurring debate about

---

*For an analytical perspective in resource allocation see Hofer and Schendel (1978); for a process perspective see Bower (1972).

short-termism (does it exist, and if so, whose fault is it?) is based on a premise that the ability of firms to act 'strategically' is imperiled by demands from impatient investors who expect uninterrupted improvement in quarterly earnings.

While there can be no argument that every firm must ultimately effect a fit between its resources and the opportunities it pursues, that resource allocation is a strategic risk and that firms must often countenance risk and uncertainty in the pursuit of strategy, the predominance of these particular notions in the strategy frame has obscured the subtle counterpoints which might suggest an alternative strategy frame. Perhaps the idea of 'fit' should be supplemented by a notion of *stretch* between existing resources and ultimate aspirations. Perhaps the concept of *resource leverage*, how to get maximum impact with the fewest possible resources, should be as central to the strategy frame as the issue of resource allocation. Perhaps the 'long term' has as much to do with *consistency* of effort and *constancy* of purpose as it does with patient money and risk taking. In the following pages I expand upon these contrapuntal themes and attempt to demonstrate how the weighting they receive in managers' strategy frames impacts competitive outcomes.

The arguments advanced represent the synthesis of 12 years of research in which the goals were to illuminate the mental frames of managers, document the ways in which those frames manifested themselves in the decisions of senior managers, and portray the interaction of competing frames within the context of protracted contests for industry leadership. The argument to be made is not that the dominant strategy frame is wrong, only that it is unbalanced; that without the counterweights suggested below, being strategic may carry as many dangers as benefits.

---

## STRATEGY AS STRETCH

Put yourself in the position of an institutional investor who, in 1970, is asked to choose between the following pairs of firms:*

---

*Of *course* this is an unrepresentative sample! The goal is to understand the process of winning and the process of losing. Yet there is no assumption of 'once a winner, always a winner,' or vice versa. Winning is only temporary (although losing may be

General Motors versus Toyota
Volkswagen versus Honda
Upjohn versus Glaxo
CBS versus CNN
Xerox versus Canon
Honeywell versus NEC
RCA versus Sony
Philips versus Matsushita
Westinghouse versus Hitachi
Pan Am versus British Airways
Burroughs versus Fujitsu
Caterpillar versus Komatsu

Where would you have put your money? Without the benefit of hindsight, most investors would probably have been tempted to invest in the firms in the left column. Why? These firms had strong reputations, deep pockets, a surfeit of technology, they would hire the most talented people in their industry, had sizeable market shares and a worldwide presence. In short, they had resources.

It is paradoxical that many managers still claim the success of Japanese firms is due to 'unfair advantages.' Having heard one too many excuses about the 'unfair advantages' of their Japanese competitors, I finally asked the senior management of a particular European electronics company just how much of their substantial resource base they would have been willing to trade, in 1970, for the unfair advantages of their competitors. The point was made. It wasn't so much that Japanese firms had unfair advantages, they merely had different advantages. But the firms in the left column were not without advantages of their own. The real issue is the relative effectiveness with which firms in both columns have multiplied their resources over time. To understand the competitive-

---

forever). Whatever a firm has done to 'win,' it will have to do again (at the level of principles, rather than tactics), if it is to win again. Neanderthal man discovered cooking, it is conjectured, when a house burned down and consumed a pig living therein. There is speculation as to how many houses were subsequently set alight in the quest for roast pork, before the distinction between tactics and principles was drawn. The firms on the left are not so much losers as firms that simply stopped winning. They continue to repeat the rituals of past success (burning down the houses, or 'corporate orthodoxies' in business school parlance), but seem unable to distill and reinterpret the principles of earlier successes.

ness dynamics at work in the illustration above, we must develop a view of strategy as *stretch* and *leverage*.

Imagine two firms, perhaps in the same industry. Alpha has a wealth of resource of every kind—human talent, technical skills, distribution access, brands, manufacturing facilities, and cash flow. These resources are the product of industry leadership (although the size of Alpha's resource base, accumulated over decades, is, of course, more a testament to past industry leadership than to present leadership). Alpha has no particular aspiration other than to remain on the perch it presently occupies. This goal has been expressed by Alpha's senior management as 'growing as fast as the industry.' Alpha's resources can thus be described as substantial, and its aspiration as modest.

Beta is a relative latecomer to the industry. It is much smaller than Alpha and has far fewer tangible resources. It has no choice but to make do with fewer people, a smaller capital budget, fewer facilities and a fraction of Alpha's R&D spend. But Beta's grand ambitions belie its meager resource base. It has every intention of knocking Alpha off its leadership perch, though Alpha would mock any such intention. To do this, Beta managers know that they must grow faster than Alpha, must thus develop both more and better products than Alpha, must be present in all the world's major markets, must build a credible worldwide brand franchise, and so on. Beta is the mirror image of Alpha: Beta is resource-poor but aspiration-rich. The extreme misfit between Beta's resources and its aspirations would cause most observers to discount the feasibility of the firm's goals.

The gap between Alpha's resources and its aspirations can be described as 'slack'; the gap between Beta's resources and its aspirations can be thought of as 'stretch.' Armed only with this knowledge, one can confidently predict that the two firms will adopt fundamentally different approaches to competitive strategy, and exhibit very different degrees of creativity in leveraging their respective resources.

Certainly Alpha is much better placed to behave 'strategically': to pre-empt Beta in building new plant capacity, to outspend Beta on R&D, to bury Beta under an avalanche of new products, to hire the lion's share of young talent, and so on. In fact, given its slack resources, this is precisely how Alpha will think about competitive battles with Beta. One would not be surprised to find Alpha managers resting easily, confident in the knowledge that they can overpower their smaller rival in any confrontation.

Alpha managers will find it hard to resist the temptation to take a World War I trench warfare approach to competitive strategy: 'We have more bullets than the enemy has bodies.' Alpha's approach to competitive warfare is to overwhelm the opposition by sheer weight of resources—however resource-inefficient this may be.

Beta has no such luxury. Facing its wealthy rival, Beta has no choice but to adopt the tactics of guerilla warfare, where the goal is to exploit the orthodoxy of the larger army. It must out-maneuver rather than overpower the enemy. This is the simple truth recognized by the North Vietnamese in their confrontation with American military might. A story is told of an American general who, while visiting Hanoi, got the chance to ask an ageing Vietnamese general a long-nagging question. How, the American soldier wanted to know, had the North Vietnamese been able to move men and *matériel* so freely across rivers, despite the attempts of the US military to locate and bomb enemy bridges? The simple answer was that the North Vietnamese had built their bridges just below the water line, so that they would be practically invisible to airborne reconnaissance, yet entirely usable by men and machines. One wonders how a resource-rich enemy would have responded to the problem of an enemy intent on destroying its bridges: probably by committing more troops to the defense of the bridges, by constructing redundant bridges, by bringing in even more engineers and heavy equipment, and by establishing even more anti-aircraft batteries. With a very clear, although daunting, goal in front of them, the North Vietnamese army hid in tunnels, sabotaged enemy facilities, co-opted civilians, laid traps and ambushed enemy soldiers with more verve and determination than could be mustered by US forces, who were pursuing a muddy and oftentimes unconvincing goal and believed they could always fall back on the 'big stick' of satura-tion bombing.

Like the well-worn aphorism about necessity and invention, tactical creativity is the child of resource scarcity. There is no reason to expect this to be any less true in competitive battles than in battles of a more deadly kind. While a galvanizing ambition and creative approach to resource utilization cannot be expected to compensate for any and all resource deficiencies, my own research evidence, and the annals of military history, suggest it is certainly the way to bet (for more historical evidence, see Tuchman, 1984).

While an abundance of resources enables strategic investments to be made, a state of plenitude does nothing to enhance the wisdom of strategic decisions. Resource abundance, and the attendant ability to make multiple bets and to sustain multiple failures, may too often be a substitute for disciplined and creative strategic thinking. Fifty billion dollars later, no one can accuse GM of not being strategic in its pursuit of factory automation, if by 'strategic' one means the willingness to make bold pre-emptive investments. Indeed, one could argue, as many who worked at the Hamtramck plant did, that GM has been *too* strategic, that the firm's ability to make strategic investments totally outpaced its ability to absorb new technology, retrain workers, re-engineer work flows, rejuvenate supplier relationships and discard managerial orthodoxies. If there is no capacity for resource leverage, if the firm has not learned how to do more with less, if, in other words, the risks of being 'strategic' are fully commensurate, or more than commensurate, with the rewards, there is no advantage in being strategic. Bigger bets sometimes bring bigger payoffs, but they're just as likely to bring bigger disasters. In the absence of an aspiration that outstrips a firm's resources, and a capacity for resource leverage, abundance is likely to be little more than a license for carelessness in strategic decision-making.

By way of contrast, what kinds of strategic decisions would be likely to emerge from Beta, whose aspirations run far ahead of its resources? First, as I have argued, Beta would eschew a 'John Wayne' approach to competitive strategy. It would exploit opportunities to change the rules of the game, rather than play by the rules of the incumbents. It would search for 'loose bricks' rather than confront its competitor in well-defended market segments. Investments would be focused on a relatively small number of core competencies where the firm felt it had the potential to become a world leader. Beta would invent lean manufacturing, with its emphasis on doing more with less. With fewer product designers than its competitors, the firm would be forced to dramatically reduce product development times in order to develop a full product line. The need to accelerate product development would spur lateral communication between functions. The growth of a vigorous and capable supplier base would be encouraged and suppliers would be asked to share a significant part of the innovation burden. The firm would be unable to support any superfluous corporate overhead or excess management layers. With a smaller human resource base, Beta would be compelled to view every employee as a contributor. To avoid any diversion of effort, top management in Beta would seek a deep consensus on strategic goals.

One could extend this illustration further, but the point is obvious. What has just been described—a view of competition as encirclement rather than confrontation, a propensity to accelerate the product development cycle, tightly-knit cross-functional teams, a focus on core competencies, close links with suppliers, programs of employee involvement and so on—is typically labeled as 'Japanese management'. Yet each of these particulars can be logically induced when one starts with a view of strategy as stretch.

So-called Japanese management may have less to do with social harmony and personal discipline than with stretch. It is this stretch—the fact that ambition forever outpaces resources—that fuels the engine of advantage creation. The disciplines of continuous improvement are the rails on which advantage creation runs, but the momentum comes from stretch. A firm that has a surfeit of ambition and a dearth of resources quickly discovers that it cannot merely imitate the advantages of more affluent competitors: it cannot match their spending dollar-for-dollar; it cannot afford the same entry costs; it cannot tolerate the same inefficiency and slack; it cannot take the risk of playing by the leader's rules. For all these reasons, a few Japanese firms were compelled to create entirely new forms of competitive advantage (à la lean manufacturing), and figure out ways of matching the existing advantages of competitors in more resource-efficient ways (for example, by initially relying more on third party channels than on a direct sales force).

Companies like NEC, CNN, Sony, Glaxo, Canon and Honda were, perhaps, united as much by the unreasonableness of their ambitions and the creativity they exhibited in getting the most from the least as they were by their common cultural and institutional heritage. If further evidence is needed, consider the less than sterling performance of Japan's largest banks and brokerages in world markets. Almost unique among Japan's multinationals, these firms already possessed immense resource advantages when they launched themselves upon world markets. Yet their material advantages have proved to be a poor substitute for the strategic creativity engendered by resource scarcity.

A view of strategy as stretch helps to de-mythologize the success of those relatively few Japanese companies that have become world leaders despite initial resource handicaps. It may be more honest to talk about the attributes of resource leverage than the attributes of Japanese management. The lesson for Western managers is not so much to become students of Japanese culture, but to ensure that there is sufficient stretch within their own bodies to compel employees at every level to challenge the orthodoxies that frustrate resource leverage.

The author was recently attempting to explain the logic of stretch to the executive committee of a large American-based multinational that was, throughout the 1970s and 1980s, one of the world's most consistently successful firms. 'Of course,' interrupted one senior executive, 'you must realize that we are number one in our industry, stretch only works if you're number two.' This manager was then asked to name a single criterion, other than revenue, market share or investment, on which his firm was still number one in its industry. The point was made: this firm was living on the momentum of the past, and had ceded intellectual leadership to hungrier, more ambitious rivals. What made stretch difficult for this firm was not that it was the biggest firm in its industry, but that it had not sought out a new definition of leadership more appropriate to its fast-changing industry, and had not re-stretched employees with a new ambition. The arrogance of leadership and the tendency towards profligacy can be avoided only by periodically raising the collective aspiration level. Industry leadership is something to be aimed for; no one should ever believe it has been achieved.

It may be that the explicit emphasis in the concept of strategy on the notion of 'fit,' and the way in which the idea of fit is implicitly embedded in strategy tools like critical success factor analysis and SWOT analysis, often deflects managers from the enormously important task of creating a misfit between resources and ambitions. Of course, as each rung of the leadership ladder is mounted, there must be a fit between the resources a firm is able to marshal and the opportunities immediately in prospect. Yet rather than resizing aspirations to fit the firm's existing resource base, the goal is to challenge managers to become substantially more ingenious in multiplying the impact of the firm's resource base. If ambition is prematurely pared down to achieve fit, there is no spur for such ingenuity and much of the firm's strategic potential will remain dormant. Tests of realism and feasibility must not be applied prematurely. Stretch, and the creativity it engenders, is the engine for corporate growth and vitality. This is why the genesis of the strategy process must be a purposefully created misfit between where the firm is and where it wants to be.

Mere ambition is not enough. Firstly, not any aspiration will do. Caterpillars can become butterflies; they are unlikely to become humming-birds. The misfit between a firm's existing resources and its desired goal may be substantial; it cannot be total. An aspiration must be grounded on the firm's competencies and its deep understanding of the potential patterns of industry evolution. The goal of becoming a world leader in 'C&C' (computers and communication) when first articulated by NEC top management might have seemed fanciful; it would have been outright absurd had it been Toyota or Sony that announced such a goal.

Secondly, stretching must become striving. Individuals at every level in the company must feel that the firm's ambition is inherently worthwhile, that it is a goal worth striving for. This suggests that the aspiration must have an emotional content as well as a numerical one. IBM's once-stated goal of becoming a $100 billion company by the end of the 1990s certainly represented a stretch— at the time IBM's sales were in the region of $50 billion—but was unlikely to capture the imagination of employees. The act of stretching is uncomfortable; it asks individuals and teams to continually teeter on the brink of what is personally and collectively possible. The more distant the prize, the more inherently worthwhile it must be if it is to inspire genuine striving. Only extraordinary goals beget extraordinary commitment and effort.

Thirdly, just as stretch is worth little without a capacity for resource leverage, a firm is unlikely to develop imaginative approaches to resource leverage in the absence of an ambition that far outstrips visible resources. A firm with an extraordinary ambition but no capacity for resource leverage is rightly dismissed as a dreamer. John Sculley at Apple Computer may dream of creating a 'knowledge navigator' to guide curious children and frustrated executives through the numbing complexity of today's multimedia data mountains, but to accomplish this dream Apple will need to match its vision with a capacity to leverage resources. Deals with Sony and IBM are a beginning. A firm with a capacity for resource leverage but no galvanizing ambition will be a 'sleeper.' A firm with neither aspiration nor a capacity for resource multiplication will be a 'loser,' while the 'winners' will be those firms that have both.

## STRATEGY AS LEVERAGE

The notion of resource leverage rests on several premises. The first is that the firm can be conceived of as a portfolio of resources (technical, financial, human, etc.), as well as a portfolio of products or market-focused business units. A growing body of academic research and writing takes such a resource-based view of the firm (Barney, 1989; Dierickx and Cool, 1989; Itami with Roehl, 1989; Prahalad and Hamel, 1990). The second premise is that resource constraints are not necessarily an impediment to the achievement of global leadership, nor are copious resources a guarantee of continued leadership. If it were otherwise, we would not have witnessed the dramatic shifts in competitive position that have occasionally put seemingly invincible incumbents like GM, Philips, IBM, Xerox and Texas Instruments on the defensive.

The third premise is that great differences do exist between firms in the market and the competitive impact they are capable of generating with a given amount of resources. Honda established leadership in its core competence area of engines and powertrains despite a much smaller R&D budget than General Motors. NEC succeeded in gaining market share against ATT, Texas Instruments and IBM despite, for most of its history, an R&D budget more modest in both absolute and relative terms than those of its rivals. Toyota develops a luxury car for a fraction of the resources required by Daimler–Benz. IBM challenges Xerox in the copier business and fails, while Canon, a firm only 10% of the size of Xerox in the mid-1970s, eventually displaces Xerox as the world's most prolific copier manufacturer. In its adolescence CNN managed to provide 24 hours of news a day with a budget estimated at one-fifth that required by CBS to turn out an hour of evening news. Such differences beg explanation.

The fourth premise is that leverage-based efficiency gains come primarily from raising the numerator in productivity ratios (revenue or profits), rather than from reducing the denominator (investment and headcount). Restructuring has reached epidemic proportions among Western firms. Whatever the name—'downsizing,' 'de-layering,' 're-focusing,' and the disingenuous 'right-sizing'—the universal goal of restructuring programs is to raise the productivity of human, physical and financial assets. The easiest, and usually the quickest, route to this goal is to cut the productivity denominators such as assets and headcount. With a goal of reducing the buck for a given bang, rather than increasing the bang for a given buck, denominator-driven corporate restructuring programs are more about cutting resources than leveraging resources.

Consider the plight of Britain's manufacturing sector during the 1970s and 1980s. Starting in 1973, Britain's manufacturing output fell, and then slowly recovered, so that by 1987 it stood at the same level it had in 1973. But by 1987, the UK had only 5.5 million people still employed in manufacturing, versus 8 million in 1973. On this basis British politicians could proudly point to a record of productivity improvement which, by the mid-1980s, was surpassed only by Japan. What was less readily admitted, and perhaps only dimly perceived, was that in the process of 'regaining its competitiveness,' Britain's share of world manufacturing had declined just about as fast as its productivity had improved.

Many companies are today in a similar predicament. Going through the same retrenchment wringer, ridding themselves of unneeded management layers, outmoded work rules and cumbersome bureaucracies, few of these firms are managing to grow in real terms. With a static revenue line, these firms are losing relative share in world markets. Yet if the typical approach to restructuring, with its denominator focus, grants productivity gains only at the expense of global market share, efficiency programs may do as much harm as good. And whereas this phenomenon was once though to be limited to the manufacturing sector, the service sector, from banking to airlines, appears to be in for the same brutal round of consolidation and constriction that has already worked its way through heavy industry.

But there is a fundamentally different way of achieving productivity gains. Imagine a company, or a country, that maintains employment at a constant level—there is no down-sizing and no blood-letting—and yet still manages to steadily increase output. This is resource leverage. While the productivity improvement numbers for the down-sizer and the leverager may appear identical, the progress made by each may not be equally sustainable. It is perfectly possible to get smaller without getting better; to cut the denominator without becoming any better at resource leverage. An inherently inefficient firm that down-sizes, without improving its capacity for resource leverage, will find that productivity improves—for a while. Technological leadership, brand loyalty, distribution coverage and customer service will not deteriorate immediately, but unless the firm discovers new approaches to resource leverage (e.g. ways of preserving its technological leadership on a smaller R&D budget, ways of building brand loyalty with fewer advertising dollars, ways of deepening distribution coverage more cost-effectively, and ways of improving customer service faster than the rate at which additional resources are committed to the task), it will find itself, in a few months or a few years, engaged in another round of non-elective surgery.

In such cases the firm will continue to ratchet down its resource base until investors locate a new owner with a proven track record of resource leverage. In a macro sense, this is precisely what is happening in the United States and Europe. An increasing share of the human and physical capital in industries like cars, consumer electronics and semiconductors are, through acquisitions and joint ventures, falling into the hands of companies, often Japanese, who better understand the process of resource leverage. And why shouldn't that be so?

What this also suggests is that while resource cutting is not an essentially creative activity, resource leverage is. It is about the continual search for new, less resource-intensive, means of achieving strategic objectives. Slimming down the work-force and cutting back on investment is inherently less intellectually demanding for top management than discovering ways to grow output on a static or only slowly-growing resource base. Cutting the buck is easier than expanding the bang; thus the preference for the former over the latter.

One manager I met early in my research career had recently left the auto industry to take a top job in a large electronics-based company. Early in his tenure he noticed that revenue per employee for the firm was just half that achieved by the industry leader. Reflecting on his experience as a tough cost cutter and down-sizer, the manager concluded that the problem he faced in his new job was simple—the company had too many employees! The idea that the firm should be growing by 20% a year, that any employees released would be immediately snapped up by faster growing competitors, and that the real problem was opportunity enlargement simply did not occur to this manager.

Managers, and operational improvement consultants, must ask themselves just how much of the efficiency problem they are actually working on. If their view of 'efficiency' encompasses only the denominator, if they do not have a view of resource leverage that addresses the numerator, then they have no better than half a chance of achieving and sustaining world-class productivity.

My fifth premise is that the allocational task of top management has received rather too much attention when compared to the role of top management in enlarging the firm's resource base and multiplying its market and competitive impact. While numerous textbooks, courses and consultants have sought to increase the allocational efficiency of top management (getting the right resources behind the most promising opportunities), there has been relatively little emphasis on top management's role in accumulating and orchestrating firm resources, particularly when the focus moves away from financial resources. If top management devotes more effort to assessing the strategic feasibility of projects in its allocational role than it does to the task of gaining resource leverage, its value-added will be modest indeed.

For whatever the starting resource advantages of industry incumbents, and whatever the efficiency of resource allocation, sooner or later, in every industry, the battle comes to revolve around the capacity to leverage resources rather than the capacity to outspend rivals. One measurement of a firm's capacity to leverage resources is the ratio of its relative market share gain (or loss) to its relative investment or resource base; revenue growth over resources would be another measure. Thus, while IBM and General Motors rate highly in terms of their ability, and even willingness, to make strategic investments (where an investment's strategic-ness is measured by the number of zeros that follow the integer), they rate no better than 'poor' in terms of resource leverage. Philips made so many 'strategic' investments, and was so poor at resource leverage, that despite the richness of its resource endowment it went to the brink of financial catastrophe. This points to the sixth and final premise: the capacity for resource leverage is the ultimate selection mechanism, sorting out the victors from the victims in prolonged battles for industry leadership.

## THE ARENAS OF RESOURCE LEVERAGE

Having a view of the firm as a portfolio of resources is one thing; understanding the basis for resource leverage is quite another. It is to this we now turn our attention. There are five fundamental ways in which resource leverage can be achieved: by more efficiently *accumulating* resources, by more effectively *concentrating* resources on key strategic goals, by *conserving* resources wherever possible, by *complementing* resources of one type with those of another in order to create higher order value, and by rapidly *recovering* resources by minimizing the time between expenditure and payback. I will now consider some of the specific components of resource leverage that make up each of these broad arenas.

---

## CONCENTRATING RESOURCES

### Converging

*The idea of convergence can be expressed as a ratio of time over the number of core strategic goals possessed by the firm.* The bigger this ratio, the greater the potential for resource leverage. The pursuit of a single 'strategic intent' (Hamel and Prahalad, 1989), over a long period of time, ensures that the efforts of individuals, functional departments and entire businesses converge on the same goal. Komatsu's goal of 'encircling Caterpillar,' Canon's goal of capturing 30% of the global copier business and 'beating Xerox,' and John F. Kennedy's challenge to 'put a man on the moon by the end of the decade,' all provided the focal point to individual and team effort.

In many of the companies I studied there was no such convergence of long-term goals. In some firms top management simply seemed to lack the discipline and intellectual courage needed to carefully think through potential patterns of industry evolution and distill an appropriate aspiration for the firm. Having established no specific aspiration, top management could not be accused of not having achieved it. In a funny kind of way, the absence of a clearly articulated stretch goal leaves top management more room for maneuver: it is difficult for anyone else in the organization to challenge the consistency or appropriateness of the stream of decisions (about acquisitions, disposals, market entry and withdrawal) that emerges from top management. Of course, the price for such maneuvering room is that there is little 'cumulativeness' to month-by-month and year-by-year strategic decisions. Going around in circles is not a recipe for resource leverage.

For example, consider NEC's relentless pursuit of its 'computers and communication' goal. While NEC was first a telecommunications equipment manufacturer, and IBM first a computer maker, both have long recognized that the two industries are converging. Yet IBM's flirtation with the telecommunications world has been an on–off affair. Satellite Business Systems, dalliances with MCI and Mitel, and the acquisition of Rolm have come and gone. Today, IBM's communications business is still very much a 'poor relation' in the IBM family. On the other hand, NEC is today the only company in the world that is a top five producer of both computer and communications equipment. NEC did not arrive here by outspending IBM; but rather by establishing, in the mid-1970s, the specific objective of becoming a leader in both computers and communications, by carefully elaborating the implications of that ambition in terms of required skills and capabilities, and then unswervingly pursuing that goal for the next decade and a half. NEC's experience suggests that resource convergence requires an intent with sufficient precision. There is no way to converge resources around a goal as amorphous as becoming a $100 billion dollar company, growing as fast as the industry, or achieving a 15% return on equity.

Almost as bad as having no clear aspirational goal is having multiple, competing goals. In several $10 billion+ companies in the study, the absence of a single, convergent goal left $1 billion or smaller sized units competing with the combined resources and singular vision of larger rivals. This is not to argue that every multi-divisional company can, or should, have an all-encompassing aspiration. Yet even in highly related multi-divisional companies, I have often found that line of business managers possessed radically different, and sometimes mutually exclusive, beliefs about future industry structure and the appropriate strategic intent of the firm. Without a mechanism to resolve such differences, and with each divisional manager jealousy protecting his or her own goal-setting prerogatives, it was not surprising that the efforts of middle and lower level managers were uncoordinated and often at cross-purposes.

For example, a divisional manager in Kodak admitted that executives in the firm's traditional film business had often viewed their colleagues in electronic imaging businesses like printers and copiers with deep suspicion—what did these new businesses have to do with Kodak's core business; didn't they represent a diversion of resources? These suspicions were not lessened by the oft-expressed views of their colleagues that electronic media would one day replace chemical-based media. Thus, despite the fact that

Kodak possessed perhaps the world's most complete portfolio of imaging capabilities, there was no convergence in long-term goals, and the two businesses fought, more or less independently, against Fuji on the one hand and Xerox on the other. More recently, Kodak has realized that it is uniquely positioned to control and shape the evolution of the information and imaging business. Kodak has a new strategic intent, and the strategies and development efforts of the chemical- and electronic-based imaging sectors are converging in important ways. The experience of Kodak demonstrates that convergence requires an understanding of how all the resources of the firm can be orchestrated to achieve a common goal, one that firms with a different portfolio of resources could not hope to aspire to.

Where core strategic goals do not outlive the often short tenures of senior executives, resource convergence is also unlikely. Even with a high degree of resource leverage, the attainment of industry leadership, on a worldwide basis, may be a decade-long quest. Recasting the firm's core ambition every three to four years is almost a guarantee that leadership will forever remain elusive. If the goal is to converge on a single distant target, the target has to sit still long enough for everyone in the organization to calibrate their sights, take a bead on the target, fire, adjust their aim, and fire again. Again, resource leverage comes only if the efforts of individuals, teams, functions and businesses are additive across time.

## Focusing

If convergence protects against the diversion of resources over time, focus protects against the dilution of resources at a particular point in time. *The idea of focus can be expressed as a ratio of resources over the number of key operating goals at any point in time.* The bigger the ratio, the greater the potential for resource leverage. I believe too many firms, finding themselves behind on cost, quality, cycle time, customer service and other parameters, attempt to put everything right simultaneously, then wonder why progress is so painfully slow. No single business, functional team or department can attend to all of these improvement goals at once, particularly if there is a sizeable gap to be closed in each area.

The effort required to embed the quality discipline, and to change the deeply-entrenched work habits, processes and management attitudes that get in the way of quality, is monumental. So too is the effort required to establish just-in-time manufacturing, as it requires a complete rethink of work flows, logistics and information systems, radical changes to plant layout, the training of both staff and suppliers, and must proceed, anyway, from a solid quality foundation. Cutting product development times by 50% and improving customer satisfaction by 100% are similarly heroic tasks. Without unrelenting attention to a very few key operational goals at any one time, improvement efforts are likely to be so diluted that the firm ends up as a perpetual laggard in every critical performance area. To take a simple military analogy, a general who arrays his or her forces against too many targets is unlikely to make much of a dent in any of them.

Consider Komatsu. Starting with products that were judged only half the quality of those of Caterpillar, Komatsu won Japan's highest quality award, the Deming prize, in three years. Many companies have been wrestling with quality for a decade or more and still cannot lay claim to world-class achievement. What accounts for this difference? When Komatsu initiated its total quality control (TQC) program, every manager was given explicit instructions: when it comes to a choice between cost and quality, vote quality. While quality may be free eventually, Komatsu managers realized that the pursuit of quality is certainly not free in the short run. It involves downtime, investment in better production equipment, training expenses, and so on. Thus, Komatsu focused almost exclusively on quality for a period of time, then, having achieved world standards there, and still keeping a close eye on quality measurements, Komatsu could focus its attention on, successively, value-engineering, manufacturing rationalization, product development speed and the attainment of variety at low cost. Each new layer of advantage provided the foundation for the next.

With a clear statement of operational priorities—the periodic 'management by policy' statements in Komatsu—top management focuses the intellectual energy and financial resources of the company on the next critical area for improvement. Such focus is not an excuse to ignore everything else—that would be naive and dangerous. Rather, in providing operational focus, top management simply predetermines the trade-offs it expects operating employees to make when, inevitably, they must decide where to allocate scarce time and resources.

Focus has brought Motorola a success as striking as that of

Komatsu. In 1987 Motorola established six sigma quality (3.4 manufacturing defects per million) as its paramount corporate goal—everything else came second. To date, defects have dropped from 6000 per million to 40 per million, and the company expects to hit six sigma within the next couple of years.

As strategic capabilities, cost and quality are mutually supportive; as operational improvement goals, reducing costs and improving quality both compete for scarce management time and employee attention. At one time, it was assumed that product variety and cost leadership were mutually exclusive. They are not: once one thoroughly understands cost drivers, one can seek ways of cost-effectively accommodating greater product variety. Yet a firm that is far from the leading edge on both cost and variety must build the capabilities in sequence.

Dividing meager resources across a wide range of medium-term operational goals is a recipe for mediocrity across a broad front. Take a simple example. Suppose someone standing three meters away suddenly hurls five golf balls at your head. What's your immediate reaction? Unless you're a world-class juggler, your first instinct is to duck. This is the same reaction exhibited by middle managers when top management attempts to push down five or six key operational goals of undifferentiated priority. Now imagine someone throwing just one golf ball at you, waiting the few seconds it takes for you to catch it, then throwing another and another. All five will be successfully fielded in around half a minute (I know, I've tried this with my students!).

Middle managers are regularly blamed for failing to diligently translate top management initiatives into action. On the other hand, middle managers may simply recognize the real risk of so diluting operational focus that little progress is made on any front. Middle management often finds itself attempting to compensate for top management's failure to sort out operational improvement priorities. Mixed messages and conflicting signals prevent a sufficient head of steam developing behind any improvement task.

Of course, once a firm is close to world standard on most key operational parameters, and well understands the interaction of cost, quality, variety, cycle time and so on, it can move forward on all fronts. Yet a challenge in a fundamentally new area would again require a clear focus, predetermined trade-offs, and a critical mass of effort. Put simply, the bigger the improvement task and the smaller the resource base, the more critical is operational focus.

Focus is as important in research and product development as it is in setting operational improvement goals. In many companies, the attitude towards innovation may be 'let 1000 flowers bloom,' but innovators soon discover that the fertilizer of corporate resources is so thinly spread that growth is prematurely stunted in each case. 3M, with more than 60 000 separate products, has long prided itself on the breadth of its innovative efforts. Yet recognizing that without more focus, big opportunities might remain small projects, 3M launched a 'pacing program,' in which each business picks one or two products or processes which it thinks offer 3M the chance for a big win. The result, 3M hopes, will be a menu of perhaps 50 key future projects that will serve as magnets for R&D resources (Anonymous, 1991a). Following a similar logic, the British-based pharmaceutical giant Smithkline Beecham has cut the number of drugs in its research pipeline by 26%, and reduced the number of diseases it aims to treat from 100 to 58 (Anonymous, 1991b).

## ACCUMULATING RESOURCES

### Extracting

A firm is a reservoir of experiences. Every day employees come into contact with new customers, managers learn more about competitors, new technological problems present themselves, product development programs are reviewed, and cross-functional disputes arise. What differentiates firms may be less the relative quality or depth of their experience stockpiles than their relative capacity to extract learning from that stockpile. *The idea of resource extraction can be expressed as a ratio of incremental skill enhancement (the numerator) per incremental experience (the denominator).* Put simply, some firms are capable of extracting greater learning from each additional experience than other firms. The capacity to maximize learning from every incremental experience and turn that learning into enhanced skills is a critical component of resource leverage.

For example, Honda has launched some small fraction of the number of small models spawned by Ford or GM. How, then, can one account for the fact that, despite its relatively scanty experience base, Honda seems capable of developing new car models in a fraction of the time, and at a fraction of the cost of Ford and GM? Honda makes a mockery of the experience curve. There is no lockstep relationship between accumulated volume and productivity improvement; rather, it is the relative efficiency with which the firm learns from each additional experience that determines the rate of improvement. The smaller a firm's relative experience base, the more systematic it must be in culling through its experiences for any hint of where and how improvements might be made.

The capacity to learn from experience depends on many things: having employees who are well-schooled in the art of problem solving; having a forum where employees can identify common problems and search together for higher order solutions (quality circles are one such forum); creating a sense of responsibility among all employees for firm competitiveness; being willing to fix things before they're broke; and continuously benchmarking oneself against best practice. For a comprehensive description of the elements of 'continuous improvement,' see Imai (1989) or, more generally, Baba (1989). A common saying in Japan is that a problem is a blessing. One has to be careful here—it is not the problem itself that is a blessing, but the opportunity it affords for improvement. This is a very different attitude from that observed in some companies, where problems are either camouflaged or shunted to someone else. The fundamental point is that each new experience, whether good or bad, must be seen as an opportunity to learn.

Whether learning actually takes place often depends on whether those closest to customers and competitors, who after all have the richest and most immediate experience base, possess the freedom to challenge long-standing organizational practices and processes. Those who really understand total quality management often say that quality is the key to management innovation. Yet in many companies, quality and innovation tend to be regarded as quite unrelated issues. The essence of total quality management is that every problem should be traced back to its roots. Often these roots are quite distant, in terms of organizational level and functional area, from where the problem was first spotted. Pulling up these roots often disturbs sacrosanct corporate policies, senior management prerogatives and revered company traditions. Yet only if every employee has the freedom to pull at these roots can learning take place. Freedom to take risks, freedom to be an entrepreneur, freedom to experiment are all important, but are no substitute for the freedom to challenge corporate dogma in the pursuit of enhanced performance.

Again, the point is simply: unlearning must often take place before learning can begin. What determines the capacity of a firm to extract learning from experience is, as much as anything else, the slope of its forgetting curve. The potential for leveraging the experiences of every employee in the quest for competitive advantage exists only when top management declares open season on precedent and orthodoxy.

---

### Borrowing

'Borrowing' the resources of other firms is yet another way of achieving resource leverage. Through alliances, joint ventures and licensing deals, a firm can avail itself of skills and resources residing outside the firm. *The extent of such leverage can be expressed by a ratio of the total resources available to the firm—those borrowed plus those internally developed—divided by internally developed resources.* The bigger the ratio, the bigger the leverage. At the extreme, borrowing involves not only gaining access to the skills of a partner but actually internalizing those skills.

Internalization is usually a more efficient way of acquiring new skills than acquiring an entire firm. In making an acquisition, the acquirer must pay both for the critical skills it wants and for other skills that it may already have or may deem less strategically valuable. Likewise, the problems of cultural integration and policy harmonization loom even larger in an acquisition than they do in an alliance.

NEC relied on literally hundreds of alliances, licensing deals and joint ventures to bolster its own development efforts and gain access to foreign markets. During the 1970s, and for most of the 1980s, as NEC was gaining market share against competitors like Texas Instruments, IBM and L.M. Ericsson, it was investing proportionately less in R&D than its rivals. NEC's alliances—with Intel, General Electric, Varian and Honeywell, to name a few—were significant multipliers of internal resources. NEC managers are quite forthright in admitting that without a capacity to learn from their partners, their progress towards the goal of C&C would have been much slower.

A senior manager in another Japanese firm expressed the simple logic of borrowing. Speaking of his firm's Western partners he remarked that 'they cut down the trees and we built the houses.' In other words, our partners do the difficult, resource-intensive work of scientific discovery, and we exploit these discoveries to create new markets. It is interesting to remember that it was Sony that first commercialized the transistor and the charge-coupled device, both technologies pioneered by Bell Laboratories. Technology is increasingly stateless: it moves quickly across borders in the form of scientific papers, foreign sponsorship of university research, cross-border equity states in high-tech start-ups, international academic conferences, and so on. Tapping into the global market for technology is a potentially important source of resource leverage.

Borrowing can be used to multiply resources at any stage of the value chain. Firms such as Canon, Matsushita and Sharp sell components and finished products on an OEM basis to Hewlett-Packard, Kodak, Thomson, Philips and others as a way of financing their leading-edge research in imaging, video technology and flat screens. For almost every Japanese firm I've studied, share of world development spending in key core competence areas was greater than brand share in end markets. Even today, around half of the output of the Korean electronics company, Samsung, is sold to downstream partners on an OEM basis. One can think of this as borrowing market share of well-positioned downstream partners in order to leverage up internal development efforts. The goal is to capture investment initiative from firms either unwilling or unable to invest in core competence leadership, in order to gain control of next generation competencies. As an example, there is currently no major American computer manufacturer that can turn out laptop or notebook computers without significant help from a Japanese partner. On the other hand, Toshiba, NEC and Sharp are quite capable of developing and marketing laptops with little or no help from Western partners.

In this case, and others, upstream partners can be expected to work hard to internalize the understanding of customer needs, buying patterns and distribution channels possessed by downstream partners. In this sense, alliances often represent a race to learn. If the upstream partner internalizes the unique skills of the downstream partner more rapidly than the reverse, bargaining power inevitably shifts to the upstream partner. More generally, whenever there is an asymmetry between partners in their relative capacity to learn from each other, bargaining power accrues to the partner that is most rapidly digesting the skills of the other. This partner may eventually be able to exit the relationship, and regain its freedom, or it may choose to exploit the fact that it has come to effectively control its partner.

If the goal is to leverage resources through borrowing, a firm's absorptive capacity is as important as its inventive capacity. In my research on strategic alliances, it was obvious that some firms were systematically better at borrowing than others. In simple terms, some firms approached alliances and joint ventures with the attitude of a teacher, and others with the attitude of a student. Suffice to say, arrogance and plenitude were not as conducive to borrowing as humility and hunger. Thus, for some firms the ratio of total resources to internally developed resources was far more than one; for others it was less than one. Some companies were more likely to inadvertently surrender skills to their partners than they were to internalize partner skills. One might term this negative leverage!

Borrowing may take a myriad of other forms: welding tight links with suppliers to better exploit their innovation, sharing development risks with critical customers, borrowing resources from more attractive factor markets (for example, when Texas Instruments employs relatively low cost software programmers in India via a satellite hook up), or participating in international research consortia (i.e. borrowing foreign taxpayers' money). Whatever the form, the principle is the same (Hamel, 1990)—how do we supplement internal resources with resources that lie outside the formal boundaries of the firm?

## COMPLEMENTING RESOURCES

### Blending

Another form of resource leverage rests on a firm's ability to blend different types of resources together in ways that multiply the value of each. This is the essence of the resource transformation process. *This notion of leverage can be expressed as a ratio of the value of combined skills over the value of discrete skills.* The bigger the ratio, the greater the leverage.

Blending involves several skills: technological integration, functional integration and new product imagination. Let us consider each in turn. It would be entirely possible for GM or Ford to outspend Honda in pursuing leadership in a set of discrete engine-related technologies like combustion engineering, electronic controls, variable valve timing, advanced materials, fuel injection, lean burn and so on, and perhaps even attain leadership in each of these areas, but still lag behind Honda in terms of all-round engine performance. What is critical is not just possessing the discrete skills, but one's capacity to blend those technologies together to create a world-class engine. This requires technology generalists, systems thinking and optimization of complex technological trade-offs. Absolute leadership in a range of technologies may count for little, and the resources expended in that quest may be substantially underleveraged, if the firm is not as good at the subtle art of blending as it is at brute force pioneering. When it comes to leveraging resources, a capacity for technological integration and harmonization may be just as important as a capacity for invention, and may represent a more resource-efficient route to best-in-class product performance.

A second notion of blending is the ability to successfully integrate diverse functional skills—R&D, production, marketing and sales—to produce a successful product. In firms where narrow functional specialization and organizational chimneys prevent such integration, functional excellence is rarely translated fully into product excellence. In such cases a firm may out-invest its competitors in every functional area, but reap much smaller rewards in the market-place.

Sometimes the issue is less the firm's ability to integrate disparate skills than its ingenuity at dreaming up new combinational permutations. Merrill Lynch's 'Cash Management Account' is such an example of resource leverage. 3M and Sony have also demonstrated great imagination in reconfiguring core technologies in novel ways. Sony's Walkman brought together headphone and tape recorder skills, and created a huge new market. Yamaha combined a small keyboard, a microphone, and magnetically encoded cars to create a play-along karaoke system for children. Resource leverage here comes not just from better amortizing of past investments in a particular skill set, but from creating entirely new forms of functionality and, thereby, value-added.

---

### Balancing

Blending and balancing are different things—one involves the creative interweaving of disparate skills, the other involves taking ownership of resources that multiply the value of a firm's unique competencies. Yet both are forms of resource complementation. *In the case of balancing, leverage impact can be expressed as a ratio between the profits gained by taking control of critical complementary resources, versus the cost of acquiring such control.* Let us start with an example. In the early 1970s the British company EMI invented computerized axial tomography, i.e. the CAT scanner. Despite having a ground-breaking product, EMI lacked both a strong international sales and service network and adequate manufacturing skills. With such an unbalanced resource profile, EMI was a bit like a one-legged stool. Because of this, EMI found it very difficult to capture and hold on to what it thought was its fair share of the CAT scanner market. Much of the financial bonanza created by EMI's innovation ended up in the pockets of General Electric, Siemens and other competitors who, having once figured out a way around or through EMI's patents, used their distribution clout and manufacturing excellence to squeeze EMI out of the market.

To be balanced, a company, like a stool, must have at least three legs: a strong product development capability, a capacity to produce the product at world-class levels of cost and quality, and a sufficiently widespread distribution, marketing and service infrastructure—in simple terms, a capacity to invent, make and deliver. If any leg is much shorter than the others, the firm will be unable to fully exploit the investment it has made in its areas of strength. The leverage impact comes when, by gaining control over complementary resources, the firm is able to multiply the profits it can extract out of its own unique resources (Teece, 1986).

Many small, high-tech firms are unbalanced in just the way EMI was. A firm that has a strong product development capacity but is relatively weak in terms of brand or distribution, or lacks the disciplines of cost and quality, is unlikely to gain much of the profit stream that ultimates accrues to its innovation. While it can certainly enter a partnership with firms that do possess critical complementary resources, the innovator is likely to find itself in a poor bargaining position with such firms when it comes to dividing up profits. This explains why every Japanese company in my study, though very willing to temporarily borrow the downstream resources of foreign partners, had also worked diligently to set up its own worldwide distribution and manufacturing infrastructure. They realized they could fully capture the economic benefits of their innovations only if they ultimately owned the critical bundle of complementary resources.

A similar logic is at work in the international alcoholic drinks industry. IDV, Seagrams and Guinness once saw themselves as primarily brand creators and managers. Yet they have come to realize that to fully leverage the equity inherent in brands like Smirnoff, Johnny Walker and Chivas Regal they must take control of distributors around the world. This realization has set off a frenzied competition for control of these distributors and agents.

Whatever the nature of the imbalance, strong on distribution and weak on product development, strong on manufacturing and weak on distribution, or some other combination, the logic is the same. A firm cannot fully leverage its accumulated investment in any one dimension if it does not control, in some meaningful way, the other two dimensions. Rebalancing leads to leverage when the additional profit the firm is able to capture by gaining control of critical complementary assets (through borrowing or outright investment) more than covers the cost of acquiring those complementary resources.

---

## CONSERVING RESOURCES

### Recycling

The more often a given skill or competence is re-used, the greater the resource leverage. *The leverage that maybe gained from resource recycling can be expressed as the number of applications per competence.* Canon applies its optics expertise in cameras, copiers, ophthalmic testing equipment, semiconductor production equipment, camcorders and other areas. Canon's cartridge-based imaging system, which first made its appearance in a line of 'Personal Copiers,' migrated to laser printers and plain paper faxes. Sharp exploits its LCD competence in calculators, electronic pocket calendars, mini-TVs, large screen projection TVs and laptop computers. Honda has recycled engine-related innovations across motorcycles, cars, outboard motors, generators and garden tractors. It is little wonder that these firms have unmatched R&D efficiency. It is said that in Japan no technology is ever abandoned, it's just reserved for future use. These firms are proof of that maxim.

Unless senior managers across the firm have reached agreement on key development priorities, the potential for recycling will be severely limited. Divisional managers will be more likely to hoard scarce resources than loan them to sister businesses. One thing I sometimes ask divisional vice presidents to do, one by one, is to rank what they believe are the company's top ten opportunities. Where rankings differ substantially across divisional managers, there is no logical basis for recycling scarce resources across unit boundaries.

Of course recycling is not limited to technology-based competencies. A brand can be recycled as well. Again, it is not surprising that resource-constrained Japanese firms have almost universally elected to use 'banner' brands rather than individual product brands; the economy of scope benefits of banner brands are obvious. Familiarity with a high quality banner brand creates a strong predisposition on the part of customers to at least consider purchasing new products that bear the banner. Think of the leverage Sony gets when it launches a new product; think of the relatively modest incremental cost that faces Sony in building credibility with retailers and consumers for a new product; consider the amount of implicit goodwill with which a new product is imbued simply because it carries the Sony brand.

Obviously banner branding cannot turn a loser product into a winner. In fact, a lousy product will undermine the brand. And in companies with a long history of product branding, like Unilever or Procter & Gamble, there can be no argument for abandoning tried and tested product brands for unknown banner brands. Yet even these companies are increasingly prone to use their corporate monikers in tandem with well-known product brands. In working to build a strong presence in Japan, where consumers were not familiar with Procter & Gamble's traditional brands, the company recognized the added 'umph' its brand building efforts would receive from a judicious use of the Procter & Gamble corporate brand. Building brand leadership on the back of a single product line is a slow and expensive process. To even begin to capture a share of mind, customers must have been exposed to the brand a dozen times or more. Fragmenting an advertising campaign across many independent brands substantially slows the pace of brand building. This was not an issue for Procter & Gamble in its traditional product categories in the US, where everybody already knew Tide, Crest and Ivory. It most certainly was an issue in Japan.

Walk through an international airport—Charles de Gaulle, Heathrow, Frankfurt or Hong Kong—and note the number of billboards bearing the corporate logos of Japan's, and Korea's, industrial giants. It is clear that for these companies brand building is, at least in part, a corporate activity. There is no expectation that each business must bear the full costs of building global share of mind. A few years ago General Electric took what, for it, was an unusual step—it erected an illuminated corporate billboard at Heathrow airport. The GE logo was accompanied by an innocuous slogan: 'GE, moving faster than the world around us.' The billboard didn't stay up long. None of the businesses, complained a senior European GE executive, were willing to pay for the sign. Hardly an example of recycling. A few days later that particular piece of English sky belonged to Toshiba.

The ability to quickly switch a production line from making widgets to gadgets, known as flexible manufacturing, is another form of resource recycling. Some Japanese car producers can make up to seven models on a single production line; American producers seldom manage more than one model per line. Such flexibility means less downtime as production shifts from one model to another, and therefore better resource utilization.

This suggests that speed is also an issue in recycling. The faster resources are recycled from project to project, the greater the resource leverage. Every firm has a given stock of resources. Like the money supply, a firm's total quantity of resources is the product of both stock and velocity—that is, how much of any scarce resource it possesses, and how quickly it can recycle that resource to support other opportunities. The faster these resources can be effectively deployed from project to project, the greater the potential resource leverage. Resources that through organizational territorialism become imprisoned in a particular part of the company will be under-leveraged.

Opportunities for recycling hard-won knowledge and resources are manifold: sharing merchandising ideas across national sales subsidiaries; migrating operational improvements from one plant to another; re-using the same subsystem across a range of products; quickly disseminating ideas for better customer service; and lending experienced executives to key suppliers. Yet every opportunity for recycling requires a view of the corporation as a pool of widely accessible skills and resources, an appreciation that unit managers are stewards over key resources, and don't 'own' them, deeply etched patterns of lateral communication that keep everyone aware of just which resources are located where, and, of course, a cooperative spirit among key managers. This is the organizational foundation for resource recycling.

## Co-opting

Sometimes it is possible to entice a potential competitor into a fight against a common enemy. Sometimes it is possible to work collectively to establish a new standard or develop a new technology. Sometimes a group of firms can be made to coalesce around a particular legislative issue. In these cases, and others, the goal is to co-opt the resources of other firms, and thereby extend one's influence and power within one's industry. In borrowing resources the firm seeks to absorb its partners' skills and make them its own; in co-opting resources, the goal is to enroll others in the pursuit of a common objective. *The ability of a firm to co-opt the resources of others can be expressed as a ratio of industry influence over size.* For some firms this ratio is more than one, for others it is substantially less than one.

A firm that seeks to co-opt other industry players must first identify a common objective—that's the carrot. The process of co-option begins with the question: how can I convince other firms that they have a stake in my success? Co-option is driven by the logic that my enemy's enemy is my friend. Philips has demonstrated a knack for playing Sony and Matsushita off against each other, selectively enrolling one as a partner to block the other. This may suggest that being slightly Machiavellian is no disadvantage when it comes to co-opting resources. Sometimes co-option requires a stick as well as a carrot. The stick is typically control over some critical resource that other players in the industry are forced to rely on. The unstated logic here is, 'unless you play the game my way, I'll take my ball and go home.'

A good example of co-option has been Fujitsu's relationship with its partners in the computer business: ICL in Britain, Siemens in Germany and Amdahl in the United States. Each of these partners shares a common objective—challenging the dominance of IBM. That is the carrot. Fujitsu's stick is the substantial, in some cases almost total, dependence of its partners on Fujitsu's semiconductors, central processors, disk drives, printers, terminals and other components.

Co-option does not require an equity stake. Although Fujitsu recently acquired the majority of ICL shares, Fujitsu was not eager to take over the company. Its hand was forced by the risk that ICL's parent company, STC, might sell Fujitsu's long-term partner to a competitor. That Fujitsu saw no great benefit in acquiring

ICL is testimony to the fact that, in many respects, Fujitsu already controlled ICL through ICL's technological dependence. In Fujitsu's mind, equity control was both redundant and politically fraught.

Staying with the computer industry, Andersen Consulting, an IT consulting specialist, has acquired a degree of industry influence out of proportion to its size. By pre-emptively building unique IT consulting skills, Andersen has positioned itself, in a number of clients, as a critical gateway to top IT decision makers. In these companies any vendor that wants to get a hearing needs first to convince Andersen that it really understands the client's needs and will bring a world-class solution to the table. Microsoft is another past expert at co-option.

## Shielding

A wise general ensures that his or her troops are not exposed to unnecessary risks. One does not attack a heavily fortified position; one disguises one's true intentions; one carefully reconnoiters the territory to be captured before advancing; one diligently studies the enemy's weaknesses; one feints in order to draw the enemy's forces away from the intended point of attack; one exploits the element of surprise, and so on. The greater the numerical advantage held by an enemy, the greater the incentive to avoid a full frontal confrontation. The goal is to maximize the losses inflicted on an enemy, while minimizing the risk to one's own forces.

*In this sense, the idea of shielding resources can be expressed as a ratio of market or competitive impact over degree of resource exposure.* Attacking a competitor in its home market, attempting to match a larger competitor strength-for-strength, accepting the industry leader's definition of market structure, or becoming a prisoner of 'accepted industry practice,' are all akin to John Wayne marching into the OK Corral. Judo may be a more appropriate metaphor for competition when the goal is to leverage resources. The first principle in judo is to use your opponent's weight and strength to your own advantage: deflect rather than absorb the energy of your opponent's attack, get him or her off balance, and then let momentum and gravity do the rest.

Dell Computer, America's fastest growing personal computer company, could not have hoped to match Compaq's dealer network or IBM's direct sales force. Instead, Dell chose to sell its computers by mail. Industry incumbents, with big stakes in their existing distribution arrangements, have found it almost impossible to match Dell—not because they don't have the resources, but because they face powerful constituents who have a big stake in the status quo. Critical success factors become orthodoxies when a competitor successfully changes the rules of competitive engagement. Such competitive innovation is an important way of shielding resources.

Searching for under-defended territory is another approach to shielding resources. Honda's success with small motorbikes, Komatsu's early forays into Eastern Europe, and Canon's entry into the 'convenience' copier segment all failed to alert incumbents whose attention was focused elsewhere. Understanding a competitor's definition of its 'served market' is the first step in the search for under-defended competitive space. The goal is to build up one's forces just out of sight of stronger competitors.

'Expeditionary marketing' is another way of shielding resources. Through a series of limited market incursions, the goal is to gain insights into customer preferences, price points and appropriate channel strategies, before launching an all-out assault. In the 1960s, while Canon was hard at work developing its own proprietary technology for electrostatic copying, it licensed technologies for coated paper copiers and distributed the resulting product in the US through Scott Paper Company. Without directly exposing itself to American competitors, Canon was able to garner insights into channels, servicing requirements and customer needs. Canon's goal was simple: to gain maximum insight into a potential market opportunity with a minimum initial commitment of resources.

---

## RECOVERING RESOURCES: EXPEDITING SUCCESS

Another important determinant of resource leverage is the elapsed time between the expenditure of resources and the recovery of those resources, in the form of revenues, via the market-place. A rapid recovery process acts as a resource multiplier. A firm that can do anything twice as fast as its competitors, with a like resource commitment, enjoys a two-fold leverage advantage. This rudimentary arithmetic explains why Japanese companies have been so intent on accelerating product development times.

It is currently estimated that Detroit's Big Three require an average of 8.0 years to develop an entirely new model line, while the figure for Japan is 4.5 years, with individual model variants developed in something close to half that time. This allows Japanese manufacturers to recoup their investments more quickly, have more up-to-date products, and give customers more excuses to abandon their traditional models. A disciplined approach to agreeing on product development priorities (focusing), seamless functional integration (blending) and tight integration with a network of capable suppliers (borrowing and co-opting) also means that Japanese car companies are capable of developing a new model with 1.7 million person-hours of effort, rather than the 3.0 million person-hours typical of American manufacturers. Not only do Japanese auto firms get a much quicker payback, they need a much smaller payback to put them into the black on any particular model (Anonymous, 1991c).

While much has been written about concurrent engineering and parallel development, fast-paced product development is only one way of shortening recovery time. A firm that has built a highly esteemed, powerful global brand will find customers eager to try out new products. This predisposition to buy, as it was earlier labeled, is another recovery accelerator. After all, recovery time is not measured from product concept to product launch, but from product concept to some significant level of world market penetration.

There has been no attempt here to present an exhaustive list of every possible strategy for resource leverage. The goal was simply to challenge managers and strategy professionals to be more imaginative in thinking up ways to get the most from the least. A firm's capability for resource leverage can be calculated, at least in part, in terms of this inventory. However, I do believe the five broad arenas of resource leverage outlined above encompass the complete domain of leverage opportunities. By efficiently *accumulating*, sufficiently *concentrating*, creatively *complementing*, carefully *conserving* and speedily *recovering* resources, firms close the gap between where they are and where they want to be.

---

## TOWARDS A NEW STRATEGY FRAME

The emergence of new competitors, dramatic changes in technology, the globalization of markets and geopolitical upheaval have profoundly shaken the foundations of the competitive environment for most Western firms. Not surprisingly, the strategy frame that rested atop this foundation is now contorted and, perhaps, even unsafe. Not that all of it must be dismantled. There is much that is right with the dominant strategy frame; much that can be built upon as we seek to construct a frame appropriate to the competitive challenges of the 21st century.

## FROM FIT TO STRETCH

I believe that the first essential element of a new strategy frame is an aspiration that creates, by design, a chasm between ambition and resources: strategy is stretch, as well as fit. For many managers, great ambition means big risk taking. Yet there is no one-to-one correlation between stretch and risk. Stretch implies risk only when there is orthodoxy about how and when the aspiration is to be achieved. If managers at Ford simply extrapolate past practices, they might be tempted to believe that developing a car five times as good as the Escort, a potential Lexusbeater, say, would require five times the resources. As long as a firm is held hostage to the orthodoxies of the past, it is unlikely to gain the courage necessary to commit to undisputed world leadership.

There is a chart in the office of a senior executive in a Japanese electronics company, that has as its *x*-axis a timeline, and along the *y*-axis a ratio of the sales and profits of its leading American competitors to its own sales and profit. In between is a plot that shows, year-by-year, the American competitor getting relatively smaller and the Japanese firm relatively bigger. Yet there is no assumption as to just when the trend line will finally intercept the timeline: maybe it will happen in 10 years, maybe in 20, maybe in 50. Nevertheless, everyone in the company knows that the goal is to continue to grow at the expense of their competitor; in other words, the line had better come down every year!

Stretch begets risk when an arbitrarily short time horizon is superimposed on a long-term leadership goal. Impatience brings the risk of rushing into markets not fully understood, ramping up R&D spending faster than it can successfully be managed, acquiring firms that cannot be easily digested, and rushing into alliances with partners whose motives and capabilities are poorly understood. If resource commitments outpace the accumulation of customer and competitor insights, risk inevitably ensues. The job of top management is not so much to boldly 'stake out' the future, but to help accelerate the acquisition of market and industry knowledge in ways that do not prematurely expose the firm to market and competitor risks. Risk recedes as knowledge grows, and as knowledge grows, so does the firm's capacity to move forward.

The notion of strategy as stretch helps to bridge, I believe, the gap that exists between those who see strategy as 'grand plans, thought up by great minds,' and those that see strategy as a pattern in a stream of incrementalist decisions. Strategy as stretch is strategy by design, in the sense that top management does possess a relatively clear view of the goal line. Strategy as stretch is strategy incrementalism to the extent that top management cannot pre-specify a 20-year plan for global leadership, and must challenge the organization to clear the path towards leadership meter-by-meter. Strategy as stretch recognizes the essential paradox that while leadership cannot be planned for, neither does it happen in the absence of a reasonably precise aspiration.

## FROM ALLOCATION TO LEVERAGE

The dominant strategy frame pays much attention to the task of resource allocation. Resources, it is rightly assumed, are scarce; top management must apportion them with all due care. But isn't it equally top management's job to effectively multiply the firm's resource base through creative approaches to resource leverage? Is leverage any less important than allocation? If not, why the almost exclusive preoccupation of managers and strategy researchers with the allocational task?

The great majority of managers I met through my research felt themselves to be resource constrained. 'If only we had more resources, we could be more strategic,' was an opinion voiced again and again. Yet with a view of strategy as leverage, it is apparent that the real issue for many of these managers is not a lack of resources, but too many priorities, too little stretch, too little creative thinking about how to leverage resources, and too little consistency in direction over time. It's no wonder that many of these managers feel that they are resource-constrained—in a sense, they were. Yet showering them with more resources, in the absence of a fundamental improvement in their capacity to leverage resources, will provide no more than temporary relief of their frustrations.

If the goal is to be 'strategic,' a sense of deprivation may not be a bad thing. I do not believe that managers in ATT, IBM, General Motors, Ford, Xerox, Du Pont, Procter & Gamble, ICI, Siemens and a host of other companies feel resource-constrained *enough*! Lean manufacturing and lean product development ain't the half of it. What is needed are fundamentally lean strategies. This is not a crash diet; this is living one's entire life lean and hungry. This is the *hyper-efficient firm*.

---

## From Patient Money to Perseverance

If stretch provides the incentive for resource leverage, it is resource leverage that allows a firm to persevere in its quest for global leadership. That strategy is about the long term cannot be denied. That the long term is about making bigger bets, having more patient shareholders, or being more courageous than the next guy is nonsense. Strategic commitment is evidenced not so much by how much is invested, but by how persistently leadership is pursued. When it comes to being strategic, too many companies pass the courage test, yet fail the consistency test.

To get off the restructuring treadmill, to escape the catch-up trap, to get back on the offensive, nothing less than an intellectual transformation of management is required. Managers must be ready to admit that half of what they know today may be toxic in the next decade. Business school academics must be ready to admit that they are not merely students of the 'competitiveness problem,' they are part of the problem. Consultants must be ready to admit that simply showing firm B how to mimic what firm A has already done—communicating the *what* of competitiveness without understanding the *why*—offers little hope of self-sustaining revitalization. Together, we must all search for an ever deeper understanding of competitiveness. Together we must first deconstruct, and then reconstruct, our managerial frames.

## REFERENCES

Andrews, K. (1980). *The Concept of Corporate Strategy.* Homewood, IL: Richard D. Irwin.

Anonymous (1991a). 3M: 60,000 and counting. *The Economist*, 30 November, 86–89.

Anonymous (1991b). A tighter focus for R&D. *International Business Week*, 2 December, 80–82.

Anonymous (1991c). Miles traveled, more to go. *International Business Week*, 2 December, 44–47.

Baba, Y. (1989). The dynamics of continuous innovation in scale intensive industries. *Strategic Management Journal*, **10**(2), 89–100.

Barney, J. (1989). Firm resources and sustained competitive advantage. Texas A&M University, unpublished manuscript.

Bower, J.L. (1972). *Managing the Resource Allocation Process.* Homewood, IL: Richard D. Irwin.

Buzzell, R.D., Gale, B.T. and Salton, R. (1975). Market share: A key to profitability. *Harvard Business Review*, January/February, 92–106.

Consumano, M.A. (1991). *Japan's Software Factories.* New York: Oxford University Press.

Deirickx, I. and Cool, K. (1989). Asset stock accumulation and sustainability of competitive advantage. *Management Science*, December, 1504–1514.

Hamel, G. (1990). Competitive collaboration: Learning, power and dependence in international strategic alliances. University of Michigan, unpublished doctoral dissertation.

Hamel, G. and Prahalad, C.K. (1989). Strategic intent. *Harvard Business Review*, May/June, 63–76.

Hofer, C.W. and Schendel, D. (1978). *Strategy Formulation: Analytical Concepts.* St Paul, MN: West Publishing.

Imai, M. (1989). *Kaizen: The Key to Japan's Competitive Success.* New York: Random House.

Itami, H. with Roehl, T. W. (1989). *Mobilizing Invisible Assets.* Cambridge, MA: Harvard University Press.

Mintzberg, H. (1979). An emerging strategy of 'direct' research. *Administrative Science Quarterly*, **24**(4), 582–589.

Ouchi, W.G. (1981). *Theory Z: How American Management Can Meet the Japanese Challenge.* Reading, MA: Addison-Wesley.

Pascale, R.G. and Athos, A.T. (1981). *The Art of Japanese Management.* New York: Simon and Schuster.

Porter, M.E. (1980). *Competitive Strategy: Techniques for Analyzing Industries and Competitors.* New York: Free Press.

Porter, M.E. (1985) *Competitive Advantage: Creating and Sustaining Superior Performance.* New York: Free Press.

Porter, M.E. (1990). *The Competitive Advantage of Nations.* New York: Free Press.

Prahalad, C.K. and Hamel, G. (1990). The core competence of the corporation. *Harvard Business Review*, May/June, 79–91.

Prewstowitz, Jr, C.V. (1988). *Trading Places: How America Allowed Japan to Take the Lead.* New York: Basic Books.

Rumelt, R.P. (1991). How much does industry matter? *Strategic Management Journal*, **12**(3), 167–186.

Teece, D.J. (1986). Firm boundaries, technological innovation, and strategic management. In L.G. Thomas (Ed.) *Economies of Strategic Planning*. Lexington, MA: Lexington Books.

Tuchman, B. (1984). *The March of Folly*. New York: Alfred A. Knopf.

Womack, J.P., Jones, D.T. and Roos, R. (1990). *The Machine that Changed the World*. New York: Rawson and Associates.

# 4

# Strategic Reference Point Theory

## AVI FIEGENBAUM, STUART HART, DAN SCHENDEL

---

### INTRODUCTION

The rational model of strategic choice has been questioned extensively. A well-established behavioral literature demonstrates that
individual cognitive limits, organizational politics and environmental change all serve to blunt rational choice (Lindblom, 1959;
Lyles and Mitroff, 1980; March and Simon, 1958; Tversky and
Kahneman, 1974). At best, according to this literature, individuals
and organizations can achieve only 'bounded rationality' (Simon,
1957). For top managers, this means that the formulation of a
deliberate or comprehensive strategy is an illusion (Mintzberg,
1978, 1990). However, abdicating responsibility for strategic choice
by allowing it to emerge from the bottom up is probably not
desirable either (Guth and MacMillan, 1986).

Given the infeasibility of the former and undesirability of the
latter, what is the appropriate role for top managers in strategic
choice? Can managers make a difference? In particular, can
managers alter the perceived risk–return position of organizations? Quinn (1978) proposed that rather than seeking to be comprehensive—the ideal of rationality—executives should work to
create a broad sense of direction, but allow the precise nature of
the strategy to emerge over time. Hart (1992) described this as the

*Building the Strategically-Responsive Organization.*
Edited by H. Thomas, D. O'Neal, R. White and D. Hurst.
Copyright © 1994 the Strategic Management Society. Published 1994 by John Wiley & Sons Ltd.

'symbolic' mode of strategy making, where executives attend primarily to crafting an ambitious mission and creating a compelling vision which helps to focus the actions of organizational members. Such a vision or 'strategic intent' should serve to inspire and motivate organizational members by creating a high level of aspiration (Hamel and Prahalad, 1989; Westley and Mintzberg, 1989).

Economic theory and organization theory have also recognized the importance of establishing targets or reference groups (and, by implication, 'gaps' and 'aspiration levels') for individual and organizational performance. Indeed, industrial economics (Porter, 1980), resource dependence (Pfeffer and Salancik, 1978), and institutional theory (Meyer, Scott and Deal, 1983), all posit, in one way or another, the importance of *external* points of reference to strategic choice or firm survival. Similarly, motivation theory (Latham and Yukl, 1975), prospect theory (Tversky and Kahneman, 1981), and the resource-based view of the firm (Barney, 1989) each emphasize the importance of *internal* goals and capabilities to organizational behavior and effectiveness.

Research applying prospect theory, for example, has demonstrated that individuals use targets or 'reference points' in evaluating risky choices and that their behavior depends upon whether they perceive themselves as above (better than) or below (worse than) a specific target they choose (Kahneman and Tversky, 1979). Moreover, Fiegenbaum and Thomas (1988) confirmed prospect theory as a descriptor of behavior at the firm level: they found that organizations behaved as risk-takers when below their reference point but avoided risk when above. An organization's (or decision maker's) selection of a 'reference point' thus appears to have important implications for strategic choice behavior. By signaling organizational priorities and overall direction, top managers, either wittingly or unwittingly, focus the attention of organizational members on particular goals and objectives; in so doing, they define the 'strategic reference point' for the firm.

According to prospect theory, choosing reference points which the firm is clearly 'below' should result in behavior and performance measurably different from cases where reference points are selected which the firm clearly exceeds. For example, it is now generally accepted that in the years following World War II, the large American market enabled many US companies to be world leaders. Under these favorable circumstances, the American incumbents maintained a steady course, minimizing risk, while reaping the financial benefits of their superior positions (Dertouzos, Lester and Solow, 1989). This philosophy led top managers to invest only in projects that promised high rates of return in the short term without risking the overall profitability of the firm. However, over the past decade, many new Japanese-based competitors entered the US market armed with equal, if not superior, technology. Adopting a longer time perspective, and driven more by quality goals and market share than profitability, these firms transformed the nature of competition (Abegglen and Stalk, 1985). Incumbent firms were slow to recognize that the 'rules of the game' had changed. Locked into a particular set of assumptions about their industry, the nature of competition, and strategic management, such firms were often unable to alter their behavior. Large-scale investments had to be made regardless of the implications for short-term profitability. Regaining competitiveness demanded frequent and extensive organizational change. Such transformation required a broader vision and greater risk-taking. In short, top managers were required to select and deploy a different set of 'reference points' than had been used in the past.

This chapter takes the position that understanding a firm's choice of reference points is an important aspect of strategic management. It argues that top management can be explicit and deliberate in the choice of reference points, rather than passive or unaware. Furthermore, the theory developed here predicts that strategic behavior and performance can be influenced directly by the choice of reference points. After a review of the relevant literatures, the chapter develops the concept of the Strategic Reference Point (SRP), which is composed of three dimensions: (i) conditions internal to the firm, (ii) conditions external to the firm; and (iii) time (i.e. future and past orientation). Taken together, the three reference point dimensions operationalize the structure of the firm's 'mission' and 'vision.' Firms are expected to vary widely with respect to which dimensions or elements of the SRP they emphasize. A theory is therefore developed which specifies the optimal SRP structure, and propositions are opposed which articulate the expected relationships between the SRP, strategic choice behavior, and firm performance. The chapter closes with some suggestions for future research using the SRP concept.

## STRATEGIC CHOICE BEHAVIOR: THE REFERENCE POINT

Previous studies have developed and tested three different models of strategic choice behavior. Findings from these studies are depicted in FIGURE 4.1 and are summarized below. The first stream of research (Curve 1) is based on the assumption that decision makers, and hence organizations, are risk-averse. Under this assumption, organizations will take risks only if they are compensated by higher returns. This means that for each strategic alternative, firms and managers will choose that alternative with the higher utility, or for actions having the same expected utility, they will choose the one with the lower risk (Schoemaker, 1982). This is the rationale for the positive slope of Curve 1 in FIGURE 4.1. Indeed, studies such as those by Conrad and Plotkin (1968), Hurdle (1974), and Bettis (1981) have confirmed aspects of this theory.

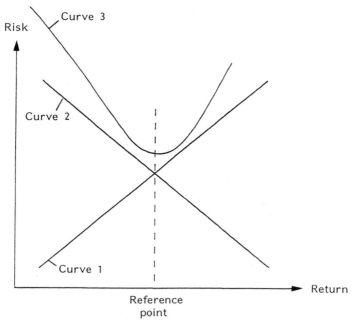

FIGURE 4.1   Three models of strategic choice behavior: Curve 1, risk-averse behavior; Curve 2, risk-seeking behavior and/or good managers can simultaneously increase return and reduce risk; Curve 3, risk-seeking and risk-averse behavior in the domains of losses and gains, respectively

A second stream of research (Curve 2), which began with the empirical findings of Bowman (1980, 1982), however, asserts that individuals, and hence organizations, may be risk-takers under certain conditions. Furthermore, well-managed firms can increase returns and reduce risk simultaneously, suggesting an apparent 'paradox' in the risk–return relationship. This kind of behavior is represented by the negative slope of Curve 2 in FIGURE 4.1. Studies such as those by Treacy (1980), Fiegenbaum and Thomas (1986), and Cool and Dierickx (1987) have found evidence for this kind of behavior.

A third approach (Curve 3) starts from a different perspective. Fiegenbaum and Thomas (1988), for example, adopted 'prospect theory' (Tversky and Kahneman, 1981) to predict strategic choice behavior. The major prediction of this approach is that organizations are *both* risk-averse and risk-seeking, depending upon whether decision makers perceive themselves to be in the domain of gains or losses, respectively. The following example is taken from Tversky and Kahneman (1986) and is used to illustrate the central concepts underpinning prospect theory:

*Problem 1.* (N = 150) choose between:
  A.    A sure gain of $240 [84%]
  B.    25% chance to gain $1,000 and 75% chance to gain nothing [16%]
*Problem 2.* (N = 150) choose between:
  C.    A sure loss of $750 [13%]
  D.    75% chance to lose $1,000 and 25% chance to lose nothing [87%]

It can be seen readily that Problem 1 deals with 'gains' while Problem 2 deals with 'losses.' While options A and B in Problem 1 and C and D in Problem 2 are equivalent in their expected monetary returns, individuals revealed very different preferences. In Problem 1, most respondents (84%) displayed risk-averse behavior since they preferred the option with the lower risk. Alternatively, the majority choice in Problem 2 (87%) was risk-seeking, since the preferred option contained the higher risk. This is a common pattern: choices involving gains are usually risk-averse while choices involving losses are often risk-seeking. Thus, prospect theory argues that individuals use targets or 'reference points' in evaluating risky choices (Kahneman and Tversky, 1979). Furthermore, individuals are not uniformly risk-averse, as has been implicitly assumed by many previous studies, but adopt a mixture of risk-seeking behavior when their expected outcomes from actions are below their reference point and risk-averting behaviour when expected outcomes are above their reference point.

This phenomenon has been confirmed by many studies where individuals, including managers, were the subjects (e.g. Crum, Laughhunn and Payne, 1980; Fishburn and Kochenberger, 1979). Furthermore, Fiegenbaum and Thomas (1988) tested and confirmed prospect theory in the context of strategic choice for an entire organization. Other studies, such as those by Singh (1986) and Chang and Thomas (1989), have found evidence for similar behavior. In addition, Fiegenbaum (1990) confirmed another prediction of prospect theory in his empirical study, where he found that the risk–return relationship for firms below the reference point was three times deeper than for the above-reference point firms. Curve 3 in FIGURE 4.1 depicts these findings.

In short, both individual and organizational choices appear to depend to a very great extent upon whether decision makers see themselves as being above or below a 'reference point' used to describe the situation. Missing from prospect theory, however, is any explicit discussion concerning the *content* of the reference point. While it seems clear that decisions can be altered depending upon how a problem is framed (as we saw in the above example), there has been no explicit treatment of what constitutes an appropriate reference point at either the individual or organizational level. Fortunately, several existing theoretical perspectives from economics, psychology and organization theory help to shed light on this problem from the standpoint of the firm.

## RELATED THEORETICAL PERSPECTIVES

A central theme in strategic management has been the challenge of matching the demands of the external environment with the internal capabilities and values of the organization (Andrews, 1971; Hofer and Schendel, 1978). Since the external environment is constantly changing, often in unpredictable ways, maintaining this match or 'fit' is no easy task and usually involves the need to overcome particular deficiencies or build new capabilities over

TABLE 4.1 Related theoretical perspectives: a summary

| Theoretical perspective | Reference point emphasized | Fundamental prescription | References |
|---|---|---|---|
| Motivation theory | Internal organization<br>• individuals<br>• groups | Design work and set goals for higher performance | Latham and Yuki (1975)<br>Nadler and Lawler (1977)<br>Hackman and Oldham (1980) |
| Resource-based view | Internal organization<br>• firm-wide resources | Build unique competencies | Wernerfelt (1984)<br>Barney (1989)<br>Prahalad and Hamel (1990) |
| Industrial economics | External conditions<br>• industry<br>• key competitors | Beat the competition | Bain (1956)<br>Caves (1970)<br>Porter (1980) |
| Resource dependence | External conditions<br>• competitors<br>• suppliers<br>• customers | Minimize constraints on resources | Pfeffer (1972)<br>Pfeffer and Nowak (1976)<br>Pfeffer and Salancik (1978) |
| Institutional theory | External conditions<br>• stakeholder<br>• interdependencies | Meet demands of society | Meyer and Rowan (1977)<br>DiMaggio and Powell (1983)<br>Meyer, Scott and Deal (1983) |
| Corporate identity | Time<br>• past traditions<br>• philosophy | The past shapes what is possible | Westley and Mintzberg (1989)<br>Torbert (1987)<br>Dutton and Dukerich (1991) |
| Strategic intent | Time<br>• long-term purpose<br>• mission | Strategic intent informs current decisions | Hasegawa (1986)<br>Imai (1986)<br>Hamel and Prahalad (1989) |

time (Galbraith and Kazanjian, 1986; Itami, 1987; Prahalad and Hamel, 1990). Thus, the creation of a high aspiration level—a gap between the current state and some desired state—has long been a part of management theory (e.g. March and Simon, 1958). In fact, several major theoretical perspectives from economics, psychology, and organization theory have sought to identify targets or reference groups that expose 'gaps' and thereby raise individual or organizational aspiration levels. Each, however, focuses upon different elements or areas of content in establishing reference points. TABLE 4.1 provides an overview of each of these major theoretical perspectives. Because of space limitations a comprehensive description has been omitted, but this may be obtained on request from the authors.

All of the perspectives from the literature appear to have one important theme in common: the selection of a benchmark or 'reference point' against which strategic choices or organizational behavior are judged. However, each perspective deals with different content and posits a different mechanism of comparison. As TABLE 4.1 indicates, the theories can be categorized broadly into three groups: those focused upon factors *internal* to the firm (motivation theory, resource-based perspective), those involving factors *external* to the firm (industrial economics, resource dependence, institutional theory), and *time-based* concerns (corporate identity, strategic intent).

Industrial economics, for example, establishes 'competition' as the primary point of reference, whereas the resource dependence perspective and institutional theory expand the set of external concerns to include suppliers, customers, and other important non-economic stakeholders. Similarly, the resource-based perspective establishes 'organizational capability' as the primary reference point, whereas motivation theory focuses more on the individual or group levels. Corporate identity and strategic intent, while clearly containing content, demonstrate the importance of the time dimension in establishing reference points—the former with respect to the past and the latter with respect to the future. Taken together, the different perspectives cover a broad range of potential reference points. Each perspective constitutes a 'piece of the puzzle' in that it defines a particular decision frame, thereby creating a 'gap' or aspiration level. To develop a theory of *strategic* reference points, therefore, it appears necessary to consider the external, internal, and time dimensions, treating them simultaneously as an integrated package.

## THE STRATEGIC REFERENCE POINT MATRIX

The first requirement for conceptualizing the 'strategic reference point' is the articulation of an appropriate set of factors and dimensions to consider. As was argued by Tversky and Kahneman (1986) and others, however, there is no formal theory available for formulating reference points. It should be noted that the concept of 'reference point' has its roots in the psychology of perception. The argument is that human perceptual mechanisms appear to consider differences, rather than absolute levels, when evaluating alternatives (Festinger, 1954).

In laboratory studies on prospect theory, researchers have defined reference points in monetary terms. Other studies have tried to test this theory in 'real' situations. In this manner, Puto (1987) used either an increasing or decreasing price trend, a difficult to achieve or an easy to achieve budget, and a gain or loss message in a sales letter to manipulate the decision reference points of industrial buyers. Fiegenbaum and Thomas (1988) and Fiegenbaum (1990), however, used the industry's median return on equity (ROE). The reason for this reference point selection reflects the financial literature's suggestion that firms adjust their performance to the industry average (Frecka and Lee, 1983; Lev, 1969).

These studies indicate that any factor(s) that highlights a particular target or objective seems capable of establishing a reference point and, subsequently, of creating a decision frame. Because there are several factors to consider, we propose a three-dimensional reference point 'matrix' which includes the wide range of factors identified in the literature review. Specifically, a strategic reference point matrix is developed consisting of three major dimensions: (i) factors internal to the firm, (ii) factors external to the firm, and (iii) time (FIGURE 4.2).

## THE INTERNAL REFERENCE DIMENSION

As motivation theory and the resource-based perspective suggest, factors internal to the firm are crucial to success and constitute important reference points for organizational members. Companies routinely set targets for *strategic inputs* (e.g. cost reduction,

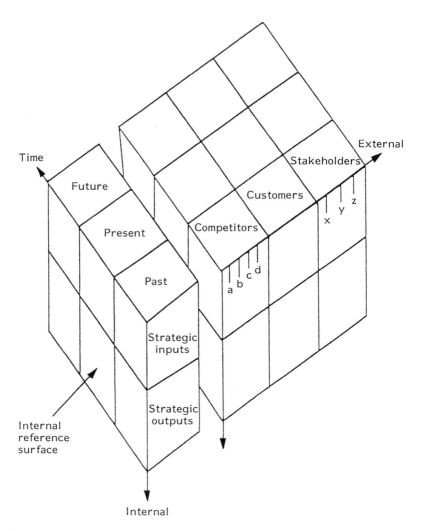

FIGURE 4.2   The strategic reference point matrix

quality improvement, new product development) and evaluate employees' performance based upon these goals. Similarly, it is customary for firms to see targets for *strategic outputs* such as profitability or sales and to hold managers accountable for performance against these targets.

## Strategic Inputs

Internal capability can be conceived as developing around particular 'functions' or 'value-added' activities (Porter, 1985). Most also emphasize one or more company-wide capabilities which serve as a backdrop to functional operations; these 'cross-cutting' capabilities include an emphasis upon cost position (Porter, 1980), quality (Imai, 1987), speed (Stalk and Hout, 1990), and innovation (Foster, 1986). While some firms may focus on one or two of these capabilities to the exclusion of others (e.g. achieving a low-cost position versus innovation), the themes are not necessarily mutually exclusive. In fact, it is becoming increasingly clear that all four competences may have to be developed simultaneously to remain competitive in the coming years (Hamel and Prahalad, 1991). For example, Toyota has achieved a low cost position through total quality management and the reduction of cycle time, investing the resulting profits in aggressive programs for further innovation.

The value-added activities and cross-cutting capabilities can be used to create a matrix of internal reference points (FIGURE 4.3).

Cross-cutting capabilities

| Value-added activities | Cost | Quality | Speed | Innovation |
|---|---|---|---|---|
| Technology | | | | |
| Product development | | | | |
| Production | | | | |
| Distribution | | | | |

FIGURE 4.3   Strategic inputs

An analysis of a firm's strategy and organization (particularly its planning, resource allocation, and reward systems) reveals which internal reference points are important in any particular case. Thus, a firm that aggressively targets cost reduction with its centre of gravity in production would establish a set of reference points quite different from a firm that emphasizes technological development and product innovation as its focal point.

## Strategic Outputs

While strategic inputs are potentially important sources of reference points, so too are the strategic outputs or 'results' of the firm's operations. As noted above, most firms set explicit performance targets such as profitability (e.g. ROA, ROE, ROS), growth (e.g. sales growth or profit growth), or value creation (Rappaport, 1986). These output measures capture different dimensions of the firm's performance level and also serve to focus employees' attention in different ways. For example, it is now generally recognized that firms strongly oriented toward year-to-year profitability make very different strategic choices from those driven by sales growth, market share, or cash-flow over the life cycle of a product (Abegglen and Stalk, 1985). Thus, the choice of which strategic outputs to emphasize is an important source of reference points for the organization.

## THE EXTERNAL REFERENCE DIMENSION

While self-reflection—the crux of the internal reference dimension—appears to be very important, so too is the comparison of oneself to external benchmarks. Indeed, as the industrial economics, resource dependence, and institutional theory perspectives make clear, it is essential to examine the position of the firm relative to important actors in its external environment. Industrial economics focuses upon the firm in reference to competitors in the industry; resource dependence extends consideration to suppliers and customers, and focuses upon the constraints or expectations that these parties impose; institutional theory is the most encompassing, and emphasizes the pressures placed upon the firm by the full range of organizational stakeholders. Given the diversity of external factors, it is useful to consider three major subsets of external reference points: competitors, customers, and stakeholders.

## Competitors

Successful strategies are often characterized as those that out-distance the competition. Indeed, the most accepted external reference point in the literature on strategic management has to do with competitors (e.g. Porter, 1980) and the concept of 'competitive advantage' is premised upon sustaining a position relative to competitors (Porter, 1985). The literature indicates that competitor reference points can be defined at several levels: the firm can compare or 'benchmark' itself to the industry as a whole, to a particular strategic group of firms in the industry, to the industry leader, or to competitors from other industries ('best-in-class' capability). For example, Lev (1969) and Frecka and Lee (1983) have shown that industry averages serve as targets for the financial goals of many companies. At Komatsu, however, the reference point is its arch-rival Caterpillar, the dominant competitor in the industry. This target is captured well by the firm's slogan, 'Maru-C,' which means literally 'to encircle Caterpillar.' Increasingly, firms also seek to identify potential competitors—firms from other industries possessing technology or capability that might be applied in the incumbent's domain (Porter, 1980). Strategic choice thus appears to be greatly affected by the choice of competitor reference point(s).

## Customers

While many firms emphasize competitors' actions as the primary external reference point, others are driven more by customer needs, and seek to develop strong relations both with customers and suppliers (Ohmae, 1988; Peters, 1987; Peters and Austin, 1985). The stated mission of Nissan, for example, has little to do with competitors; instead, the goal is to develop 'life-long customers.' This means painstaking assessment of customer needs and an analysis of the company's degrees of freedom in responding to those needs. A 'customer' orientation has important implications for organizational actions and strategic choice (Cornish, 1988;

Shapiro, 1988). SAS provides a compelling example of this in the airline industry, where changing customer needs precipitated a wholesale reorientation of competitive strategy and corporate culture around the 'business flyer.' Thus, a 'gap' between customers' needs and the organization's ability to deliver on those needs constitutes an important external reference point.

---

## Stakeholders

The third component of the external reference dimension relates to those concerns which historically have been treated as issues of 'social responsibility' (Anshen, 1980; Freeman, 1984). Here again, reference points can be formed at several levels, including local community relations (Henderson, 1990), national competitiveness (e.g. Dertouzos, Lester and Solow, 1989), and environmental quality (e.g. Davis, 1991; Perrow, 1984).

Many companies are concerned with sustaining good community relations. Being a good 'corporate citizen' means providing stable employment and contributing, where possible, to local economic development (Freeman, 1984; Henderson, 1990). Johnson & Johnson, for example, has long stressed the importance of corporate citizenship in its 'credo.' The issue of national competitiveness also provides a reference point for many firms. This is most evident among firms from developing countries. Consider, for example, the Korean firm Daewoo. In 1967, it started with an investment of $18 000; by 1985, its revenue was $14 billion. When Mr Kim, the founder and CEO of the company, was asked to explain why they have been so successful, he attributed his firm's success to his desire to show people around the world that Korea can produce the highest quality products at the lowest prices. Increasingly, firms also measure their success against how well their products or services contribute to environmental quality and sustainability (Davis, 1991; Piasecki and Asmus, 1990; Woodruff and Peterson, 1991). Dupont, for example, aims to anticipate, seek, and respond to public values concerning the environmental impacts of their operations and has incorporated environmental concerns into the corporate mission. Their recent decision to phase out the production and sale of CFCs because of their ozone-depleting properties is a good example of a 'stakeholder' issue supplying a reference point for a firm.

## Time as a Reference Dimension

As the corporate identity and strategic intent perspectives suggest, time is a critical source of reference points for the firm. The time dimension can be divided readily into two major categories—*past and future*. Today's strategic choices can thus be heavily affected by references to either the past (where the firm has been) or the future (where the firm would like to be).

The past is often an important factor in establishing reference points. Organizational learning studies have shown that firms that accumulate knowledge over time can use it as a source of competitive advantage (e.g. Fiol and Lyles, 1985; Levitt and March, 1988; Shrivastava, 1983). Building upon past excellence provides a reference point to spur continued achievement. Indeed, the financial literature has shown that investors and organizational decision makers look at past performance in evaluating future alternatives (Lev, 1969). However, using the past as a reference point can also serve to constrain the strategic options perceived as viable by the organization. Dutton and Dukerich (1991), for example, have shown how the long-standing mission of New York's Port Authority as a 'transportation agency' limited its ability to recognize homelessness as a problem at its various facilities throughout the city. Only by redefining its identity as an organization—a break with past tradition— was it able to reframe the issue and adopt a different set of policies and behaviors towards homeless people.

The future also serves as a source of decision frames and reference points. Firms with a strong sense of strategic 'intent,' for example, may think a great deal about the 'deep' future—10 or 20 years out—when making strategic choices. Hamel and Prahalad (1989) noted that companies that have risen to global leadership invariably began with ambitions that were out of all proportion to their resources and capabilities. But they created an obsession with winning at all levels of the organization, and then sustained the obsession over the 10 to 20 year quest for global leadership. At Matsushita, for example, founder Konosuke Matsushita developed a grand 250-year mission which is expressed through the 'Seven Spirits of Matsushita.' Each year, Matsushita rededicates the company to its long-term mission by embedding its short-term goals within the strategic intent, captured through a slogan which serves as the theme for the year.

## THEORY DEVELOPMENT

The strategic reference point matrix could be applied descriptively in virtually any organizational setting. Beyond its use as a descriptive or diagnostic tool, however, the SRP concept should also have predictive (and ultimately, normative) value. In this section, we therefore develop a basic theoretical framework that can be used to help guide future empirical work. Theory and associated propositions are developed around two major themes: (i) the linkage between the SRP and *strategic choice behavior*; and (ii) the relationship between the SRP and *firm performance*.

## STRATEGIC CHOICE BEHAVIOR

The position of the firm relative to its strategic reference point would be expected to relate to a number of significant cognitive, organization process, and behavioral characteristics. TABLE 4.2 contains a summary of these expected relationships. Jackson and

TABLE 4.2   Strategic choice behavior propositions

|  | Above reference point | Below reference point |
|---|---|---|
| Current situation | Satisfied<br>'Sitting on top of the world' | Dissatisfied<br>'At the bottom looking up' |
| Perception of new issues (Jackson and Dutton, 1988) | Threat<br>Potential loss<br>Negative | Opportunity<br>Potential gain<br>Positive |
| Organizational processes Staw, Sandelands and Dutton, 1981; Dutton and Jackson, 1987) | Constricted<br>Rigid<br>Centralized | Open<br>Flexible<br>Decentralized |
| Nature of response or behavior (Kahneman and Tversky, 1979) | Risk-averse<br>Conservative<br>Defensive | Risk-taking<br>Daring<br>Offensive |

Dutton (1988) have demonstrated empirically that issues categorized as 'threats' imply a negative situation in which loss is likely, whereas those categorized as 'opportunities' imply a positive situation in which gain is likely. The former set of cognitions would be expected for firms above their SRP and the latter for those below. Thus, firms with 'everything to lose' (above the SRP) will tend to see new issues as threats, whereas those with 'nothing to lose' (below the SRP) should tend to see the same issues as opportunities.

Staw, Sandelands and Dutton (1981), and Dutton and Jackson (1987) also proposed a number of links between issue categorization and organizational processes. They hypothesized that when confronted with a 'threat' issue (above the SRP), decision makers will constrict information flow, become rigid by applying only tested repertoires, and engage in centralized decision making. In contrast, decision makers facing an 'opportunity' issue (below the SRP) will tend to be more open to new information, more flexible and willing to try new repertoires, and more willing to decentralize decision making.

Finally, as prospect theory predicts, responses or behaviors should be risk-averse (conservative, defensive) where the firm's perception places it above its reference point, and risk-seeking (daring, offensive) where below. The decision maker's attitude toward risk is based upon their framing of the situation. In the case of the risk-taker, the decision maker is *dissatisfied* with their current situation, seeing themselves as below where they would like to be. Conversely, the risk-averter is *satisfied* with their situation—they see themselves as 'sitting on top of the world.' An industry leader, for example, should be less inclined to take risks if decision makers saw a particular action as carrying the potential of unseating the firm from its position of advantage. Thus, conservative behavior is expected in cases where firms have clearly met or exceeded their goals, whereas active risk-taking is anticipated in cases where firms are clearly below their target (Fiegenbaum and Thomas, 1988; Kahneman and Tversky, 1979). These expected relationships can be summarized in the following propositions:

*Proposition 1a:* Firms above their SRP will perceive new issues as threats, engage in constricted, rigid and centralized decision making processes, and behave in a risk-averse, conservative, and defensive manner.

*Proposition 1b:* Firms below their SRP will perceive new issues as opportunities, engage in open, flexible, and decentralized decision making processes, and behave in a risk-seeking, daring, and offensive manner.

---

## SRP and Firm Performance

Four characteristics of the SRP are expected to have significant implications for firm performance: content, configuration, change, and consensus. The theory for each of these aspects is developed below, along with propositions for each.

---

### Content

Since strategic choice behavior is expected to vary depending upon whether the firm sees itself as above or below its SRP, the content of the reference point(s) is of critical strategic concern. The literature suggests that top managers play a central role in managing organizational attention through the articulation of the firm's vision and mission (Bennis and Nanus, 1985; Hart, 1992; Quinn, 1978; Westley and Mintzberg, 1989). Therefore, by choosing carefully which dimensions of the SRP to emphasize, it would seem that top managers could influence the framing of issues in a way that motivates organizational members and focuses their actions. The firm's performance should thus be directly influenced by its choice of strategic reference point.

The three dimensions of the strategic reference point matrix can be seen as capturing the basic 'structure' of the firm's vision and mission. Given the complexity of the matrix, however, it would be expected that great variation will be observed with respect to the actual configuration of reference points adopted by firms. Some firms, for example, might be primarily *internally*-oriented, emphasizing one or more internal reference points to the virtual exclusion of external concerns. Others, however, might be primarily *externally*-oriented, focusing mainly upon competitors or customers, while downplaying the importance of strategic inputs or outputs. In addition, some firms may be preoccupied with the *past*, basing important decisions upon history or tradition, while others are concerned more with the *future* trajectory of the firm.

Each element of the SRP matrix might also be expected to correlate with particular aspects of firm performance. A focus on competitors, for example, might be expected to result in market-share gains; a strong customer focus might result in higher product quality; and a concern with stakeholder issues should be associated with strong social and environmental performance. Similarly, an internal emphasis upon cost position and production might relate strongly to profitability, whereas an emphasis upon speed and product development might correlate more strongly with growth. Finally, a 'mission' orientation might be expected to produce a strong emphasis on future positioning whereas pre-occupation with the firm's past successes might translate into a focus on greater efficiency and profitability.

Recently, a few authors have begun to argue that effective strategic management requires a balancing and simultaneous mastery of seemingly contradictory or 'paradoxical' capabilities— broad vision and attention to detail, an external as well as internal focus, and emphasis upon both flexibility and stability (Bourgeois and Eisenhardt, 1988; Hart and Quinn, 1991; Mitrof, 1983; Quinn, 1988; Quinn and Cameron, 1988; Torbert, 1987). Applying the logic of the 'paradox' perspective to the SRP suggests that the most effective firms should evidence reference points that emphasize simultaneously all three dimensions of the matrix. Such organizations should possess a superior understanding of the situation, thereby facilitating performance on several dimensions. This suggests the following four propositions:

*Proposition 2a:* Firms possessing both internal and external reference points will outperform firms that emphasize one dimension over the other.

*Proposition 2b:* Firms possessing both past and future orientations will outperform firms that emphasize one element over the other.

*Proposition 2c:* Firms possessing multidimensional SRPs—a simultaneous emphasis upon internal, external, and time dimensions— will outperform firms with less complex reference points.

*Proposition 2d:* Firms possessing multidimensional SRPs will perform on more dimensions (e.g. profitability, growth, quality, innovation, social responsibility) than will firms with less complex reference points.

## Configuration

Beyond the specific content of the SRP, it is also important to examine the configuration of the firm's reference point—the relationships among the different dimensions and elements. Contingency theorists (e.g. Lawrence and Lorsch, 1969; Thompson, 1967) and management theorists (e.g. Galbraith and Kazanjian, 1986; Miles and Snow, 1978; Peters and Waterman, 1982) have long emphasized the importance of *fit* between the different elements of the firm (strategy, structure, technology, systems, processes) and its environment. Applying this logic to the SRP concept, it might be expected that where multiple reference points are evident, the most effective firms will demonstrate *internal consistency* among the elements of the SRP. For example, where a firm identifies an industry leader as its primary external reference point, then its targets for strategic inputs and outputs should be visibly connected to the goal of overtaking that rival. If the rival possesses strong technological and distribution capability, then an internal reference point targeted at cost reduction and efficiency introduces inconsistency and, it is hypothesized, a destructive tension within the organization. Even where long-term mission or 'strategic intent' has been adopted that is far beyond current capabilities, the associated internal and external reference points should be identifiably connected to and consistent with the long-term aim: they should be *mutually reinforcing*—on the 'critical path' to the ultimate goal. Where organizational members perceive mixed motives or conflicting targets, the effectiveness of the SRP will be blunted. This suggests the following proposition:

> *Proposition 3:* The most effective firms will possess multi-dimensional SRPs that are internally consistent and mutually reinforcing. That is, the demands placed upon the organization for improvement, change, or performance by the reference points will align, producing a mission and vision with integrity.

## Change

It is essential to consider the *dynamic* aspects of the SRP. While Proposition 3 suggests that the structure of the SRP should be internally consistent and mutually reinforcing *at any given point in time*, this is not to suggest that the SRP should remain *fixed* over time. In fact, the literature on strategic change and adaptation suggests that organizations pass through periods of relative stability and equilibrium, punctuated with episodes of 'revolution' characterized by disequilibrium and divergence from the status quo (e.g. Greiner, 1972; Miller and Freisen, 1980; Romanelli and Tushman, 1986). The concept of 'dynamic fit' (Itami, 1987) asserts that a key role for top management is to create both order and chaos. Management must work hard to send consistent messages and align organizational strategies, systems, and processes to achieve high performance (Proposition 3). However, management must never allow the organization to settle into complacency. As soon as 'balance' or 'alignment' has been achieved, it must be destroyed. The organization must be challenged to acquire new competencies so that it might be positioned for the future. Thus, the SRP should continually evolve and change if the organization is to achieve *sustainable* performance. A static SRP might eventually lead to stagnation. This suggests the following proposition:

> *Proposition 4:* The most effective firms will periodically revise or alter their SRP to focus attention on new challenges and avoid complacency and stagnation.

---

### Consensus

The last characteristic to consider relates to perceptions about the SRP within the organization. The literature on top management team consensus indicates that agreement among top managers about strategic goals and competitive strategies is an important predictor of firm performance (Bourgeois, 1980; Dess, 1987; Hrebiniak and Snow, 1982), although the nature of the relationship appears to vary depending upon competitive environment and the nature of the strategy making process utilized (Wooldridge and Floyd, 1989). There is also growing evidence that agreement *across* organizational levels concerning these issues is an important predictor of firm performance (Hart, 1991, 1992; Yeung, 1990). Indeed, the literature on corporate culture has long asserted the importance of shared values and understandings to organizational effectiveness (Pascale, 1985; Peters, 1987; Weick, 1987). Thus, while the CEO, or even the top management team, may have a clear image concerning the firm's SRP, organizational members may not share the same perception, or may have conflicting images. Indeed, organizational members may interpret the signals being sent by top managers very differently than intended, resulting in a perceived reference point that diverges from the 'intended' SRP (e.g. Weick, 1979). But if organizational members do not share the same perceptions about the SRP, then issues will be framed and decisions made in ways that run counter to the desired direction. A lack of consensus concerning the firm's SRP would thus be expected to have negative consequences for strategic behavior and firm performance. This suggests the following, final, proposition:

> *Proposition 5:* The most effective firms will be characterized by high levels of agreement among top managers and organizational members regarding the content of the firm's SRP.

---

## FUTURE RESEARCH

To apply the concept of the strategic reference point, both in theory and practice, it must first be operationalized: variables must be defined and a system of measurement and scoring devised. Operationalization should be pursued both objectively and subjectively. *Objective* indicators for each of the elements of the SRP matrix could be defined through both secondary and primary sources. For example, R&D-, capital-, and advertising-intensity data could be used to indicate the level of firm focus on key 'internal' factors such as technology, production, and distribution. To create a reference point, these data could be benchmarked against the industry leader, a particular strategic group, or the overall industry average. Its placement 'above' or 'below' each element of the SRP matrix, coupled with a scoring system that could be devised, would lead to classification of the firm in the matrix and would allow systematic investigation into the linkages between SRP, strategic choice behavior, and firm performance.

While objective measures of the SRP should prove to be very useful, it will also be necessary to develop a *subjective* measurement system. Here, sets of survey items could be crafted to tap each of the elements in the SRP matrix. Perceptual measures must be designed to determine both *if* a respondent perceives a particular dimension as a reference point for the firm (e.g. competitors versus customers) and *whether* the respondent sees the firm as 'above' or 'below' the SRP. To be complete, data must be collected at multiple levels within the organization, including top managers, middle managers, and line employees. Such a strategic reference point survey would enable researchers and top managers to take the pulse of organizations and determine the extent of understanding and agreement concerning their SRPs. Comparing the objective and subjective results would yield important insights into firms' strategic positioning and provide a basis for management intervention. Indeed, such a set of diagnostic tools could have important implications for both research and practice.

Once operationalized, strategic reference point theory could be used to analyze several specific issues of current strategic relevance. For example, it could be usefully applied to the study of *innovation* and *entrepreneurship*. An accepted belief is that entrepreneurship deals with risk-taking behavior (e.g. Smith and Miner, 1983; Van de Ven, Hudson and Schroeder, 1984). If high risk-taking behavior is a necessary condition for success, the SRP concept suggests that entrepreneurs and innovators probably see themselves as below a reference point(s). What are the reference points used by successful entrepreneurs? Do innovative firms emphasize a different set of strategic reference points than firms that defend established strategic positions? Empirical research applying the concepts developed in this chapter could help to answer these questions.

A related research question is how *small firms* compete successfully against large ones. Previous research has indicated that an important element for small firm success is a 'focus' strategy, which means high risk-taking behavior (e.g. Porter, 1980). The SRP concept could aid in answering such questions as: what are the reference points that successful small firms use? What is the relative importance of the distance from different reference points? In addition, *interfirm collaboration* has become an increasingly important phenomenon over the past decade. While previous research has explored how to manage joint ventures and strategic alliances (e.g. Hamel, Doz and Prahalad, 1989; Kogut, 1988), there are still many questions remaining. For example, which firms are the best candidates for strategic alliances? What reference points do they use? How much risk are they willing to take and why? Do they differ systematically with regard to reference points?

Another important strategic issue has to do with the appropriate level and type of *diversification*. Previous research has focused upon the concepts of relatedness, risk, and firm performance (e.g. Montgomery and Singh, 1984; Rumelt, 1982). The SRP concept offers a new point of view on this issue. For example, what is the reference point for firms that change their diversification strategy? Are there distinctive reference points for firms that diversify through acquisition as opposed to internal development? What is the reference point that firms use when deciding to enter new markets? Can we predict which firms will enter new markets (e.g. Eastern Europe, Middle East)?

Finally, the issue of *environmental sustainability* is emerging as a key concern for the 1990s (e.g. Davis, 1991). Beyond the immediate demand for 'green' products, governments around the world are requiring that firms adopt a more systematic approach to product and process technology to save energy and materials, prevent pollution, and minimize waste. The response to these demands by corporations has been highly variable, with some taking a strongly proactive orientation while others delay or resist the call for 'greening.' This raises several interesting questions: how can multinational corporations manage cross-border and international environmental problems most effectively? Is innovation within existing large corporations or the creation of new 'green' start-ups the most effective way to respond to environmental demands? In terms of the SRP concept, what differentiates those firms that move rapidly toward environmental sustainability from those that resist? Are there fundamental differences in the reference points adopted by 'green' firms?

## ACKNOWLEDGEMENTS

The authors acknowledge the support provided for this research by the Michigan Business School (US) and the Technion (Israel). We would also like to thank Jane Dutton and Susan Schneider for their comments on earlier drafts.

# REFERENCES

Abegglen, J. and Stalk, G. (1985). *Kaisha: The Japanese Corporation*. New York: Basic Books.

Andrews, K. (1971). *The Concept of Strategy*. Homewood, IL: Richard D. Irwin.

Anshen, M. (1980). *Corporate Strategies for Social Performance*. New York: Macmillan.

Bain, J. (1956). *Barriers to New Competition*. Cambridge, MA: Harvard University Press.

Barney, J. (1989). Firm resources and sustained competitive advantage. Texas A&M University, unpublished manuscript.

Bennis, W. and Nanus, B. (1985). *Leaders*. New York: Harper and Row.

Bettis, R. (1981). Performance differences in related and unrelated diversified firms. *Strategic Management Journal*, **2**, 379–393.

Bourgeois, L.J. (1980). Performance and consensus. *Strategic Management Journal*, **1**, 227–248.

Bourgeois, L.J. and Eisenhardt, K. (1988). Strategic decision processes in high velocity environments: Four cases in the microcomputer industry. *Management Science*, **14**, 816–835.

Bowman, E. (1980). A risk/return paradox for strategic management. *Sloan Management Review*, **21**, 17–31.

Bowman, E. (1982). Risk seeking by troubled firms. *Sloan Management Review*, **23**, 33–42.

Caves, R. (1977). *American Industry: Structure, Conduct, Performance*. New York: Prentice Hall.

Chang, Y. and Thomas, H. (1989). The impact of diversification strategy on risk–return performance. *Strategic Management Review*, **10**, 271–284.

Conrad, G. and Plotkin, I. (1968). Risk return: US industry pattern. *Harvard Business Review*, **46**, 90–99.

Cool, K. and Dierickx, I. (1987). Negative risk return relationships in business strategy: The case of the U.S. pharmaceutical industry, 1963–1982. INSEAD working paper.

Cornish, F. (1988). Building a customer-oriented organization. *Long Range Planning*, **21**, 105–107.

Crum, R., Laughhunn, D. and Payne, J. (1980). Risk preference: Empirical evidence and its implications for capital budgeting. In F. Derkindren and R. Crum (Eds), *Financing Issues in Corporate Project Selection* (pp. 99–117). Boston: Martinus Nijhoff.

Davis, J. (1991). *Greening Business*. Oxford: Basil Blackwell.

Dertouzos, M., Lester, R. and Solow, R. (1989). *Made in America*. Cambridge, MA: MIT Press.

Dess, G. (1987). Consensus on strategy formulation and organizational performance: Competitors in a fragmented industry. *Strategic Management Journal*, **8**, 259–277.

DiMaggio, P. and Powell, W. (1983). The iron cage revisited: Institutional isomorphism and collective rationality in organizational fields. *American Sociological Review*, **48**, 147–160.

Dutton, J. and Dukerich, J. (1991). Keeping an eye in the mirror: The role of image and identity in organizational adaptation. *Academy of Management Journal*, **34**, 517–554.

Dutton, J. and Jackson, S. (1987). Categorizing strategic issues: Links to organizational action. *Academy of Management Review*, **12**, 76–90.

Festinger, L. (1954). A theory of social comparison processes. *Human Relations*, **7**, 117–140.

Feigenbaum, A. (1990). Prospect theory and the risk-return association: An empirical examination in 85 industries. *Journal of Economic Behavior and Organization*, **14**, 187–204.

Feigenbaum, A. and Thomas, H. (1986). Dynamic and risk measurement perspectives on Bowman's risk–return paradox for strategic management: An empirical study. *Strategic Management Journal*, **7**, 395–407.

Fiegenbaum, A. and Thomas, H. (1988). Attitudes toward risk and the risk return paradox: Prospect theory explanations. *Academy of Management Journal*, **31**, 85–106.

Fiol, M. and Lyles, M. (1985). Organizational learning. *Academy of Management Review*, **10**, 803–813.

Fishburn, P. and Kochenberger, G. (1979). Two-piece Von Neumann–Morgenstern utility functions. *Decision Sciences*, **10**, 503–518.

Foster, R. (1986). *Innovation: The Attacker's Advantage*. New York: Summit Books.

Frecka, T. and Lee, C. (1983). Generalized financial ratio adjustment processes and their implications. *Journal of Accounting Research*, **21**, 308–316.

Freeman, R. (1984). *Strategic Management: A Stakeholder Approach*. Boston, MA: Pitman.

Galbraith, J. and Kazanjian, R. (1986). *Strategy Implementation*, St Paul, MN: West Publishing.

Greiner, L. (1972). Evolution and revolution as organizations grow. *Harvard Business Review*, July/August, 37–46.

Guth, W. and MacMillan, I. (1986). Strategy implementation versus middle management self-interest. *Strategic Management Journal*, **7**, 313–327.

Hackman, R. and Oldham, G. (1980). *Work Redesign*, Reading, MA: Addison-Wesley.

Hamel, G., Doz, Y. and Prahalad, C.K. (1989). Collaborate with your competitors—and win. *Harvard Business Review*, January/February, 133–139.

Hamel, G. and Prahalad, C.K. (1989). Strategic intent. *Harvard Business Review*, May/June, 63–76.

Hamel, G. and Prahalad, C.K. (1991). Expeditionary marketing and corporate imagination. *Harvard Business Review*, July/August, 81–92.

Hart, S. (1991). Intentionality and autonomy in strategy-making process: Modes, archetypes, and firm performance. *Advances in Strategic Management*, **7**, 97–127.

Hart, S. (1992). An integrative framework for strategy making processes. *Academy of Management Review*.

Hart, S. and Quinn, R. (1991). Roles executives play: CEOs, behavioral complexity, and firm performance. University of Michigan Business School, unpublished manuscript.

Hasegawa, K. (1986). *Japanese-Style Management*. Tokyo: Kodansha International.

Henderson, D. (1990). The influence of corporate strategy, structure, and technology on location of procurement and sales. University of Michigan, unpublished doctoral dissertation.

Hofer, C. and Schendel, D. (1978). *Strategy Formulation: Analytical Concepts*. St Paul, MN: West Publishing.

Hrebiniak, L. and Snow, C. (1982). Top management agreement and organizational performance. *Human Relations*, **12**, 1139–1158.

Hurdle, G. (1974). Leverage, risk, market structure, and profitability. *Review of Economics and Statistics*, **56**, 478–485.

Imai, M. (1956). *Kaizen*. New York: Random House.

Itami, H. (1987). *Mobilizing Invisible Assets*. Cambridge, MA: Harvard University Press.

Jackson, S. and Dutton, J. (1988). Discerning threats and opportunities. *Administrative Science Quarterly*, **33**, 370–387.

Kahneman, D. and Tversky, A. (1979). Prospect theory: An analysis of decisions under risk. *Econometrica*, **47**, 1979, pp. 262–291.

Kogut, B. (1988). Joint ventures: Theoretical and empirical perspectives. *Strategic Management Journal*, **9**, 319–332.

Latham, G. and Yukl, G. (1975). A review of research on the application of goal setting in organizations. *Academy of Management Journal*, **18**, 824–845.

Lawrence, P. and Lorsch, J. (1969). *Organization and Environment*. Homewood, IL: Richard D. Irwin.

Lev, B. (1969). Industry averages as targets for financial ratios. *Journal of Accounting Research*, **7**, 290–299.

Levitt, B. and March, J. (1988). Organizational learning. *Annual Review of Sociology*, **14**, 319–340.

Lindblom, C. (1959) The science of 'muddling through'. *Public Administration Review*, **19**, 79–88.

Lyles, M. and Mitroff, I. (1980). Organizational problem formulation: An empirical study'. *Administrative Science Quarterly*, **25**, 102–119.

March, J. and Simon, H. (1958). *Organizations*. New York: John Wiley and Sons.

Meyer, J. and Rowan, B. (1977). Institutionalized organizations: Formal structure as myth and ceremony. *American Journal of Sociology*, **83**, 340–363.

Meyer, J., Scott, R. and Deal, T. (1983). Institutional and technical sources of organizational structure: Explaining the structure of educational organizations. In J. Meyer and R. Scott (eds) *Organizational Environments: Ritual and Rationality*. Beverly Hills, CA: Sage.

Miles, R. and Snow, C. (1978). *Organizational Strategy, Structure and Process*. New York: McGraw-Hill.

Miller, D. and Friesen, P. (1980). Momentum and revolution in organizational adaptation. *Academy of Management Journal*, **23**, 591–614.

Mintzberg, H. (1978). Patterns in strategy formation. *Management Science*, **24**, 934–949.

Mintzberg, H. (1990). The design school: Reconsidering the basic premises of strategic management. *Strategic Management Journal*, **11**, 171–195.

Mitroff, I. (1983). Archetypal social systems analysis: On the deeper structure of human systems. *Academy of Management Review*, **8**, 387–397.

Montgomery, C. and Singh, J. (1984). Diversification strategy and systematic risk. *Strategic Management Journal*, **5**, 181–191.

Nadler, D. and Lawler, E. (1977). Motivation: A diagnostic approach. In R.

Hackman, E. Lawler and L. Porter (Eds) *Perspectives on Behavior in Organizations*. New York: McGraw-Hill.

Ohmae, K. (1988). Getting back to strategy. *Harvard Business Review*, November/December, 149–156.

Pascale, R. (1985). The paradox of 'corporate culture': Reconciling ourselves to socialization. *California Management Review*, **27**, 26–41.

Perrow, C. (1984). *Normal Accidents*. New York: Basic Books.

Peters, T. (1987). *Thriving on Chaos*. New York: Alfred A. Knopf.

Peters, T. and Austin, N. (1985). *A Passion for Excellence*. New York: Warner Books.

Peters, T. and Waterman, R. (1982). *In Search of Excellence*. New York: Harper and Row.

Pfeffer, J. (1972). Merger as a response to organizational interdependence. *Administrative Science Quarterly*, **17**, 382–394.

Pfeffer, J. and Nowak, P. (1976). Joint ventures and interorganizational interdependence. *Administrative Science Quarterly*, **21**, 398–418.

Pfeffer, J. and Salancik, J. (1978). *The External Control of Organizations*. New York: Harper and Row.

Piasecki, B. and Asmus, P. (1990). *In Search of Environmental Excellence*. New York: Touchstone Books.

Porter, M.E. (1980). *Competitive Strategy: Techniques for Analyzing Industries and Competitors*. New York: Free Press.

Porter, M.E. (1985). *Competitive Advantage: Creating and Sustaining Superior Performance*. New York: Free Press.

Prahalad, C.K. and Hamel, G. (1990). The core competence of the corporation. *Harvard Business Review*. May/June, 79–91.

Puto, C. (1987). The framing of buying decisions. *Journal of Consumer Research*, December, 56–65.

Quinn, J.B. (1978). Strategic change: Logical incrementalism. *Sloan Management Review*, **20**, 7–21.

Quinn, R. (1988). *Beyond Rational Management*. San Francisco, CA: Jossey-Bass.

Quinn, R. and Cameron, K. (1988). *Paradox and Transformation*. Cambridge, MA: Ballinger.

Rappaport, A. (1986). *Creating Shareholder Value*. New York: Free Press.

Romanelli, E. and Tushman, M. (1986). Inertia, environments, and strategic choice. *Management Science*, **32**, 608–621.

Rumelt, R. (1982). Diversification strategy and profitability. *Strategic Management Journal*, **3**, 359–369.

Schoemaker, P. (1982). The expected utility model: Its variants, purpose, evidence and limitations. *Journal of Economic Literature*, **20**, 529–563.

Shapiro, B. (1988). What the hell is 'market oriented'? *Harvard Business Review*, November/December, 119–125.

Shrivastava, P. (1983). A typology of organizational learning systems. *Journal of Management Studies*, **20**, 7–28.

Simon, H. (1957). *Administrative Behavior*. New York: Free Press.

Singh, J. (1986). Performance, slack, and risk-taking in organizational decision making. *Academy of Management Journal*, **29**, 562–585.

Smith, N. and Miner, J. (1983). Type of entrepreneur, type of firm, and managerial motivation. *Strategic Management Journal*, **4**, 325–340.

Stalk, G. and Hout, T. (1990). *Competing Against Time*. New York: Free Press.

Staw, B., Sandelands, L. and Dutton, J. (1981). Threat-rigidity cycles in organizational behavior: A multi-level analysis. *Administrative Science Quarterly,* **26**, 501–524.

Thompson, J. (1967). *Organizations in Action.* New York: McGraw-Hill.

Torbert, W. (1987). *Managing the Corporate Dream.* Homewood, IL: Richard D. Irwin.

Treacy, M. (1980). Profitability patterns and firm size. Sloan School of Management, Massachusetts Institute of Technology, unpublished manuscript.

Tversky, A. and Kahneman, D. (1974). Judgment under uncertainty: Heuristics and biases. *Science,* **185**, 1124–1131.

Tversky, A. and Kahneman, D. (1981). The framing of decisions and the psychology of choice. *Science,* **211**, 453–458.

Tversky, A. and Kahneman, D. (1986). Rational choice and the framing of decisions. *Journal of Business,* **59**, S251–S278.

Van de Ven, A., Hudson, R. and Schroeder, D. (1984). Designing new business start-ups: Entrepreneurial, organizational, and ecological considerations. *Journal of Management,* **10**, 87–107.

Weick, K. (1979). *The Social Psychology of Organizing.* New York: Random House.

Weick, K. (1987). Organizational culture as a source of high reliability. *California Management Review,* **29**, 112–127.

Wernerfelt, B. (1984). A resource based view of the firm. *Strategic Management Journal,* **5**, 171–180.

Westley, F. and Mintzberg, H. (1989). Visionary leadership and strategic management. *Strategic Management Journal,* **10**, 17–32.

Woodruff, D. and Peterson, T. (1991). The greening of Detroit. *Business Week,* 8 April, 54–60.

Wooldridge, B. and Floyd, S. (1989). Strategic process effects and consensus. *Strategic Management Journal,* **10**, 295–302.

Yeung, A. (1990). Cognitive consensuality and organizational performance: A systematic assessment. University of Michigan, unpublished doctoral dissertation.

# 5

# Corporate Strategy and Parenting Maps

MICHAEL GOOLD, ANDREW CAMPBELL

## INTRODUCTION

Most large companies today are made up of a number of separate divisions or business units. In such companies, there is a need for a corporate level strategy which transcends the strategies of each of the individual businesses. Few companies, however, possess a corporate strategy that is clear, convincing and powerful. Indeed, many chief executives find it difficult to determine what topics a corporate strategy should cover, what concepts should be used to express it, and by what criteria its validity and usefulness should be judged. We believe that the fundamental question for corporate strategy is whether and how the corporate centre, or parent, adds value to the individual businesses in the company. Do the businesses make better decisions and achieve better results than they would achieve if they were independent entities or if they were part of some other parent organization? And, if so, how does the parent makes its contribution? Or, as is all too often the case, does the relationship with the parent lead to worse decisions, more overheads and depressed profitability? The objective of corporate strategy must be to add value to the businesses in the portfolio. Ideally, the businesses should be better off as part of the parent company than they would be under any other ownership.[1]

An added value corporate strategy can depend on what

*Building the Strategically-Responsive Organization.*
Edited by H. Thomas, D. O'Neal, R. White and D. Hurst.
Copyright © 1994 the Strategic Management Society. Published 1994 by John Wiley & Sons Ltd.

Michael Porter calls 'horizontal strategy':[2] the attempt to achieve synergies and coordination across businesses in the portfolio. It can also be created by what we have begun to call 'stand-alone parenting': situations in which the parent company uses its influence to improve and add value to the decisions being taken in each business unit as a stand-alone entity. While much has been written about horizontal strategy, the subject of stand-alone parenting as a basis for corporate strategy has received less attention. This chapter therefore focuses on stand-alone parenting.

In many companies, corporate strategy is conceived primarily in terms of what are the most attractive businesses for the company to be in. In our view, a corporate strategy that focuses exclusively on selecting attractive businesses for inclusion in the portfolio is liable to miss the crucial question of whether the parent can add any value to the businesses it owns. By contrast, a corporate strategy that is built on the notion of added value by the parent provides a firm foundation for portfolio selection, since acquisitions, divestments and other resource allocation decisions can be tested against and follow from it. Such a strategy requires a sense of what sorts of business the company is able to add value to, or as we shall put it, in what sorts of businesses it possesses an appropriate parenting map.

The chapter is organized in five sections:

- The decentralization contract: the nature of the relationship between the centre and the business
- 'Stand-alone' parenting and parenting maps: how the centre adds value to each business as a stand-alone entity
- Opportunities to add value: the circumstances in which the parent can add the most value
- Parenting maps, diversification and corporate strategy: the implications of parenting maps and added value for portfolio selection and resource allocation
- Management implications: a summary of some practical guidelines for corporate strategists.

## THE DECENTRALIZATION CONTRACT

To understand how the parent adds value, we must begin by examining the nature of the relationship between the centre as corporate parent and the business units that make up the portfolio. In any multi-business company (MBC), each individual business has a line reporting relationship to upper levels of general management. In smaller companies, this relationship focuses essentially on the corporate chief executive and his personal staff. In larger, more complex companies, the business may report to the corporate centre through intermediate levels (e.g. the division, the group); and in a matrix organization such as Unilever there may be a variety of overlapping reporting relationships (e.g. to the region and to the sector). The business may also have functional relationships with corporate or divisional staffs or services, such as finance or research and development. In complex MBCs, the influence of 'the centre' is therefore distributed across a number of levels, functions and staff groups, and it may be far from easy to define and disentangle the roles of each of them. However, from the perspective of the business unit, the combined impact of all of these organizational entities makes up the centre's influence. It is therefore still possible to refer to the reporting relationship between the business unit and the centre.

In theory, a line reporting relationship gives the centre or parent the right to involve itself in any aspect of the business's affairs that it chooses. In practice, in decentralized companies, our research shows that there tends to be an understanding between the parent and the business about where and when the parent will exercise its influence. This understanding, which we shall call the decentralization contract, is frequently as much a matter of custom and practice as of explicit agreement.[3] Hence, it is seldom precisely defined. But anyone who accepts an appointment as managing director of a business will almost always have an understanding in his mind of the terms of the contract that will apply, and will rapidly begin to explore any areas of uncertainty. For, without such an understanding, he does not know what issues he can decide for himself, what needs to be discussed with his boss, what policies or constraints he must accept, what his objectives are, or, indeed, what will be regarded as 'good performance' in his job. The decentralization contract amplifies the bare job description and, *de facto*, establishes the nature of the roles, responsibilities and relationships between the levels in a company.

The decentralization contract differs between companies, and in some cases, between subsidiaries within a given company. However, there are certain issues that all parents tend to decide centrally. These include:

- Organization structure: what the overall business definitions in terms of product–market responsibilities will be for the business units that report to the centre, and what the structure and remit of corporate functions and services will be.
- Senior appointments: whom to appoint to run the units that report to the centre.
- Plans and investments: what sorts of budgets, medium term or strategic plans and investment proposals must be submitted to the centre for approval,[4] and whether specific plans and investments that are proposed by the businesses should be approved.
- Targets: what targets to agree with the businesses, in association with budgets, plans or investments that are approved.
- Exceptions: how to react to major deviations from plan, or to other major problems or opportunities that could have corporate-wide impact.

In addition, the centre may choose to be more or less active in:

- Giving directions: on certain issues of importance to the company as a whole, or to the business in question, the centre may act as primary decision maker. In decentralized companies, the centre avoids such interventions, leaving the strategic initiative with the business unit management unless it feels that important overall corporate interests are threatened.
- Offering advice: both the range of issues covered and the degree of pressure to act on the advice can vary. By giving advice on more issues and, in particular, by pressing more strongly for the advice to be accepted, the centre reduces decentralization.
- Establishing corporate policies: the extent and nature of issues covered by mandatory corporate policies and guidelines can also vary, thereby giving more or less discretion to business managers.
- Providing incentives and sanctions to business managers: the nature and 'tightness' of the control process varies between companies.
- Establishing a common corporate culture: the centre may promote a shared set of values, standards of behaviour and decision processes between the businesses, at least on certain issues.
- Helping to develop and transfer skills: if there are skills that are of value across different businesses in the company, the centre may choose to play a role in facilitating their development and use.

- Coordinating strategies between businesses: if businesses have strategies that overlap, for example in terms of resources used or markets served, the centre may decide to arbitrate between the businesses on trade-off decisions, or to propose coordinated strategies in the areas of overlap.

In previous research,[5] we have shown that, even among companies that all profess a belief in 'decentralization', the nature of central influence is very different. It ranges from the highly decentralized approach of financial control style companies such as Hanson, which have very small corporate centres and rely mainly on financial targets and monitoring to exert their influence, to the more involved approach of strategic planning style companies such as IBM or Shell. In strategic planning companies, the decentralization contract gives the centre a much more active role in terms of directing and advising the businesses on the strategies they are planning to pursue and on how they should work together with other businesses in the portfolio, which tends to lead to larger corporate staffs and functions.

Although the terms of decentralization contracts may differ from company to company, for any given parent–business relationship the contract needs to be reasonably clear to both sides; otherwise the centre will lack a framework for deciding when to intervene in the business, and the business will see the centre's interventions as arbitrary and unpredictable. Equally, interventions by the parent that are viewed as unilateral attempts to change the contract are liable to be strenuously resisted by the business as *ultra vires*. Our current research shows that companies in which the decentralization contract is clearly understood, normally as a result of long periods of stability in the relationship between the parent and the businesses, have a more trusting and productive working relationship, which, in turn, enables the parent to add more value.

The decentralization contract therefore describes the areas of the business that the parent expects to influence, and, hence, the ways in which it can add value to (or subtract value from) the business. Since corporate strategy is about how the parent can add value to the businesses, the terms of the contract provide a vital background for any thinking about corporate strategy.

In analysing the decentralization contract, it is useful to distinguish between those decisions or interventions that focus purely on a specific business, aiming to improve the quality of decisions within that business as a stand-alone entity, and those that aim to achieve synergies through getting different businesses to work together in ways that would not have been possible for separate companies. In the former case, the emphasis is exclusively on the 'stand-alone' parenting relationship between a business and the centre. In the latter, the horizontal relationships between the businesses are more important, with the centre mediating, facilitating and, in some cases, directing these relationships. The centre can add value either directly through the stand-alone relationship or indirectly by influencing the horizontal relationships. A full discussion of corporate strategy needs to cover both of these dimensions. The remainder of this chapter will, however, focus on stand-alone parenting relationships.

## STAND-ALONE PARENTING AND PARENTING MAPS

Much of the literature on corporate strategy emphasizes 'horizontal strategy'. In our research, we have become increasingly aware, however, that the corporate strategies of many successful companies avoid any attempt at horizontal synergies, particularly where the similarities and overlaps between the businesses are limited in terms of markets and technologies. Furthermore, we have observed the great potential, both for adding and for subtracting value, that is inherent in the stand-alone parenting relationship, and that, although there are many different types of stand-alone relationship, some such relationship invariably exists in every parent company. What, then, is the key to adding value through the stand-alone parenting relationship?

To add value the corporate parent must possess insights that are better than or different to those of the business on at least some of the issues that it can influence according to the decentralization contract. In other words, the centre's views on the matters it gets involved with must be superior to those of the businesses sufficiently frequently to offset both the added cost and time of involving the parent and the negative value of the parent's influence on issues that it is wrong about. Given that the team running the business will be spending much more time on the issues and will be much closer to the detailed operations of the business, this is evidently a tall order.

Our research suggests that corporate parents that do add value possess certain essential skills.[6] In particular:

- They have a good 'feel' for the business, which allows them to provide a new and useful perspective on certain issues.
- They are selective in their influence, and are aware that on many issues, and indeed on the vast majority of operating matters, they have little or nothing to contribute.

The concept of stand-alone parenting therefore implies *both* a good sense of what issues to select for involvement (what sort of decentralization contract to establish) *and* good insights about the selected issues (what decisions to press for). A parent can add value through focusing only on certain issues, but choosing issues that are important and on which it has good insights. Hanson, for example, focuses on financial, budgetary targets and succeeds in stretching performance by so doing, while successful venture capital companies,[7] such as Apax Partners, focus on the financing of growth and the composition of the management team in companies in which they invest. Alternatively, the parent can choose to cover more issues, provided it has enough knowledge of the business to be able to contribute to them. Shell has extensive staffs at the centre to provide advice on functional, business sector and regional issues, and expects to influence the local operating companies on a variety of matters in these areas, but on issues of day-to-day management and on questions concerning the local market and environment the Shell centre leaves the operating company to make its own decisions. A part of the skill of a good corporate parent is therefore to know its own limitations.

But the more positive component of stand-alone parenting is the feel, the judgement and the insight that allow good decisions and advice on the areas of involvement and intervention. What is the basis of this ability?

It is in the nature of the parenting relationship that the parent will normally be dealing with issues on which it is less fully informed, and on which it has spent less time, than the managers of the business. Of course, the chief executive should aim to be well briefed, and of course he can draw on corporate staff work to help him. But there is something wrong with the decentralization contract if he and his team are putting in anything like as much effort on the problems of a single business[8] as the management of that business. Much more typically, the chief executive must react quickly to propositions, without the time, resources or desire to duplicate the work already done by the business. There-fore, diligent homework and issue-specific analysis are not the answer to good parenting. Indeed, business heads will more fre-quently complain about interference and nitpicking than praise the insight of chief executives who try to second-guess decisions by knowing more about the detail of the businesses than the management team in charge.

The skilful chief executive, then, manages to make insightful contributions on issues where, almost by definition, he is imper-fectly informed. 'He [the CEO] leaves me pretty much alone to run the business, and I don't see him that often. But, whenever I do, I always pick up some interesting ideas from him,' was the comment from a business head in one successful MBC in our research. Ideally, the chief executive of the decentralized company leaves the initiative and the detail firmly in the hands of business management, but still seems able to provide valuable guidance when, infrequently, he does choose to get involved.

This rather remarkable capacity depends on the parent having a feel for what matters most and for how to succeed in the business. Different chief executives use different phrases to describe the phenomenon, but we shall call it a 'parenting map'.[9] The parenting map provides a means of interpreting information about the business. It allows the parent to identify the most important features in the business and to determine in which direction it should be developing. Its essence is an understanding of certain aspects of the business that gives a frame of reference against which to test specific proposals or initiatives. The parent-ing map will cover issues such as:

- What sorts of managers succeed in this sort of business?
- What are the key success factors to focus on?
- What are the key risks to guard against, and how heavily should different risks be weighed?
- What are suitable performance targets and ratios?

Depending on the nature of the decentralization contract, it may also cover a range of other issues.

The parenting map may amount to a comprehensive sense of what sorts of strategies and investments succeed and fail in the business. However it can also be limited to a single insight ('invest in the downturn') or rule of thumb ('anything less than

10% return on sales is unacceptable performance'). Where the parenting map focuses on a single insight, however, the parent must nevertheless have a sufficient appreciation of other aspects of the business to be confident that the insight is valid for the business in question. Hanson's financial control formula covers only certain aspects of a business, in particular suitable short-term profit targets. But Hanson also knows that this formula is only valid in certain sorts of businesses (low-tech, mature, competitively stable) and must satisfy itself that a business has these broad characteristics before using its map, otherwise the 'insight' provided by the map may turn out to be false for the business, and may damage its performance rather than help it. A crucial component of Hanson's success has been to avoid businesses such as pharmaceuticals or oil exploration in which a primary focus on short-term profits is incompatible with the strategies necessary for sustained success.

It is the parenting map that allows a chief executive to react quickly and with insight to issues that arise. Rather than conducting an exhaustive assessment of all possible courses of action, he reaches a judgement based on his sense of what matters most. Thus, for example, we were told about an investment proposal put to the centre of a natural resources company. The investment involved accepting a minority position in a joint venture in a Latin American country to produce a commodity whose price was then at the bottom of a deep cyclical trough. For most parent companies, let alone banks, such an investment would have seemed terrifyingly risky: lack of management control, a volatile and depressed local political environment, the need to assume a major recovery in the price of the commodity to achieve adequate returns. But for the company in question, the investment seemed attractive. It knew that many good natural resource investments involve joint ventures without management control, and are located in politically 'difficult' regions. It was able to help the business to put together sophisticated financing deals that laid off much of the political risk onto suppliers and eventual customers. And, most importantly, it was more interested in the very low prospective cost position of the mine than the depressed price level, since its parenting map stressed long-term cost advantage, not the current price level. Although a full analysis of the investment was of course undertaken, the basic confidence to proceed with what became an immensely profitable investment turned much more on the parent company's feel for what investments were appropriate in cyclical commodity businesses of this type. This is what a parenting map is all about.

From where does the parenting map that guides a chief executive come? Obviously, it builds on the data, information and briefings about the business that the CEO receives. It will also factor in other information that the CEO acquires from field visits, from acquaintances, from background reading, from one-off external studies and from many other sources. But digesting the vast array of information available is a major task, let alone converting it into an intuitive feeling for what works best in the business. Therefore, chief executives are frequently guided by their personal experience with the business or with other similar businesses, either as manager or parent. Strategies and tactics that the CEO has himself tried, or directly observed, provide the basis for judgements about what succeeds and what fails, about how to handle different situations, about how to react to crises. It is the personal experience base that creates good intuitions, a good 'gut-feel' for a business; and, in the area of parenting, we must be as concerned with experience and intuition as with analysis.

Just as parents that add value have a suitable parenting map, parents that subtract value either lack a feel for the business, and hence have no parenting map to guide them, or else, perhaps more dangerously, use an inappropriate map. The basic reason given for Courtaulds' demerger of its textile interests from its chemicals, coatings and fibres businesses was that the board, collectively, did not have a good feel for the sorts of strategies that are valid in textiles businesses. The parent company was therefore not in a position to react sensibly, far less insightfully, to proposals put forward by the textiles businesses. A demerger freed these businesses from what would otherwise have been negative parenting influence. In our research, we have encountered numerous examples of negative parenting, but few companies with the courage to demerge as Courtaulds did. We believe that corporate strategy must be as concerned with avoiding businesses in which the parent does not have a good parenting map, and so subtracts value, as with finding ways to add value.

To add value to a business, the parent therefore needs to possess a parenting map that is valid for the business. Given such a map, the parent has the potential to add value. But the amount of added value created will depend on the circumstances of the business and the opportunities they provide for the parent to intervene constructively.

## OPPORTUNITIES TO ADD VALUE

Value added by a parent depends on adding something to the proposals, perceptions and strategies of the management of the business. If the managers share the same appreciation of the strategic logic of the business that the parent has, the opportunities to add value are reduced, even if the parenting map is appropriate. In these circumstances, the parent and the business will usually get along well, decisions will be reached speedily and with little contention, and the most serious source of subtracted value, inappropriate influence, will be avoided. But the corporate overhead remains, and may deliver little positive benefit.

The opportunities for a parent to add value are much greater where the parenting map provides new insights for the business team. This most frequently occurs where the business is facing an important but unfamiliar change situation, where the management of the business is inexperienced or unsophisticated in certain areas, or where there are particular pressures on the business that may cloud the judgement of its management. We shall discuss each of these situations in turn.

Where a business faces the need for major change, the parent may be able to bring to bear insights based on similar transitions in other businesses. The parent can then help the business to deal with such transitions by drawing on skills and experience not likely to be possessed by its management. In our research we have come across a number of parents who specialize in change situations of this sort. For example, the British TI Group has helped a number of its businesses to build up an international network of companies in what were previously essentially national businesses; Grand Met has prospered by acquiring weakened branded goods companies, and then strengthening and capitalizing on their underexploited brands; and Emerson has been especially successful in parenting businesses that had opportunities for rationalization, cost reduction and margin improvement. These parent companies have developed skills in how to manage the relevant change situations that have allowed them to provide added value insights to their businesses. Many of the most significantly successful parent companies fall into this category.

High added value can also be delivered to relatively unsophisticated business managements. A parent that is experienced in the techniques of strategic planning (Emerson), the methods of financial control (BTR) or manufacturing efficiency (Cooper or Williams) has much to contribute to a management team that lacks these skills. In our research, we have, for example, come across several cases in which a corporate parent was able to catalyse important new initiatives in its businesses through the introduction of a new approach to strategic planning. But, as the new approach became familiar to the businesses, its impact, and hence its added value, diminished. The value added depends on the parent being able to introduce effective approaches to management that are new to the businesses. It is for this reason that portfolios consisting of small, relatively unsophisticated companies often provide some of the most fertile ground for parenting added value.[10]

There is, however, something essentially transitory about both change situations and unsophisticated management teams. In a sense, the successful parent works itself out of a job, since it is aiming to help the business to complete the change needed or to acquire the skills that were previously lacking. Once these goals have been reached, the parent needs to find fresh opportunities to add value to justify a continuing parenting role. Perhaps the most fruitful continuing opportunities arise in businesses that face systematic pressures that may cloud their judgement. For example, in cash cow businesses whose internally generated cash flow is far in excess of what they should sensibly re-invest, there are pressures to over-invest or to diversify unwisely; tight control from a separate parent company might have prevented much wasteful investment in industries such as tobacco. Alternatively, in businesses with long investment time cycles, there may be a temptation to pay too little attention to the need for short-term performance. In some chemical companies, the parent has played a useful role by pressing its pharmaceutical businesses to show a consistent annual growth in profits. Without this pressure, there would have been a tendency to focus too much on major, long-term research developments and not enough on smaller, more incremental improvements in formulations, delivery mechanisms or packaging. Where such pressures exist, the parent can usefully counterbalance them, providing an alternative view of how to weight opportunities, strategies and targets.

There are other situations in which a corporate centre with a suitable parenting map can add value. The parent can provide a sounding board for the business and help it to refine and clarify its own thinking. It can identify mistakes, caused perhaps by overcommitment to a strategy or by overlooking some important features of a situation. It can elicit higher standards of performance through tough, objective and dispassionate control processes. We have encountered real added value in each of these instances. But it remains important to recognize that unless the parent has insights that are in some way different from those of the business, the scope for adding value is much reduced. All too frequently, the parent then fails to add sufficient value to justify the costs it causes. If this is the case, the time has come to consider divestment of the business. There are, unfortunately, few companies that are willing to recognize when this situation has been reached, and to act upon it.

## PARENTING MAPS, DIVERSIFICATION AND CORPORATE STRATEGY

In an MBC, the parent must be able to focus on suitable issues and have a feel for an appropriate parenting map for *each* business in the portfolio. If the sort of parenting map that is appropriate is quite different in each business, the task of creating an added value parenting relationship becomes daunting. Where the sorts of issues that matter most, the sorts of managers who succeed and the sorts of strategies and investments that pay off are different, the parent must fine-tune its relationship for each business, drawing on different skills and experiences in each case. If, however, a similar parenting map can be applied across the different businesses, the centre's task is much easier.[11] The parent can then rely on similar intuitions, gut-feel and experience across the portfolio.

It follows that a corporate strategy that takes a company into a range of businesses with widely different appropriate parenting maps is much more difficult to make successful than a corporate strategy that focuses on businesses that share a common strategic logic, and can be managed with similar parenting maps. Many of the most spectacular failures in managing MBCs have been caused by entering businesses that were not amenable to the same parenting map as the core, original business areas. Exxon's misguided foray into the office equipment business is only one case in point.

This does not mean that all of the businesses must come from the same industry. Indeed, businesses that come from widely different industries may all respond to a similar parenting map. This is a point that financial control companies such as Hanson have long appreciated, and which underlies the ability of venture capital companies to parent businesses from many different industry sectors, provided they are all passing through the same phases of growth, and therefore facing similar issues.

Conversely, businesses that all come from one industry sector are often not amenable to the same parenting map. For example, the parenting maps that are appropriate in ethical pharmaceutical businesses are very different from those needed in either OTC or generic pharmaceuticals. The same is true of prestige, mass-market and own-brand consumer goods in most, if not all, product areas. Thus, a parenting map that works well for one business in an industry is often wholly unsuitable for other businesses in the same industry. Similarly, businesses that share a common technology, a common customer group or common distribution channels may nevertheless require very different parenting maps. This means that the traditional dimensions of 'relatedness' between businesses in the portfolio do not ensure that similar parenting maps, the real test of parenting relatedness, can be applied.[12]

To judge the diversity of a portfolio, it is therefore necessary to assess the extent to which a common parenting map can be applied. It is commonality of parenting maps that matters in determining the diversity of a portfolio, not the spread of industries or the number of businesses. Successful MBCs whose portfolios are largely made up of businesses that respond to similar parenting maps include:

- 3M: innovation and new product driven businesses, based around selected core technologies
- Unilever/Procter & Gamble: multi-local, branded, fast-moving, packaged, mass-market consumer goods
- RTZ: cyclical, capital-intensive mining and minerals businesses
- TI Group: high added value, safety critical engineering components and sub-systems for international markets.

There are some successful MBCs whose corporate strategies involve applying different parenting maps in different parts of the portfolio; GE is perhaps an example. However, our research suggests that this sort of strategy requires an unusually able and adaptive corporate team, and that the success rate is low. Instead, we see many MBCs that diversified widely in the 1960s and 1970s retrenching to their so-called 'core' businesses.[13]

Parenting problems most frequently arise when companies diversify into businesses that cannot be successfully managed with the sort of map employed in the base businesses of the company. To some extent, this is commonly recognized, and many companies are guided in their portfolio building decisions by some sort of 'comfort factor' or sense of 'fit'. But comfort factors are typically soft, subjective, and ill-defined. Often, they express the prejudices and preferences of the chief executive rather than a grounded assessment of the real parenting skills of the company. What is needed is an honest review of the businesses that the company has succeeded and failed in adding value to, and of the experience and skills of the corporate team. Such a review is often not openly undertaken, perhaps because it might lead to unpalatable conclusions, but appears to offer a sounder basis for decisions on new business entry. It may not be possible to define the boundaries around the businesses that a company can successfully parent with precision, but the broad outlines are normally clear.

When diversifications are undertaken that require parenting skills that a company lacks, the parent company tends either to pull back substantially from exercising any influence, or to settle into an unproductive, subtracted value relationship. There is therefore much to be said for a corporate strategy that limits the portfolio to businesses where similar parenting maps are applicable. In most companies, this is the only way to achieve a genuine added value relationship between the centre and its business units.

---

## MANAGEMENT IMPLICATIONS

The implications for senior central management of this view of corporate strategy and parenting maps are profound. They may be summarized in four main points.

1. Lay out the decentralization contract and the parenting map for each business in the portfolio as fully and clearly as possible. By doing so, senior central managers:
   i. show the basis on which the parent believes it can add value
   ii. help to communicate with business managers
   iii. help to define the limits on the businesses that the parent thinks it can handle.
2. Conduct an honest audit of your successes and failures with diversifications. Such an audit provides a means of testing where the limits of existing parenting skills and parenting maps lie.
3. Make the possession of suitable parenting skills the key criterion for assessing diversification proposals. In the first instance, limit diversification to businesses that respond to parenting maps similar to those in the core businesses. This does not necessarily imply sticking to a single industry sector, but does underline the importance of:
   i. building on established areas of parenting success
   ii. avoiding diversifications whose rationale does not focus on parenting added value.
4. Constantly review whether you are adding sufficient value to justify retaining each business in your portfolio. In particular:
   i. once a transition is complete during which you have been able to add substantial value, review whether steady-state value-added is likely to be enough to offset the continuing costs caused by or attributable to the parent.
   ii. be willing to sell or demerge businesses to which you do not believe you add sufficient value.

By following these principles, we believe that many corporate parents will be able to clarify their thinking about corporate strategy and achieve greatly improved results for their stakeholders.

---

## NOTES

1. See Goold, M. and Campbell, A., and Alexander, M. (1994). *Corporate Level Strategy: Creating Value in the Multibusiness Company*. New York: John Wiley, for a fuller statement of many of the arguments in this chapter. In this book, we argue that the objective of corporate strategy

must be for the parent to add more value to its subsidiaries than any other potential parent. We refer to this as achieving 'parenting advantage'. Thus, parenting advantage becomes the key underlying objective for corporate level strategy, in the same way that competitive advantage is for business level strategy.

2. Porter, M.E. (1987). From competitive advantage to corporate strategy. *Harvard Business Review*, May/June, 43–59.

3. The idea of a decentralization contract was first articulated in an unpublished Ashridge Strategic Management Centre working paper on skill sharing in decentralized companies, 'Learning and sharing in multi-business companies', A. Campbell, November 1990. The decentralization contract is one key element of what Bartlett and Ghoshal call 'administrative heritage'. See Bartlett, C.A. and Ghoshal, S. (1989). *Managing Across Borders: The Transnational Solution*. Cambridge, MA: Harvard Business School Press.

4. In complex, multi-level MBCs, the centre also determines who needs to be consulted or advised as part of the decision process.

5. Goold, M. and Campbell, A. (1987). *Strategies and Styles: The Role of the Centre in Managing Diversified Corporations*. Oxford: Blackwell; Goold, M. and Quinn, J. (1990). *Strategic Control: Milestones for Long-Term Performance*. London: The Financial Times/Pitman.

6. There are also parenting skills associated with management process and the means by which corporate influence can be most effectively exercised. However, this topic is not covered in this chapter.

7. The relationship between venture capital companies that attempt to do more than simply invest and their portfolio of companies is similar to that between a parent company and its subsidiaries.

8. The assumption here is that the portfolio is not dominated by any one business.

9. The importance and influence of the mental maps that lie behind 'experienced based' decisions has been documented by several writers. See Spencer, J.-C. (1989). *Industry Recipes: The Nature and Sources of Managerial Judgement*. Oxford: Blackwell; Nelson, R.R. and Winter, S.C. (1982). *An Evolutionary Theory of Economic Change*. Cambridge, MA: Harvard University Press; Miller, D. and Friesen, P.H. (1984). *Organisations: A Quantum View*. Englewood Cliffs, NJ: Prentice Hall; Mintzberg, H. (1978). Patterns in strategy formulation. *Management Science*, 24(9), 934–948; Prahalad, C.K. and Bettis R.A. (1986). The dominant logic: A new linkage between diversity and performance. *Strategic Management Journal*, 7, 485–501.

10. We noted that companies that concentrate on stand-alone as opposed to horizontal parenting often have such portfolios. Venture capitalists are perhaps the most extreme example.

11. Prahalad, C.K. and Bettis, R.A. (1986). The dominant logic: A new linkage between diversity and performance. *Strategic Management Journal*, 7, 485–501.

12. This observation may be one explanation of why the research on performance and relatedness in diversification has proved so inconclusive.

13. Porter shows the high proportion of diversifying acquisitions that are subsequently divested (Porter, M.E. (1987). From competitive advantage

to corporate strategy. *Harvard Business Review*, May/June, 43–59). The role of 'non-core' businesses is particularly problematic in the portfolio. Once a business has been categorized as non-core—either because it is too small to be material, or because it does not fit the main thrust of the parenting strategy or for other reasons—an unsatisfactory parenting relationship almost always ensues. See Goold, M. and Campbell, A. (1987). *Strategies and Styles: The Role of the Centre in Managing Diversified Corporations*. Oxford: Blackwell, pp. 188–189, for an enumeration of some of the problems that arise. The right course is to move speedily to disposal once a business is no longer part of the core.

# 6

# Removing Intermediaries from Distribution Channels

## Kim Warren

---

### ALTERNATIVE PERSPECTIVES ON DISTRIBUTION CHANNELS

Strategy research regarding the business unit has in recent years had two distinct areas of focus. Attention has been given to issues internal to the firm, such as the building of resources and capabilities, while a further focus concerns external issues, such as the competitive forces determining industry profitability. However, most such consideration has been conditioned by the presumption that the supply chain in which the firm operates is relatively fixed. Little attention has been given to the potential for competitive advantage through reconsidering the role of distribution channels. Here, the term 'distribution channel' does not mean simply the physical transportation of physical product, but encompasses every business activity after a product or service has been created in the form ultimately consumed by the final buyer. It therefore includes import agencies, distributorships, wholesalers and retailers, and covers both the supply of physical goods and the provision of services, whether to individual consumers or to commercial end users.

---

*Building the Strategically-Responsive Organization.*
Edited by H. Thomas, D. O'Neal, R. White and D. Hurst.
Copyright © 1994 the Strategic Management Society. Published 1994 by John Wiley & Sons Ltd.

The relative inattention given to the strategic impact of distribution channels is surprising, considering the multi-stage process through which many products have to move to reach the final consumer, and the considerable value added between the cost of manufacture and the price paid by the final buyer. Starting from the final productive stage, a product may be launched into a complex and costly system of distributorships, wholesalers and retailers. Each participant has to search for the goods it chooses to stock, negotiate and buy, arrange inward delivery, market its portfolio to the next in the chain and arrange outward distribution. At each stage, people are employed, property constructed, systems administered and costs incurred. Yet after all this activity, the consumer still does not have the product. He has to find it, look for the best terms, and spend time and money collecting it from the retailer.

*Strategy* concerns itself with a firm's search for sustainable competitive advantage. It has long been recognized that distribution channels represent an important factor in determining an industry's profitability and a firm's search for advantage. Powerful buyers bear down on the profitability of an entire market of competing suppliers. They are able to do this more easily if those suppliers have a limited choice of alternative distribution channels. Having gained access to channels of distribution, this advantage to incumbent suppliers provides a barrier to entry against other suppliers wishing to enter the market.

This framework, however, *assumes* the existence of the multi-stage distribution chain, and pays little attention to the possibility of challenging conventional channel structures. Yet industry profitability and individual firm performance are likely to be substantially affected by distribution channel structure. Small firms or new entrants to a market may be at a substantial disadvantage if access to powerful distributors is a critical factor for success in a market. Moreover, the balance of power is clearly different between, on the one hand, the case of producers selling to major retailers and, on the other, producers selling direct to individual consumers.

*Economics* offers its own perspective on distribution channels. Transaction costs feature at least two levels: those incurred in setting up a supplier/customer relationship in the first place, and those incurred in adjusting the relationship over time (Williamson, 1975). One might expect transaction cost economics to consider the multiple costs incurred if a product has to flow through a number of stages between producer and consumer, yet little attention has been paid to this issue. Economists instead focus their attention either on who *owns* the various stages of distribution or on competition to optimize the costs of supply, given the existence of distribution stages. Empirical studies focus on issues such as vertical integration, rather than on comparing supply chains with different numbers of stages. Information economics also concerns itself mostly with the power balance between supplier and buyer, assuming both to exist (Jonscher, 1983; Perry, 1989; Tirole, 1988). Little consideration is given to questioning that assumption.

*Marketing* writers have given perhaps the greatest attention to the management of distribution channels (Day, 1990; Cespedes and Corey, 1990; Christopher, 1972; Rosenbloom, 1990; Stern, El-Ansary and Brown, 1989; Takeuchi, 1980). Such attention generally considers the options a firm faces in selecting a mix of channels: some options may involve intermediaries, while others consist of direct dealing.

This work, though, is limited in two respects. Firstly, much of the debate about direct trading from producer to user focuses on industrial products where direct dealing is taken to be economic only in the case of trade with major users. Secondly, marketing writers take it as axiomatic that, although one may eliminate the middle-man, one cannot eliminate the function he performs. This accepted wisdom misses two important points:

- While a supplier may not eliminate the function that the middle-man performs, he may nevertheless eliminate part of his own function of dealing with that middle-man. If a wholesaler were eliminated, the supplier would have to take on distribution to retailers, but would save himself the need to market his products to that wholesaler.
- The intermediary's function itself is only necessary if the next firm in the chain exists. To extend the example, if consumers bought directly from the producer rather than through a retailer's store, the function of the wholesaler would indeed be obsolete.

*Technological change* also features in the likely evolution of distribution channels. Two important technologies impact on distribution channels: physical transport and information technology (IT). Physical transport has been something of a poor relation in analysis of distribution channels, being considered as merely the carrier, used by the various traders to move goods from A to B. Yet its role need not be so humble. If a producer wishes to deal directly with consumers, rather than through wholesalers and retailers, an effective door-to-door delivery facility becomes of paramount importance (Sekita, 1990).

IT features in channel structures because the producer has to inform the potential user of his product about its existence and its qualities. He may also need to find out more about the user's needs and desires. The user, on the other hand, has to discover the product, its availability, price and performance, and must inform the supplier of his needs. The problems of both parties can be addressed by IT. To date, interest in IT has been in its potential for 'locking-in' customers by creating switching costs. However, this perspective also assumes the existence of the immediate customer, which will generally be an intermediary, rather than considering the final consumer. Indeed, some of the most powerful strategic applications of IT have been made by intermediaries, who have created for themselves an electronic market-place of products from alternative producers. Little thought has been given to the use of IT by producers for direct trading with the ultimate end user.

---

## SOURCES OF POTENTIAL ADVANTAGE FROM DISINTERMEDIATION

### CURRENT CHANNEL STRUCTURES: PRODUCER/RETAILER/ CONSUMER

The following analysis takes the case of a typical consumer product, manufactured by a producer, sold to a multiple retailer, and finally bought and used by a private consumer. The starting point is the cost of the product at the point where it leaves the production plant, and therefore assumes for simplicity that earlier costs (e.g. product development) are unaffected by the method of subsequent sales and distribution, although in practice such costs may be affected.

## Producer Channel Costs

From the end of the production stage, the producer faces the following principal cost elements in dealing with his retailer buyer (FIGURE 6.1):

- costs of physical distribution, either directly to retailer store locations or to a retailer's central warehouse
- marketing costs, both consumer advertising and retailer sales/ promotion
- follow-up service, either retailer servicing (e.g. faulty goods) or service provided directly to the consumer (e.g. product maintenance)
- transaction costs in dealing with the retailer (e.g. order processing, obtaining payment, negotiation and financing the 30 days or more to receive payment from the retailer).

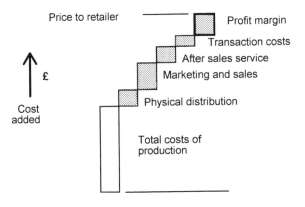

FIGURE 6.1   Producer's cost structure: dealing via a retailer

## Retailer Channel Costs

Moving to the next stage in the chain, the retailer makes no actual change to the product, so his channel costs encompass the whole of his value chain (FIGURE 6.2):

- sourcing the goods from the producer, including costs of the retailer's internal distribution from warehouse to store

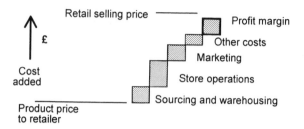

FIGURE 6.2   Retailer's cost structure

- store operating costs, in particular the cost of physical premises and staff
- marketing costs, consumer advertising
- other costs, largely administrative (e.g. human resource management, finance and data processing).

---

### Consumer Channel Costs

The consumer also faces costs in the purchasing process (FIGURE 6.3):

- search costs: all of the direct and opportunity costs incurred from the moment the consumer identifies a need to the time when he knows which product he wants, and where it will be obtained (e.g. consulting others about their experience, calling alternative stores to identify range, price and availability, consulting consumer reports on the desired type of product, and visiting alternative stores to physically compare alternative products)
- sourcing costs, including both the time and financial cost of visiting the store to collect the desired goods, and returning with them
- consumption costs, such as consumable accessories or energy.

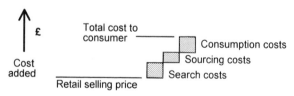

FIGURE 6.3   Consumer's cost structure

It is apparent that the total cost to the consumer may be substantially above the retail price charged in the store. However, consumers may not explicitly recognize the search and sourcing costs they incur in making buying decisions.

---

### Total Channel Costs

Taking all three players in the multi-stage process, it can be seen that the final cost of products to the consumer may be substantially raised by conventional distribution channels (FIGURE 6.4).

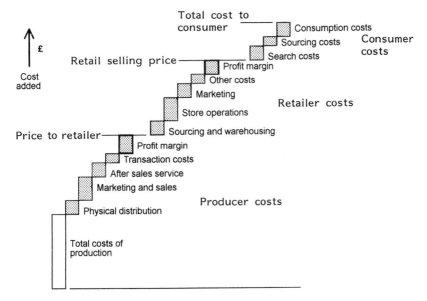

FIGURE 6.4   Total cost: producer/retailer/consumer channel

---

## SIMPLIFIED CHANNEL: PRODUCER TO CONSUMER

In the example considered here, disintermediation implies direct trading between producer and consumer. Under such conditions, the producer's costs are substantially altered, retailer costs are eliminated and consumers' costs differ, as compared with the con-

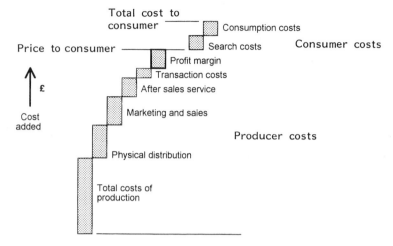

FIGURE 6.5   Total cost: direct dealing

ventional supply chain. The producer's costs will alter as follows (FIGURE 6.5):

- Physical distribution to retail stores or warehouses may be eliminated, to be replaced with the costs of delivery to consumers' premises. This may incur a much higher unit cost than store delivery. Indeed, it may only be feasible if 'bundled' with other doorstep delivery opportunities, such as mail.
- Within marketing, the considerable cost of consumer advertising may not be significantly altered, since consumers must still be made aware of the product and persuaded to pay. There may be savings in advertising if producers no longer have to commit heavy advertising budgets simply to get their products accepted onto the retailer's shelves. Retailer promotion and the costs of a sales force to sell to retailers can both be eliminated, to be replaced with the cost of capturing consumer orders.
- Servicing costs can be handled directly with the consumer—not significantly different from the case of dealing through a retailer.
- Transaction costs may be altered. Each consumer purchase would create a discrete transaction directly on the producer. However, the transaction is likely to be significantly simpler than when dealing with a retailer. Contract terms will be relatively trivial, specifications of quality and delivery may be simpler, and the order process itself may require little more

than a credit card number and an address.

- Financing costs will be significantly reduced, since payment can be obtained from consumers within days, though perhaps with some offset for credit card charges.

Whether the product price charged by the producer in these circumstances is higher or lower than it was when dealing with retailers will depend on the relative balance of the savings and increased costs. For most products, the high cost of physical transport to consumers' premises would outweigh any savings the producer could make. However, the retailer costs eliminated may be considerable, ranging from 10–20% on top of the producer's price in the case of fast-moving consumer goods to 50–100% on clothing and premium goods. This saving offers considerable potential to offset the additional costs for the producer in direct dealing.

The consumers' costs may be reduced, since it will no longer be necessary to visit stores to compare and select the goods. Against this saving, there may be small additional costs in adding producers to the early search process. However, as this can often only be done remotely, for example by telephone or catalogue, the costs need not be substantial.

## POTENTIAL SAVINGS FROM REMOVING INTERMEDIARIES

It is now possible to arrive at a framework for comparing the costs of the multi-stage and direct-dealing distribution channels. For any category of goods or services, the costs of conventional channels can be calculated, and the costs of direct dealing estimated with reasonable accuracy. From this data, potential savings can be identified (FIGURE 6.6).

In addition to the financial savings involved, further benefits may arise from eliminating time delays and information inefficiencies. When dealing through retailers, a producer will be isolated from the consumer's purchase event by the time it takes for the retailer's stock and order generating processes to respond. This may be quite quick—in the case of perishable foods, only a matter of days. In other cases, however, retailers may stock a month's supply of goods, and producers may receive orders only several weeks after the consumer purchase which triggered the eventual need for the retailer to replace his stock.

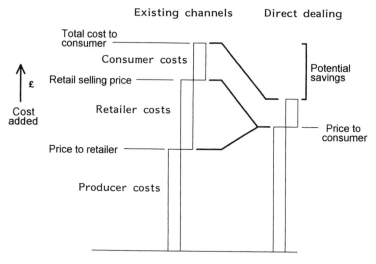

FIGURE 6.6  Potential savings from disintermediation

These delays isolate producers from the purchase event, and expose them to additional variability imposed by the retailer. For example, if retail sales decline, the retailer may deliberately reduce ordering levels on the producer by more than the percentage fall in retail sales so as to reduce stock. Further information inefficiencies occur in the producer–retailer–consumer case. The retailer's staff may simply not know about a product's qualities, specification or performance as well as the original producer, and may therefore be unable to communicate this information to the consumer. If a consumer has a complaint, there may be delay and distortion of the message between consumer and producer in the process of solving the problem.

## FACTORS DETERMINING THE TREND TO DISINTERMEDIATE

Given the cost added by multi-stage distribution channels, and the impact of supplier/buyer relationships on the profitability of product markets, a truly strategic perspective on the supply chain would encompass a fundamental challenge to existing structures.

The likely impact of such a reconsideration to the case of any particular product will be conditioned by two distinct sets of issues:

- the strength of any *driving forces* tending to bring about the removal of intermediaries (the costs and delays already mentioned and the incentives facing producers or consumers), balanced by
- the strength of any *constraints* that may obstruct the process (such as the investment needed to set up alternative channel structures, or the vested interests of the existing parties).

The implications of this balance between the two sets of forces include:

- that the relative balance between intermediated and direct channels will vary significantly, but predictably, between different categories of goods and services
- that the relative balance between intermediated and direct channels will alter over time, as changes occur to the relative costs of the two alternatives, and to the influence of the moderating factors
- that as intermediaries are removed, substantial changes will occur in the structure of affected markets, altering the prospects for those firms involved.

## DRIVING FORCES

It is in the producer's interest to concern himself with the cost of his goods to the final consumer. He thus has an incentive to examine the costs of multi-stage channels and seek to reduce the final price. The potential savings will be a function of the product's characteristics:

- *Its unit value*: the higher the unit value, the greater (in general) the cash margin taken by distribution channels.
- *Its bulk*: less bulky goods can be transported easily through existing, low-cost mail and parcel services, whereas larger items require more specialist transport.
- *Its urgency and perishability*: if a product is required urgently (e.g. a medical prescription) waiting for home delivery may be

unacceptable, even if that wait is reduced to a matter of hours. Similar considerations apply to perishable goods.

- *The efficiency of existing channels*: if current distribution channels get the goods to the final consumer relatively quickly and cheaply, the potential savings from disintermediation are reduced.

Producers of goods and services have a strong interest in challenging the time delays inherent in current multi-stage channels and seeking to eliminate them. Many have been placed under great pressure by powerful buyers, such as retail groups, to respond 'just in time' to orders. Yet between their premises and the consumer, goods may still experience considerable delays, waiting in warehouses and in retail stores, before finally being selected and taken by the consumer. These delays incur financing costs, lead to obsolescence of the goods, and expose goods to loss, theft and damage.

End user service may be improved by direct producer–consumer trade in some circumstances. Many goods and services are not straightforward for consumers to buy, collect, install, use or have serviced (e.g. washing machines or fax machines). With intermediaries involved in the supply chain, producers are isolated from consumers' difficulties in these matters. Producers may thus suffer consumer dissatisfaction with their product or service, perhaps through no fault of their own, yet may not be able to correct matters or, may not even be aware that a problem exists.

---

## CONSTRAINTS

### Producers

Various constraints can be expected to slow or prevent any tendency to disintermediate, even where the simple cost equation would indicate that it should be possible. Producers themselves are constrained by lack of appropriate capabilities and infrastructure:

- *Capabilities*: the ubiquity and efficiency of existing supply channels have made it unnecessary for producers to have any capability for dealing directly with end users. Their marketing, sales and distribution efforts are highly tuned to meeting the onerous demands of supplying the powerful intermediaries through whom they have to sell. Such specialism is one of the hallmarks of an efficient and advanced economy. However, if economic activities can be eliminated through simpler supply structures, cost saving to the economy may outweigh the benefits of specialization.

- *Infrastructure*: with decades of heavy investment directed towards current supply arrangements, some infrastructure elements needed for direct dealing do not exist. Few marketing media lend themselves naturally to direct-to-consumer methods. To be suitable, a medium would need to provide the 'comparison' of alternative products currently provided by retail stores, much as mail-order catalogues already offer. The French Minitel service, based on simple computer terminals in a large proportion of homes, is an example of the facility required. Current distribution arrangements have developed to serve present-day sales channels, in particular the multiple retail chains, and are rarely appropriate for direct-to-consumer channels. Telephone ordering is now quite feasible for many products. However, for many items, such as a regular grocery order, the task is daunting, and errors may later cause disputes between buyer and supplier. Direct channels would be more widely practical with communications systems that allowed easy data transmission to and from consumers' premises.

## Investment in Direct Channels

For a firm accustomed to conventional multi-stage channels, achieving the new capabilities needed for a direct dealing operation can be regarded as a conventional investment decision. Initial costs may include new facilities, in particular new information and distribution systems, recruitment and training of staff, and pre-marketing of the new service to consumers. Incremental income could comprise additional sales volume, gained from attracting new consumers who would not otherwise have access to the firm's goods through existing channels. Other gains might arise from capturing some of the savings made as additional profit margins. On the other hand, there might be some loss of sales through channels previously employed, either as a result of consumers switching to the new service, or from current distributors and retailers de-listing the firm's products.

Given these sources of cost and benefit, it may be easier for new market entrants to develop direct-to-consumer channels than it would be for established products. Firstly, a new entrant would not risk having to write off capital and human investments in existing channels. Secondly, a new entrant risks no loss of sales from existing channels.

## Resistance from Intermediaries

Existing channel structures exhibit an established balance of power between the various players in the chain. An importing distributor of goods, for example, has power over his supplier arising from his knowledge of the local market and his reputation among those in his home country to whom he sells. Some of the most powerful channel members are large retail chains, whose access to large proportions of the consumer market gives them considerable power over suppliers. They may demand special packaging, provision of point-of-sale equipment, in-store demonstration staff, producer-financing of consumer credit and more. They may also obstruct producers' efforts to get closer to the end consumer. A major retail chain, hearing that a producer of consumer durables intended to put reply cards in their packaging to learn about their buyers, de-listed the supplier's goods.

Having adapted to this balance of power, suppliers will be reluctant to undermine existing channels by trying to sell direct. If producers were to make direct sales to consumers, existing retail stockists would suffer, might de-list the producer's range and hence cause the producer to suffer lower rather than higher sales.

## Consumer Behaviour

Retailers give consumers the opportunity to compare different brands of products, each of which might meet their need. This advantage should not be overstated, however, since retailers frequently face incentives to minimize the range held and may feature only brand leaders in any category. Consumers may also gain assurance from knowing that the retailer of the goods is reputable, and thus likely to supply a reliable quality of products.

The usage of direct channels will thus depend on consumers' willingness to buy without advance contact with the goods, a willingness that in turn depends on the nature of the product being purchased (Tirole, 1988):

- *Search goods* are those where the product's qualities can be ascertained before purchase, e.g. fashion clothing. Direct producer-to-consumer channels will be appropriate for search goods if an alternative to the search process is provided (e.g. 'approval' periods or provision of independent evaluation reports).
- *Experience goods* are those where the quality of goods is ascertained after one purchase, and used to judge whether to make repeat purchases (e.g. packaged foods). Direct channels will not be inhibited by the consumer's need to ascertain quality in the case of experience goods.
- *Credence goods* are those where certain qualities of goods or services are not known, even after a purchase has been made (e.g. toothpaste). Direct channels will be feasible for credence goods, where other constraints do not exist.

The development of direct channels will be slowed by the reluctance of buyers to change embedded habits. Consumers are used to buying through retailers and may not be content to rely on remote supply, even where direct contact with the goods does not help the buying decision, or is uneconomic from a rational viewpoint.

Consumers may not be aware of the opportunity to use direct buying channels, even when they exist, so awareness will depend on efforts by suppliers to promote such channels. A further requirement for direct channels to be effective is that the consumer should know how to use them. Information needs would include, for example, contact phone numbers of suppliers, or specification of the buyer's requirements in a form to which the supplier can respond, such as model number, colour and other specifications.

---

## A MODEL OF DISINTERMEDIATION

Given the foregoing argument, it is possible to produce a model of the tendency to disintermediate, which can be applied in a pre-

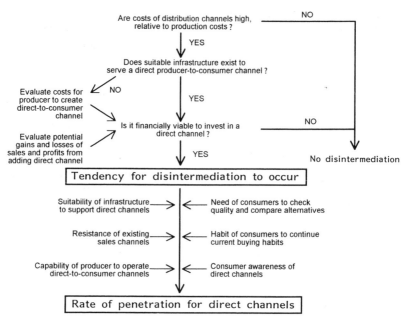

FIGURE 6.7   Model of the tendency to remove intermediaries

dictive manner (FIGURE 6.7). The benefits available from removing intermediaries will vary between different types of goods and services, as a function of the driving forces and the moderating constraints. The relative viability of intermediated and direct channels will thus vary significantly, but predictably, between different types of goods and services. The model in FIGURE 6.7 will produce outcomes specific to the nature of the good or service being considered, the efficiency of existing supply channels, the economics of current and possible direct channels and the particular constraints that apply (TABLE 6.1).

## TRENDS AFFECTING MULTI-STAGE CHANNELS

One feature of the model is that it can reflect the dynamics of market evolution. Since the relative costs of multi-stage and direct channels will alter over time, their relative attractiveness will also alter, and removing intermediaries will become more or less

TABLE 6.1   Comparative tendency to remove intermediaries

| Nature of good or service | Potential savings from disintermediation | Ability to deal with constraints | Likely rate of disintermediation |
|---|---|---|---|
| Financial services: banking, insurance | ***** | ***** | High |
| Large, high value consumer durables: car, fridge, television | ***** | *** | Medium |
| Lower value consumer durables: books, electrical goods | *** | ***** | High |
| Fashion goods: clothing, cosmetics | **** | ** | Low |
| Non-perishable consumables: coffee, photo film, detergents | *** | ** | Low |
| Perishable consumables: fruit, meat, vegetables | ** | * | Very low |

TABLE 6.2   Cost trends for multi-stage channels

| Factors raising long-run costs of multi-stage channels | Factors reducing long-run costs of multi-stage channels |
|---|---|
| Increasing real wages of employees in retail operations | IT enabling improved inventory and supply management |
| Increased real cost of retail premises, driven by planning restrictions and rivalry | Continued consolidation of retail chain ownership, leading to improved buying power and distribution economics |
| Escalating spend on producer and retail advertising | Continued escalation of average store size |

feasible. The relative balance between intermediated and direct channels should thus alter over time, as various factors reduce or raise costs over the longer term. In the case of multi-stage channels, cost trends are moving as shown in TABLE 6.2.

## COST TRENDS AFFECTING DIRECT PRODUCER-TO-CONSUMER CHANNELS

The cost factors applying to direct channels can be expected to respond rather differently. Few significant costs are likely to rise, with the possible exception of the marketing expenditure needed to establish a new channel. Two substantial factors, though, should reduce in cost:

- Communications and information processing costs should fall substantially as IT becomes cheaper and more powerful, and as deregulation reduces the charges levied by telecommunications providers.
- The cost of physical door-to-door delivery should fall as deregulation of postal services progresses and rival delivery firms build scale and technological capabilities.

If these trends in costs for the two types of channel continue, direct channels will become more economic relative to multi-stage channels (FIGURE 6.8). Thus, not only will different products and services show different tendencies to switch to direct channels at any point in time, but direct channels will also become feasible over time for products where they were previously not economic.

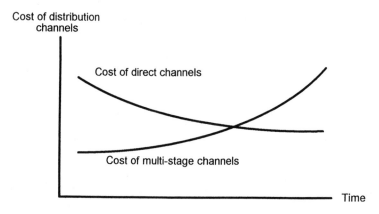

FIGURE 6.8   Cost trends for multi-stage and direct channels

## CONCLUSIONS

This chapter argues that strategy researchers and practitioners should be taking an active interest in the role of distribution channels, and the possibility of transforming firms' competitive advantage by reappraising that role. It takes little more than an analysis of industry forces to appreciate the potential impact.

In conventional, multi-stage channels, there is a balance between increasingly large supplier firms (whether of products or services) and comparably large retailers, wholesalers and other intermediaries. New entry by would-be suppliers is hindered by access to powerful distribution channels. New entry to the retail or other intermediary stage is hindered by the considerable investment and scale economy advantages enjoyed by incumbents. Consumers' options are limited by the provision of retail outlets in the area where they happen to live—in many product categories and many localities this provision is increasingly dominated by large stores.

When suppliers of goods and services are able to transact directly with consumers, the power balance is fundamentally shifted. Although it may appear that the individual consumer has limited bargaining power in comparison with large supplying firms, electronic markets can reduce consumer switching costs substantially. Under such circumstances, existing barriers to entry for suppliers are sharply reduced. A new supplier wishing to get his product to the consumer no longer has to gain access to powerful intermediaries. The prospect is open, then, for the vertical structure of many consumer markets to be fundamentally realigned. Indeed, the firms least able to adapt may well be those large suppliers who are already intimately dependent upon the major retailers through whom they currently distribute their goods.

## REFERENCES

Cespedes, F.V. and Corey, E.R. (1990). Managing multiple channels. *Business Horizons*, **33**(4), 67–77.
Christopher, M. (1972). *Marketing Logistics and Distribution Planning*. London: George Allen & Unwin.

Day, G.S. (1990). *Market-Driven Strategy*. New York: Free Press.

Jonscher, C. (1983). Information resources and economic productivity. *Information Economics and Policy*, **1**(1), 13–66.

Perry, M.K. (1989). Vertical integration: Determinants and effects. In R.L. Schmalensee and R.D. Willig (Eds) *Handbook of Industrial Organisation*. Amsterdam: North-Holland.

Rosenbloom, B. (1990). Motivating your international channel partners. *Business Horizons*, **33**(2), 53–57.

Sekita, T. (1990). Value added distribution of parcels in Japan. *Long Range Planning*, **23**(6), 17–25.

Stern, L.W., El-Ansary, A.I., and Brown, J.R. (1989). *Management in Marketing Channels*. Englewood Cliffs, NJ: Prentice-Hall.

Takeuchi, H.J. (1980). Strategic issues in distribution. Harvard Business School note, 581-026.

Tirole, J. (1988). *The Theory of Industrial Organization*. Cambridge, MA: MIT Press.

Williamson, O.E. (1975). *Markets and Hierarchies*. New York: Free Press.

# Section II

# Managing Strategic Change

Although sustaining competitive advantage requires effective strategy formulation, without equally effective implementation even the most ingenious strategy has little opportunity to contribute to corporate success. Consideration of the firm's internal capabilities and processes (distinctive competences) is critical to successful implementation. Yet, since virtually all organizations are open systems, depending on the external environment to provide inputs and to accept/absorb outputs, the external environment is at least as important to corporate success as are the firm's internal processes. A firm's external environment is, at once, its most pervasive source of a need to change and the fountain of opportunities and threats that are inherent in competitive markets.

It is appropriate, then, that the chapters in this section address issues relating to strategy implementation; the first four emphasizing the need for a firm to be interactive with its external environment, and to be responsive to changes in that environment.

Deiser refutes the belief that nature and society are relatively stable and predictable, and suggests that intuitive, rather than rational, evaluation of information is essential to a firm's ability to respond to changing circumstances.

Chilingerian discusses an alternative to overt action during a crisis: enacting the appearance of 'normal' behavior, to maintain a non-crisis mode.

Egri and Frost explore the organizational power and politics involved in addressing environmental issues, suggesting that who wins and who loses is largely influenced by the audience. By this they mean that corporate strategists must be more attentive to the environmental consequences of their actions, more politically informed as to the power they and others have to influence outcomes, and more aware of the cultures and values of other players.

Lindell and Melin present a longitudinal perspective on acquisition, focusing on the long-term strategic change process. Their results suggest that the process may not be controlled by top management, but instead influenced by internal politics.

The final two chapters in this section examine current research in the strategic management process.

One of the most elusive concepts in strategy is how to manage the increasing complexity and ongoing change that are inherent in strategic processes. Toward that end, Melin and Hellgren offer two typologies to help to illustrate the complexity of strategic processes in practice, and the changing nature of strategic processes over time. They emphasize the necessity of taking a long-term perspective (as opposed to cross-sectional snapshots) in strategic management research, in order to fully capture the changing strategies of firms.

Chakravarthy, Doz and Lorange discuss new developments in strategy process research, and attempt to pinpoint critical challenges in complex multi-business firms.

The chapters in this section emphasize the importance of change, the external environment, organization structure, and power/politics in strategy implementation. Each of these areas has been extensively addressed by previous researchers, attesting to their ongoing importance to strategic management. Following are some suggested readings.

Andrew Pettigrew's title, Director, Centre for Corporate Strategy and Change, at Warwick Business School suggests not only the close linkage between strategy and change but also the thrust of much of his research. He has discussed the *management of change* in such books as *The Awakening Giant: Continuity and Change in ICI* (1985) and *Managing Change for Competitive Success* (1991). Other writings by Pettigrew address equally germane areas of strategy, such as Information control as a power resource, *Sociology*, May, 1972, *The Politics of Organizational Decision Making*, 1973, and On studying organizational culture, *Administrative Science Quarterly*, December, 1979.

David Whetten's writings, which examine the use of life-cycle stages to characterize organizational evolution, address change from the perspective of *organizational growth and decline*, and include Organizational decline: A neglected topic in organizational science, *Academy of Management Review*, October, 1980, Organizational growth and decline processes, *Annual Review of Sociology*, 1987, and Organizational effects of decline and turbulence, *Administrative Science Quarterly*, **32**, 1987.

James March and Herbert Simon's *Organizations* (1958), challenged the notion that managers make rational and optimal decisions. They were among the first to suggest that individuals' *limited rationality* restricts their ability to consider more than a few alternatives, and that 'satisficing'—selecting from alternatives that were 'good enough'—becomes the standard mode of decision making.

Jeffrey Pfeffer, in *Organizational Design* (1978) and *Power in Organizations* (1981), builds on the work of March and Simon, introducing the effects of *power coalitions, goal conflict,* and *individuals' self-interests* on the design of organizations.

James Brian Quinn is perhaps best known for his *Strategies for Change: Logical Incrementalism* (1980), in which he suggests that managers in large organizations consciously develop strategies *incrementally*, rather than through formal planning processes.

Alfred Chandler's *Strategy and Structure* (1962) is a seminal discussion of how an organization's growth may dictate the need for a change in *organizational structure*.

Richard Rumelt's *Strategy, Structure and Economic Performance* (1974) defines related and unrelated *diversification* and examines their implications for corporate success.

Howard Aldrich, in *Organizations and Environments* (1979), and Paul Lawrence and Jay Lorsch, in *Organizations and Environment: Managing Differentiation and Integration* (1987), discuss the strategic importance of considering the threats and opportunities in a firm's *external environment*.

# 7

# Post-Conventional Strategic Management: Criteria for the Postmodern Organization

### Roland Deiser

## INTRODUCTION

In one of his recent articles, Igor Ansoff embarks on a journey through the historical development of the strategic management discipline (Ansoff, 1991). He analyses the history of prevailing 'schools of thought' and links them with the phenomena of environmental 'speed' and 'turbulence'. In a nutshell, Ansoff's historical reconstruction can be interpreted as the steady decrease in importance and usefulness of the traditional 'technocratic' paradigm.

Indeed, in a relatively stable and predictable environment, it is possible to plan for the long term by extrapolating trends and adjusting one's organization accordingly. As long as the environment behaves in a 'rational' way, it makes sense to develop technical tools for the purpose of handling it effectively. However,

*Building the Strategically-Responsive Organization.*
Edited by H. Thomas, D. O'Neal, R. White and D. Hurst.
Copyright © 1994 the Strategic Management Society. Published 1994 by John Wiley & Sons Ltd.

during past decades, mainly due to the dynamics of technological development, environmental 'speed' has continuously increased. Phenomena of discontinuity and surprise have become an everyday ingredient of a firm's strategic challenge (Peters, 1987). At the same time, the strong belief in the predictability, controllability and malleability of the world has turned out to be a myth and an ideology (Habermas, 1968), and is eroding fast.

The belief that nature and society can be instrumentally managed is weakening for several reasons. First of all, we are beginning to realize that we are not able to predict even a fraction of all internal and external consequences of managerial decisions, even using the most elaborate information processing tools. On the contrary, the overwhelming amount of information available today demands intuitive, rather than rational, criteria of selection (Etzioni, 1989). Secondly, the technical–instrumental paradigm, as such, has turned out to be incapable of coping with complex economical, social and ecological system dynamics (Capra, 1985). Increasingly, in the world of global business, issues beyond the immediate context of 'the industry' must be taken into account. Apart from Porter's five competitive forces (Porter, 1980), the impact of organizational actions on regional and global ecological, social and political systems has become not only a question of ethics but also a key question for long-term corporate survival. Facing this challenge, strategic management becomes a complex systemic task which is no longer solvable through mechanistic 'figure-management' alone.

The traditional technocratic planning approach, with its relatively static and mechanistic view of the world, must be given up, at least to a certain extent, in favour of a paradigm better able to deal with the phenomena of dynamics and ongoing change. Paradigms like system theory and the interactionistic approach seem to satisfy better the emerging needs of managing complexity and unpredictability. The following arguments are grounded in these theory systems.

## THE INTERACTING ORGANIZATION

Today, organizations striving for 'success' have to regard themselves as ever-changing, ever-learning systems, reacting with creative, successful and valuable 'real-time responses' to their changing arena. In so doing, they become permanently involved in *interaction processes* with environmental systems crucial to their own survival. Most of these systems are other organizations, like customers, suppliers, competitors, shareholders, unions or public institutions, facing similar challenges navigating through rapid change and uncertainty. The sum of all interactions of a firm makes up the strategic process, which is the engine and the medium that shapes both the firm and its environment.

It is important to keep in mind that the organizational system, as such, is composed of numerous subsystems, following the rationale of functions and/or distinctive product–market combinations. These subsystems are organized by differentiated structures and linked by managerial systems and mechanisms. They develop specific cultures and particular perceptions of the world according to the peculiarities of their tasks, leading inevitably to contradictions and tension.

In order to adapt the firm as closely as possible to different technologies, markets or functions, organizational design must provide an optimal differentiation of subsystems. The more an organization allows multicultural subsystems to exist, the more easily it can match differentiated needs in the market-place. At the same time, too much differentiation leads to centrifugal and fragmenting forces, threatening the coherence of the firm. Integrating structures and mechanisms aids in the realization of synergies, focuses resources and energies, and leads to a more efficient market approach: acting with 'one voice' against other external players. Too much focus on integration, however, threatens multicultural diversity and differentiated adaptability. Therefore, only an optimal balance between differentiation and integration leads to a high degree of customer orientation and specialization, and ensures, at the same time, a joint strategic perspective and a strong corporate identity.

In this respect, the boundaries of an organization play an important role. Clear boundaries lend stability and orientation to the members of a firm. They provide a superordinate identity to the different subsystems within. On the other hand, boundaries must not be too rigid. A lack of permeability may lead to organizational introversion and, finally, to loss of 'touch' with the external environment, threatening the very sense and legitimacy of the firm. As it is the subsystems of a firm that interact with distinctive environments, 'holes' in the boundaries enhance diversity within the firm.

The exchange that takes place between an organization and its environment is a dynamic interactive process, and through this process an organization attempts to create the environment most suitable to its particular competences. The attainment of this goal can be accomplished on two levels. Firstly, a company may define itself and its market by means of a *creative strategic self-definition*. Secondly, the firm acts within this arena and tries to *establish competitive advantages*.

Given this approach, each company is, at least partially, responsible for its own environment. The strategic arena of a firm depends on the conscious or unconscious answers to basic strategic questions such as: 'Which industry am I in?', 'Who are my customers?' or 'How do I define my industry boundaries?' These answers shape the cornerstones of a firm's identity and self-concept, just as they shape the structural and cultural aspects developed within an organization over time.

A representative case from my own consulting experience illustrates the importance of strategic self-perception. At the outset of a strategy formulation process, the welding wire division of a large European steel manufacturer perceived itself as a major player in the highly specialized *steel* industry, being the technological and market leader in the world of stainless steel welding wire. However, strengths, like the high degree of vertical integration and the outstanding know-how in stainless steel processing, suddenly lost their importance when their perspective shifted. By perceiving themselves as a player in the *welding* industry, they suddenly found themselves to be small players in a rapidly changing environment, where 'steel' may easily lose its importance against laser-based welding technologies. Furthermore, in the welding world, products such as equipment and gases play a very important role, making the close connection to 'steel' a problematic one.

Once a firm has chosen its basic frame of reference and, by doing so, has created its specific environment, it attempts to shape its chosen context as a proactive and/or reactive player that wants to maximize interests within the multi-stakeholder game. If managed well, organizations develop competences through this process, embodied in specific structures, mechanisms and cultures that support their strategic intent (Hamel and Prahalad, 1989, 1990).

Interaction is the core of strategic and organizational change. However, by definition, an interactive process occurs *between* distinctive players at their respective organizational boundaries. Therefore, in order to understand phenomena of strategic and organizational learning and change, it is important to pay attention not only to processes *within* the particular firms as single entities, but also—and even more so—to the superordinate system constituted by the interactive process. This superordinate system works as the relevant context for the actors involved and, as 'constructed reality' (Berger and Luckmann, 1969), comprises their orientation.

This carries fundamental implications for the traditional concept of strategic management and the strategy process. The classical iterative algorithm of (i) analysis, (ii) formulation, and (iii) implementation is not coherent with the logic of real-time interactive skills, for several important reasons. Firstly, it is too slow to cope with current requirements stemming from complex change, environmental speed and discontinuity. Today, management does not have time to carry out scientifically tested studies and thorough, exhaustive analyses of the organization and its environment, but must act and react spontaneously and intuitively. As the classical steps of the strategy process merge into each other, analysis, formulation and implementation must continuously occur at the numerous boundaries of the firm and cannot be separated in staff functions only.

Secondly, and more fundamentally, the traditional approach to strategy is a paradigm taking the system of the 'acting organization' as the central point of reference. The 'acting organization' represents a 'player' challenged to position itself successfully in a given environment. The criteria for success are defined solely from the perspective of the player and relate directly to the amount of tangible and sustainable competitive advantages held, as compared to other players within the (enlarged) industry. This is an inadequate, restricted perspective.

But, from an interactionistic and systemic point of view, 'success' should not be measured from the perspective of a single player only. The decisive criterion for an 'ethical' assessment of organizational action becomes the homeostatic balance of the superordinate system which, in the long term, guarantees the survival of *all* players. Therefore, individual 'success' must be defined according to universal ethical standards that transcend the rationale of the single firm. As long as a firm's success is 'payed for' by other stakeholders, who are exploited or even destroyed, it is a failure from an interactive point of view. This differentiation is not only academic. A short-sighted effort towards short-term profits may, in the long term, destroy the customer base, disrupt the profitability of the industry as a whole, hurt the loyalty of employees and/or damage the environment. Each of these initially unintended consequences can threaten the very existence of the firm in the long run. So, taking the perspectives of external players and the superordinate context into account is not only an ethical category, but a *conditio sine qua non* for the long-term survival of a firm.

## STRATEGIC COMPETENCE

Therefore, the traditional algorithm of the strategy process should be substituted by the concept of the 'strategic competence of the firm'. I define 'strategic competence' as an *organization's ability to interact, at any given time and under changing circumstances, with and within the relevant environmental context, in an efficient and effective way, leaving all players in a win–win situation.* This paradigm reaches well beyond the numerous concepts addressed in standard managerial techniques. It perceives the firm as a dynamic sociotechnical system and views the development of strategic competences as a matter of both 'social' and 'instrumental' learning.

Strategic competence requires *strategic–interactive skills* in order to handle responsibly one's own organization and its relations to all the players involved in the joint context (FIGURE 7.1). These skills relate to the paradigm of social learning and follow the requirements of mutual understanding. The achievement of an enlarged understanding of the superordinate system is a complex task. Firstly, in order to interact successfully from a systemic point of view, an organization needs to gain an in-depth understanding of the processes guiding its behaviour (A in Figure 7.1). Secondly, in order to understand the motives and driving forces of other external players, management must be able to assess the internal processes within those firms that guide their behaviour (B). Finally, in order to understand the dynamics of the total system (E), it is not only necessary to look at the dynamics between the firm and its partners (C), but also to watch and understand the processes going on between the external systems themselves (D). FIGURE 7.1 illustrates the different processes at stake.

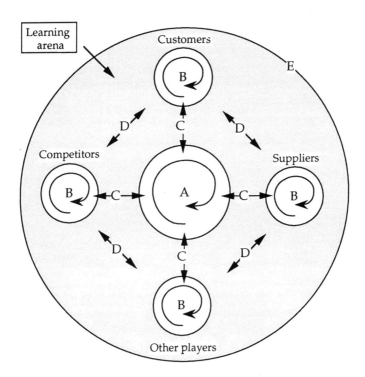

FIGURE 7.1 Levels of strategic–interactive skills. Levels of processes to understand: A, within own organization; B, within external players; C, between own organization and external players; D, between external players; E, superordinate system as a whole

However, strategic–interactive skills alone are inadequate without the *operational skills* that enable an organization to produce a desired output, whatever that output may be. Operational skills are vital for a firm's ability to implement its strategic intent, and they are an important basis for successful action within the industry. Operational skills relate to internal efficiency and require the ability to establish an appropriate internal organizational context (structures, mechanisms, culture) suited to build on the very competences that are required to meet, successfully, the needs of an ever-changing external environment.

Therefore, at its core, strategic management is a 'janus-faced' affair. In the strategic process, managing the internal organizational system and managing (interacting with) external systems represent two sides of one coin that must be managed coherently.

Only a dynamic balance between internal and external perspectives can produce the necessary 'semipermeability' of the boundaries between the organizational system and its environment. Strategic competence can be acquired only through structural and cultural institutionalization of an intraorganizational, as well as an interorganizational, learning process.

---

## STAGES OF INTERACTIVE COMPETENCE: AN APPLICATION OF KOHLBERG'S THEORY ON MORAL DEVELOPMENT

From its conceptualization, the idea of strategic competence can be compared with Habermas' theory of 'communicative competence' (Habermas, 1981). For Habermas, interaction is successful if it remains undistorted and unbiased. These criteria require socially and ethically mature individuals, interacting for the purpose of achieving mutual understanding (not with the goal of mutual instrumentalization). In this respect, Kohlberg's model of the moral development of children can serve as an excellent reference theory (Kohlberg, 1969). Habermas uses Kohlberg's stages to define three different levels of identity, each of them corresponding to various stages of interactive competence (Habermas, 1984).

Kohlberg's considerations are centred on the question of how children deal with normative prescriptions during the socialization process. In a nutshell, children may progress to more mature moral orientations by acquiring cognitive structures that enable them to perceive the world in an increasingly differentiated way. Following a process of emancipation, they become able to handle standards autonomously. In the last stage, finally, the adult can criticize existing prescribed standards according to universal ethical principles. In the following pages this theoretical framework will be applied to the concept of strategic competence.

As Habermas' perception of Kohlberg stems from a completely different context, an application to complex systems like organizations may be criticized as 'anthropomorphism'. However, the heuristic value of the argument should balance that disadvantage. Perceiving the strategic process as an interactive and dynamic exchange between sociotechnical systems justifies the application of related theories. The following description of the levels of moral orientation already includes an 'organizational translation' of Kohlberg's socialization theory. In his original work, Kohlberg distinguishes between six stages. For the sake of simplicity, his model is reduced here to three substantially different levels: the pre-conventional, the conventional, and the post-conventional levels (following Döbert and Nunner-Winkler, 1975).

## PRE-CONVENTIONAL LEVEL

At this stage, actions are directly and exclusively oriented on needs and short-term profits. Only the immediate context of action and counteraction, for the best short-term results, serves as a basis of the orientation for the actors involved. Consequences of actions are only important as far as they touch the immediate interest of an actor. External actors are treated as instruments that either promote or inhibit the success of oneself. Ethical yardsticks relate only to personal benefits. If it serves self-interest, rules are violated without further consideration.

Typical examples include firms that attempt to 'escape' environmental legislation by hiding their toxic waste; firms that try to exploit their customers and/or suppliers for short-term profits; or firms that follow rules only grudgingly and only if strong measures of control are in place.

'Social' skills do not play a role in the process at this level. The actor does not possess the (structural) cognitive requirements for understanding the complex external context. Interactive competence is virtually non-existent, because the actor is neither able to see nor understand the systemic interdependence of all the players involved, and therefore, his is unable to reflect on the impact of a given action on the enlarged system's context. If learning happens at all, it happens unconsciously and on a very direct and uninstitutionalized basis.

## CONVENTIONAL LEVEL

At the conventional stage, actions are oriented on a commonly accepted set of rules or standards. Environmental standards have been internalized, and the actor follows them without any further critical assessment. As long as other players adhere to these rules too, they are treated as equal partners. Whether or not the rules themselves are appropriate is not brought into question. Law and order is the prevailing ethical yardstick, counting more than personal, short-term interest.

Typical examples are firms that follow environmental legislation according to the requirements of the law. They do this because they think that it is immoral to violate the law. Customers and/or suppliers are treated according to 'fair contracts'. The relationships are expected to remain stable and predictable according to existing rules. Change is threatening.

At this level, the actors possess a certain degree of interactive skills. They are able to understand the present normative structure of their environment and to 'behave well' within it. However, as mentioned, change is a threat to those who depend on law and order. Learning proceeds, but it is restricted to the limited frame of reference that is established by the self-perception of the organization. Therefore, real *inter*action does not take place.

## POST-CONVENTIONAL LEVEL

Actions in the spirit of post-conventionality gain their orientation from guiding principles that are valid beyond presently existing rules of the game. These principles are derived from universal ethical imperatives. The point of reference is not the single actor within the interactive context, but the homeostatic balance of the superordinate system itself. The interests of all players involved are taken into consideration, equally. According to these principles, prevailing rules are assessed and altered (if necessary).

Typical examples include firms that proactively generate standards that transcend the prevailing rules of the game. Instead of waiting for environmental legislation, they actively set the pace themselves. They involve customers and/or suppliers permanently in a joint creative process of improving mutual satisfaction. Relationships are regarded as dynamic and changing. Change is actively managed and promoted.

Apart from the high ethical standards implied by this orientation, the ability to bring prevailing rules into question has tremendous implications for the strategic capability of a firm. Rewriting the rules of the industry according to the firm's own principles, justifiable according to a superordinate rationale, means active creation of reality in a most responsible way. By doing so, the firm acts consciously at the edge of the development and will be able to adapt more quickly to change and discontinuity.

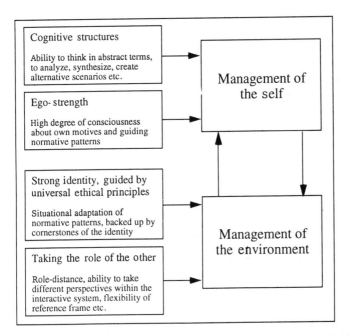

FIGURE 7.2   Requirements for post-conventional organization (individual)

Obviously, there exists a strong connection between the different stages of moral orientation and respective interactive skills. Following Kohlberg and Habermas, but introducing elements of the psychodynamic approach as well, Döbert and Nunner-Winkler (1975) have formulated criteria that enable an individual to act at the post-conventional stage. FIGURE 7.2 summarizes briefly the requirements, illustrating, as well, the interdependence of managing the self and the environment.

### STRATEGIC COMPETENCE AND POST-CONVENTIONAL MANAGEMENT: CRITERIA FOR THE POSTMODERN ORGANIZATION

Referring to the concept of *strategic competence* described above, the quality of an organization's strategic–interactive skills is decisive for its ethically reflected success in the market-place.

While being aware of the problematic implications of a psychologically-based approach, it is nevertheless an exciting exercise to transfer the insights of Habermas and Döbert and Nunner-Winkler to the world of strategy and organization. Through this transfer, it is possible to develop criteria for the post-conventional organization. A closer look at these criteria, however, reveals none other than the organizational and managerial profile for Ansoff's postmodern 'real-time-responding' firm.

The following subsections relate to the four boxes in FIGURE 7.2. After a short referral to 'individual' and 'interaction', the analogy 'organization' and 'strategy process' will be addressed.

## INSTITUTIONALIZE REFLEXIVITY AND CREATIVITY

In order to be able to act as a fully competent partner in an interactive context, an individual must possess appropriate cognitive structures. If successful interaction implies the possibility of a conscious change of frames of reference, a person must be able to analyse alternatives, build hypotheses, assess different probabilities and measure experiences according to grounded principles. If these requirements are not fulfilled, the acting partners will not be able to progress beyond the conventional level.

For the strategic process, the analogue of the cognitive structures are the institutionalized organizational structures and mechanisms that guarantee permanent collection, processing and utilization of relevant knowledge about the company itself and its environment (strategic intelligence systems). Additionally, in order to capitalize on experiences resulting from interactions with markets, competitors and other environmental systems, it is necessary to allow enough room for reflexivity and creativity. Only with these factors accounted for can a systematic and relatively undistorted assessment of processes in the environment occur, which is, in turn, a precondition for the development of thoughtful strategic responses.

A major obstacle for company-wide intelligence systems and institutionalized topoi of creativity is the unavoidable distortion and fragmentation of communication within organizations (Claessens, 1985). If management does not invest constant efforts to overcome these barriers, the firm will not be able to capitalize on valuable information from the market-place that has been collected, for instance, by the sales force. The 'cognitive structure' of an organization can unfold its potential only on the basis of extensive communication flows.

## ABILITY TO TRANSCEND EXISTING REFERENCE PATTERNS

In order to act as a competent partner in an interactive context, an individual must be knowledgeable about him or herself. If a person's behaviour is blindly driven by internalized norms or values that he or she is unable to reflect upon or call into question, the options of his or her behaviour will be restricted to the existing normative patterns. Such an individual will not be able to transcend the rationale of the existing frame of reference and will be forced to maintain a 'conventional' orientation.

The less an individual's behaviour is steered by 'blind spots', the more it will be capable of developing creative alternatives that transcend the state of the art. It will be able to decide consciously what to do, and it will be able to assess the consequences of its behaviour within the enlarged context of communication. A conscious 'ego-driven behaviour' is a major requirement for post-conventional orientation.

What is the analogue for 'ego-driven behaviour' for the complex system of an organization? As previously mentioned, the 'inside' of the organization is a direct result of its experiences 'outside'. Therefore, the existing structural, cultural and strategic cornerstones can only be understood within a historical context. At the conventional level, an organization will not undertake this historical reconstruction and is, therefore, unable to properly understand its own identity. Organizational behaviour is justified by traditional standards ('We have always done these things this way successfully; why should we change?'). However, even if present patterns of action are appropriate, the members of the organization do not really know *why* they work in this specific way. Often, they will continue to follow old patterns even as the strategic environment changes.

In order to overcome these 'blind spots', which limit options when dealing with environmental systems, all members must develop a historically reflected consciousness as to their structural and strategic cornerstones, as well as to the most important elements of their organizational culture (processes, myths, hidden standards, etc.). In order to understand these *organizational* issues, people need to look beyond the narrow boundaries of the organizational subsystems they belong to and obtain a holistic perspective of the total system. Such a holistic perspective can be achieved through *institutionalized* discussions on overlapping organizational issues. This implies the necessity to overcome traditional barriers between departments, and/or hierarchical layers, to make conscious use of existing interorganizational networks (customers, suppliers and competitors). Interdisciplinary and interorganizational cooperation, carefully nurtured by top management, leads to integration of the fragmented perspectives of individuals and groups. It leads to a multicultural organization, one that can act in a differentiated and a coherent way at the same time. Moreover, this cooperation enhances both individual and organizational patterns of perception and opens new and creative options that go beyond the standardized, well-known solutions.

## DEVELOP A STABLE YET FLEXIBLE IDENTITY

A third important prerequisite for successful interaction is a strong, stable identity, supported by reflected and proven principles. At the conventional level, an individual's identity is weak and rigid. It is dependent upon prescribed normative patterns and is threatened by any change in the normative structure. At this stage, different cultures with different standards are perceived as 'aliens', to be converted to the given cultural patterns. This ethnocentric attitude (Adorno, 1973) inhibits the development of mutual understanding and leads to a myopic perspective of the world. In the case of post-conventional orientation, on the other hand, identity is grounded in consciously reflected principles that transcend the social prescription of standards. Orientation according to *principles*, instead of standards, guarantees flexibility, as differing normative cultures are acceptable as long as they do not violate universally justifiable ethical principles. Therefore, it is possible to find mutual understanding, accommodating often very different perspectives (Habermas, 1984).

What is the analogue of the 'stable and flexible identity' for the organizational system? At the conventional level, an organization follows the prescribed rules of the game, which are the present 'state of the art' of the industry. Through a more or less unconscious historical process, the firm finds itself playing a certain role within the industry and tries to optimize its position by trying to 'play the game better than the others'. The firm is not able to transcend the existing rules, and expects all other players to remain in their established roles. A substantial change in the behaviour of customers, suppliers and/or competitors is perceived as a major threat. As the management of the firm is only able to think in established patterns, they neither understand nor accept a change in the rules, and attempt to impose their perspective onto the arena, if possible. If they are too weak to do so, they may not survive a major change.

In the post-conventional stage, an organization is not only able to follow the existing rules of the game but to *bring the game itself into question* (Hamel and Prahalad, 1989). This requires creativity and a willingness to leave the 'safe' path of established industry standards. The courageous move of playing the game with new and hitherto unknown rules must be grounded in a strong, clear identity, independent of historically proven and generally accepted patterns of strategic action. It is an identity centred on some core principles that lend orientation and vision to the members of the firm beyond its existing role within the industry.

This identity can be developed through a clearly formulated and continuously communicated basic strategic–ethical orientation, built around the core competence of the firm (Hamel and Prahalad, 1990). It is the responsibility of top management to care for appropriate structures and mechanisms that enhance the internalization of the cornerstones of this identity. Every member of the firm must be aware of the fundamental goals and the core competence of the firm. This awareness provides continuity during the necessary change, reduces uncertainty and ensures coherent action in the market-place.

---

## UNDERSTAND ONE'S OWN ROLE WITHIN THE GAME

In order to act as a competent partner in an interactive context, one must have the ability to take the role of the other and become more objective with regard to one's own perception of the world. At the conventional level, an individual is bound to prescribed patterns of perception that have been internalized and generalized. In other words, it is 'centred' on its distinctive 'reality', unable to see the world from a different view. Role configurations are perceived as rigid structures, defined according to the ego-centred perspective. The result shows an extremely restricted and unrealistic picture of the social system as a whole.

At the post-conventional level, interaction processes are driven by a *decentred attitude* (Deiser, 1987). Given this attitude, one is able to step out of the self-centred frame of reference in order to see the world as a complex network of interrelations, one's own system being just a part of it. Through the act of changing and enlarging perspectives, roles become more understandable. Thus, aspects of one's own role can be brought into question and, therefore, become openly negotiable.

In this case, one can easily see the analogue for organizations. At the conventional level, a firm cannot see its competition and markets except through lenses coloured by its own self-perception and self-centred interest. Customer satisfaction, for example, is defined from the perspective of the firm's existing capabilities. Customer needs that do not fit into prescribed organizational patterns cannot, by definition, be perceived and, therefore, cannot be satisfied. This leads to a very limited understanding of the mindset of other players, completely determined by the rationale of the firm. The rationale of the market, which deviates from one's own perspective, cannot be taken seriously and will be disqualified as 'irrational'.

At the post-conventional level, an organization is able to see itself and the world through the eyes of other relevant players. This enables the firm to achieve a realistic picture of itself from a *superordinate* perspective of market needs and required strengths and capabilities. This realistic picture is a precondition for developing the ability to fulfil the needs of the market most accurately. Moreover, it opens a path to participation in the creative process, through which the rules of the game may be redefined in innovative ways. Being able to distance oneself from the company's present role is a prerequisite for finding innovative solutions.

*Managing across boundaries* is the catchphrase for developing the competencies required for this aspect of post-conventionality. Companies can substantially improve in their ability to take the perspective of other players by establishing *interorganizational learning structures and mechanisms*. For instance, those structures could be frequent, facilitated retreats with core customers and/or suppliers, driven by the goal of trying to understand each other's mindset. Another fruitful exercise is developing scenarios of multidimensional moves and countermoves within the industry ('If I am moving towards X, what will be the moves of my most important customers, suppliers, and competitors?'). Systematically applied, the members of an organization will increasingly develop sensitivity towards other cognitive maps.

## SUMMARY

Increasing environmental speed and discontinuity forces companies to learn the art of creative real-time response. Issues like *organizational learning* and *managing across boundaries* become more and more important. At the same time, the awareness of systemic interdependencies that transcend the narrow rationale of the single firm increases. The 'conventional' attitude of perceiving one's own company as the centre of the world and regarding one's own standards, values and perceptions as 'the right ones' leads not only to ethical problems but inhibits the development of creativity and may, in addition, damage the system upon which the company depends.

Post-conventional orientation, on the other hand, is based on a decentred, holistic view. This view transcends the narrow perspectives of one's own system, opening the cognitive frame to alien cultures, and leading to a different understanding of the total game from a superordinate perspective. Changing from organizational and strategic ethnocentrism to 'decentrism' entails a complex learning process. However, companies that undertake that managerial effort will be rewarded by an increased ability to act quickly, successfully and in an ethically responsible way in changing environments. This flexibility, together with a clear orientation to core competences, will prove to be a major element in sustaining competitive advantage.

## REFERENCES

Adorno, Th.W. (1973). *Studien zum autoritären Charakter*. Frankfurt: Suhrkamp.
Ansoff, I.H. (1991). Strategic management in a historical perspective. *International Review of Strategic Management*, **2**(1), 3–72.
Berger, P.L. and Luckmann, T. (1969). *Die gesellschaftliche Konstruktion der Wirklichkeit*. Frankfurt: Fischer.

Capra, F. (1985). *Wendezeit*. Bern: Scherz.

Claessens, D. (1985). *Das Konkrete und das Abstrakte*. Frankfurt: Suhrkamp.

Deiser, R. (1987). Systemisch-interaktionistische Aspekte des Lernens von Individuen, Gruppen und Organisationen. In Kailer, N. (Ed.) *Neue Ansätze der betrieblichen Weiterbildung in Österreich. Band 1: Organisationslernen*. Wien: IBW Forschungsbericht 54.

Döbert, R. and Nunner-Winkler, G. (1975). *Adoleszenzkrise und Ich-Identität*. Frankfurt: Suhrkamp.

Etzioni, A. (1989). Humble decision making. *Harvard Business Review*, July/August, 122–126.

Habermas, J. (1968). *Technik und Wissenschaft als 'Ideologie'*. Frankfurt: Suhrkamp.

Habermas, J. (1981). *Theorie der kommunikativen Kompetenz*. Frankfurt: Suhrkamp.

Habermas, J. (1984). *Moralbewußtsein und Ich-Identität*. Frankfurt: Suhrkamp.

Hamel, G. and Prahalad, C.K. (1989). Strategic intent. *Harvard Business Review*, May/June, 63–76.

Hamel, G. and Prahalad, C.K. (1990). The core competence of the corporation. *Harvard Business Review*, May/June, 79–91.

Kohlberg, L. (1969). Stage and sequence. The cognitive–developmental approach to socialization. In Goslin, D.A. (Ed.) *Handbook of Socialization Theory and Research* (pp. 367–480). Chicago: Rand McNally.

Luhmann, N. (1981). *Soziale Systeme*. Frankfurt: Suhrkamp.

Peters, T. (1987). *Thriving on Chaos*. New York: Alfred A. Knopf.

Porter, M.E. (1980). *Competitive Strategy* New York: The Free Press.

# 8

# Managing Strategic Issues and Stakeholders: How Modes of Executive Attention Enact Crisis Management

JON A. CHILINGERIAN

## INTRODUCTION

A crucial test of executive leadership occurs whenever significant external pressures and unexpected threats are translated into internal corporate action (Ottensmeyer and Dutton, 1989; Schein, 1985). In these crisis situations, the classic two-pronged prescription to executives is (i) avoid crises by noticing the early warning signals, and (ii) translate external pressures immediately into internal action. As one analyst puts it, effective leaders 'improvise staff into new combinations and arrangements . . . they attack problems frontally and aggressively, interpret their powers expansively, and radiate confidence' (Koenig, 1964, p. 383).

*Building the Strategically-Responsive Organization.*
Edited by H. Thomas, D. O'Neal, R. White and D. Hurst.
Copyright © 1994 the Strategic Management Society. Published 1994 by John Wiley & Sons Ltd.

The literature notes that effective crisis management upsets organizational routines by exacting its own distinctive pattern of social organization (Janus, 1989; Koenig, 1964; Vroom and Jago, 1988; Weinberg, 1977). In other words, during a potential crisis, the chief executive officer (CEO) is expected to take observable and extraordinary *social* action. For example, CEOs are expected to prod and mobilize stakeholders (especially staff) into new *ad hoc* arrangements. To acquire and process information swiftly, they are expected to recentralize their authority over routine tasks, relationships, and work schedules. Thus, what is regarded as routine work and ordinary hierarchy is interrupted.

The reason why a crisis situation exacts an executive response may be related to a widespread belief that *some* executive action is better than inaction (Weick, 1983). Consequently, when a potential crisis threatens, the decision not to act is very tenuous. The executive who appears to be slow in responding to crisis signals may be blamed for producing a worse outcome. Historians have labeled executives who carried on with routine behavior, or who declared 'business as usual' in situations that deteriorated into 'real' crises as monumental failures. So, if an executive senses a potential crisis, he or she may be more apt to act than to 'thoughtfully' ignore the problem because of the possibility of making matters worse.

The literature alludes to a second basic proposition. That proposition states that routine behaviors improve crisis conditions if, and only if, it turns out that a full-blown crisis never materializes. The following excerpt may help to clarify that position: 'In fact, situations are not crises if normal behaviors produce improvements. Crises are dangerous, in part, because normal behaviors make them [crises] worse' (Starbuck, Greve and Hedberg, 1988, p. 691). So, if conditions improve after an executive chooses to delay action or to *consciously ignore* the problem, then his or her 'crisis denial' response is interpreted as effective behavior (Drucker, 1967). This suggests that there are cases in which a more passive, *cognitive response* from the CEO is the best available choice. However, effective behavior can be seen only in retrospect, and is effective simply because crisis signals do not always mean that a real crisis is coming.

There is another way to interpret executive inaction in such a situation. One could say that perhaps the situation evolved into a non-crisis because of the way in which the CEO attended to it. That is, perhaps because the CEO chose to deny, suppress, or otherwise re-interpret the ambiguous crisis signals, without inter-rupting the routine, the situation did not develop into a full-blown crisis. The inverse is also true. Perhaps because a CEO chose to respond, react, and mobilize stakeholders, an ambiguous threat *did* develop into a full-blown crisis.

If, as this interpretation suggests, some CEOs have the ability to shape a crisis outcome simply by their action or inaction, there may be a place for 'perceived' inaction among leaders whose ability to understand and respond to crisis situations is well honed. Some executives may choose to carry on with routine behaviors, because they possess the capacity to translate their visions into a shared reality. In other words, these are leaders who have an ability to construct expected environments (Bennis, 1983; Berger and Luckmann, 1966). For such CEOs, normal beha-viors may culminate in a non-crisis because 'enactment' of routine is the reality they have constructed (Weick, 1979). Thus, perhaps an alternative to declaring a crisis is 'acting out' a non-crisis by maintaining routine behaviors.

This chapter examines the idea that a non-crisis can result from an 'enactment' of routine behavior. In so doing, a cognitive mode of managing disturbances and crises is articulated, in contrast to the more aggressive, social mode mentioned earlier. Executives who approach crisis situations in a cognitive mode maintain the appearance that the problem is routine. They exclude everyone from becoming involved with the issue except themselves. The demands of the crisis are met and resolved with minimum upset to the organization's routine. Consequently, inaction can be viewed as an alternative strategy of control to manage a potential crisis situation.

The context for the discussion is a case study, describing how one hospital CEO handled a series of potential crises around a controversial hospital policy—a policy that allowed a nurse with AIDS to continue to treat patients in the surgical intensive care unit of the hospital. Despite the potential gravity of the situation, the CEO categorized the incident as a routine problem; further-more, the enactment of a non-crisis was achieved by maintaining the appearance that everything was normal. Hence, the situation became an occasion in which a chief executive effectively managed a real disturbance with 'normal behaviors.'

When the incident occurred, the author was inside the organi-zation studying the CEO. This research was part of an observa-tional study of six hospital chief executives, following Henry

Mintzberg's methods (see Mintzberg, 1973). The author had an opportunity to watch the events as they unfolded and to see how they ultimately would resolve.

Ethnography was used as a field method to capture the fine details of the chief executive's situation (Van Maanen, 1988). However, the whole case is not reported here.* The story is summarized, with noting of the key events, and explanation of what happened by inferring a strategy from the CEO's behavior (Crozier and Friedberg, 1980).†

To orient the reader, the chapter begins with a short description of the case, focusing on what the CEO did and what the outcome was. In order to analyze what happened, three research questions will be answered:

1. How do CEOs translate external threats and pressures into internal responses?
2. What choices are available to the CEO during a potential crisis?
3. How does the CEO communicate with people during emergencies?

To answer these questions, three conceptual ideas about handling disturbances, crises, and other pressures are developed. Firstly, Harvey Leibenstein's (1987) hypothetical model of pressure translation is adapted and extended to CEOs. Secondly, borrowing from Goffman (1971), two choices for handling crises and disturbances are identified. Thirdly, executive attention structure is offered as the mechanism that CEOs use to communicate with key stakeholders. The chapter concludes by suggesting how understanding the attention behavior of the CEO in the case offers new insights for effective crisis management.

---

*The case, entitled Baker Medical Center (A), (B), and (C) (Chilingerian, forthcoming), may be obtained from the author.
†While it is dangerous to draw lessons of broader applicability from a single case study, this analysis has benefited from the studies the author conducted of five other chief executives. Although the chapter draws heavily on this single case, the other cases helped the author to develop the basic ideas and analytic framework used here.

## A CASE STUDY OF EXECUTIVE CRISIS HANDLING

In 1985, a reporter for a nationally syndicated newspaper learned that a nurse at Baker Medical Center,* a first-rate American hospital, carried the AIDS virus and continued to treat patients. At the time there was much public hysteria, very little scientific knowledge, and virtually no precedents to follow.† Since the chief of infectious diseases and the director of nursing had made a conscious policy decision to let the nurse continue to treat patients, the reporter wanted to do a feature story for the Sunday edition. The reporter also wanted to find out the nurse's name.

Except for the people working with the nurse with AIDS, few hospital employees (including the physicians) knew of the incident or the policy. The hospital's stated policy was to protect employee and patient confidentiality. Moreover, the Board had not formally approved the policy. It was difficult for the CEO to predict everyone's reaction.

The reporter called the public relations office and asked for an interview with the CEO that afternoon, and the right to talk with the hospital's employees. On the Tuesday morning when the public relations department informed the CEO of the interview, the CEO's calendar was jammed with scheduled meetings from 8 a.m. to 6 p.m. The schedule looked that way every day that week.

## WHAT DID THE CEO DO?

The CEO, who is called by the pseudonym Dr Hunt in this chapter, did not interrupt his schedule. In fact, he announced to everyone that the issue was a routine matter. The CEO moved in a relaxed manner throughout the week, casually mentioning the 'news' to stakeholders in a tranquil, yet potent, way. He never interrupted his schedule, but went on with the agenda of each meeting. During each scheduled meeting, no more than a few

*Disguised name.
†Between 1980 and 1985, AIDS had transformed from a medical curiosity into a deepening national (and global) crisis. Because of its deadly nature, it was a disease shrouded in myths and half-truths. Since there were no precedents around the issue of health workers with AIDS, there was a potential for public hysteria and patient lawsuits.

minutes were spent on the AIDS issue. Moreover, he never called for any special meetings, or held any *ad hoc* meetings, apart from a few phone calls with the public relations office.

From the author's field notes and accounts from insiders, other more important issues dominated the agenda that week. The author observed, however, that at each scheduled meeting, among the other issues, he developed a theme. He told each group that there was going to be some publicity that they should know about. He said that Baker Medical Center was employing a nurse with AIDS, and that it had been decided that he could continue caring for patients. The CEO articulated that the policy was very 'rational and appropriate—in accordance with the Center for Disease Control's guidelines.' He admonished everyone that, despite the fact that other hospitals had handled AIDS in a 'medieval way,' Baker was not about to 'fall prey to unfounded fears.'

---

## WHAT WAS THE OUTCOME?

Hunt opted to handle the interview with the reporter by phone, and thus handled the interview alone. During the interview, Hunt 'played it straight,' offering facts and data about AIDS. However, he gave only some of the facts to the reporter: for example, he did not correct the reporter's confusion over the difference between surgery and surgical intensive care. When the reporter asked if the nurse had been working in surgery, the CEO quickly answered, 'No!' He did not volunteer that the nurse worked in surgical intensive care—a fact that the reporter may have blown out of proportion. He told the reporter that this unusual situation was not only handled well, but that the policy in question was 'safe, appropriate, intelligent, and morally correct.'

During the interview, the reporter claimed to have obtained the name of the nurse from 'other sources.' The CEO informed the reporter that the hospital had an obligation to let the 3000 members of the 'Baker' family know what was happening. Ostensibly, he wanted the employees to know that Baker's policy of employee confidentiality had not been violated. Because the CEO said he would personally write a story that would *appear on Friday morning* in the employee newspaper and the physician newsletter, the reporter was forced to release the story on Friday instead of Sunday. The story came out on page 20, and the headline read:

*Case of Nurse with AIDS Poses Difficult Issues: Despite Fears, No Risk, Specialists Say*

The article emphasized the rational side of the argument, suggesting that Baker had made a sound choice, and ended with a powerful quotation from the interview with the CEO:

> In these instances there are two choices: one is more hysterical and emotional, and the other is more rational. In the last analysis, if the hospital does not choose the more rational option it will not fulfill its responsibility. We can't go back to the middle ages and start persecuting people who have diseases of one kind or another. The hospital has to take the most rational viewpoint it possibly can.

This case provides a dramatic example of an event that might have crippled the CEO and the organization for days, or weeks. If the story had come out the wrong way and been picked up by the 'yellow press,' the hospital could have been beset by lawsuits from patients and employees. In fact, no newspapers ever picked up the story, and no lawsuits ever arose. Given the way in which American courts have recently handled discrimination suits regarding employees with AIDS, Baker Medical Center looks like a leadership institution in this important area of social policy.

---

## AN ANALYSIS OF EXECUTIVE BEHAVIOR

No CEO can ignore the pressures exerted by the 'external' environment, especially when public awareness of a deadly disease was rising and a newspaper reporter was around the corner. All of these pressures came to bear on Dr Hunt as he faced the potential crisis. The stakeholder notion recognizes that beyond the stockholders (or Board of Trustees), there are people internal and external to the organization who also have a stake in an AIDS policy. When crises are brewing, stakeholder support, commitment and acceptance are desirable (Bourgeois, 1980). FIGURE 8.1 identifies some key stakeholders in this type of situation.

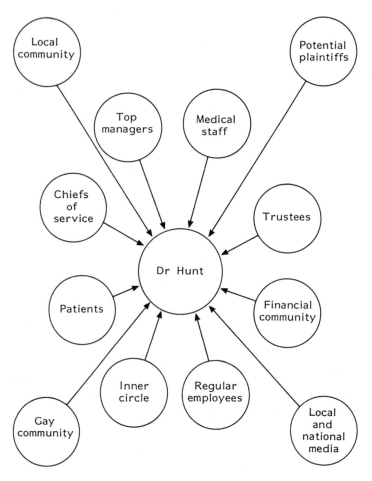

FIGURE 8.1   Key stakeholders for the Baker Medical Center (adapted from Blair and Fottler, 1990)

The behavior of this executive raises many interesting questions about how strategic issues are noticed and managed, how information is processed, and how strategic policy is imprinted in complex organizations. While there are several plausible hypotheses that explain Dr Hunt's behavior, based on observation and extensive interviews, the following view profile emerged.

Hunt was a thoughtful CEO with 20 years' experience as chief executive officer. Both his medical background and experiences helped him to realize that AIDS was a complex, volatile, and emotional issue. Since there were many stakeholders with short attention spans for this issue, it would be difficult to carry on a rational discussion with everyone.

Thus, the CEO appears here in the characteristic executive role of disturbance handler: 'The manager acts because he or she must, because pressures brought to bear on his or her organization are too great' (Mintzberg, 1973, p. 82). Mintzberg's term 'disturbance-handler role' is a convenient notion that describes a complex bundle of activities and interactions, but masks how the executive negotiates that behavior. In other words, what choices are available to the executive when acting this role out (Stewart, 1982)?

## EXECUTIVE CRISIS INTERPRETATION

In their day-to-day work activities, chief executives must be alert to alarming signs, ambiguous information, and unstable incidents and events. A manager exposed to risks and opportunities must come to terms with them. However, these external pressures are ambiguous; underlying problems are not obvious (Ottensmeyer and Dutton, 1989). Real disturbances and strategic issues are embedded in a steady stream of raw data processed through various types of communication media, such as meetings, memos, reports, rumors, tours, telephone calls, and so on (Mintzberg, 1976; Chilingerian, 1987). Somehow, the manager must anticipate the likely consequences of what is going on 'out there' by translating external pressure into various levels of action inside the organization.

From a normative standpoint, Ansoff (1984) has written extensively about the need to anticipate threats and opportunities by 'reading' weak or risky signals. Future crises can be avoided by carefully managing events and anticipating strategic issues in a way that avoids overreaction and underreaction. Clearly, anticipation buys the time needed to achieve a full-scale response.

To anticipate effectively, three things must happen. Firstly, signals must reach the people who have authority to act. Secondly, those decision makers must detect, interpret and communicate these signs and signals—does the information signal a clear and imminent danger, or will it go away? Thirdly, a decision must be reached on whether to turn the volume up or down on an alarming event or threatening incident by deciding who to involve, and how much pressure (if any) to put on select participants or stakeholders.

Under conditions of uncertainty, managers can make two types of mistakes. The manager may either under-interpret a real crisis or over-interpret a minor disturbance (Kiesler and Sproull, 1982). In either case, managers who enact crises face problems of effectiveness (Drucker, 1967; Weinberg, 1977).

Assume for a moment that the executive is accurately perceiving (and not distorting)* the environment. FIGURE 8.2 differentiates between the strategic significance of an incident or event (major strategic issue versus minor strategic issue) and the risk of a negative outcome (low versus high). Strategic significance, as it is used here, refers to the potential impact of an incident or event on the organization's performance and/or survival (Dutton and Ottensmeyer, 1987), and risk of a negative outcome is defined as the likelihood that a threatening incident or event will have a negative outcome. The cells reveal the range of executive options.

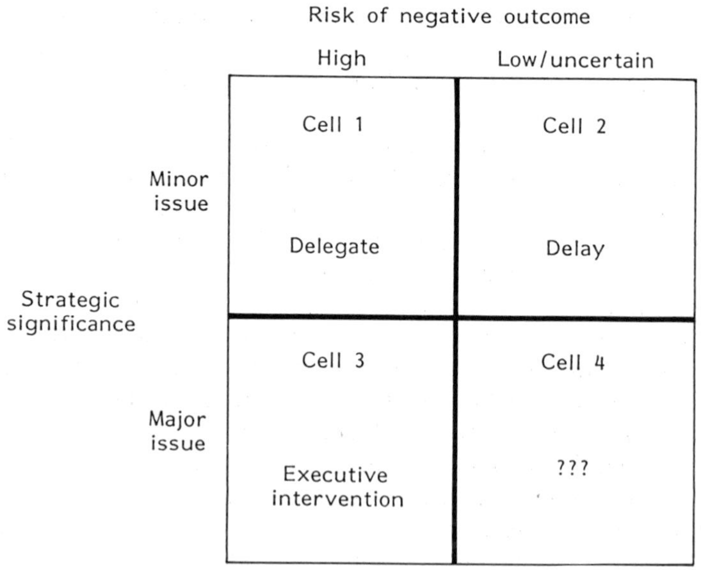

Risk of negative outcome

| | | High | Low/uncertain |
|---|---|---|---|
| | | Cell 1 | Cell 2 |
| Strategic significance | Minor issue | Delegate | Delay |
| | Major issue | Cell 3 | Cell 4 |
| | | Executive intervention | ??? |

FIGURE 8.2   A model of executive crisis management

---

*There is a literature that explains why executive perceptions can become distorted (for examples, see Starbuck, Greve and Hedberg, 1988; McCaskey, 1982).

Not every threatening signal deserves full-scale executive attention. When the CEO (or some group) anticipates that a problem will have a minor impact and will eventually go away, crisis denial or suppression occurs. In these situations, the action taken depends on whether the CEO perceives the risk of a negative outcome to be high or low. Hence, in Cells 1 and 2 some signals are either ignored or go unnoticed. Cell 1 describes a situation in which the risk of a negative outcome is so great, despite its minor strategic impact, that the CEO assigns to someone else the responsibility for handling the disturbance. Cell 2 describes a situation in which there is sufficient uncertainty that a tactic of delay is chosen.

Cell 3 describes a matter of major significance that is imminent—a crisis is declared because the disturbance requires executive attention now. Finally, Cell 4 describes a more ambiguous situation; one in which there is no prescription about what to do. Since the correct technical recipe for responding to this situation is not well understood, a variety of responses are possible, ranging from denial, suppression, or inattention to a 'call to arms.' Thus, we need a way of understanding how the CEO translates pressure when the external signals are ambiguous.

## A NORMATIVE MODEL OF EXECUTIVE PRESSURE TRANSLATION

There are several ways of analyzing executive behavior when external pressures are ambiguous (see, for example, Mitroff, Shrivastava and Udwadia, 1987). To shed light on the problem of executive crisis interpretation, Harvey Leibenstein's (1987) hypothetical model of pressure translation is adapted and extended. The essence of Leibenstein's model focuses on two variables: the relation between internal pressure and real external pressures and disturbances. To this model a third variable is added—programs of organized managerial action (i.e. the bundle of managerial work activities and social interactions taken in response to an external threat or pressure).

Leibenstein argues that external pressure must be translated into pressure on people inside the firm. He postulates three possibilities: (i) 'accurate' interpretations, in which each unit of external pressure is converted into a unit of internal pressure; (ii) optimistic interpretations that introduce less pressure inside than outside;

(iii) pessimistic interpretations that introduce more pressure inside than would otherwise seem warranted.

FIGURE 8.3 is a simple diagram that illustrates the hypothetical relation between two variables: (i) real external pressures and disturbances, and (ii) internal pressure translated by the CEO. In this model, external pressures which exist in the form of market signals, threats from the press or other stakeholders, observable social or economic conditions, and so on, are translated into internal pressure through executive pressure and organizational hierarchy.

To cope with massive amounts of information, executives learn to translate external threats and pressures into categorical responses or programs of action. Although internal pressure cannot be measured precisely, it becomes meaningful in relation to the existence of external pressure. For example, given an average degree of external pressure, a range of executive responses are

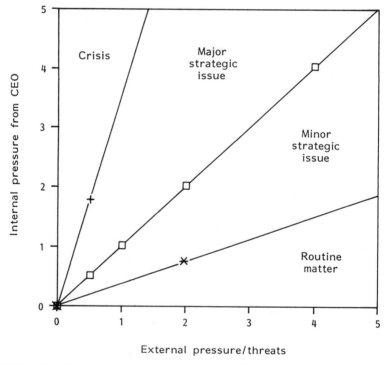

FIGURE 8.3  Executive pressure translation problem: varieties of executive attention. –□– Matching proportions; –×– Relaxed attention; –+– Heightened attention.

possible. The external–internal pressure responses can be broadly categorized into four possible programs of action: major strategic issues, minor strategic issues, crisis activation, or routine problem solving (i.e. a crisis suppression or crisis denial response). Each sector in FIGURE 8.3 contains a different executive reaction to the pressure and can be interpreted as follows:

1. For the sectors along either side of the 45° line, the CEO translates an external pressure into either a major or minor strategic issue. If the executive believes that a signal portends a major issue, then proportionally greater pressure will be applied—the internal pressure will be above the 45° line.
2. If the manager anticipates that the disturbance will pass, a threat might be ignored, or the CEO might buffer the organization from the issue. Since the problem can be treated as a routine problem, everything appears to be normal inside the organization.
3. If the manager anticipates serious consequences, he or she might crank the organization up for a crisis. Here, proportionally greater pressure is applied inside than might otherwise be justified. However, the manager has to be careful of 'crying wolf.'

FIGURE 8.3 hypothesizes that a particular organizational situation 'never completely constrains' the CEO (Crozier and Friedberg, 1980). FIGURE 8.4 hypothesizes that while the CEO retains an ability to choose and negotiate the social reality, it is bounded. When potential crises are a low probability or an uncertain event (see FIGURE 8.2, Cell 4) and the external pressure is low, the CEO can categorize the situation as somewhere between a routine, a minor or major strategic issue, or an imminent crisis. As FIGURE 8.4 reveals, when the signals get stronger and real pressure increases, the ambiguity is reduced and the executive is driven into crisis mode (for examples, see Mintzberg, 1973). Thus, 'You can fool some of the people some of the time, but not all of the time.'

By all accounts from insiders, it appeared that Hunt had placed the incident within the 'routine problem' sector (see FIGURE 8.3). Although it appeared to everyone that he had withdrawn his main attention from the issue to get on with other work, each social interaction was in fact carefully planned. Hunt was not slow at recognizing the problem, nor was he placidly dissociated. He was mindful of the problem and its threatening possibilities; moreover, he was fully mobilized.

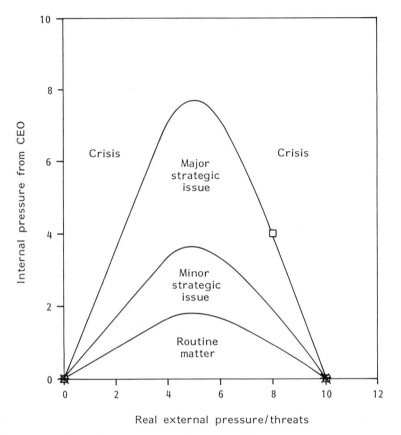

FIGURE 8.4   Executive pressure translation problem: executive attention strategies

## TWO CHOICES FOR HANDLING EXTERNAL THREATS AND DISTURBANCES

Goffman (1971) argues that our immediate world divides into two types of places: one where 'easy control' is sustained, and a second in which the individual is enveloped in a fury of 'self-preserving action.' For the manager, the first situation describes routine, day-to-day management; the second the critical situation or *ad hoc* disturbance (Selznik, 1957). Managers are taught that there are routine situations that are amenable to programming, e.g. coordination by rules, goals, performance standards, and hierarchies

TABLE 8.1 Two modes of crisis management: organizing socially versus cognitively

| Social Mode | Cognitive Mode |
|---|---|
| Declares a 'crisis' by recentralizing control | Maintains 'normal' appearances |
| Identifies key participants | Identifies key participants |
| Generates series of *ad hoc* meetings | Avoids *ad hoc* meetings |
| Stalks and mobilizes people into active awareness | Attends meetings placidly |
| Echoes interests of key stakeholders | Articulates interests of stakeholders |
| Interrupts schedules | Maintains schedules |
| Brings managers physically together to achieve time compression | Maintains normal information channels |
| Requires no detailed knowledge | Requires some expertise |
| Focuses more on process | Focuses more on content |

(Galbraith, 1977). Then, there are unique or non-routine situations that require either: (i) rapid information processing in which tasks are handled on an *ad hoc* basis (task forces, teams, and so on); or (ii) reduced information processing in which task deadlines are extended, goals are lowered, and so on (Galbraith, 1977).

On the basis of observations and analysis of six chief executive officers (Chilingerian, 1987), disturbance and crisis handling could also be characterized by two modes: a social mode and a cognitive mode. TABLE 8.1 shows some of these characteristics.

## Characteristics of the Social Mode

If the CEO adopts the social mode, the chief executive declares (either explicitly or implicitly), that there is an unusual disturbance or crisis. The organization's routines are upset. The CEO's immediate objective is to recentralize control over some organizational/issue domain. The management process involves stalking and mobilizing stakeholders into active awareness and involvement with the incident. The executive's scheduled meetings are replaced by a series of *ad hoc* meetings to acquire and process information and also to obtain qualified opinions on key decisions.

To achieve time compression, key managers are physically brought together, often in a 'command center.' The command center can be located in a conference room or in the CEO's office. All participants' work schedules are suddenly disrupted. As events unfold, other stakeholders may or may not become involved with the problem.

By engaging a group process, the executive is not required to possess detailed information or be the most informed member. Since other stakeholders are involved, the CEO must echo their interests or persuade them otherwise. The CEO exercises control by selecting the stakeholders, determining the rules, and imposing the performance standards. The CEO is still a more powerful player, but must use that power to ensure that the views of no single stakeholder dominate. The executive's focus is on managing the process and interpreting the events, rather than on controlling the issue content.

If Hunt had adopted the social mode of crisis handling, he would have had to cancel the unimportant meetings and mobilize an inner circle: e.g. in a 'fury of intent' call the chief of infectious disease, the executive vice president, director of nursing, and vice president of public relations into action. In other words, he would symbolically declare that a potential crisis exists. This is largely the response received when MBA students and practicing managers are asked how they would handle the situation faced by Hunt.

## Characteristics of the Cognitive Mode

Research suggests that within organizations, individuals' reactions (cast in terms of attitudes and perceptions, rather than substantive behaviors) to incidents and events are determined from information and social pressure in the work environment (Salancik and Pfeffer, 1978). To put it another way, when the chief executive attends to a crisis by disrupting 'normal behavior,' others will read a message of alarm (Schein, 1985). While sounding an alarm can be useful for obtaining undivided (or heightened) attention, it commits the CEO to a highly specific bundle of activities and involvements. Therefore, an alternative way to influence everyone's perceptions is by directing everyone's attention to the normal routines in the work environment (Sproull, 1984; Chilingerian, 1987).

When CEOs decide to enact 'unalarm,' executives must 'consciously act out a style of behaving that is in fact their own' (Goffman, 1971, p. 269). The CEO may not be concealing the true crisis nature of the situation. On the one hand, the decision may be based on a genuine belief that there is no cause for alarm. On the other hand, it may be based on a belief that there is cause for alarm, but that signalling alarm will be counterproductive. In either case, the executive must be vigilant and alert—ready to improvise or switch to a social mode.

TABLE 8.1 highlights some of the behaviors displayed when a cognitive mode is used. As TABLE 8.1 suggests, when the executive chooses a cognitive mode of control, the CEO role is qualitatively different from those of the other stakeholders. The CEO is no longer just a more powerful player among less powerful stakeholders; the CEO has near-complete control. Executive attention is more focused on content than process. Rather than seeking 'qualified opinions,' the CEO must test his or her version of 'what is going on' on everyone, making adjustments as needed.

## WAS THE COGNITIVE MODE EFFECTIVE?

Ostensibly, Hunt went on with 'business as usual.' In fact, he went on a quiet, novel campaign. Hunt's major objective was to create and/or confirm a confident attitude among stakeholders within the organization. He called no *ad hoc* meetings; he merely adapted his normal routine to process information. Throughout the episode, Hunt maintained normal information channels and telegraphed no sense of an emergency.

TABLE 8.2 reveals how Hunt managed communications with key stakeholders that week. He used regularly scheduled meetings to 'mention' the publicity Baker might receive, which included large group meetings and private face-to-face meetings with key managers. Dr Hunt relied on the telephone for continual information updates. Finally, he published information about the incident in two in-house organs: one for physicians and one for lay employees.

In Baker Medical Center, if there was a plausible crisis it was declared cognitively, in the executive's mind. The CEO, Dr Hunt,

TABLE 8.2 Communicating with key stakeholders: information processing strategies

| Key stakeholders | Work modality |
|---|---|
| Department heads | Scheduled meeting/group |
| Chiefs of service | Scheduled meeting/group |
| Newspaper reporter | Telephone interview |
| Trustees | Scheduled meeting/group |
| Chair of trustees | Routine telephone call |
| Non-management employees | Employee newsletter |
| Medical staff | Physician newsletter |
| Assistant vice president public affairs | Telephone |
| Legal counsel | Scheduled meeting |
| Chief of infectious disease | Routine telephone call |
| Executive vice president operations | Unscheduled meeting |
| Director of nursing | Unscheduled meeting |

did not mobilize and attack the problem by calling *ad hoc* meetings with stakeholders—an action that would have symbolically enacted a crisis. Rather, he casually moved through the week, placidly attending to his schedule, displaying 'normal appearances.'

To understand why Hunt managed to do so well, a strategy needs to be inferred from his behavior. More importantly, there is a need to understand the mechanism by which the CEO enacts either of these modes of managing—a mechanism referred to as attention structure (Sproull, 1984; Chilingerian, 1987).

## EXPLAINING HUNT'S BEHAVIOR: EXECUTIVE ATTENTION STRUCTURE

One feature of every manager's information processing activities is the need for a mechanism to deal selectively with a problem-filled environment. The concept that describes this mechanism is

TABLE 8.3  Attention structure

| Aspects of attention | Dr Hunt's behavior |
| --- | --- |
| Focus of attention | Time evenly divided among:<br>External contacts (33%)<br>Subordinates (31%)<br>Other stakeholders (34%)<br>Focus on quality of care<br>and clinical policy |
| How information was<br>acquired and processed | 75% of time spent in<br>formally scheduled meetings<br>with large groups |
| Attention spans | Spent more time with<br>each activity<br>Allowed few interruptions |

attention structure (Sproull, 1984; Chilingerian, 1987, 1989). Attention structure is the manner in which a manager's attention is organized and allocated to people and problems through various work modalities over time. It describes the manager's pattern of personal involvements with his or her task environment. Managerial attention has three aspects:

1. Where executive attention is positioned, in terms of organizational domains
2. How information is generally acquired and processed
3. The time spans of executive attention.

To illustrate these ideas, Dr Hunt's attention structure will be described. TABLE 8.3 indicates that in a typical week 75% of Hunt's time was spent in scheduled meetings with large groups of 'key' decision makers. He had many more formal weekly meetings than did other CEOs in the study, and displayed longer attention spans (more time on the phone and in scheduled meetings) than average. He allowed the fewest interruptions. The object of his attention was strategic management focused on quality of care and clinical policy.

Over the past 20 years, Dr Hunt had learned where he might focus his attention to improve his chances of obtaining usable information and shared understandings. He had also learned how frequently he needed to check those information sources. His attention structure shifted from short, informal attention spans to formal, carefully planned social interactions. So, even during this potential crisis, he achieved active but orderly information processing.

Thus, a consequence of viewing how Dr Hunt handled a potential crisis requires an understanding of how he structured his attention. Attention structure, as it is used here, refers to an information processing strategy that helps the CEO to *translate external pressures into internal responses*. Through attention structure, the CEO at Baker Medical Center achieved a 'quasi-programmed' response to an otherwise unusual disturbance; that is, he behaved as if he had already established procedures for handling any threat or disturbance. Attention structure defines the executive's capacity to maintain normal behaviors while tacitly looking for alarm signals; thus, it is a mechanism that mediates between the two managerial states of crisis and routine management.

By analyzing Hunt's attention structure, several lessons were revealed about executive leadership during crises. Firstly, it suggested that in order to manage stakeholders, CEOs must exploit a variety of communication media. Secondly, it reveals that a thoughtful, well-designed attention structure allows some disturbances to become subject to programming and routines. In Dr Hunt's case, his daily, weekly, and monthly scheduled meetings were carefully planned social interactions with key stakeholders. Hence, the micro-structure of executive attention contains a web of relationships with various stakeholders that becomes an 'ensemble of means' to acquire and process information, and to imprint new policy.

## IMPLICATIONS FOR EXECUTIVE LEADERSHIP

This chapter has considered how CEOs translate external pressure into internal programs of actions. To explore these ideas, the author analyzed how a chief executive handled a series of potential crises around a controversial policy. The implications for executive leadership will be summarized here.

A key idea from the analysis of this case is that CEOs may not only be capable of enacting a plausible crisis out of a non-crisis situation, but are also capable of enacting a non-crisis out of a crisis situation. The way that CEOs 'turn the volume down' on an issue involves maintaining 'normal appearances'; the way they 'turn the volume up' is by upsetting normal behaviors. Thus, CEOs may possess far greater discretion in interpreting threats and disturbances than was previously realized.

A second idea from the analysis of this case is the existence of at least two modes of handling crises and strategic problems. If the role undertaken by CEOs facing a crisis is 'disturbance handler' (Mintzberg, 1973), then a core idea from this analysis is that this role might be carried out either socially or cognitively. The social mode involves stalking and mobilizing people into active awareness through their personal involvement. The cognitive mode involves making 'normal appearances,' excluding everyone from becoming personally involved with the 'issue as crisis,' except the CEO. The cognitive mode translates into minimum upset to the routine.

Each mode of enacting a crisis is *sui generis*. Each one requires very different attention structures and engenders different managerial behaviors. Thus, depending on the attention structure adopted:

1. the strategic content of managerial work is different,
2. the process of managerial work is different, and
3. the outcomes may be different.

On this last point, however, more work is needed before we can predict under which set of conditions one mode of handling disturbances will be more effective than another.

## FUTURE RESEARCH

This chapter has challenged the idea that 'normal behavior' aggravates a crisis, raising a number of questions about executive pressure translation and crisis enactment; however, it has only scratched the surface. There are many interesting questions that might be addressed in future research. For example, how does pressure translation change when the task is made very difficult or when the manager is already under stress? To what extent are cognitive skills involved, such as the capacity to make a series of adaptive responses while the events are still unfolding? To what extent have plausible crises gone unnoticed or been indecipherable because organizational routines were not upset?

Future studies of crisis management should pay particular attention to both social and cognitive perspectives as modes of crisis handling. Studies that contrast these modes might discover attention rules for translating external pressures into internal programs of action. These attention rules may be influenced either by organizational hierarchy or by rank-ordering stakeholders. For example, an attention rule might be to allow only the important stakeholders to feel the pressure of 'crisis,' while less important stakeholders feel less pressure.

Future studies should also focus on how managers learn from the crisis experience. As Goffman reminds us, nearly every activity that is now easily performed and allows for normal behavior appearances used to require 'anxious mobilization of effort' (1971, pp. 248–249):

> The individual's ease in a situation presumes that he has built up experience in coping with the threats and opportunities occurring within the situation. He acquires a survivably short reaction time—the period needed to sense alarm, to decide on a correct response, and to respond. And as a result, he has not so much come to know the world around him as he has become experienced and practiced in coping with it.

Novice managers who have little perceptual grasp or experience in handling disturbances acquire the experience over time. Sudden and surprising events will validate, extend, or disconfirm the less experienced manager's prior knowledge about organizing to do something. We do not have a clear understanding of the knowledge embedded in a crisis situation, especially in terms of the awareness and judgments required. Thus, comparisons of novice and experienced managers may increase our understanding of the role of executive intuition and tacit knowledge (Polanyi, 1958).

The tendency for CEOs to oscillate between critical and routine decision-making situations is more complex than understanding normal and 'other-than-normal' behavior. If 'full calm may in nature be a very few steps away from full agitation' (Goffman, 1971, p. 329), then the existence (or avoidance) of a crisis should not solely be determined by the appearance of 'normal behaviors.' Consequently, students of executive leadership might pay closer attention to the appearance of normal behavior.

This chapter points out some good and bad news for students

of strategic management behavior. The bad news is that executive leadership appears to be an even more complex phenomenon to understand than when Mintzberg (1973) first described executive work. To describe how executives carry out roles such as 'disturbance handler,' research methods are required that capture the inner structure of executive work. The good news is more compelling. Observational research that describes the micro-structure of executive leadership not only tells interesting classroom stories, it has the potential to teach us new theoretical lessons about the practice of management.

## ACKNOWLEDGEMENTS

The helpful comments of Henry Mintzberg, Paul Shrivastava, Leonard Sayles, Nanette Fondas, Barbara Bigelow, Mitchell Glavin, and Dianne Chilingerian are gratefully acknowledged.

## REFERENCES

Ansoff, H.I. (1984). *Implanting Strategic Management*. Englewood Cliffs, NJ: Prentice Hall.

Bennis, W. (1983). The artform of leadership. In S. Srivastava (Ed.) *The Executive Mind*. San Francisco, CA: Jossey-Bass.

Berger, P. and Luckmann, T. (1966). *The Social Construction of Reality*. New York: Doubleday.

Blair, J. and Fottler, M. (1990). *Challenges in Health Care Management: Strategic Perspectives for Managing Key Stakeholders*. San Francisco, CA: Jossey-Bass.

Bourgeois, L.J. III (1980). Performance and consensus. *Strategic Management Journal*, 1, 227–248.

Chilingerian, J. (1987). The strategy of executive influence: An analysis of the attention structure of the hospital chief executive officer. MIT, unpublished doctoral dissertation.

Chilingerian, J. (1989). Analyzing the attention structure of the chief executive officer. In W.A. Ward and E.G. Gomulka (Eds) *Eastern Academy of Management: Proceedings of the 1989 Meeting*.

Chilingerian, J. (forthcoming). Baker Medical Center (A), (B), and (C). In P. Shrivastava (Ed.) *Strategic Management: Conceptual and Practical Frontiers*. Cincinnati: Southwestern Publisher.

Crozier, M. and Friedberg, E. (1980). *Actors and Systems: The Politics of Collective Action*. Chicago, IL: University of Chicago Press.

Drucker, P. (1967). *The Effective Executive*. New York: Harper and Row.

Dutton, J. and Ottensmeyer, E. (1987). Strategic issue management systems: Forms, functions and contexts. *Academy of Management Review*, April. 355–365.

Fink, S.L., Beak, J. and Taddeo, K. (1971). Organizational crisis and change. *The Journal of Applied Behavioral Science*, **7**(1), 15–41.

Galbraith, J. (1977). *Organizational Design*. Reading, MA: Addison-Wesley.

Goffman, E. (1971). *Relations in Public: Microstudies of the Public Order*. New York: Harper and Row.

Janus, I.L. (1989). *Crucial Decisions: Leadership in Policymaking and Crisis Management*. New York: Free Press.

Kiesler, S. and Sproull, L. (1982). Managerial response to changing environments: Perspectives on problem sensing from social cognition. *Administrative Science Quarterly*, **27**, 548–570.

Koenig, L. (1964). *The Chief Executive*. New York: Harper and Row.

Leibenstein, H. (1987). *Inside the Firm: The Inefficiencies of Hierarchy*. Cambridge, MA: Harvard University Press.

McCaskey, M. (1982). *The Executive Challenge*. Mansfield, MA: Pitman.

Mitroff, I.I., Shrivastava, P. and Udwadia, F. (1987). Effective Crisis Management. *Executive*, **1**(4), 283–292.

Mintzberg, H. (1973). *The Nature of Managerial Work*. New York: Harper and Row.

Mintzberg, H. (1976). Patterns in strategy formulation. McGill University, Montreal, Faculty of Management Working Paper.

Ottensmeyer, E. and Dutton, J. (1989). Interpreting environments and taking action: Types and characteristics of strategic issue management systems. In C. Snow (Ed.) *Strategy, Organizational Design, and Human Resource Management*. Greenwich, CT: JAI Press.

Polanyi, M. (1958). *Personal Knowledge*. London: Routledge & Kegan Paul.

Salancik, G. R. and Pfeffer, J. (1978). A social information processing approach to job attitudes and task design. *Administrative Science Quarterly*, **23**, 224–253.

Schein, E. (1985). *Organizational Culture and Leadership*. San Francisco, CA: Jossey-Bass.

Selznik, P. (1957). *Leadership in Administration*. New York: Harper and Row.

Simon, H.A. (1983). *Reason in Human Affairs*. Stanford, CA: Stanford University Press.

Sproull, L. (1984). The nature of managerial attention. In P. Larkey and L. Sproull (Eds) *Advances in Information Processing in Organizations*, Vol. 1. Greenwich, CT: JAI Press.

Starbuck, W.H., Greve, A. and Hedberg, B.L.T. (1988). Responding to crisis. In J.B. Quinn, H. Mintzberg and R.M. James (Eds) *The Strategy Process: Concepts, Contexts and Cases*. Englewood Cliffs, NJ: Prentice Hall (pp. 687–696).

Stewart, R. (1982). *Choices for the Manager*. Englewood Cliffs, NJ: Prentice Hall.

Van Maanen, J. (1988). *Tales of the Field: On Writing Ethnography*. Chicago, IL: University of Chicago Press.

Van Maanen, J. (1981). Working the street: A developmental view of police behavior. In H. Jacob (Ed.) *The Potential for Reform of Criminal Justice* (pp. 83–130). Beverly Hills, CA: Sage.

Vroom, V. and Jago, A. (1988). *The New Leadership: Managing Participation in Organizations*. Englewood Cliffs, NJ: Prentice Hall.

Weick, K. (1983). Managerial thought in the context of action. In S. Srivastava (Ed.) *The Executive Mind*. San Francisco, CA: Jossey-Bass.

Weick, K. (1979). *The Social Psychology of Organizing*, 2nd edn. Reading, MA: Addison-Wesley.

Weinberg, M.W. (1977). *Managing the State*. Cambridge, MA: MIT Press.

# 9

# The Organizational Politics of Sustainable Development

CAROLYN P. EGRI, PETER J. FROST

Perhaps nowhere have environmental issues gained more prominence than in the natural resource industries. However, we will
focus on only one, the forestry industry, where there are highly
visible political contests between industry, government, and
environmental and native groups over the management and use
of the old growth forests of British Columbia (BC), Canada. In
this chapter, we present a conceptual framework to explore the
organizational power and politics surrounding the social and
technological innovations currently under way which focus on
achieving environmental sustainability in forestry. As we shall
see, many of the political games that are being played are socially
innovative in their own right.

## ORGANIZATIONAL POWER AND POLITICS AND THE KEY PLAYERS IN THE FORESTRY INDUSTRY

In our perspective on organizational power and politics, we see
two levels in operation: (i) the surface political games that take

*Building the Strategically-Responsive Organization.*
Edited by H. Thomas, D. O'Neal, R. White and D. Hurst.

place at the observable level of human interaction; and (ii) the less observable politics in the deep structure of relationships within society. It is useful to conceive of the deep structure as a world view, a way of perceiving and acting. The deep structure is the frame that sets the rules of the games, thereby influencing the types of political games that are played by human actors. We argue, with others, that this world view is the outcome of political forces and actions, typically those that have occurred in an earlier era, or earlier in an era, and that are no longer in our everyday awareness or consciousness (Clegg, 1981; Deetz, 1985; Frost and Egri, 1991).

In forestry in BC, there are four main players in these political contests for change: (i) forest industry firms; (ii) environmentalist groups; (iii) native aboriginal groups; and (iv) the provincial government of BC. These groups differ on a number of dimensions such as their value positions, perceptions and behaviours, and the political games that they are playing in this contest over the forests. The stereotypical or extreme categorization of each of these players is discussed in the following subsections.

<hr>

## FOREST INDUSTRY FIRMS

The major players in this group are firms such as MacMillan Bloedel, Fletcher Challenge and Canadian Forest Products. These players have an economic stake in the forests as a resource for their operations. Their view is that trees are resources that are primarily in existence to serve humankind. Most typically, forests are a harvestable resource seen as a means of generating profits (Drushka, 1985; Mahood and Drushka, 1990; Marchak, 1983; Swift, 1983).

Forest industry firms admit that they have made mistakes in the past as far as minimizing the environmental impact of their forest harvesting practices. But they also contend that they are making significant progress in implementing sustainable forestry practices that protect the forest ecosystem (Forest Alliance of BC, 1991; Smith, 1990; Stewart and Apsey, 1991).

The forest industry says that hard choices are required to balance environmental pressures and our economic needs according to what we, as a society, value and the price we are willing to pay for these values. They argue that the forestry industry is responsible for over 250 000 direct and indirect jobs—almost 1 out of every 5 jobs in the province (Pacific Logging Congress, 1990). Drastically restricting the logging of old growth forests would result in a significant cut in social services and the quality of life in BC.

Their main message is that industry, environmentalists, politicians, scientists and concerned citizens need to communicate and cooperate in order to work out their differences and arrive at a common solution with regard to environmental issues in forestry (Forest Alliance of BC, 1991).

## ENVIRONMENTALIST GROUPS

There are two major types of environmentalist groups involved in forestry issues in BC. One type includes the mainstream groups such as the Sierra Club of Western Canada and Greenpeace. Another type includes the more radical groups such as the Western Canada Wilderness Committee, Friends of Clayoquot Sound, Friends of the Earth and Earth First!

The stereotypical environmentalist view is that trees exist as part of ecosystems that sustain a diversity of life forms, only one of which is human. Forests are a harvestable resource for present and future generations. Environmentalist groups differ as to whether forests should be preserved in their original state or should be maintained with minimal cutting because of their sustaining role in the ecosystem (Manes, 1990; Norse, 1990; Sierra Club of Western Canada, 1990; *The New Catalyst*, 1990; Western Canada Wilderness Committee, 1990a,b; Zuckerman, 1991).

While they differ in their influence tactics and the degree and speed of change that they envision for forestry in BC, environmentalist groups generally agree on the following three issues:

1. The restriction of clearcutting as a means of forest harvesting, especially in watershed areas. Instead, they advocate selective logging as a more ecologically sustainable alternative.
2. The preservation of old growth forests as wilderness areas.
3. The need for the regeneration of forests through the intensive planting of a diversity of tree species rather than monocultured replacement.

Environmentalist groups also agree that there are hard choices to be made in balancing the environmental and economic needs of society. In contrast to industry, they give more weight to the local and global environmental benefits resulting from the preservation of old growth forests. They also contend that there is a moral obligation to protect the forests for the benefit of future generations even if it means forgoing current economic benefits.

## NATIVE ABORIGINAL GROUPS

Native aboriginal groups are beginning to make their presence felt through native land claims and challenges over land use practices. They are, in many instances and respects, closely aligned with environmentalist groups (Caulfield, 1990; Parfitt, 1991h; Pynn, 1990; Simpson and Jackson, 1990).

## PROVINCIAL GOVERNMENT OF BC

The provincial government plays a key role in forestry given that 85% of the province's total area is designated as public provincial forest. Of that, 26 million hectares or 30% of the total is suitable for forest harvesting (Vance, 1990). The provincial government is charged with the responsibility for managing the forests in a way that meets 'The goal of sustainable development [which] is to achieve economic benefits without depleting natural resources or damaging the environment' (Government of BC, 1990, p. 2).

Government perspectives will vary according to the ruling party's ideology and political realities of the day. In the era we describe, now at an end we think, the ruling party's ideology was primarily free enterprise with forests as a harvestable resource—a means to earn revenue for business and government, and a source of employment (Marchak, 1983; McKillop and Mead, 1976; Vance, 1990).

But the government has been forced to change as a result of pressures from a public which is proving to be increasingly receptive to the environmentalists' message. The recent independent Forest Resources Commission (the Peel Report) and professional foresters within and outside of the Ministry of Forests are also providing evidence regarding the inadequacy of government planning and controls to ensure that the provincial forests are managed in an environmentally sustainable manner (Baldry, 1991a; Hammond, 1989; Mahood and Drushka, 1990; Parfitt, 1991b,e,f). Caught in the middle of the political contest between the forest industry, environmentalists and native groups, the provincial government is being forced to act.

While here we are presenting a generalized view on the parties involved, we recognize that there is diversity within these groups in terms of beliefs, attitudes and actions in regards to the natural environment. In environmentalist terms, some are not green at all, some are a moderate light green while others are a deeper green. This tension within adds another dynamic to the political contests and change that we are witnessing in BC.

## A FRAMEWORK OF STRATEGIC RESPONSES OF INTEREST GROUPS IN FORESTRY

There are two basic dimensions of our framework for describing the strategic responses of interest groups in forestry: (i) paradigmatic world views; and (ii) perceptions of the change process with respect to the environment (TABLE 9.1).

### PARADIGMATIC WORLD VIEWS

A paradigmatic world view represents a set of fundamental beliefs, values and assumptions that influence how one views and interprets reality. We present these paradigmatic world views as two extremes. Each extreme encompasses the natural environment, the economic order, the social order and political factors. At one extreme is the *dominant social paradigm*, which traces its origin to the Age of Enlightenment. In this paradigm, humans dominate and control the environment as the natural order of things. There is a hierarchical relationship of entities with humans at the apex and other species and entities below to serve humans. Inherent in this world view are the espoused free market competitive principles. Paradoxically, it also includes actual strong centralized government control. Essentially, the dominant social paradigm

TABLE 9.1   Strategic responses of interest groups in forestry

| Perception/ experience of change process | Beliefs regarding environmental sustainability | |
| --- | --- | --- |
| | Dominant social paradigm | Radical deep ecology paradigm |
| Evolutionary | Routine response: Compete Innovative response: Collaborate and negotiate | Routine response: Withdraw Innovative response: Educate by example and by teaching |
| Revolutionary | Routine response: Resist React Innovative response: Confront own reality | Routine response: Attack Sabotage Innovative response: Develop alliances to gain strength |

reflects the standard conservative position on what the world is (Bookchin, 1990).

At the other extreme is the *radical deep ecology paradigm*, which traces its origin to the Age of Environmentalism. This paradigm is based on an egalitarian world view in which there is harmony and balance between humans and other entities and Nature. Humans are only one group equal to other biospecies and natural elements: in this world view, the Earth itself has rights. The deep ecology paradigm promotes a vision of bioregional autonomy and control. Economics is incomplete in that it does not include the costs of pollution. The standard deep ecology perspective on what the world is and should be is found in the writings of deep ecologist philosophers (Devall and Sessions, 1985; Tobias, 1988).

## THE PERCEPTION AND EXPERIENCE OF CHANGE WITH RESPECT TO THE ENVIRONMENT

The traditional way of viewing change in the world has been based on Darwin's *evolutionary model*. In this model, change is seen as an incremental progression of small changes with change equalling progress.

Recently, a new model of change based on the idea of punctuated equilibrium has gained prominence in the biological sciences (Gould, 1989) and social sciences (Gersick, 1991; Tushman and Romanelli, 1985). In this model, periods of incremental evolutionary change are interrupted, or punctuated, by periods of revolutionary change.

The combination of these two dimensions gives us a way of representing strategic responses between interest groups with regard to environmental issues in forestry. We draw on published reports of environmental actions in the media and elsewhere for illustrations of routine and innovative strategic responses.

## DOMINANT SOCIAL PARADIGM: EVOLUTIONARY CHANGE PROCESS

### Routine Response: Compete

The BC forest industry has hired a public relations firm with a history of assisting other industries to conduct damage control in the wake of environmental disasters (Parfitt, 1991d). As part of their campaign to influence public opinion, they have produced a series of television commercials featuring forest industry executives and professional foresters to defend their logging practices.

### Innovative Response: Collaborate and Negotiate

There have been several joint task forces and committees involving industry, government, environmental and native groups, e.g. the provincial Roundtables on the Economy and Environment, and the Clayoquot Sound Sustainable Development Steering Committee. One issue that surrounds these collaborations is the degree to which they represent *true* or *false* collaborative intent and action. For example, environmentalist members of the Springer Creek Integrated Watershed Plan Committee (a joint industry–government–environmentalist initiative) walked out after 4 years and 42 meetings and consultations when it became evident that there was no real intent to alter existing logging practices (Glavin, 1991). A similar fate currently threatens the Clayoquot Sound Sustainable Development Steering Committee, where industry and local government representatives contend that their intents are sincere while environmentalist members charge that the committee has been ineffectual and a means of stalling any change (Hume, 1990b; Irving *et al.*, 1991; M'Gonigle, 1991).

## DOMINANT SOCIAL PARADIGM: REVOLUTIONARY CHANGE PROCESS

### Routine Response: Resist and React

This response to the perception of revolutionary change is to play the victim role and to deny reality by fighting to keep the revolution at bay. For example, the forest industry successfully pressured the Canadian Imperial Bank of Commerce to pull their ads from David Suzuki's television program 'The Nature of Things' following a feature that compared land clearing in the Amazon to clearcutting in BC (Hume, 1991a; Parfitt, 1991a). Another example concerns MacMillan Bloedel filing a civil suit against 34 people and the Western Canada Wilderness Committee for 'damages for trespass, harassment, intimidation and conspiracy to injure' (Anonymous, 1991a).

### Innovative Response: Confront Own Reality

This response recognizes the revolution as real. For example, a consultant was engaged by the forest industry to conduct an analysis of the underlying beliefs and values of the industry (Hume, 1990a). One intent was to gain a better understanding of sources of resistance to change as they relate to environmental practices. One conclusion of the study was that the language and terminology of the practices and goals of the industry supported the dominant social paradigm.

## RADICAL DEEP ECOLOGY PARADIGM: EVOLUTIONARY CHANGE PROCESS

### Routine Response: Withdraw

One response is to quietly withdraw and isolate oneself, as found among the 'back to the landers'. Their intent is to minimize contact with others but these players remain confident that eventually others will join them.

## Innovative Response: Educate by Example and by Teaching

These are the ones who visibly practice their deep ecology beliefs. They influence others to adopt their course of action through apprenticeships or by writing about their practices and experiences in ecological forestry (Camp, 1981; Hammond, 1989, 1991).

## RADICAL DEEP ECOLOGY PARADIGM: REVOLUTIONARY CHANGE PROCESS

### Routine Response: Attack and Sabotage

There has been an increasing trend of confrontations between radical environmental groups and the forest industry over clearcut logging methods, logging of old growth forests and watersheds, logging road construction and so on. The record of direct action in forestry for only four months in BC has been as follows:

1. In the old growth forests, environmentalist protestors have blockaded logging roads.
   i. Thirty-four environmental protestors in the Walbran Valley have been arrested—10 of those arrested were teenagers (Bohn, 1991d).
   ii. Around 250 environmentalists protested against logging in the Slocan Valley—84 were arrested and fined $500. If they refrain from protesting against forest activities for 2 years, the fines will not be collected (Bohn, 1991b). However, two weeks later, 64 people were arrested from a group of 350 to 400 protesters who were blocking the construction of a logging road into the Slocan Valley (Parfitt, 1991g).
2. Two logging bridges have been destroyed—one by fire and one by dynamite (Bell and Simpson, 1991; Hume, 1991b).
3. Monkeywrenching in the form of tree spiking and the destruction of heavy logging equipment (Bohn, 1991c; Buttle, 1991).

4. During the recent provincial election campaign, the Sierra Club of Western Canada paid for a full page advertisement in the *Vancouver Sun* newspaper which encouraged voters to defeat the ruling political party (Sierra Club of Western Canada, 1991).

Environmentalist protests have also gone to the provincial government legislature. For example,

1. Thirty high school students occupied the offices of the BC Minister of Forests to protest against logging of old growth forests (Bohn, 1991a).
2. Around 140 environmentalists protested against the arrest of environmentalist protestors in the Walbran Valley (LeGuilloux and Bohn, 1991).
3. Fifty high school students, members of the Environmental Youth Alliance, protested on the lawn of the provincial legislature (Baldry, 1991b).

While radical environmentalist groups often disavow themselves of any responsibility for destructive incidents of sabotage, they do not condemn them either, as illustrated by the following statement by Paul Watson (quoted by Pynn, 1991), President of the Sea Shepherd Society and member of the radical Earth First! organization.

The environment movement is for the most part rhetoric, paper-pushing and bureaucracy. Environmentalists have shown too much restraint in light of massive global destruction. Tree-spiking has done more to save old-growth forests than negotiations between environmentalists and the forest industry.

In contrast, while mainstream environmentalist groups such as the Sierra Club express an understanding of the frustrations that lead to violent acts, they firmly advocate the use of non-violent civil disobedience as the most appropriate method of environmental protest (Bohn, 1991c).

---

**Innovative Response: Develop Alliances to Gain Strength**

BC environmentalist groups have joined forces with European environmental groups to organize a consumer boycott of BC wood products (MacQueen, 1991; Parfitt, 1991c). They have also formally developed an alliance with another environmentalist group, the New Zealand Rainforests Coalition, to coordinate boycott action against and share information about Fletcher Challenge, a multinational corporation based out of New Zealand (LeGouilloux, 1991). In October 1991, environmental groups (Sierra Club of Western Canada, and Western Canada Wilderness Committee) and BC forest labour unions announced that they had formed a joint committee to draft a 'Peace in the Woods' treaty (Anonymous, 1991b).

## INSIGHTS INTO THE FRAMEWORK OF STRATEGIC RESPONSES

These are only a few examples of strategic responses within this framework. What we have presented is a simplified model of the pure types of strategic responses. Three things should be noted about how this plays out in reality. Firstly, all of these strategic responses are taking place simultaneously. Secondly, these are stereotypical representations of these interest groups. In reality, there are radical agents within the mainstream industrial and government groups, just as there are environmentalists who are more closely aligned with a conservative ideology. Thus, there is a wide diversity of both beliefs and values as well as perceptions of the change process in each interest group.

Thirdly, these types of strategic responses we have described serve as conceptual anchors for the morass of beliefs and perceptions present in a reality that is not as clear cut as a two-by-two matrix. It is in this middle, messy world that most of the politics, tensions and movement for change are taking place. For example, the Forest Alliance of BC, subtitled Citizens for Shared Environmental Responsibility, started in April 1991. Largely industry financed, it now has over 3000 members. The Citizens Advisory Board of the Forest Alliance of BC is chaired by IWA union president, Jack Munroe, and is comprised of 30 members from the forest industry, local governments and concerned citizens—including Patrick Moore, a founding member of Greenpeace (but not an official Greenpeace representative). One of the Alliance's goals is to provide a 'true picture of what is occurring in the forests' through public educational programs, television commercials, tours of the forests and so on (Forest Alliance of BC, 1991). They have also produced six half-hour television programmes, which were broadcast province-wide during 1991 to convey their essential message. To ensure that this message receives wide coverage, all of the programmes are available free of charge to the public at retail video rental outlets. Another initiative of the Forest Alliance of BC is the development of a 'code of environmentally, economically and socially responsible forest practices and to monitor the forest industry's performance with respect to this code' (Forest Alliance of BC, 1991). It is notable that in the face of calls for stricter government regulation and monitoring of industry practices, the forest industry advocates a system of voluntary self-regulation.

One thing that should also be recognized is the simultaneous operation of both competitive and collaborative strategies *within* each interest group. This offers yet another level of complexity to the dynamics of environmental change in regard to forestry. For example, formal collaboration between environmentalist groups is most visible in the BC Environmental Network, which is a loosely coupled association of over 250 environmentalist, union, native groups and government agencies. Another is the Tin Wis Coalition of environmental, native, union and legal representatives. Within the forest industry, there are numerous associations such as BC's Council of Forest Industries and the Pacific Logging Congress.

## CONCLUSIONS

We have suggested that the politics of sustainable development is shaped by the deep structure from which the major players operate and is influenced by the day-to-day political actions they use. We add that who wins and who loses is influenced in large part by the audiences to the game—including the paying and voting public.

We believe that the various collaborative and confrontational games will continue to be played with increasing intensity and with mixed results for those who are involved. The games will continue to attract public attention while the very arena in which they operate, the natural environment, is defined politically. We note that the terms 'environment' and 'crisis' are themselves highly politicized and contestable terms.

We think that what we have discussed here has implications for the greening of strategy in at least the following ways:

- Strategies of forest companies and governments must become more intensively green, i.e. attentive to the environmental consequences of their actions. Governance is a key. They must also become more politically informed, i.e. attentive to the power that they and others have to influence outcomes.
- While environmental groups already attend to these issues, they need to attend more to economics, i.e. to the costs and benefits of ways of resolving competing choices.
- All players need to be more cross-culturally aware of the cultures and the values of the other players if we are to move to satisfactory resolutions of environmental issues.

And finally, some closing comments on collaboration and confrontation. Collaborative strategies will only work between players where:

- World views are compatible.
- Management and bridging of competing world views is done, and done skillfully.
- There is acceptance that this collaboration takes place in a politicized arena. Each player plays to a different audience and needs credibility before that audience.

Strategies of confrontation are needed to stimulate the innovation process. It serves as a wake-up call to complacent organizations. Furthermore, confrontational tactics accompanied by collaborative initiatives may be our best hope for really surfacing and dealing with the fundamental environmental issues.

---

## ACKNOWLEDGEMENT

We would like to thank David Farrell, a law student at UBC, who assisted us in our analysis of information on the forestry industry.

## REFERENCES

Anonymous (1991a). Earth Day activists served with writ. *Vancouver Sun*, 23 April, A12.

Anonymous (1991b). Peace in the woods treaty signed. *Vancouver Sun*, 11 October, A1.

Baldry, K. (1991a). Forestry controls faulty, inaccurate, auditor finds. *Vancouver Sun*, 15 May, A1.

Baldry, K. (1991b). Legislature protest backs Walbran. *Vancouver Sun*, 17 August, A6.

Bell, S. and Simpson, S. (1991). Loggers scared, angered by bridge dynamite blast. *Vancouver Sun*, 18 April, B1, B2.

Bohn, G. (1991a). Forestry position protested: Richmond's office occupied over Walbran Valley logging. *Vancouver Sun*, 20 July, A4.

Bohn, G. (1991b). 84 arrested in logging protest. *Vancouver Sun*, 7 September, A1.

Bohn, G. (1991c). Violent group linked to Walbran battle: Forestry industry officials warn Earth First! hurts everybody. *Vancouver Sun*, 20 September, B4.

Bohn, G. (1991d). Arrests, injury, tree spiking escalate battle over Walbran. *Vancouver Sun*, 24 September, B9.

Bookchin, M. (1990). *Remaking Society: Pathways to a Green Future*. Boston, MA: South End Press.

Buttle, J. (1991). Logging equipment sabotaged. *Vancouver Sun*, 14 August, B1.

Camp, O. (1981). *The Forest Farmer's Handbook: A Guide to Natural Selection Forest Management*. Ashland, OR: Sky River Press.

Caulfield, C. (1990). A reporter at large: The ancient forest. *The New Yorker*, 14 May, 46–84.

Clegg, S. (1981). Organization and control. *Administrative Science Quarterly*, **26**, 545–562.

Deetz, S. (1985). Critical-cultural research: New sensibilities and old realities. *Journal of Management*, **11**(2), 121–136.

Devall, B. and Sessions, G. (1985). *Deep Ecology: Living as if Nature Mattered*. Salt Lake City, UT: Peregrine Smith Books.

Drushka, K. (1985). *Stumped—The Forest Industry in Transition*. Vancouver: Douglas and McIntyre.

Forest Alliance of BC (1991). The forest and the people: Are we the Brazil of the north? Transcript of video program. Vancouver: Forest Alliance of BC.

Frost, P.J. and Egri, C.P. (1991). The political process of innovation. In L.L. Cummings and B.M. Staw (Eds) *Research in Organizational Behavior*, Vol. 13 (pp. 229–296). Greenwich, CT: JAI Press.

Gersick, C. (1991). Revolutionary change theories: A multilevel exploration of the punctuated equilibrium paradigm. *The Academy of Management Review*, **16**(1), 10–36.

Glavin, T. (1991). Watershed clearcuts hasten fall of local resource committee. *Vancouver Sun*, 24 June, B2.

Gould, S.J. (1989). Punctuated equilibrium in fact and theory. *Journal of Social Biological Structure*, **12**, 117–136.

Government of BC (1990). *Environment BC: A Special Edition of BC News.* Victoria, BC.

Hammond, H. (1989). Public forests or private timber supplies? The need for community control of British Columbia's forests—Summary. Unpublished manuscript, 4 January.

Hammond, H. (1991). *Seeing the Forest Among the Trees: The Case for Wholistic Forest Use.* Vancouver: Polestar Book Publishers.

Hume, M. (1990a). Kinder image seen in gender: Masculine, feminine formula to guide MB through the woods. *Vancouver Sun,* 6 March, A1.

Hume, M. (1990b). BC peacemaker walks through trail. *Vancouver Sun,* 7 September, D10.

Hume, M. (1991a). Forest industry ties to silence Suzuki—and Suess. *Vancouver Sun,* 16 March, B5.

Hume, M. (1991b). Environmentalists talked sabotage but expressed shock at bridge fire. *Vancouver Sun,* 2 May, B8.

Irving, W. and Ucluelet Village Council (1991). Stop throwing stones at the people who are trying to help. *Vancouver Sun,* 29 August, A17.

LeGouilloux, M. (1991). Trio focuses on BC logging. *Vancouver Sun,* 24 September, B9.

LeGouilloux, M. and Bohn, G. (1991). Environmentalists' arrests protested. *Vancouver Sun,* 16 August, B4.

MacQueen, K. (1991). Forest product boycott by Europe possible, documents say. *Vancouver Sun,* 23 November, D5.

Mahood, I. and Drushka, K. (1990). *Three Men and a Forester.* Madeira Park, BC: Harbour Publishing.

Manes, C. (1990). *Green Rage: Radical Environmentalism and the Unmaking of Civilization.* Toronto: Little, Brown & Company.

Marchak, P. (1983). *Green Gold—The Forest Industry in British Columbia.* Vancouver: University of British Columbia Press.

McKillop, W. and Mead, W.J. (Eds) (1976). *Timber Policy Issues in British Columbia.* Vancouver: University of British Columbia Press.

M'Gonigle, M. (1991). Wood wars: Industry more committed to public posturing than to implementing long sought reforms. *Vancouver Sun,* 9 July, A13.

Norse, E.A. (1990). *Ancient Forests of the Pacific Northwest.* Washington, DC: Island Press.

Pacific Logging Congress (1990). Report on Forestry. Vancouver: Pacific Logging Congress.

Parfitt, B. (1991a). Forest industry demands CBC give other side of 'biased' show. *Vancouver Sun,* 6 February, B3.

Parfitt, B. (1991b). Changes in cutting rights urged in forestry report. *Vancouver Sun,* 3 May, A1.

Parfitt, B. (1991c). BC gets black eye in Europe. *Vancouver Sun,* 21 May, B4.

Parfitt, B. (1991d). PR giant in forestry drive linked to world's hot spots. *Vancouver Sun,* 8 July, D8.

Parfitt, B. (1991e). Province's top foresters fear forests being overcut: Report claims ministry losing track of fellings. *Vancouver Sun,* 11 September, D3.

Parfitt, B. (1991f). Two top forest ministry executives say inventory-taking must change. *Vancouver Sun,* 20 September, D2.

Parfitt, B. (1991g). 64 arrested at logging protest in watershed. *Vancouver Sun*, 25 September, D3.

Parfitt, B. (1991h). Nisga'a demand audit of forest practices. *Vancouver Sun*, 11 October, D4.

Pynn, L. (1990). Loggers armed with court order move to resume work in Tsitika. *Vancouver Sun*, 6 November, B1.

Pynn, L. (1991). Protester wants clearcut logging phased out: Army of eco-climbers sought to disrupt loggers. *Vancouver Sun*, 12 July, B6.

Sierra Club of Western Canada (1990). The Sierra Report, Vol. 9, No. 4. Vancouver: Sierra Club of Western Canada.

Sierra Club of Western Canada (1991). Still stumped for a choice on election day. Advertisement, *Vancouver Sun*, 9 October, B3.

Simpson, S. and Jackson, B. (1990). 50 arrested at Duffy blockade face supreme court appearance. *Vancouver Sun*, 7 November, B1.

Smith, R. (1990). Let's look at the facts. *Vancouver Sun*, 30 November, A15.

Stewart, M. and Apsey, M. (1991). Industry has changed its ways; so should its critics. *Vancouver Sun*, 12 June, A11.

Swift, J. (1983). *Cut and Run—The Assault on Canada's Forests*. Toronto: Between the Lines Press.

*The New Catalyst* (1990). Let BC forests live! Community forest strategies, No. 19 (Fall). Gabriola Island, BC: The New Catalyst.

Tobias, M. (Ed.) (1988). *Deep Ecology*. San Marcos, CA: Avant Books.

Tushman, M.L. and Romanelli, E. (1985). Organizational evolution: A metamorphosis model of convergence and reorientation. In L.L. Cummings and B.M. Staw (Eds) *Research in Organizational Behavior*, Vol. 7 (pp. 171–222). Greenwich, CT: JAI Press.

Vance, J.E. (1990). *Tree Planning: A Guide to Public Involvement in Forest Stewardship*. Vancouver: Public Interest Advocacy Centre.

Western Canada Wilderness Committee (1990a). Carmanah: Canadian rainforest deserves protection. *WCWC Educational Report*, Vol. 8, No. 8. Vancouver: WCWC.

Western Canada Wilderness Committee (1990b). Crisis in the woods. *WCWC Educational Report*, Vol. 9, No. 8. Vancouver: WCWC.

Zuckerman, S. (1991). *Saving Our Ancient Forests*. Los Angeles: Living Planet Press.

# 10

# Acquisition and Realization of Vision: Diversification through Strategic Bridging

MARTIN LINDELL, LEIF MELIN

## INTRODUCTION

The general freedom of strategic action for business firms can be categorized as a few pairs of alternatives. The firm can choose (i) to penetrate existing business area or diversify into new ones; (ii) to grow through internal development or through alliances and acquisitions; (iii) to reach market dominance or find a niche position; and (iv) to be domestic in its market orientation or become more international/global. The combined choice of (intensified) internationalization and acquisition seems to be a very common corporate growth strategy. Based on an in-depth study of a large Scandinavian corporation showing such a strategic pattern, we have found that contemporary knowledge about strategic change through acquisition ought to be supplemented with new understanding. A more longitudinal and contextual perspective on acquisition is needed, with the focus on the long-term process of strategic change as the relevant setting. The purpose of this chapter is twofold: to present some empirical evidence for

*Building the Strategically-Responsive Organization.*
Edited by H. Thomas, D. O'Neal, R. White and D. Hurst.
Copyright © 1994 the Strategic Management Society. Published 1994 by John Wiley & Sons Ltd.

this perspective and to formulate tentative propositions about the acquisition process and the role of strategic visions in such processes.

---

## Two Streams of Acquisition Research

The main stream of research on acquisitions and mergers has been focusing on strategic and financial fit between the acquirer and the acquired firm (Nahavandi and Malekzadeh, 1988). Most of these academic studies have been devoted to the consequences and especially the synergies achieved by acquisitions (Trautwein, 1990). This research is based on the assumptions of capital market efficiency and rational choices of the acquiring firm (Song, 1983). The most popular research question has been to decide whether the *related acquisition* will result in higher profitability and create more value than the *unrelated acquisition* (Rumelt, 1974). The related acquisition is characterized by similar markets, similar production technology and/or similar R&D orientation between the two companies in question. The purpose is to try to achieve both financial and operating synergies (through transfer of functional skills etc.), while the motive behind unrelated acquisitions is limited to the achievement of financial synergy.

Traditionally, the acquisition process has been described through a sequential and rather rational model where the process is divided into three phases (Lindgren, 1982). The *pre-acquisition phase* consists of the formulation of the overall corporate strategies and the establishment of acquisition policies and guidelines. The *acquisition phase* involves planning for the acquisition, the assignment for carrying out the acquisition, the identification and evaluation of suitable candidates, negotiating with the acquisition candidate and the conclusion of the financial acquisition agreement. The *post-acquisition phase* includes the design and implementation of coordination and control systems in order to achieve potential benefits from integrating the operational systems of the acquired units so as to fit with those of the rest of the group.

The above description represents a limited view of the acquisition process, especially in a diversification context. An earlier stream of research is subject to criticism from an increasing number of representatives of an emerging, alternative stream of research on acquisitions, including Nahavandi and Malekzadeh

(1988), Trautwein (1990) and Walsh (1988). At least three types of criticism and alternative frameworks can be stated.

### Bridging of the Strategy Process and Acquisitions

When a business environment is complex and unpredictable, a variety of actors in the organization must be able to respond to it. The pattern of organizational action cannot be set deliberately from the top of the organization. It is not always possible to identify the strategic fit and formulate acquisition guidelines, especially not early in a diversification situation. From the perspective of the leadership, therefore, strategies are allowed to emerge (Mintzberg and Waters, 1985). Instead of a specific action agenda of the desired outcome of a strategic transformation, a vision that provides a sense of direction may be formulated and communicated. The vision is further developed and refined in the reorientation process itself. A vision gives room for adaptation: the details of vision can emerge 'en route' (cf. Wrapp, 1967).

Child (1987) proposes that vision has the capacity to inspire cognitive reformulation in the minds of their managers, but retain flexibility with regard to the form and timing of their application. This flexibility allows others to work on the specifications of vision and in so doing, to attach their commitment to it. Only by understanding the whole organizational process through which visions emerge can we understand the driving forces of vision. The visionary process can have a strong cumulative quality. The strategic effect of a number of separate decisions and acts of implementation may be so powerful that it overwhelms the original intention. The cumulative result may even be an entirely new context for future strategic decision making through a reshaped vision (Whipp and Pettigrew, 1990). The subsequent interpretation by different actors and all local adjustments are of equal importance. Those who have shaped the vision do not control its realization; but the vision at least puts some constraints on the actions of others and, ideally, provides a sense of direction as well. The visionary process seems to be about maintaining a subtle balance between proaction and reaction.

The bridging between a corporate vision and specific acquisitions can be expected to be a bottom-up as much as a top-down process. The vision has more of a legitimizing role. Acquisition initiatives may be established at the business unit level based on the general manager's individual way of thinking (Hellgren and Melin, 1989). All of these forces and interactions strengthen the picture of an emergent process, and when vision plays a role, bridge activities between the vision and individual acquisitions.

## The Character of the Acquisition Process

The complexity of the acquisition process is not realistically interpreted by the rational model. It is a far more complex learning process. The new stream of acquisition research mainly emphasizes the acquisition process: the human aspects of acquisitions; the non-rational aspects; the cultural dimension of integrating two organizations; the motives behind acquisitions (besides financial motives). Adapting to this mode of thought, we want to stress the acquisition process in order to understand the determining forces that drive acquisition and the integration processes forward. Difficulties in integrating two companies might depend on the different value systems in the two organizations. Value systems are historical products, and counteract changes. Because of actor-specific cognition, managers recruited from the acquirer will use an action logic that will create confusion in the acquired company. Buono, Bowditch and Lewis (1985) refer to this kind of post-acquisition experience as 'culture shock' and 'culture clash'. Cartwright and Cooper (1990) regard mergers and acquisitions as the greatest disturbers of 'cultural peace' in organizations. The result is most often 'culture collisions'. The sociocultural integration occurs on a time scale of five years or even longer (Cartwright and Cooper, 1990). Graves (1981) has proposed that successful mergers cause new cultures to evolve, cultures that differ from those of the preceding organizations.

Jemison and Sitkin (1986) identify four groups of impediments that concern the whole acquisition process. They propose that these factors might be an answer to why so many well-intended and well-advised acquisition efforts result in disappointing outcomes. The *first factor* has to do with the technical complexity of the activities surrounding an acquisition and the resulting task segmentation. This segmentation produces different and poorly integrated analyses. Another result will be disproportionate attention to the more analytical and financial strategic fit over organizational fit. The *second factor* concerns the forces that stimulate momentum in the acquisition process. Factors stimulating momentum are participants' commitment, secrecy, decision-maker isolation, overconfidence, and participants' self-interest. These factors cause the acquisition process to take on a life of its own. Once begun, the process may be very difficult to stop. The *third factor*, expectational ambiguity, points out that the presence and use of ambiguity during the negotiating phase of an acquisition are often quite purposeful and provide manoeuvring room. But if this ambiguity is carried to the integration phase, it can become a major source of conflict. Finally the *fourth factor*, management system misapplication, expresses that the parent's desire to help the new subsidiary and its confidence about its own capabilities often lead to a misapplication of management systems. Due to pressures to obtain rapid financial return on the acquisition, the acquiring firm often imposes its approaches and practices on the subsidiary in a heavy-handed fashion. Fundamental competencies and capabilities of the subsidiary may be dismissed.

The argument for a more behavioural approach in acquisition research is based on the view that it is the acquisition process and integration processes themselves that produce the outcome (Jemison and Sitkin, 1986). Evidence indicates that it is especially the period after the acquisition agreement that determines the result (Walsh, 1989). Human merger problems (Cartwright and Cooper, 1990) as well as unsuccessful merger attempts should also be considered. In focus is the match between personal characteristics, administrative practices and cultural practices of the target and parent firms (Shrivastava, 1986). As the combination of people, competencies and organizational cultures is regarded as the most fundamental factor to acquisition success, the whole acquisition and integration process must be emphasized.

## Integration of a Series of Acquisitions

The literature focuses mainly on one isolated acquisition. But when diversifying into a new business area, it seldom occurs that only one acquisition is made, but several are carried out in order to build up a strong position and a competitive unit. The competitiveness of a company depends on how the different acquisitions are coordinated and integrated, an issue that has received very limited attention in the literature. Mintzberg says in an interview that top management takes the broad decision without any intimate feeling or understanding of its impact on the small operations (Lloyd, 1992). The integration process of several acquisitions is a learning process with many bridging activities during a long time period. Local adaptation and system-wide economies must be tuned together. Global-scale efficiency, local responsiveness, and the ability to leverage learning worldwide is needed (Bartlett and Ghoshal, 1992).

In summary, central to the mainstream of literature on acquisition is the logical decomposition of the acquisition process into a well-structured decision making process where analyses of risk and value creation for the stock holders are in focus (cf. Salter and Weinhold, 1979). However, the initiation of acquisitions is often a result of political games, personal relations, chances and so on, without any immediate strategic intention in the acquiring company. Furthermore, the development of a new business is a 'trial and error' process, where a vision may play a role. There are no ready-made solutions concerning strategy and organization. Therefore a long-term process perspective on acquisitions has been taken, emphasizing political, chances and learning elements. Our ambition is to supplement the rational sequential view with a more contextual and incremental view, and to emphasize the overall visionary process as an important driving force for acquisitions.

The case describes the visionary process in a Finnish company, Nokia, with the focus on the diversification and growth process that led the company into the consumer electronics sector. Nokia Consumer Electronics ranks third on the European market, a position attained through rapid acquisition of four European companies between 1983 and 1988. The case description is based on an in-depth study of the change process over time through interviews, observation and documentary archival data.

## THE NOKIA CASE

In 1989, after 16 years of internationalization, diversification and rapid growth, about 70% of Nokia's turnover (22.795 MFIM) derived from export and more than 50% of its personnel (41 300) were working outside Finland. Nokia was the biggest computer company on the Nordic market. Of total turnover, 47% came from the Nordic countries and 40% from the rest of Western Europe. Nokia was one of the world's leading producers of mobile phones and cable machines.

---

## FORMULATION OF THE LONG-TERM VISION FOR THE COMPANY

After the oil crisis in 1973 new strategic directions were drawn up for Nokia. The basic industry (paper, tyres and power) was expected to see more limited growth. The ambition was to enter industrial sectors with growth potential. The top management set forth the following basic strategic goals for future development.

- internationalization
- increase in high-tech products
- maintaining the competitiveness of the basic industry.

These visionary goals highlighted the strategic direction for the company and have had an evident effect on later strategic actions, especially in relation to a number of acquisitions. In our study, we concentrated on Nokia's diversification into the consumer electronics industry. The realization of the vision to ensure growth through diversification and internationalization was accomplished by four major acquisitions, which created the bridge into consumer electronics.

---

## THE ACQUISITION OF SALORA–LUXOR: NOKIA ENTERS THE CONSUMER ELECTRONICS INDUSTRY

During the early 1970s Nokia had an interest in all areas of telecommunication. At that time there were three firms—Salora, Nokia and Televa–in the radio telephone business in Finland. Nokia believed that three domestic companies in this area were too many and determined to reduce the total to one. Salora was slightly ahead in R&D activities so Nokia signed its initial contract with that company. A *cooperation agreement* was signed in 1975. In 1980 the cooperation agreement was extended and a *joint venture* on a fifty/fifty basis—Mobira, a mobile telephone business unit—was formed. In 1982 Mobira became a subsidiary to Nokia. Nokia later acquired Televa as well and became a leading company, first in the Nordic countries and then worldwide.

Salora was also the biggest TV producer in Finland, and during the late 1970s had experienced great problems with its TV sector. Salora was offered to Nokia, but the head of the electronics division was only interested in Salora's mobile telephone business, and not in the consumer electronics. He saw no competitive advantages for Nokia in the consumer sector.

The difficulties for Salora continued and the firm suffered huge losses. The recently appointed president of Salora was forced to resign after only a few years. Salora was offered for sale, but Nokia still showed no interest. The top management of Nokia just wanted Mobira, while the owners of Salora connected the divesture of Mobira with the divesture of the rest of Salora. The result was that Nokia acquired 18% of Salora's shares in 1982. At the same time, Nokia acquired the remaining 50% of Mobira from Salora.

The new president of Salora succeeded in producing a turnaround: already 1982 was a good year and 1983 was expected to be even more successful. Markets were growing rapidly. Salora obtained two big orders for colour TV sets and encountered *capacity problems*. The president, looking for more production capacity, became interested in Luxor, a Swedish competitor. Luxor had such great problems during the late 1970s that the Swedish state first acquired the company for the symbolic sum of one krona, and then poured in large sums of money in an attempt to save it. The Swedish Minister of Industry wanted a final solution for Luxor, and was looking for a large-scale corporation partner. The Minister held the opinion that Salora was not strong enough for this role. Other firms, including Philips, showed an interest in acquiring Luxor but none found favour with the Swedish government.

The president of Salora turned to Nokia. Although Nokia's previous interest in Salora was lukewarm, a Salora–Luxor combination put the matter in quite a different light. As pointed out earlier, internationalization was an important ingredient in the Nokia corporate vision, and Finnish firms have traditionally made their initial expansion on the Swedish market. A common opinion then was that the demarcation between consumer and professional electronics was going to disappear, and Nokia was also interested in 'know-how' in mass production and marketing. The production capacity of Salora and Luxor combined made a strong production unit. Relations between the Nokia CEO and the Swedish government were good, and Sweden was willing to accept Nokia as the acquiring company. After many twists and turns Nokia had entered the consumer business area and was making a serious foray into the international market. However, the integration between Luxor and Salora was arduous, and made no real progress until the president of Luxor left the company.

## THE ACQUISITION OF OCEANIC

After the Luxor–Salora purchase was completed and integration under way, Nokia began to think of the future. Profitability was good, especially in 1987. One possibility was to continue with Salora–Luxor dominating the Nordic markets for three or four more years, using this business as a cash cow. No further growth would then be possible, as the company already had 40% of the Nordic markets. The other alternative was to turn to Europe.

Nokia chose the European option. The fixed R&D costs were expected to rise in the near future and needed a large volume. The strategy was to purchase TV brands in Europe. There were negotiations with different sellers, including the French company Oceanic. Personal relationships established between Nokia's top management and the owners of Oceanic, the Swedish Electrolux Group, resulted in the rapid acquisition of Oceanic.

Together with striving for scale of economy, the possibility of entering the EC arena seemed to be the most important reason for the acquisition of Oceanic. The French market is rather closed and difficult to penetrate for an outsider. The CEO emphasized that the motives behind the acquisition were to gain both new markets and increased market share.

## THE ACQUISITION OF STANDARD ELECTRIC LORENZ

Nokia negotiated with several other European firms, besides Oceanic, without success. Their biggest competitors, Philips and Thompson, acquired some American and European competitors.

Furthermore, Philips, Thompson and Eureka planned to develop an HDTV concept. Nokia, afraid of failing to gain access to this new key technology, had to react.

At the time, an internal fight was also going on for future top positions in the Nokia corporation. Top managers were traditionally recruited internally. In 1985 a new manager for professional electronics was appointed after a tight internal competition. He was seen as the probable next CEO of Nokia. However, the earlier successful president of Salora, now general manager of the consumer electronics business unit in Nokia, had strong personal ambitions to advance to the top. This ambition became a driving force behind the next acquisition. This manager made the initial analysis that resulted in the proposal to acquire a major competitor, Standard Electric Lorenz (SEL). At the same time, the manager responsible for professional electronics acquired the whole information business of the Ericsson company in Sweden— an acquisition of the same size as SEL.

For Nokia the result of all these external forces, internal ambitions, and striving for power was the acquisition of SEL in West Germany from ITT. The acquisition was made early in 1988, just a few months after the Oceanic acquisition. Production capacity increased from one million TVs per year to over two million. Opinion in Nokia was that SEL completed Nokia's consumer electronics business, both technically and regionally. SEL was ahead of Nokia in digital TV technology. Regionally, Nokia now became strong in France (10% of market share), in German-speaking Europe (15%), and in Southern Europe, since SEL exported to Italy, France, Spain, and Portugal. Market share was greater than 14% in Europe. New brand names were ITT, Schaub-Lorenz and Graetz.

The integration and coordination of Salora–Luxor, Oceanic and SEL started with the appointment of an integration group in February 1988, led by the general manager in charge of consumer electronics. However, the CEO of Nokia was of the opinion that Nokia had insufficient internationally experienced personnel. The then general manager was not given the responsibility to lead Nokia Consumer Electronics into Europe, and in summer 1988 a new managing director was appointed. Corporate headhunters found him in France. The head office was established in Geneva in order to facilitate recruitment and establishment of an international business unit. In 1989 a new integrated organizational structure for consumer electronics was established, one year after the last acquisition. Nokia lost at least a year before the necessary integration between all acquired units was started. Nokia's choice was to try to integrate the acquired companies as one organization. Several new international senior managers were recruited and a centralized organization was created.

In 1989, after thorough discussions, the top management of this business unit was ready to decide policy matters. They had to choose among all products and brands that the acquisitions had given: which to drop; which to continue with; which development project to accelerate. On the marketing side they built up complete strategies with channels and brands. Generally, Nokia Consumer Electronics combined a universal brand, Nokia ITT, a middle range product, with other brands, including one high end product on each local market. After the product, channel and brand strategies were determined, the next task was to decide the future of the five production sites (in Finland, Sweden, Germany, France and Portugal). So far, the result has been the closure of three of these plants, and the acquisition of one further production site.

A Euro-manager programme has been started, into which new and recently employed graduates are taken from all countries involved. As the strategies have been decided gradually, a new corporate culture is expected to emerge for this business unit. The attempt to create a new 'Euro-Culture' will continue during the following years. It is a long process—the Euro-strategy is not yet completed—but many important decisions have already been made. The vision from the mid-1970s has been realized, at least partly, through the creation of this 'Europeanized' business unit, Nokia Consumer Electronics. However, the profits for this unit have not so far been satisfactory.

---

## DISCUSSION AND IMPLICATIONS

Our main critique of earlier mainstream acquisition research is the limited concentration on strategic and financial fit and the description of the acquisition process as a planned, linear, step-by-step process. The propositions and related discussions below present our generalized conclusions on acquisition processes, visionary processes and bridging activities as important parts of a theory of strategic change. Just a note of 'bias': the acquisition and integration processes in this case are characterized by a high degree of emergent and incremental actions. Presumably this picture represents just one—but still significant—type of change process based on acquisition activities. Our propositions show one type of acquisition process. There may be other types showing other patterns of choice, integration and so on. However, a good insight is given into the difficulties of reaching a high degree of integration in a short time with a new management.

## CORPORATE LEVEL INPUT IN STRATEGIC CHANGE PROCESSES

The main role of a new vision is as an indicator for changes in strategic direction and wished-for future action. In Nokia's vision of the mid-1970s, internationalization and high-tech products were main factors. A new vision informs which type of actions have high priorities and will be legitimized—a corporate vision may create a freedom of strategic actions for members throughout the corporation. The formation of a new strategic vision means that dominating perceptions of the firm and its environment are challenged. A precondition for strategic reorientation is a changed perspective on the environment, i.e. a shift in the cognitive maps in use within the organization (Melin and Alvesson, 1989). Doz and Prahalad (1987) found in their studies that it is unlikely that a new strategy can be provided or a reorganization implemented without first achieving a cognitive shift, which provides a new strategic context with the new strategy or reorientation. Legitimacy is needed for a new strategy to take root.

In a non-crisis situation, strategic redirection is managed as a sequence of changes (Doz and Prahalad, 1987), not as rapid comprehensive restructuring (cf. Tichy and Devanna, 1986). Comparing knowledge in the mid-1970s with the situation in 1990, no one could have predicted the steps that Nokia took in its internationalization and diversification. Few would have believed that Nokia should be in consumer electronics. Vision is a tool in the learning process (Normann, 1977) but at the same time it is also subject to the learning process. In the beginning the vision may be rather diffuse, but specific enough to communicate the new freedom of action.

## BRIDGING VISIONS AND STRATEGIC ACTIONS: REALIZATION THROUGH ACQUISITIONS

The realization of vision in a large organization involves many parties. The realization process determines the strategic outcome of the original vision. Lindgren (1982) found, in a study of 100 acquisitions, that acquisitions mainly originate from levels below corporate levels. In our case, corporate management created a freedom of strategic action through repeated communication of the original vision. But the initiative in each acquisition process was held by managers on the next level. As noted by Westley and Mintzberg (1989), visionary leadership is a dynamic, interactive phenomenon. Strategic processes of change are widely accepted as multi-level activities (Burgelman, 1983). The CEO has substantial, but limited, power in implementing strategic change. The management of strategic change has to be understood as a jointly analytical, political and learning process which weaves together the content and context of change (Whipp, Rosenfeld and Pettigrew, 1987). Our conclusion on the visionary process is that the realization of a vision can be seen as a series of actions made in response to emergent problems and possibilities—often as part of internal power games—with a relatively weak overall integration (cf. Lindgren, 1982).

## BRIDGING INTO NEW BUSINESS AREAS: THE LOGIC OF ACQUISITIONS

Short-run profit is not a decisive factor for acquisitions. The basic reason for acquisitions seems not to be to raise the profitability level of the company. There is evidence that acquisitions do not reliably yield increased financial returns. As in the Nokia case, Rydén and Edberg (1980, p. 208) found after studying 40 acquisitions in large firms that acquisition contributes more to growth and size than to profits.

Managers' networks influence the choice of acquisition target. Child (1987) notes especially the contribution of *social networks*. Top managers in Nokia had very good relations with Salora before the acquisition. Also, in the case of Luxor, well-established personal relationships played an important role. Competitors can be future cooperators. In the case of Oceanic, the top managers in Nokia had a previous acquaintance with the Swedish owner of the French company. An established social network gives managers information about companies for sales and seems to result in early proposals.

An acquisition may also be a *solution of coincident strategic problems*. This was especially the case for Nokia's first two acquisitions in the area of consumer electronics, the Salora–Luxor acquisition. Generally, an acquisition may result not only from the acquiring firm's readiness to purchase but also from the willingness of the owners of the target firm to divest. The willingness of the original owners to sell might even be the main driving force behind an acquisition, i.e. an acquisition target may proactively seek acquirers. The final solution is the result of a chain of events, including random factors, and involving many parties. Many factors have to fit together when an acquisition decision is made.

Further, Jemison and Sitkin (1986) talk about the *escalating momentum* that characterizes some acquisition processes. This was the case in Nokia's fourth acquisition, because of personal interests in gaining increased power. Politicking in the pre-acquisition phase may create increased momentum in order to complete the acquisition. Mintzberg says that many acquisitions become a power game, a growth game, where shareholders' money gets thrown around. Acquisitions in these circumstances are usually mistakes and have destructive effects on the companies that are bought (Lloyd, 1992).

## BRIDGING BETWEEN ORGANIZATIONS: THE INTEGRATION DIMENSION OF ACQUISITIONS

Integration of an acquired firm is a balance between control and autonomy. It is difficult to maintain the right amount of control during the integration phase. In a study of a merger between Burroughs and Sperry in Denmark, the first year was very successful (Molin and Strandgaard Pedersen, 1991). However, the deeper integration two years later resulted in huge losses. Many efforts in the beginning were staked on reaching harmony between the two units. But the internal efforts to reach a unified unit resulted in neglect of market adaptation. No criticism was allowed to disturb the picture of harmony. A long-term perspective on the integration process is needed. Concerning the mode of accomplishing this, Hellgren and Melin (1991) have found evidence in their studies that a two-stage method—with the first stage being limited collaboration—will lead to a higher degree of 'permeability' (Borys and Jemison, 1989) after the final acquisition. Cultural barriers, governance, and legitimacy problems may be prevented or better treated in the two-stage model. Our findings support their observations. However, this model may prolong the acquisition process and final integration.

## BUILDING A NEW BUSINESS POSITION

A new business area based on acquisitions must balance strategic uniformity and central control with local autonomy and differentiated market behaviour. The first acquisition made to create a new business area can, in a learning stage, remain quite independent. Several companies, however, must be able to move beyond the assembly mode and compete in a more integrated form. There is a need to streamline the collection of designs, product lines and brands to achieve the order and logic inherent in the strategy (Haspeslagh and Jemison, 1991). An integrated network of operations is needed in order to exploit possible scale benefits. A strong management is required to avoid redundance and fragmentation. The process is not an easy one. Elimination of duplication is difficult to complete without losses in market position. Nokia's total market share in Europe declined from 14% to 10% in three years. Above all, a new way of thinking is demanded. Instead of a loosely coupled holding structure, an integrated multinational management approach must be implemented.

At the same time it seems to become imperative to avoid a uniform global strategy. The biggest challenge and opportunity is to present the best adapted offering in each national market and exploit the fact that these segments, when summed across country boundaries, provide potential for economic efficiency. Combining local adaptation and learning benefits across a range of newly acquired businesses is, above all, an organizational challenge (cf. Haspeslagh and Jemison, 1991).

Nokia Consumer Electronics combined a universal brand,

Nokia ITT, with local brands in each market. Three distribution channels were utilized: the specialized independent retailer, the large specialized channels selling only electronics, and the super-markets. They all use different selling styles. A large firm must handle them all. The strategy should simultaneously make it possible to exploit system-wide economics and learning, and to facilitate renewal without losing the unit's original ability to adapt to local requirements. The strategy must be much more sophisticated for a large company than for a small one. Integration of several acquired companies means major change and requires a turnaround in the behaviour of a large number of individuals, as well as virtually all the systems in the organization.

## IMPLICATIONS

Our in-depth study of four acquisitions made by a single corporation shows no evidence that increased profits or other financial factors should be the main motives and driving forces behind acquisitions. Instead, we found a pattern, with a web of motives, partly more rational, such as the prevailing business logic in this industry, partly less rational (from an economic performance perspective), such as personal aspirations for empire-building. Influential vision seems to be connected to top leaders, but only regarding the original formulation of the vision. Regarding the whole visionary process—with the realization and modification in focus—the most suitable framework seems to be the combination of an emergent and incremental view.

In a *theoretical* context our type of acquisition has many characteristics in common with an incremental type of strategic change. However, in our view the top management team cannot control the result of the process in the same way as the top leaders are expected to do in the logical incrementalism (Quinn, 1980). Another difference is that we believe that the internal political game may result in rather unexpected strategic steps, while politics in Quinn's view are more purposeful in order to create support and harmony around which strategic steps to take. Furthermore, Quinn's logical incrementalism is rather proactive, while our propositions illustrate a much more reactive pattern of strategic actions.

Regarding the *practical* manager, the creation of a coherent business unit is the main issue. The operationalization and modification of a corporate vision in the light of local conditions is a major requirement. Instead of emphasizing financial and profitability consequences, the basic focus ought to be on the possibilities of post-acquisition integration. Key success factors are the appointment of new managers in order to generate new ideas and handle the new whole unit in a different way than the individual companies. As Graves (1981) has noticed, successful mergers cause new cultures to evolve, cultures that differ from the preceding organizations. In addition there is a strong need to develop integrated and coordinated purchase, production and marketing strategies, and to eliminate competing products, brands and so on. All of these activities are so complex that a long-term integration perspective is required. They cannot be planned in any detail in advance. All in all, the focus in the acquisition process should be much more on the implementation and coordination phase than is suggested in the mainstream literature. Diversifying into a new market requires local adaptation, system-wide efficiency and cross-border learning.

## REFERENCES

Bartlett, C.A. and Ghosal, S. (1992). What is a global manager? *Harvard Business Review*, September/October, 124–132.

Borys, B. and Jemison, D.B. (1989). Hybrid arrangement as strategic alliances: theoretical issues in organizational combination. *Academy of Management Review*, **14**(2), 234–249.

Buono, A.F., Bowditch, J.L. and Lewis, J.W. (1985). When cultures collide: The anatomy of the merger. *Human Relations*, **38**, 477–500.

Burgelman, R.A. (1983). A process model of internal corporate venturing in the diversified major firm. *Administrative Science Quarterly*, June, 223–244.

Cartwright, S. and Cooper, C.L. (1990). The impact of mergers and acquisitions on people at work: Existing research issues. *British Journal of Management*, **1**(2), 65–76.

Child, J. (1987). Commentary on Chapter 2. In A. Pettigrew (Ed.) *The Management of Strategic Change* (pp. 84–88). Oxford: Basil Blackwell.

Doz, Y.L. and Prahalad, C.K. (1987). A process model and strategic redirection in large complex firms: The case of multinational corporations. In A. Pettigrew (Ed.) *The Management of Strategic Change* (pp. 63–83). Oxford: Basil Blackwell.

Graves, D. (1981). Individual reactions to a merger of two small firms of brokers within the re-insurance industry. *Journal of Management Studies*, **18**, 89–113.

Haspeslagh, P.C. and Jemison, D.B. (1991). *Managing Acquisitions: Creating Value through Corporate Renewal*. New York: Free Press.

Hellgren, B. and Melin, L. (1989). Managerial thinking and strategic transformation. Paper presented at the Working Conference on Managerial Thought and Cognition, Washington DC.

Hellgren, B. and Melin, L. (1991). Corporate strategies in Nordic firms facing Europe—Acquisitions and other collaborative strategies. In L.-G. Mattsson and B. Stymne (Eds) *Corporate and Industrial Strategies for Europe*. Amsterdam: North-Holland.

Jemison, D.B. and Sitkin, S.B. (1986). Corporate acquisitions: A process perspective. *Academy of Management Review*, 1, 145–163.

Lindgren, U. (1982). *Foreign Acquisition. Management of the Integration Process*. Stockholm: Stockholm School of Economics.

Lloyd, B. (1992). Mintzberg on the rise and fall of strategic planning. *Long Range Planning*, 25(4), 99–104.

Melin, L. and Alvesson, M. (1989). Strategic change and entrepreneurship. Linköping University, working paper.

Mintzberg, H. and Waters, J.A. (1985). Of strategies, deliberate and emergent. *Strategic Management Journal*, 6, 257–272.

Molin, J. and Strandgaard Pedersen, J. (1991). Myths and mergers. Paper presented at the 'Valhalla' conference, Copenhagen, 25–28 June.

Nahavandi, A. and Malekzadeh, A.R. (1988). Acculturation in mergers and acquisitions. *Academy of Management Review*, 13(1), 79–90.

Normann, R. (1977). *Management for Growth*. New York: John Wiley & Sons.

Quinn, J.B. (1980). *Strategies for Change*. Homewood, IL: Richard D. Irwin.

Rumelt, R.P. (1974). *Strategy, Structure and Economic Performance*. Cambridge, MA: Harvard University Press.

Rydén, B. and Edberg, J.-O. (1980). Large Mergers in Sweden 1962–1976. In D.C. Mueller (Ed.) *The Determinants and Effects of Mergers: An International Comparison*. Cambridge, MA: Harvard University Press.

Salter, M.S. and Weinhold, W.A. (1979). *Diversification through Acquisition: Strategies for Creating Economic Value*. New York: Free Press.

Shrivastava, P. (1986). Postmerger integration. *Journal of Business Strategy*, 7(1), 65–76.

Song, J.H. (1983). Diversifying acquisitions and financial relationships: Testing 1974–1976 behaviour. *Strategic Management Journal*, 4(2), 97–108.

Tichy, N.M. and Devanna, M.A. (1986). *The Transformational Leader*. New York: John Wiley & Sons, Inc.

Trautwein, F. (1990). Merger motives and merger prescriptions. *Strategic Management Journal*, 11(4), 283–295.

Walsh, J.P. (1988). Top management turnover following mergers and acquisitions. *Strategic Management Journal*, 9(2), 173–183.

Walsh, J.P. (1989). Doing a deal: Merger and acquisition negotiations and their impact upon target company top management turnover. *Strategic Management Journal*, 10(4), 307–322.

Westley, F. and Mintzberg, H. (1989). Visionary leadership and strategic management. *Strategic Management Journal*, 10, 17–32.

Whipp, R., Rosenfeld, R. and Pettigrew, A. (1987). Understanding strategic change processes: Some preliminary British findings. In A. Pettigrew (Ed.) *The Management of Strategic Change* (pp. 14–55). Oxford: Basil Blackwell.

Whipp, R. and Pettigrew, A. (1990). Managing change for competitive success: Bridging the strategic and operational. Paper presented at the 10th International Conference of the Strategic Management Society on Strategic Bridging, Stockholm, 24–27 September.

Wrapp, H.E. (1967). Good managers don't make policy decisions. *Harvard Business Review*, September/October, 91–99.

# 11

# Patterns of Strategic Processes: Two Change Typologies

## LEIF MELIN, BO HELLGREN

## INTRODUCTION

The strategic management paradigm must incorporate more of the complexity of strategic issues and strategic processes in practice (Freeman and Lorange, 1985; Melin, 1989). We need new and valid descriptions, which cover more of the apparently non-rational and multi-dimensional character of these processes. These descriptions must consider (i) contextual (both internal and external) aspects of strategic processes; (ii) the inherent rationale—not always economically based—of these processes; and (iii) a long-term perspective in order to supplement the cross-sectional and at most episodical character of dominating theoretical statements in strategic management. The flavor of this chapter is to put a very strong emphasis on the long cycles so characteristic of strategic processes in organizational life.

The subject of this chapter is the processes in which realization of strategies take place. The changing nature of strategic processes over time, expressed in the literature as alternating cycles of more incremental/evolutionary and more radical/revolutionary strategic change as one important discriminatory feature, will be

*Building the Strategically-Responsive Organization.*
Edited by H. Thomas, D. O'Neal, R. White and D. Hurst.
Copyright © 1994 the Strategic Management Society. Published 1994 by John Wiley & Sons Ltd.

addressed. Through a number of case studies of long cycles of strategic change in different firms, we have found different patterns of strategic processes. However, from these company-specific patterns, two more *general typologies of strategic processes* have been identified. Before presenting these two, partly overlapping and partly supplementary, typologies of strategic processes, we will give a brief overview of some existing theoretical schools on strategic processes.

## THEORETICAL HETEROGENEITY IN STRATEGIC MANAGEMENT: TIME FOR SYNTHESES

Several theoretical schools are competing within the field of strategic management knowledge. On a general disciplinary level, theoretical contributions to strategic management have their roots in such different (sub)disciplines as industrial organization economics, decision theory, marketing theory, interorganizational theory (including resource dependence), economic history, population ecology and so on. Looking at one important issue in strategic management, namely the strategic change process, Mintzberg (1987, 1990) has identified three main groups of schools:

1. Rather normative schools, which emphasize analytical, rational and sequential aspects of strategic processes.
2. Descriptive schools, which describe the process from a specific theoretical perspective.
3. Synthesizing schools, which try to integrate different apparently contradictory theories.

In the first group we find the strategy design approach (e.g. Andrews, 1971), the strategic planning paradigm (e.g. Ansoff, 1965; Lorange, 1980), and the positioning school (e.g. Porter, 1980).

In the second group, a large number of descriptive but rather partial (i.e. limited in scope) schools can be categorized. These schools emphasize such different aspects as:

- cognitions and cognitive limitations in strategy making
- the strategy process seen as a learning process

- the logical incrementalism characterizing the process
- political dimensions of strategic change
- culture and ideology as dominating aspects of strategy
- entrepreneurship and strategy as a visionary process
- networks and networking as a mode of organizing and positioning
- the environmental selection process.

The third group is represented by different integrative approaches, such as the configurative approach, which characterizes most of the work of Henry Mintzberg; the contextual approach (Pettigrew, 1985a; Pettigrew and Whipp, 1991); and the field-of-force metaphor (Melin, 1989; Hellgren, Melin and Pettersson, 1993).

This enumeration of different schools illustrates the heterogeneity and the contradictory situation that characterize the field of strategic management. However, the richness that is expressed by this summary of schools with ambitions to describe/explain/prescribe strategic processes tells us something about the complexity in the reality that we try to understand. Now, we need to base our theoretical development more upon syntheses of these apparently conflicting and diverging schools. We need synthesizing theories, without reducing too much the inherent complexity of organizational life. Furthermore, we need a more genuine process approach in our empirical efforts to map out and comprehend strategic change. In fact, we see and learn rather different things in an in-depth study of a strategic process, capturing a period of 20–30 years, compared with a study of a strategic episode of 2–3 years. For example, the interesting classification of four typical strategic decision making processes presented by Shrivastava (1983)—the managerial autocracy, systemic bureaucracy, adaptive planning, and political expediency models—is based on studies of strategic decisions—i.e. short episodes, not long processes—which reduces its value as a process typology.

In our research program on strategic change, we have conducted in-depth studies of the strategic development of seven Scandinavian firms. These case studies are characterized by a true longitudinal, processual and historical approach. The purpose has been to categorize and characterize the whole strategic process in each of our case companies, by dividing the long-term process over a period of 15–40 years into a number of significant strategic epochs.

The identified patterns of strategic change form the empirical basis for the development of two general typologies of strategic change processes. These typologies are the result of the iterative process of case study interpretations and analysis of contemporary knowledge on strategic change. In this chapter, results from three of our case studies are used both to illustrate and to validate our two conceptual typologies.

---

## CHANGE TYPOLOGY I

### A MATRIX TYPOLOGY OF STRATEGY CHANGE

The first stage in our search for patterns of strategic processes resulted in the typology of a 2 × 2 matrix. This typology can be used to categorize the long strategic processes in our studied companies into more distinct periods, each characterized by the typology's two dimensions. These dimensions express two different aspects of strategic change: (i) the degree of change intensity, and (ii) the degree of voluntarism in actions taken.

The first dimension refers to the degree of change, i.e. the change intensity in the strategic process. On one hand, *continuous adaptation* is characterized by a step-by-step refinement of current strategies. We assume that this type of change has a stabilizing effect on the organizational structure and culture. On the other hand, *revolutionary change* is a more radical strategic transformation which breaks down the prevailing congruity between leadership, strategy, structure, and culture. The assumption in theory (Greiner, 1972; Miller and Friesen, 1984; Pettigrew, 1985b) is that long periods are characterized by strategic refinement in small steps in order to defend established positions. These periods are sometimes interrupted by shorter periods of revolutionary change, i.e. a much more radical type of change in order to develop a new and more competitive position for the company.

Consequently, the second dimension in this typology focuses on the degree of voluntarism in taken strategic actions. *Proaction* implies an active search for new strategic options and strategic steps taken in new directions, although neither the external nor the internal situation obviously requires new strategic actions. *Reaction*, on the other hand, implies strategic measures taken to adapt to obvious changes in the industry.

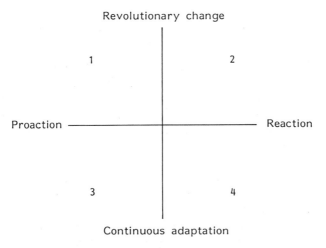

Revolutionary change

1          2

Proaction ——————————————— Reaction

3          4

Continuous adaptation

FIGURE 11.1    Four types of strategic change

Through combining these two dimensions we get two kinds of revolutionary change and two kinds of continuous adaptation (FIGURE 11.1). In quadrant 1, with proactive and revolutionary change, we identify major and radical strategic changes done by a firm, even though it is not facing any severe problems. The firm actively challenges the prevailing opinion in the industry about what strategic actions are possible and right to take and about what role the focal firm should play in that industry.

In quadrant 2, with reactive and revolutionary change, we recognize the typical turnaround. This means a radical reaction—a sharp bend (Grinyer, Mayas and McKiernan, 1988). A serious crisis forces the firm to make extensive changes. Such an adaptation to a new situation may imply both changes in product portfolio, control systems and so on, and an evident repositioning on the market.

In quadrants 3 and 4 we find step-by-step modifications of current strategies. Reactive and continuous adjustments mean 'fine tuning' to defend or strengthen an existing market position. Proactive and continuous adaptation means more voluntary strategic actions, which gradually may change the focal firm, although not in a more fundamental way.

As a basis for a discussion of the descriptive value of this matrix typology, we present results from one of our case studies.

## Interpretation of the Pharmacia Case in Terms of Typology I

Pharmacia was a Swedish company with business units within the pharmaceutical and biotechnology industries. The company was growing very quickly during the 1970s and the 1980s, the period of strategic change on which our case study was focusing. (In 1990 the company was acquired by a Swedish conglomerate, the Procordia Group.)

When presenting Pharmacia's strategic process through the framework of the matrix typology, the company seems to have gone through five epochs, i.e. five steps of strategic development, each step with its own inherent characteristics (FIGURE 11.2).

During the epoch 1973–1974 Pharmacia was a subsidiary in a diversified company, Fortia. After a 'palace revolution' the division manager of Pharmacia became CEO for the whole company, with Pharmacia as its main business. One year later, Pharmacia decentralized its organization into three divisions: drugs, separation products, and diagnostics, where the two latter divisions were fast-growing spin-offs from the traditional pharmaceutical business.

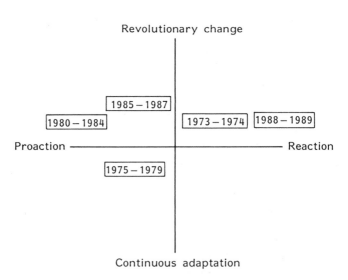

FIGURE 11.2   Five epochs in Pharmacia's strategic development

During the period 1975–1979, the CEO continuously fulfilled the strategic ideas developed in the previous epoch. Both turnover and profits increased during this period, as well as Pharmacia's international activities.

During the epoch 1980–1984, a new CEO was recruited (in May 1980). He introduced proactive strategic planning and a number of means to increase the communication of strategic issues both vertically and horizontally (between the business units) in the whole corporation. He introduced efforts to increase the 'multi-purpose competence' through 'cross-fertilization' (in fact, an early type of 'core competence,' in a development of the meaning given by Prahalad and Hamel, 1990). The strategy of the drugs division changed radically to become based more on biotechnology. Their new biological product Healon (used to facilitate surgical operations of ophthalmic diseases) became a sales success. Pharmacia was introduced on the stock market in both New York and Tokyo. Furthermore, a new marketing strategy was formed and implemented, with consequences for the organizational structure. The product and the customer should be the basis of how to organize the businesses. To summarize, this epoch is characterized as revolutionary mainly because of the radical shift in the strategic way of thinking.

The period 1985–1987, again with a new CEO, resulted in a number of radical changes, such as a change in ownership (Volvo Corporation became the new main owner), acquisitions of two Swedish competitors (LKB and LEO) and some international competitors, partly to strengthen the new strategic business unit, opthalmics (e.g. the acquisition of Intermedics, producing lenses). Although some of these acquisitions were rather defensive and partly reactions to external threats, the communication of Pharmacia as being a fast-growing biotech company—differentiating from the traditional pharmaceutical firm—continued and was strengthened during this period.

The period 1988–1989 should have been a period of consolidation. However, the market for the biotech business went down, and the integration of the acquired firms caused problems. The company's reaction was increased control, cost reductions and reorganization. The spirit of growth and success slowly disappeared, the stock market reacted negatively and finally Volvo sold its majority share to another Swedish corporation, Procordia.

## COMMENTS ON THE MATRIX TYPOLOGY

There are a number of contributions in the field of strategic management that categorize strategic processes as rather long but smooth periods of evolution and convergence, which are sometimes interrupted by more dramatic strategic reorientations, i.e. short revolutionary periods of substantial turbulence (Greiner, 1972; Miller and Friesen, 1984; Pettigrew, 1985b; Tushman and Romanelli, 1985). Our matrix typology is an effort to further develop these contributions to understand and characterize strategic change processes.

Based on the matrix typology, our conclusions are partly in line with the conventional wisdom on strategic change. The continuous strategic adaptation means (i) fine-tuning of current strategies (Brandes and Brege, 1990); (ii) the defense and development of an occupied competitive position; (iii) convergence and stabilization in the organization (its structure, competences, systems, and culture); and (iv) an unthreatened power structure. On the other hand, the revolutionary change means that (i) strategic change occurs in radical packages (Pettigrew, 1985); (ii) the change is entrepreneurial (the 'entrepreneurial revitalization' type of transition identified by Miller and Friesen, 1984) and innovative; (iii) the harmony between strategy–structure–culture–leadership is broken and must be renewed; and (iv) the dominating strategic way of thinking (the recipe or the paradigm) is punctured and replaced by new dominating ways of thinking.

However, we also have findings that lead to some conclusions that diverge from the conventional wisdom on these two types of strategic change:

- A revolutionary epoch is not necessarily shorter than the intervening periods of evolution.
- A revolutionary epoch may not necessarily follow after a period of continuous adaptation. Two revolutionary processes, with partly different characteristics, may follow sequentially.

To conclude, we believe that our matrix typology gives some new information to the evolutionary/revolutionary dichotomy. However, despite the fact that we have enriched this dichotomy with the proactive/reactive dimension, the matrix typology suffers from two main shortcomings:

1. Two descriptive dimensions are not sufficient to capture the complexity of strategic processes.
2. The construction of the matrix typology implies that the four types of strategic change are mutually exclusive and that they appear sequentially. A more realistic assumption is that there are a number of *process types* latent in a company at every moment and that they will be triggered to enter the arena in different situations. Furthermore, this implies that different process types may occur simultaneously, parallel to each other, even if one type dominates the strategic process.

Consequently, a more elaborate typology—compared with the matrix typology based on the evolutionary/revolutionary dichotomy—is needed in order to achieve a more comprehensive language for descriptions of strategic processes.

The second step of our analysis has been to develop such a typology, based on our processual case descriptions and current schools of thought on strategic processes. Our proposal for such a strategic process typology is now presented, followed by two empirical illustrations.

---

## CHANGE TYPOLOGY II

### A SEVENFOLD TYPOLOGY OF STRATEGIC PROCESSES

Different sets of dominating characteristics have here been isolated to express specific types of strategic processes in a sevenfold typology. These sets alternately characterize different periods of long-range strategic change processes.

---

### The Visionary Type

Visions may always play a role in the realization of strategies. However, this process type involves merely focusing on the early formulation and creation of a vision, i.e. the envisioning of a desired future organizational state and position (Westley and Mintzberg, 1989). The vision provides a kind of roadmap or 'guiding star' and gives information on which types of strategic action have priority and will be legitimized. A new corporate vision opens possibilities of taking actions outside the current strategic direction. This process type is connected with creative thinking, but also with the mobilization of commitment. The vision has to be recognized and owned by followers. The leader persuades the followers to see a new way of thinking and acting through the new vision. As this process type is dominated by the creation, formulation and communication of a new vision, it is not especially action-oriented. Instead, the new vision is an indicator for a changed strategic direction and future strategic actions. Of course, this process type is focused on top leader(s). However, visionary leadership is a dynamic and interactive phenomenon, not a unidirectional process (Westley and Mintzberg, 1989). Within this process type, different visionary styles can be recognized, some of which appeal more to emotion than to logic. Furthermore, some visions develop rather deliberately, while others emerge through a less conscious learning process.

### The Rational Planning Type

Like the former, this process type has its focus on formulation, but here of concrete strategies instead of rather vague visions. The rational planning process type is characterized by its sequential shape: logical analysis—rational choice—programmed planning. This process type may very well lead to intended and deliberate strategic actions, but also to implementation problems or totally unrealized actions.

### The Programmatic Implementation Type

This process type is action-oriented. The deliberate realization of a strategic plan or a shared vision is the typical pattern of this process type. The top-down perspective is dominating, as in the commander and change models of Bourgeois and Brodwin (1985). Some adjustments of the master plan in response to changes may occur.

### The Action Type

This process type is characterized by a large degree of freedom of strategic actions. The actions taken are rather big steps (such as sudden acquisitions). In order not to miss emerging opportunities, top management is 'shooting from the hip' when chances turn up. Strategy making is more parrying than planning. The big actions can follow a pattern, e.g. implying the realization of a vision. But they can also imply sudden and radical strategic reorientation.

## The Incremental Type

This process type is action-oriented, but actions are mainly taken in small steps, 'strategic increments.' The complexity of strategic issues is handled through a bounded rationality approach (March and Simon, 1958). The strategic actions will not imply any sudden reorientation. On the other hand, the pattern of actions does not follow any detailed strategic plan, since strategy making must deal with the necessary lack of completeness of a strategy. The unknowable factor becomes reality and must be adapted to. One important dimension of the incremental process type is the ambition from top management to obtain commitment through building understanding, credibility, and legitimacy before strategic actions are taken (Joyce, 1986). Note that this process type is not identical with the 'logical incrementalism' of Quinn (1980).

## The Politicking Type

This process type is related to the incremental type, but implies— in contrast to the latter—internal jostling for power (Butler *et al.*, 1977) between different internal interest groups. Such a politicking organization is still capable of strategic actions, but the choice of action will be determined by the result of the struggle for power. Political activities may include agenda control, withholding of information, behind-the-scenes coalition formation, and cooption (Eisenhardt and Bourgeois, 1988; Pettigrew, 1973).

## The Paralytic Type

An organization can, during some periods, lose its freedom of strategic action, which means that no strategic actions take place. The reason could either be that external power groups (such as suppliers and customers) become too powerful (Butler *et al.*, 1977) or that the organization becomes paralyzed by destructive internal struggles for power. The paralytic process type is then character-ized by an inability in the organization to move or to use its free will. A paralytic period implies a vacuum in terms of strategic actions: nothing happens.

STRATEGIC PROCESSES IN LUXOR AND ITS NEW PARENT COMPANY

In December 1983 Nokia, Finland's largest corporation, went into a new industry, consumer electronics, through two acquisitions. Nokia acquired the two leading TV manufacturers in Scandinavia: Luxor in Sweden and Salora in Finland. However, our analysis goes back to 1970 and the strategic development of Luxor. In 1970 the then president was fired by the company owner, who at the age of 81 still took an active part in the daily life of the organiza-tion. The new president, recruited internally, was the same kind of demanding person as the factory owner. Both were regarded as strong and aggressive.

Luxor introduced its first color TV in 1969. In 1970 Luxor increased its market share for TV sets in Sweden from 18% to 30%. Furthermore, the Scandinavian market as a whole, where Luxor was number 2 (after Philips), was growing very rapidly, from 180 000 color TV sets in 1970 to 580 000 in 1974. Luxor was growing with the market without any distinct vision or developed strategic plans. The sales orientation was heavy in the company.

1976 became the peak year for color TV sets, after which the Scandinavian market declined for a long period. Luxor tried to manage the expansion through internationalization, but without managerial competence for heavy internationalization the export business was run at a loss. At the same time, in 1977, Luxor as a whole started to suffer from a large overcapacity. Some managers questioned the export efforts, which were led by the president. But he did not accept this kind of overt opposition. One of the questioning managers was removed from his post. However, the company owner had his informants, and also started to question actions taken by the president. In 1978 more and more people in Luxor began to realize the precariousness of the situation. But no radical steps were taken until the family-dominated board was supplemented with two professional members. In January 1979 the president was forced to leave his position immediately.

The Swedish Government intervened and Luxor became state-owned for the nominal sum of one Swedish crown in February 1979. Until a new permanent president took over in April 1980, the company was financially reconstructed. During the period 1980–1982 Luxor was still an unprofitable company, with a number of internal conflicts, a lot of managers coming and going and with no radical strategic or organizational changes. Efforts were made to analyze the situation and to implement different plans. In 1981 a number of employees were fired and Luxor received millions from the Swedish state in order to once more reconstruct the company financially. In 1982 there was a recovery in demand for color TV sets in the Scandinavian market.

Turning to Nokia, its basic businesses (paper, tires, cables) was expected to meet with limited growth. The CEO formulated three visionary strategic goals during the late 1970s for the further development of the corporation: internationalization, increased growth, and more high-tech products. These visionary goals showed a new strategic direction for Nokia and the company later became very aggressive in its efforts to grow in a number of diversified business areas, one of which was consumer electronics.

However, the choice to diversify into consumer electronics was not a deliberate one: rather the opposite. Nokia had entered into a joint venture with Salora, a Finnish TV manufacturer, regarding Salora's second and smaller business unit, radiotelephones. In 1982 Nokia acquired the radiotelephone business (called Mobira) from Salora. Part of this deal was that Nokia also acquired 18% of the shares in Salora. But the R&D managers of Nokia were not at all interested in consumer electronics. However, in 1983 the president of Salora was able to sew up an acquisition offer for Nokia. The background was that Salora was growing and had capacity problems regarding the manufacturing of TV sets. On the other hand, Luxor, its strongest competitor still had problems and the Swedish Minister of Industry was now looking for a new private owner for Luxor. He considered Salora not to be strong enough, but was much more satisfied with the possibility of selling Luxor to a big corporation, such as Nokia. The combination of Salora and Luxor made the Nokia CEO very interested, despite resistance from his leading technicians. Furthermore, he had a good relationship with the Swedish government, something that facilitated the negotiations regarding the acquisition of Luxor. In January 1984 Nokia acquired majority stakes in both Luxor and Salora, and had quite suddenly entered the consumer electronics business.

---

### An Interpretation of Dominating Process Types in the Consumer Electronics Case

The strategic change processes of Luxor and Nokia can be categorized into our process types in the way shown in FIGURE 11.3. What is shown in the figure is mainly the dominating process type at each period. These process types are not only appearing sequentially (following on from each other) but also parallel to each other, simultaneously, indicated by the process types in parentheses. The process type that dominates during one significant period—strategic epoch—decides the time limits of the epoch, despite the fact that other (parallel, but not so strong) process types show other periodical patterns. For example, the epoch in Nokia during the late 1970s, here characterized as mainly visionary, also had rather strong features of the incremental process, which dominated in the next epoch. Another example is the epoch in Luxor between 1980 and 1983, dominated by the politicking type of process. During this period, a number of efforts were made to act more in the mode of the rational planning type. But this strategic style did not receive broad acceptance in the organization.

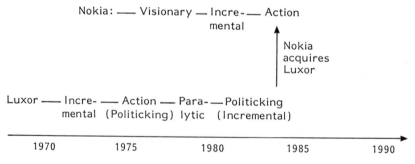

FIGURE 11.3    The strategic processes in Luxor and Nokia divided into different types

## THE STRATEGIC PROCESS IN HOLMEN

The Holmen mill was founded in 1609. In 1633, the manufacturing of hand-made paper in Holmen's name started. Early in its history, Holmen became a company based on two main operations, paper production and textile production. In 1968, Holmen was in a slight crisis, with one declining and unprofitable textile unit and one pulp and paper unit, based partly on very old manufacturing mills but still profitable. On the basis of rigorous strategic analyses, the new CEO soon made a major strategic decision to wind up the textile operations and to concentrate the strategic development on printing paper. The whole textile sector was systematically closed down during 1970, and a 10-year long-range plan was decided by the board in order to develop the printing paper sector. The business idea was to supply the market with customer tailored paper for newspapers and journals, and to grow with the market.

The long-range plan was continuously implemented and resulted in heavy investment in one of the existing production plants for printing papers and in a totally new plant on the east coast of Sweden. Between 1970 and 1984, Holmen fulfilled its expansive concentration strategy, which led to its position as the largest producer of newsprint in Europe. At this time, Holmen reached the position of number 6 in size in the Swedish pulp and paper industry. The company made some small efforts to diversify during this period, through efforts oriented towards product areas outside the forest industry, but with related production technology.

During 1985–1986 the main strategies of Holmen changed significantly, essentially not because of environmental changes. The new strategic view followed the appointment of a new CEO. The business idea was still based on a growth philosophy, but was now much more aggressive. The objective was to become one of the leading Scandinavian pulp and paper companies and to become one of the leading European suppliers in Holmen's main product areas. The strategy was to grow in two business areas: wood-containing printing paper and woodfiber-based hygiene products (i.e. tissue paper and sanitary products). Holmen acquired the latter product group through its purchase of Fiskeby in December 1985. Other products gained by this acquisition were not given priority in the new strategy by the CEO.

In the product range of wood-containing printing paper, Holmen decided to grow not only in newsprint, but also in magazine paper and coated paper, especially low weight coated (LWC) paper, the fastest growing printing paper quality during the 1980s.

The growth strategy of printing paper implied expansion of production capacity. During 1986, the strategic discussion in Holmen was focused on how to achieve increased production capacity in both newsprint and LWC paper. Despite the fact that LWC consumption was growing rapidly, there were reasons to expect an overcapacity of this type of paper in Europe around 1990 because of huge investments in LWC machines. Because of this, Holmen either had to make a very quick decision to invest in a new LWC machine or, as an alternative way of achieving LWC capacity, to search for possible acquisition objects. During spring 1986 Holmen was contacted by a West German firm about a possible collaborative arrangement. This firm, MD Papierfabriken, would, after ongoing investments, be the largest producer of LWC paper in Europe. The CEO of Holmen saw the strategic possibilities for Holmen, and in January 1987 Holmen acquired a 25% stake in MD Papierfabriken with an option to increase this. Holmen had not only found a solution to its LWC problem, but also a direct channel to the Common Market from inside the EC.

In September 1987 Holmen acquired Modo Consumer Products, the hygiene products division of Modo, one of Holmen's main Swedish competitors. This acquisition made the hygiene division of Holmen Europe's third biggest tissue producer and also an important producer of sanitary products. As a whole, Holmen Hygiene became the second biggest producer in Scandinavia of hygiene articles.

However, through this aggressive growth, the CEO of Holmen had challenged the growth strategy of its competitor Modo. After a surprising acquisition in October 1987 of a minority stake in Holmen, Modo succeeded in gaining 100% ownership in June 1988. In March 1988 the CEO left Holmen. During the end of 1988, the structure of the new Modo group was presented, with Holmen Paper (the former printing paper division of Holmen) and Holmen Hygiene (the former hygiene division) constituting two of eight large strategic business units. However, in February 1989, Holmen Hygiene was sold to a Finnish company. One reason was that Holmen Hygiene had suffered from profitability problems, but the main reason seemed to be that the CEO of

Modo—who had sold Modo's hygiene business area to Holmen less than two years earlier—still did not believe in the future of this business sector.

## An Interpretation of Dominating Process Types in Holmen

The Holmen case shows a totally different pattern to that of the Luxor/Nokia consumer electronics case. One important reason is the rather successful and strong role of both CEOs in Holmen during this 20-year period. They represented two very different strategic ways of thinking, both of which, however, were broadly accepted in the company. Both CEOs can be characterized as energetic, but while the first based all of his actions (after the first turbulent year) on careful strategic analysis and planning, the other was keener to 'shoot from the hip,' when opportunities occurred, based on his vision of growth and dominance positions.

Also, in the Holmen case, other process types 'competed' with the ones that we have interpreted as being dominant. For example, the first period of the second CEO, 1984–1985, is characterized as visionary. However, already in this period the strong action drive of the CEO was obvious, and this resulted in a number of important changes, such as the first acquisition and a radical internal organizational change. Parallel to these visionary and action processes, the earlier, strong rational planning played some role. However the result of this process was mainly analyses of the present situation, which formed one basis for the formulation of the new strategic vision (FIGURE 11.4).

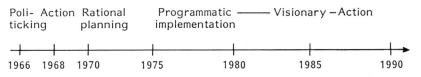

FIGURE 11.4 The strategic process in Holmen divided into different types

## CONCLUDING REMARKS

We need real long-term perspectives in strategic management research in order to be able to develop a valid theory of strategy. The cross-sectional snapshots that have been dominating the field of strategic management have made us 'half-blind,' i.e. have made us unable to see the consequences of quite another time perspective for our understanding of the mechanisms, dynamics, and complexity of strategic processes. A theory of strategy must also, to a much larger degree than up to now, become a theory of change. Strategic processes show inertia and stability, but the purpose of strategy making is to have the flexibility to carry through strategic shifts when necessary.

The two change typologies suggested in this chapter emphasize different aspects of strategic processes. Together, they can provide a step towards more holistic characterizations that capture the complexity and dynamics of strategic change. An advantage of the matrix typology is its inherent possibility of describing how a company's strategy changes over time, while focusing on both strategic content *and* strategic interruptions, thereby illuminating the differences between strategic epochs. Although the matrix typology also gives some understanding of why a strategy or a strategic interruption occurs—through the proactive/reactive dimension—its usefulness in describing, characterizing, and explaining the long cycles of change is still limited.

The second typology, characterizing different types of processes, is superior to the matrix typology in at least three aspects. Contrary to the latter, it binds different epochs together to provide more longitudinal and processual descriptions of long cycles of change. Furthermore, it has potential for understanding how different change mechanisms are related to and interact with each other. Finally, the process typology permits 'competing' process types to occur at the same time. The different types expressed in our process typology are not mutually exclusive: rather the opposite (even if some can be combined only partially, referring to our definitions).

When using a multi-perspective approach, such as our two typologies, to characterize strategic development in a business, the long-term sequence of dominating process types (following on from each other) can take a large number of different shapes. This means that the patterns of strategic change processes in different organizations seem to be very company-specific. The number of different strategic patterns, each expressing a sequence of process types acting in reality, seems to be infinite (in comparison with the limited number of available generic strategies).

Obviously, research findings like this, based on multi-perspective theories, are not easily translated to general management applications. On the other hand, if such theories develop understanding of strategic change, they will also have practical benefits for managers. They will not offer handy recommendations, but will help managers to understand and to learn from their local situations and thereby increase their managerial capability. Theory-building, as Daft and Buenger (1990) state, often ends up having more practical value for managers because it offers deeper understanding than research designed to answer practical questions relevant to the problems faced by managers. We believe (as Wilson, 1992) that there is still a need for more basic research in the field of strategic change, before move valid applied research can be conducted.

This chapter represents an initial step in developing a language to better understand strategic change. The next step involves further clarification of both typologies. We need to specify which dimensions discriminate between our seven types in the so-called process typology. A number of important dimensions can be identified, such as degree of action; freedom of action; power structure; degree of sequential decision making process; behavior versus result; individual versus organizational actions; and inherent logics (or rationales) in each process type.

## REFERENCES

Andrews, K.R. (1971). *The Concept of Corporate Strategy*. Homewood, IL: Dow-Jones/Irwin.

Ansoff, I. (1965). *Corporate Strategy*. New York: McGraw-Hill.

Brandes, O. and Brege, S. (1990). *Market Leadership*. Kristianstad: Liber (in Swedish).

Bourgeois, L. and Brodwin, D.R. (1985). Strategic implementation: Five approaches to an elusive phenomenon. *Strategic Management Journal*, **5**(3), 241–264.

Butler, R. J., Hickson, D.J., Wilson, D.C. and Axelsson, R. (1977). Organizational power, politicking and paralysis. In M. Warner (Ed.) *Organizational Choice and Constraint*. London: Sage.

Daft, R. and Buenger, V. (1990). Hitching a ride on a fast train to nowhere: The past and future of strategic management research. In J. Fredrickson (Ed.) *Perspectives on Strategic Management* (pp. 81–103). New York: Harper Business.

Eisenhardt, K.M. and Bourgeois, L.J. (1988). Politics of strategic decision making in high-velocity environments: Towards a midrange theory. *Academy of Management Journal*, **31**, 737–770.

Freeman, R.E. and Lorange, P. (1985). Theory building in strategic management. In R. Lamb and P. Shrivastava (Eds) *Advances in Strategic Management*, Vol. 3. Greenwich, CT: JAI Press.

Greiner, L. (1972). Evolution and revolution as organizations grow. *Harvard Business Review*, July/August, 37–46.

Grinyer, P., Mayas, D.G. and McKiernan, P. (1988). *Sharpbenders: The Secrets of Unleashing Corporate Potential*. Oxford: Basil Blackwell.

Hellgren, B., Melin, L. and Pettersson, A. (1993). Structure and change: The industrial field approach. *Advances in International Marketing*, **5**, 87–106.

Joyce, W. (1986). Towards a theory of incrementalism. *Advances in Strategic Management*, **4**, 43–58.

Lorange, P. (1980). *Corporate Planning: An Executive Viewpoint*. Englewood Cliffs, NJ: Prentice Hall.

March, J.G. and Simon, H. (1958). *Organizations*. New York: Wiley.

Melin, L. (1989). The field-of-force metaphor. *Advances in International Marketing*, **3**, 161–179.

Miller, D. and Friesen, D. (1984). *Organizations—A Quantum View*. Englewood Cliffs, NJ: Prentice Hall.

Mintzberg, H. (1987). The strategy concept I: Five PS for strategy. *California Management Review*, **30**, 11–23.

Mintzberg, H. (1990). Strategy formation: schools of thought. In J. Fredrickson (Ed.) *Perspectives on Strategic Management* (pp. 105–210). New York: Harper Business.

Pettigrew, A. (1973). *The Politics of Organizational Decision Making*. London: Tavistock.

Pettigrew, A. (1985a). Examining change in the long-term context of culture and politics. In J. Pennings (Ed.) *Organizational Strategy and Change*. San Francisco, CA: Jossey-Bass.

Pettigrew, A. (1985b). *The Awakening Giant: Continuity and Change in Imperial Chemical Industries*. Oxford: Basil Blackwell.

Pettigrew, A. and Whipp, R. (1991). *Managing Change for Competitive Success*. Oxford: Basil Blackwell.

Porter, M.E. (1980). *Competitive Strategy: Techniques for Analyzing Industries and Competitors*. New York: Free Press.

Prahalad, C.K. and Hamel, G. (1990). The core competence of the corporation. *Harvard Business Review*, May/June, 79–91.

Quinn, J.B. (1980). *Strategies for Change*. Homewood, IL: Richard D. Irwin.

Shrivastava, P. (1983). Variations in strategic decision-making processes. *Advances in Strategic Management*, **2**, 177–189.

Tushman, M.L. and Romanelli, E. (1985). Organizational evolution: A metamorphosis model of convergence and reorientation. In L. Cummings and B. Staw (Eds) *Research in Organizational Behavior*, Vol. 7. Greenwich, CT: JAI Press.

Westley, F. and Mintzberg, H. (1989). Visionary leadership and strategic management. *Strategic Management Journal*, **10**, 17–32.

Wilson, D. (1992). *A Strategy of Change: Concepts and Controversies in the Management of Change*. London: Routledge and Kegan Paul.

# 12

# The Greening of Strategy Process Research

BALA CHAKRAVARTHY, YVES DOZ, PETER LORANGE,

## INTRODUCTION

The main emphasis of this chapter is on a series of new developments relating to strategic process research. It is, perhaps, to an extent a matter of semantics to sort out what is strategic process and what is strategic content research. Many of the more visible research results over the last decades have taken place within the content area. Thus, the process side of research in our strategy area needs careful attention as we go along, because we cannot make progress unless there is some harmony between the various dimensions along which we are evolving.

This chapter is divided into three sections that address the process side of strategy research: (i) strategic process challenges in today's complex multibusiness firms, (ii) strategic alliances and the process challenges they face, and (iii) processes for dynamic change.

*Building the Strategically-Responsive Organization.*
Edited by H. Thomas, D. O'Neal, R. White and D. Hurst.
Copyright © 1994 the Strategic Management Society. Published 1994 by John Wiley & Sons Ltd.

## STRATEGIC PROCESS CHALLENGES IN TODAY'S COMPLEX MULTIBUSINESS FIRMS

At a recent research seminar, four interesting themes emerged, with implications for both managers and researchers (Lorange *et al.*, 1992). The first is the role of process itself: do we need process? 'Process', in this context, is not to be confused with planning, but is something beyond planning. The second has to do with the role of cognition in the strategy process. The third is organizational learning and how it can be used to enhance competitive advantage. And, finally, the fourth is perhaps a new view of the process of strategic change itself.

To illustrate the first theme, consider a presentation by Ulrich Schmauke from IBM France on IBM's efforts at organizational transformation (Schmauke, 1991). What he was essentially arguing was that if you are IBM you recognize that the firm has many competencies and that it also uses different strategy logics, i.e. different ways of competing across different market segments, different businesses, different products, and so on. Large, diversified multinationals have different strategy logics. They have to manage them all, and the classical method of focusing primarily on organization coordination is perhaps not enough.

The best way to empowerment, or what IBM calls 'ownership', is to let people take charge of ideas lower down in the organization. One solution is to create '50-member organizations' where everybody would have more power. But the next problem then becomes: what about synergy? You still have to use these competencies and logics in some economical fashion and thus create economies of scale. Another problem is one of learning—not just learning individually, but as a '50-person unit' and across these 50-person units. IBM's challenge, therefore, is to achieve coordination, ownership, synergy and learning. But is achieving this a question of reconfiguring the strategy process or of redesigning the structure?

The second issue has to do with the role of cognition. What researchers are asking us to look at are teams which are not necessarily well endowed with a whole lot of competencies but who still compete on the basis of a new concept. It is well accepted that the number of concepts you carry as a management team allows you to consider possibilities that can help you to beat your competition. Are you capable, as a management team, of generating conceptual alternatives? Consider, for instance, technology trees in the particular area of technology. It is the richness of the forest you grow that determines your competitive advantage.

Another interesting aspect of cognition relates to building cognitive distance from one's competitors. There is a distinction between invention and innovation. Conceptual distance does not call for invention, it calls for innovation. The way that Canon lead Xerox, or that Timex beat the Swiss watch companies, was not because of new technology alone. In fact, it was based on a creative conceptual repackaging of old technology. While what an innovator does, in retrospect, may seem obvious and old-fashioned to its competitors, it is still conceptually far from them. They are, therefore, unable to 'see' it. The challenge for strategy process research then is: how do you build perceptual distance so that even while you are building competitive advantage you are left alone—given some breathing space?

Concept championing is yet another difficult cognition-related challenge for the strategy process because it means being the first to 'sell' the concept to a large number of stakeholders. The key here is to create a learning architecture where you persuade customers, suppliers and yourself into joint learning. This leads to high switching costs for the parties concerned. People do not want to give up their ideas even though hindsight might tell us that they were not such exciting ideas. Competing through concepts, as opposed to competing on the basis of freestanding competencies, is a novel source of competitive advantage.

The third issue, the challenge to achieve organizational learning, has been highlighted well by the Swedish and Japanese scholars, Hedlund and Nonaka (1992). They ask us to view learning not only in terms of an organizational or interorganizational phenomenon, but also as an individual and group phenomenon. Also, the nature of knowledge can be tacit, articulated or asset-embodied. When it is asset-embodied it is called a competency. Thus, instead of being preoccupied with concepts such as core competencies and strategic alliances, and focussing on asset-embodied competencies at the organizational or interorganizational level, why not attempt to understand how organizations actually learn? In Japanese companies knowledge is assimilated from the outside and then is transferred down into teams and individuals, becoming more and more tacit in the process. Appropriation is the way in which it goes to the individual, internalization is the way in which it becomes more tacit. In many western companies, we practise exactly the reverse. We try to articulate knowledge, which is individual, make it into an organizational property, and then transfer it from a tacit to an embodied asset. We move it quickly away from the individual because we fear we might lose this individual knowledge worker.

A contrasting view on learning has been taken by Bonora and Revang (1992), who claim that learning implies the need to worry about diffusion, i.e. 'snatching' knowledge from the individual and making it a group property. We thus have to worry about de-skilling what is tacit, i.e. making it articulate and embodying it in assets. We also need to worry about fragmentation, what is tacit-individual, making it an asset and organizational property. Individuals can walk out of the organization—we want learning how it can be an organizational asset. We thus may be setting into motion a process that is perhaps counter to what may be to our competitive advantage. The kind of process we have for managing learning within organizations undoubtedly has an impact on competitive advantage. However, what do we know about it as managers or as researchers?

The fourth issue, strategic change, builds on the realization that we have competencies and we have strategic logics. What we need to do in terms of managing change is really to work ourselves out of some of the dominant boxes that we tend to be very happy with, and try to cope with new environments in a controlled, experimental fashion. These 'experiments' will tell us what competencies we need to add to our current skills. What is needed is a step-by-step iteration between trying new logics and building new competencies, and, at the same time, getting rid of old logics and old competencies.

## STRATEGIC ALLIANCES AND THE PROCESS CHALLENGES THEY RAISE

Let us now turn to the challenge of examining strategic processes as they relate to organizations in networks, such as strategic alliances. There are at least four types of process issues that might be raised regarding strategic alliance networks. One has to do with the formation of strategic alliances. The key here is to consider the gathering of information as an opportunity-seeking activity so that you can guide the push to look for interesting business. You may also want to manage the various process steps needed in order to get partners together. A second issue is the accumulation of core competencies and how to protect your own core competencies in these networks. Approaches for signalling your own skills, thus increasing the chance that the partner perceives you as a winner—as opposed to relying solely on formal processes, such as patents and legal agreements—represent important management processes for succeeding in networks.

Organizational learning also becomes an issue when attempting to succeed in networks. The one partner who is better at learning and faster at building competencies will have a better strategic resource core later on. Organizational learning, at least at a level sufficient to stay abreast of one's partner, thus becomes key. Finally, the issue of coping with cultural distance becomes a key component of management processes for successful strategic alliances.

These issues, taken one by one, are perhaps not particularly startling as such, but they signal the need for a more proactive role of strategic process thinking in the case of alliances. Strategic alliances cannot function without proper processes.

When studying strategic alliances, we see that they can very much be seen as indeed being learning processes. In research over the past few years, tracking a number of alliances in real time, it has been shown that learning processes and alliances are quite synonymous. This implies learning about partners' cultures, learning about the process of effective interaction, learning about the evolution of the outcomes and the vested interests that may exist in partners' organizations, not to mention the learning of more tacit skills and competencies.

We do not have a great deal of administrative insight regarding the management of multiple alliances in the context of one single organization. Networks are extraordinarily complicated to analyse, and one of the great challenges, both in strategy analysis and strategy process research, is to better understand these typically very complex relationships. Increasingly, companies are doing a lot of things together. Sometimes they are partners, sometimes they are even *equal* partners, and sometimes they actually have some subsidiary operations which are partners in 'local' joint ventures. Sometimes they are very transient partners. Sometimes they are also competitors in the market-place. Sometimes they are involved in very complex customer and supplier relationships. At any given point in time a firm may be involved in dozen's of partnerships, probably competing in dozen's of businesses, and there are probably some supplier–customer relationships with several hundred different components—product lines, and so on. How do they manage such webs of relationships? You find that, increasingly, the net result of these networks is creating extremely complex, extremely mixed-motive relationships among companies, which indeed may challenge many of the assumptions we have previously had about strategic management in general. As noted, we really know little about how to manage such network issues so far. To add to this we thus have the problem of instability around networks (Bartlett and Nande, 1990).

There are a number of intriguing paradoxes in alliances, one of which—and perhaps the most obvious—is that the greater the complementarity between companies, the greater the distance—geographical, cultural and/or skill-based—and therefore the greater difficulty executives will have in communicating and working together. You can start with the notion that alliances with the highest potential, because of the fact that they are based on potentially complementary, co-specialized assets, are also the alliances that are often the most difficult because of distance.

A second paradox, none the least, relates, to the fact that the very reason why companies have to enter into an alliance in the first place is also very often containing the seed of warning that is going to make them fail in future alliances. Companies may enter into a strategic alliance because they have not successfully developed new products, for instance. When you find this, typically the firm did not develop new products because it does not communicate very well between functions, it is very parochial in subunits, and so on. You bring those companies into an alliance and things often get even worse, rather than better. The same factors that made internal product development foul play havoc with many alliances. In a sense, once you start digging into these alliances, you see that there are a number of reasons why they should not work. And the fact that some of them work at all is perhaps really quite remarkable.

A methodological question that might be pertinent when it comes to researching these issues is how to take models that are tested out in other contexts and apply them to the strategic alliance process context. For instance, we have relatively well-developed models for learning that have been tested out. How do we build on these models and findings so that they provide a basis for further testing in strategic alliance contexts? Our understanding of administrative processes, accumulated over the years, may also largely assume a different corporate context than what we find in an alliance. Many of these basic underlying models may indeed no longer be of much help.

As we know, strategic alliances are inherently unstable in that they always tend to evolve towards something else. This poses another methodological question: how can we develop replicable results if there is a fundamental lack of stability when it comes to the phenomena we are looking at? Furthermore, what are relevant success criteria, keeping in mind that even these may be changing over time? We are indeed faced with some difficult and challenging methodology problems when it comes to doing research on strategic processes as they apply to the area of strategic alliances.

## PROCESSES FOR DYNAMIC CHANGE

Why is it that so much focus has been put on a variety of aspects of strategy process research by so many people but with comparatively few new breakthrough results? Many articles and scores of books have been published on these subjects; however, the cumulative impact may not have been as great as it should have been. Much of this research has concentrated on aspects of the tasks of strategic management, rooted in strategy content and the substantive strategy agendas of companies. Examples of such research areas are administrative processes, organizational structures, communication systems, reward systems, performance measurement, budgeting and planning. These are essentially all tools that were intended to support the strategic process. A lot of this research has actually been very configurational—attempting to prescribe how various types of strategic issues can be matched with certain features of administrative processes. The aim is to prescribe what are configurational linkages between strategic characteristics of a given position of the firm and the kind of administrative processes that are going to be reasonably effective in such contexts.

What we have not yet done enough of in our research, and what may be thus at least a partial explanation for why we have not had many breakthroughs in our process research, may have to do with a failure to look at the dynamics of strategic processes, above all in terms of creating transitional knowledge. A lot of the academic work has been too focused on a fairly static configuration. It has not raised the question of how to embed or build new organizational capabilities. How do we do things that are going to make companies more able to cope with various kinds of new strategic circumstances? It takes an understanding of what the strategic agenda is to achieve this. Furthermore, it requires some development of fairly concrete management processes around competitive analysis, market analysis and competency analysis. It also takes specific competencies to ask: how do we create a process whereby the mindsets of our people evolve? How do we create a process whereby roles, behaviours and skills become more adaptive and more fluid?

In order to accomplish continuing change in an organization, one might need to have a process that could act on three issues, at least. One is having a process that makes the mindsets of managers—their world views—evolve. The second is having a process rooted in substantive issues, i.e. not one that might address cultural change for the sake of cultural change, nor organizational development as an end in itself, but one that addresses specific changes, for example in competition, in technology, among one's customers, and so on. The third is having a process that modifies the organizational context, modifying the set of management systems and management processes that provide direction in the organization, i.e. an evolution of situationally tailored processes.

If you look at these change processes, both in observing how companies go about addressing them and in summarizing some of the key points from experience regarding helping companies to cope with them, a few tentative conclusions can be made. One is contrary to the kind of teaching that takes place in many business schools, and contrary to the kind of intervention that many consulting companies are doing, namely that there seems to be tremendous value in learning by doing. There is a need for personal discovery, the process whereby people in the management of companies have to find out for themselves. Our role as researchers is not to tell them, our role is to 'help' them along their journey of discovering themselves. 'Our role' may be more or less the same whether we focus on the practice of strategy consulting or whether we consider the more academic business schools and the kind of teaching they deliver.

It is also interesting that we may have to be more action-oriented, rather than conceptual. What we observe in many companies is that there can be tremendous discrepancies between thinking and action. So, if one really wants to start to induce change, this begins with asking oneself to think differently at the micro level. Top-down induced change processes typically do not work. Such large-scale cascading processes, unrolling from the top, tend not only to be hazy, they are also likely to be fairly sterile. The reason for this is that you need to get commitment from people at various levels by, in a sense, them being the true process engineers of the transition.

In this change scenario, you also have a pivotal role of key integrators. It used to be that such roles belonged to senior management. Then these roles were transferred to middle management. Now, however, companies have fewer and fewer middle managers. Some companies are making the bold next step of going after more front-end integration; some companies, for instance, now look at themselves as a collection of account managers managing major accounts. These are the integrators of the company, a large number of entrepreneurs who mobilize the resources of the multinational company behind them. This very different approach implies that change is going to come from the front-end integrators—not from the top management.

Another process principle that seems to be emerging has to do with the need for having, and sticking to, a given language, a set of words, concepts, frameworks and the like. A great danger in many companies is that top management could get enamoured with one set of 'in' concepts after another and not really use a specific language and concept system over a sufficient time period to get capabilities embedded in the organization. There is a need to be very consistent and to strive for some continuity over time in the use of language and in the use of concepts and frameworks.

Moving from the basic underlying design principles for creating dynamic change to what are the typical steps in a change process, there is typically a first step that may be summarized as: rather than confront the pre-existing mindsets in the organizational logic, existing roles, behaviours and management systems, why not bypass them, or circumvent them, by creating temporary systems? Temporary systems can be of a whole range—workshops and seminars, task forces or gatherings of various kinds. Essentially, the members of the firm are asking: can we create the opportunity for our organizations members to experiment with new behaviours, and can we do it at three levels? Firstly, an intellectual understanding of something different is needed. This is essentially what people in business schools and people in the consulting profession attempt to do every day for a living. The second—and more difficult—level involves creating an emotional commitment to a different type of behaviour. How do you actually stimulate elation? How do you create a process where people suddenly feel unshackled and liberated? Here, again, there have been many approaches, back to, for instance, T-groups and all of those approaches of some 10 years ago. These approaches were, however, not specifically linked to any strategic agenda or to any real change process. The third level is relational. Discussing issues of networks—organizational and interorganizational—puts a large set of relational demands on managers that they are typically inexperienced in dealing with, given the levels of ambiguity and confusion that often surround such alliances, partnerships and new interorganizational relationships. But the investment in relational knowledge-building and change must be considerable.

In summary, what those temporary systems can do is create an opportunity to manage by following three threads of change over time: the intellectual one, which is what we do easily; the emotional one, which is more difficult; and the relational one, which is a lot more difficult to manage successfully.

In addition to the temporary systems, there can be a series of processes and an architecture of conforming the processes over time, where one moves from the temporary systems to more quasi-permanent themes that are intended to enforce very specific results. One starts to 'nibble' at the existing administrative structure as one changes underlying determinants of the rules of the game, such as measurement, communication, information, reward systems and so on. The net result of making such changes feasible and legitimate, in essence, is an increased capability to create empowerment and personal growth. This implies a much more dynamic, transitional view of strategy processes, and we have not yet sufficiently researched these issues.

---

## CONCLUSION

We have attempted to identify a number of challenges facing the strategy field, taking a strategic process point of view. Our discussion has attempted to pinpoint what might be the critical strategic processes ahead, when seen from a practitioner point of view, as well as when it comes to the research challenges that the study of these issues will raise. Given that we are possibly facing relatively new contexts within which to cope with how effective strategic processes work—such as complex network configurations, accelerated dynamism and instability in environmental conditions, increasingly multicultural management learning and so on—there may be a need to call for a *fundamental* effort to attack these research issues.

For those of us who do research in this field and use clinical studies, we know that by their very nature clinical studies call for extraordinary involvement and take forever to do. Then there are large-scaled studies, but, by definition, they cannot be clinical because the volume of work is too great, the cost of the research is excessive and the size of the team to do them is unmanageable. This raises an interesting question when you think of process research in strategy: have we been hampered by our inability to do large-scale clinical research? We do not really know. What about an in-depth process study involving a few hundred cases? None of us knows; none of us even dreams of that. But does it make any sense? Some people probably say that it is too big, it would be a gigantic waste of time, and it is a very good thing that no one has done it. There are indeed some interesting issues here about how one really does move strategic process research forward, and we hope the commitment will be made!

---

## REFERENCES

Bartlett, S. and Nande, A. (1990). Corning incorporated: A network of alliances. Harvard Business School, case no. N9-391-102.

Bonora, E. and Revang, Ø. (1992). A framework for analyzing the storage and protection of knowledge in organizations. In P. Lorange, B. Chakravarthy, J. Roos and A. Van de Ven (Eds) *The Challenges of Strategic Processes*. Oxford: Basil Blackwell.

Hedlund, G. and Nonaka, I. (1992). Models of knowledge management. In P. Lorange, B. Chakravarthy, J. Roos and A. Van de Ven (Eds) *The Challenges of Strategic Processes*. Oxford: Basil Blackwell.

Lorange, P., Chakravarthy, B., Roos, J. and Van de Ven, A. (Eds) (1992). *The Challenges of Strategic Processes*. Oxford: Basil Blackwell.

Schmauke, U. (1991). Strategic processes and information technology. Working paper presented at the Innovation, Integration and Strategic Processes Conference, Norwegian School of Management, Oslo/Sandvika, June.

# Section III

# Implications of Industry Evolution and Competitive Dynamics

Competition and the quest for sustainable competitive advantage are the very essence of strategy. Competitive advantage results from the successful exploitation of resources, market structure, and competition, all of which are examined by the chapters in this section.

Building on Section II's discussion of managing change, the chapters in this section address changing industry dynamics, and offer strategies to help firms to recognize threats and capitalize on opportunities.

Hariharan and Prahalad highlight the importance of the need for strategies to change as an industry develops. They describe the necessity for firms in an emerging industry to shift from the traditional focus on competition among firms within the industry to that of competitors battling to define and structure the industry in their favor.

Smith and Cooper study innovations that represent not only important new products but also define the emergence of new games and new industries. They focus on the challenges facing firms attempting to enter such new industries.

Verdin and Williamson describe a concept called 'barriers to survival,' which makes competitive survival difficult for new entrants, even after they have successfully scaled an industry's entry barriers. New entrants consequently have to build asset investments around their perception of the long-term survival characteristics (competences) of the industry.

Östlund and Larsson describe how organizations facing environmental pressures can, instead of resisting these threats to their existence, address them through strategic alliances within the industry network. They, therefore, highlight the role of strategic alliances in capturing the sources of competitive advantage.

Recommended readings:

Elizabeth Bailey and Ann Friedlaender (1982). Market structure and multiproduct industries. *Journal of Economic Literature*, September. Theorizes that *all markets*, even monopolies, duopolies, and oligopolies are *contestable*.

Michael Porter (1981). The contributions of industrial organization to strategic management. *Academy of Management Review*, **6**. Discusses the past, current and potential future relationships between the industrial organization and strategic management fields.

S. Balakrishnan and Birger Wernerfelt (1986). Technical change, competition and vertical integration. *Strategic Management Journal*, **7**. Suggests that *vertical integration* becomes less desirable as competition increases, and as technological change becomes more frequent.

Gordon Walker and David Weber (1984). A transaction cost

approach to make-or-buy decisions. *Administrative Science Quarterly*, **29**. Comparative production costs are the strongest predictor of *make or buy* decisions, as are, to a lesser extent, volume uncertainty and competition among suppliers.

William Abernathy and Kim Clark (1985). Innovation: Mapping the winds of creative destruction. *Research Policy*, **14**. Introduces the idea of 'transilience'—the capacity of an *innovation* to influence the established systems of production and marketing.

Eric von Hippel (1986). Lead users: A source of novel product concepts. *Management Science*, July. Suggests how *lead users*—those whose current strong needs are likely to become those of the general market-place in the future—can be the source of valuable inputs to market researchers.

Agha Ghazanfar, John McGee and Howard Thomas (1986). The impact of technological change on industry structure and corporate strategy: The case of the reprographics industry in the United Kingdom. In Andrew Pettigrew (Ed.) *The Management of Strategic Change*. Examines firms' strategic responses to *technological change* at three levels: product, business and corporate. Suggests that successful firms continually redefine their industry boundaries and engage in ongoing innovation.

William Abernathy and James Utterback (1988). Patterns of industrial innovation. In Michael Tushman and William Moore (Eds) *Readings in the Management of Innovation*. Provides a model to explain how the character of *innovation* changes as a successful firm matures.

Hans Thorelli (1986). Networks: Between markets and hierarchies. *Strategic Management Journal*, **7**. Describes *networks* as the alternatives that lie between the open market and internalization of activities, and examines the roles of power, influence and trust in networks.

Bryan Borys and David Jemison (1989). Hybrid arrangements as strategic alliances: Theoretical issues in organizational combinations. *Academy of Management Review*, **14**. *Hybrid arrangements* (e.g. mergers, acquisitions, joint ventures, license agreements, etc.) offer new ways of increasing organizational efficiency and flexibility, but offer new challenges for managers in contrast with their past experience.

Appropriate books include:
Michael Porter (1980). *Competitive Strategy: Techniques for Analyzing Industries and Competitors*, and (1985). *Competitive Advantage:*

*Creating and Sustaining Superior Performance,* both of which were mentioned in Section I.

Robert Grant (1991). *Contemporary Strategy Analysis.* The author appropriately describes this book as a 'guide to *business strategy analysis* which combines rigor with relevance and applicability.'

Sharon Oster (1990). *Modern Competitive Analysis.* Focuses on the *competitive nature* of competitive strategy, the importance of *change,* and the theme that strategic choices are generally made with *limited information* in the face of *market friction.*

# 13

# Strategic Windows in the Structuring of Industries: Compatibility Standards and Industry Evolution

SAM HARIHARAN, C.K. PRAHALAD

Under the prevailing wisdom on strategy formulation, managers are advised to start with a structural analysis of an industry and then develop a generic competitive strategy (cost leadership or differentiation applied either to the entire industry or to a focused niche in the industry) designed to provide the firm with a sustained competitive advantage. While such a methodology and analytical sequence may be useful in industries with stable structures, strategy development as a process of creating new industries as well as influencing its structure has received very little academic attention. Indeed, what is the meaning of strategy and the process of strategy development in the absence of a relatively stable or identifiable industry structure?

*Building the Strategically-Responsive Organization.*
Edited by H. Thomas, D. O'Neal, R. White and D. Hurst.
Copyright © 1994 the Strategic Management Society. Published 1994 by John Wiley & Sons Ltd.

The importance of strategy in influencing the emerging phases of an industry is increasing. What should managers have done in the early days of the development of the VCR industry? How does a firm develop a strategy to tackle the emerging market in UNIX systems with competing and multiple versions all vying to become the standard UNIX? How will the emerging high definition television (HDTV) industry be structured? How will the emergence of the Manufacturing Automation Protocol (MAP) affect vendors of factory automation equipment and other networking products? How will digital audio tape (DAT) standards affect the consumer electronics industry? By what process will the infrastructure for intelligent vehicle highway systems (IVHS) be developed? At a general level, what strategies should firms follow to influence the emerging structure of the industry?

When applied in emerging industries, conventional strategic analysis faces considerable hurdles. Conventional strategic analysis assumes a clearly defined industry, a well-defined and identifiable value-added structure in the industry, known competitors, well-understood patterns of competition as in strategic groups, and a well-known demand structure. In emerging industries, seldom do any of the above conditions hold. Emerging industries are characterized by a high degree of uncertainty. Traditional economic analysis has focused attention on uncertainty of a particular kind: the variation in the quantity demanded. What is neglected is an even more fundamental source of uncertainty in emerging industries: uncertainty concerning the features of a product, i.e. the product concept desired by the customer. Since the value-added structure is still evolving in the case of emerging industries, strategic analysis cannot assume that the current structure of an industry is any reasonable guide to the development of strategy for the industry in the future.

In this chapter, we describe our research on the nature of competition for structuring industries and the strategies of firms in the process. Breaking with traditional strategy research, we focus not only on the competition among firms within a given industry structure but also on the competition for structuring an industry. Appendix A describes our research design.

# A THEORETICAL PERSPECTIVE ON THE EMERGENCE OF INDUSTRY STRUCTURE

Static and equilibrium notions of industry structure are the staple of economists. The traditional perspective in economics examines a static industry structure, where basic conditions of supply and demand govern the equilibrium industry structure. This is the basis of the structure–conduct–performance 'paradigm' which underpins much research in strategy (see Porter, 1980). But there is little research on how industry structures are 'formed' and how they 'evolve' over time, notable exceptions being Spence (1979) and David (1985).

Our perspective of the process by which the structure of an industry emerges is (i) dynamic, (ii) evolutionary, and (iii) incorporates industry level and firm level learning. The evolution of an industry is the result of a 'rich' process of competitive interactions between firms. The process is also evolutionary and path dependent, in the sense that the options open to a firm at each stage depend on previous stages. In this evolutionary process, the strategies followed by firms also evolve.

Our theoretical framework explicitly incorporates the role of learning in the evolution of the industry, in the strategic choices of firms and in the processes by which industries are structured. The study of industry evolution was part of a larger study on the emergence of compatibility standards. Our theoretical perspective is, however, in direct contrast to the formal game-theoretic models that have been used to study compatibility standards and their effect on industry structure. These formal models do not sufficiently incorporate the dynamic and evolutionary process of industry evolution; they assume one-time commitments to standards and perfect foresight, with no scope for learning from early outcomes that can be incorporated into future strategies (see Katz and Shapiro, 1985, 1986a, 1986b).

The dynamic and evolutionary perspectives along with industry and firm learning are critical components in our conceptualization of the process by which an industry is structured. Since uncertainty is inherent in emerging industries, learning from the market is the basic mechanism by which the uncertainty faced by the firm is reduced. This learning is then incorporated into the revision of a firm's strategic choices. It is this ability to revise strategies based on market learning that accounts for the evolution of firm strategies and the structure of the industry.

## INDUSTRY STANDARDS, COMPETITION AND INDUSTRY STRUCTURE

The emergence of industry standards is often a watershed event in the evolution of an industry. It (i) plays a critical role in the emergence of a major market, (ii) is responsible for the emergence of a stable value-added structure for the industry, (iii) affects the competition in the industry, and (iv) has a potentially large impact on the competitive positions of firms in the industry. In this section, we discuss the salient characteristics of compatibility standards, and how standards affect the evolution of an industry and the competitive positions of firms in the industry.

## THE EMERGENCE OF A MAJOR MARKET

A major market rarely emerges until after the establishment of industry standards. The growth in the market occurs because of the following reasons. The development of complementary products and other supporting infrastructure is accelerated after the issue of standards is resolved. In the absence of standards, these activities are rarely supported aggressively because of the risk of choosing the 'wrong' standards. The majority of customers and producers of complementary products (e.g. software) are also unwilling to choose systems until the issue of standards is resolved, since they could be stranded with the 'wrong' standard.

## STABLE VALUE-ADDED STRUCTURE FOR THE INDUSTRY

Before the establishment of standards, the value-added structure of the industry is still evolving. This is partly because investments in developing the infrastructure for the delivery of functionalities to the consumer remain to be made. The value-added structure that would be used in providing value to the customer is still in a state of flux. It is the establishment of the infrastructure and the development of mechanisms to provide the activities valued by customers that leads to the value-added structure of the industry. The value-added structure attains stability with the emergence of standards when specific investments are made to deliver the functionalities desired by the consumer.

## EFFECT ON COMPETITION IN INDUSTRY

The emergence of standards changes the competition among firms in the industry. Before the emergence of standards, firms compete with a wide variety of product concepts that conform to different standards. Competition among firms in the early stages of industry evolution is characterized by competition among a variety of product concepts, often using a diversity of technologies. This diversity of products reflects the uncertainty regarding which product concept will be preferred by customers, or which technologies will be able to deliver the functionalities desired by customers. The emergence of standards represents a resolution of this uncertainty. After the emergence of standards, the diversity of product concepts reduces considerably, as does the variety of technologies used in the product concepts, since certain technologies are invariably better suited to the delivery of particular functionalities.

## EFFECT ON COMPETITIVE POSITIONS OF FIRMS IN INDUSTRY

The emergence of standards affects the relative competitive positions of firms. The domination of the industry by a standard may be translated into a position of competitive advantage for the firm or consortia of firms whose product concept/standard became dominant. To the extent that the firm has proprietary know-how or other proprietary assets in the production or marketing of the product, these asymmetries may be translated into a competitive advantage for the firm. An additional advantage in the emergence of one's product concept as the dominant standard is that it becomes the base for leveraging the technologies for future products and markets. The technologies used in the product become the basis for a family of products.

---

## THEMES FROM TWO INDUSTRIES: VCR AND HDTV

### THE VCR INDUSTRY: THE FORMAT BATTLE

The video cassette record (VCR) is a ubiquitous component in most home entertainment systems, having a market penetration of around 60% in the US. The home VCR market is dominated globally (with a few exceptions in some country markets) by the VHS format. This outcome was the result of a long drawn battle—a battle among firms to develop product concepts that would appeal to customers and to influence the standard adopted by the industry. The process of evolution of the industry started in 1956 with the introduction of magnetic tape as a medium to record images. FIGURE 13.1 shows the evolution of the VCR industry. Detailed descriptions of the evolution of the industry and the products introduced over time are provided by Hariharan (1990).

A mass market for VCRs did not emerge immediately. While a number of video recording products were introduced between 1956 and 1976, none of them managed to create a market. The reasons why a mass market failed to emerge were as follows: (i) the presence of a number of competing standards, (ii) the lack of features that customers desired, (iii) prices were too high to induce a mass market, and in the absence of a potential mass market, (iv) the lack of a system of complementary products that increased the value of the product. The watershed event was the introduction of the Betamax format by Sony in 1975 in Japan (and in 1976 in the US). The Betamax format provided, for the first time in any VCR, the functionality of 'time-shift' which gave the customer the ability to record a program and watch it at a later time. This functionality was provided by incorporating within the VCR a television tuner. It was the functionality of time-shift that proved to be the impetus for the development of the market. But the functionality of time-shift was very easily imitated, and very soon JVC announced the VHS format, which not only provided the viewer with the same capability as the Betamax format, but also provided a longer

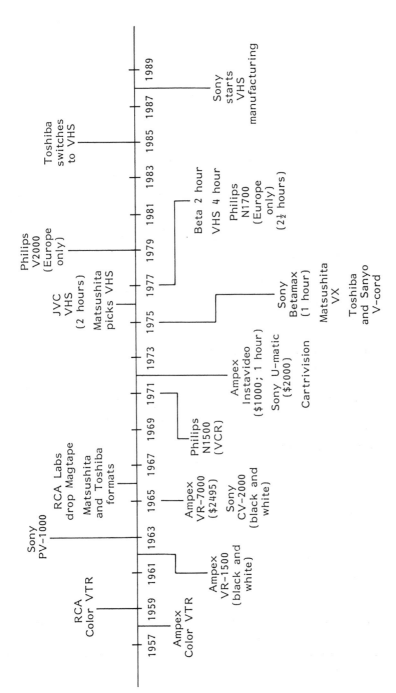

FIGURE 13.1 Chronology of key events in the VCR industry

recording time (2 hours relative to the 1 hour available for the Betamax format).

---

## HDTV: The Battle for Infrastructure Standards

The ongoing battle for standards in HDTV encompasses not only display standards (for the television receiver) but also standards in the process of delivery of the images, i.e. in production (creating programming in the studio), transmission (the process of sending the programming from the programmer such as CBS or HBO to the local broadcasters and cable operators) and emission (the delivery of programming by the local broadcasters or cable operators to the viewers at home). The standards battle, therefore, is not so much for a single product as for an entire infrastructure.

The battle for HDTV standards represents an excellent contrast to the battle for standards in the VCR industry. To begin with, the standards for HDTV spanned a number of products and were in the nature of infrastructure standards, while the standards for VCR were related to a single product. Relatedly, the setting of standards in HDTV demanded considerable coordination among a variety of players at different stages in the vertical chain of activities, while in the case of VCR, standards setting required much less coordination. The emergence of a standard in the case of VCR was essentially through market con petition. In the case of HDTV, the coordination required, the nature of the investments required, and the regulatory regimes under which broadcasting operated (such as ownership restrictions, licensing requirements of the Federal Communications Commission (FCC) for using the frequency spectrum, and broadcasting standards such as bandwidth usage) made such a market choice of standards impossible. Considerable coordination (and competition) in the choice of standards was played out in the context of meetings of standards committees. Figure 13.2 shows the development of the HDTV 'industry'; the industry is still evolving in the sense that we discuss below.

Technical research for building an HDTV system was initiated at NHK, the Japanese state-owned broadcaster, as early as 1971. A number of product prototypes were demonstrated, starting in 1981. At the same time, attempts at choosing standards were

297

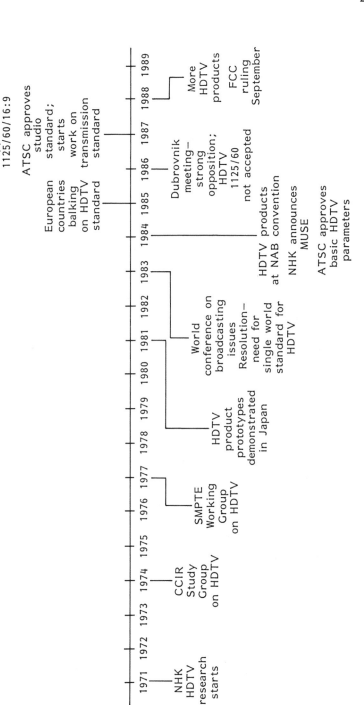

FIGURE 13.2  Chronology of key events in the HDTV industry

made, with the World Conference on Broadcasting issuing a resolution on the need for a single world standard for HDTV in 1983.
Additional products were demonstrated in 1984 as NHK
announced a transmission standard called MUSE, and there was
also support for these standards in the US. However, by 1985,
there were significant concerns in Europe that the choice of standards developed by and favorable to Japanese producers would
lead to domination by Japanese producers of the worldwide
consumer electronics market. The product concept for HDTV
allows wide screen displays with an aspect ratio (length to height
ratio) of 16 : 9 as against the usual 4 : 3 aspect ratio in current television standards. The product concept also promises much higher
resolution than current television standards (having more than
1000 lines relative to the 525 lines of resolution in current television).

While the product concept in general has seen agreement, the
parameter choices have divided firms. Choices of certain parameters would provide substantial advantages to some firms over
others, and choices that favor some technologies would also favor
some players over others. Some of the technologies needed to
provide effectively and efficiently the functionalities in the
product concept remain to be refined, especially if digital transmission and large flat screen displays are foreseen as essential in
the development of HDTV. Detailed descriptions of the evolution
of the industry, the prototypes of products introduced over time,
and the positions of firms within standardization committees are
provided by Hariharan (1990).

The vigor of the battle for HDTV standards reflects the strategic
importance of standards to the competitive positions of firms. The
choice of 1125 lines for HDTV was proposed by NHK and
adopted for the Japanese market as a compromise between the
markets that now operate under the NTSC standard of 525 lines
(such as North America and Japan), and those that operate under
PAL or SECAM standards of 625 lines (such as European countries and the majority of countries elsewhere in the world). But
the choice that was made to facilitate the adoption of a global
standard for HDTV has failed to satisfy the firms that dominate
either market. The confrontation between consumer electronics
firms from Europe and Japan has centered on standards, although
the fundamental concerns are related not to the technical super-
iority of one set of standards over another but to the competitive
consequences of adopting one set of standards.

TABLE 13.1    The phases of industry evolution

| Phase I | Phase II | Phase III |
|---------|----------|-----------|
| Product concept and technology development | Structuring of the industry | Market expansion |
| Product concept competition | Competition for structuring the industry | Product–market competition |
| Competition in developing viable products and required technologies | Competition between coalitions of firms | Standards established in the market<br><br>Competition for profits |

The difficulty in arriving at a set of standards for HDTV reflects the difficulty of setting standards for an infrastructure. In particular, infrastructure standards involve multiple stages, and coordination among a multitude of players is required. The process of standardization by committees can also be used effectively by 'laggard' firms (who are behind in technology) to delay the choice of standards. This is possible because the threat of a *de facto* standard emerging is minimal given (i) the investments (especially the irreversible components) that are necessary at various stages of the industry and (ii) the coordination that is needed to introduce the product to the customer.

## PHASES IN THE EVOLUTION OF INDUSTRY STRUCTURE AND FIRM STRATEGIES

This section describes the patterns in the evolution of the industry structure and the strategies of firms in the emerging industry. Three phases are identified in the evolution of an industry, which are shown in TABLE 13.1. We now describe the three phases, the nature of competition in each phase, and the strategic imperatives for 'success' in each phase. We illustrate this conceptualization with examples from the two industries discussed above.

The first phase in the evolution of the industry is characterized as *competition for product concepts*. The uncertainty inherent in emerging markets creates the problem of 'discovering' the product functionalities desired by customers, and the prices at which the product will be able to penetrate the market. The process of discovering the features and functionalities that products should have is a process of *active experimentation and learning* from the market and incorporating the learning in subsequent actions. This learning by the firm may come from the outcomes of its own choices and actions as well as from the outcomes of choices and actions of other firms in the market. In the case of the VCR industry, the long sequence of product introductions, none of which managed to achieve a level of sales consistent with a mass market, reflects the dimensions along which the product concept had to improve before it became a true 'home VCR.' Such learning from the market and the associated technological progress was necessary to find a viable product concept. In particular, this process of learning was necessary to discover the *price–performance–feature mix* and the *unique value bundle* (such as time-shift, compact size, longer recording times and affordable prices) which led to the development of the mass market for the home VCR.

The second phase commences *after the appropriate product concept has been 'discovered'* and is the phase in which multiple product standards compete to become the dominant design (or industry standard). The second phase is therefore characterized as the *competition to structure an industry* or to *set industry standards*. The growing acceptance of the product (even though from a small base) indicates the arrival of the 'winning' product concept. In the second phase, the competition among firms is to set industry standards, since the arrival of standards affects the competitive positions of firms. This is also the phase in which the structure of the industry achieves some stability as investments are made by firms to perform the various value-adding activities. With the emergence of standards and the growth in the market, firms now make large irreversible investments for the delivery of the product and auxiliary services to the customer.

Compatibility standards lead to installed base benefits so that the value of a particular product or format is higher corresponding to the number of compatible products in use. This installed base benefit arises from (i) increased variety of complementary products that are available, (ii) lower prices for complementary products, and (iii) the ability to share complementary products.

Some of these benefits have been discussed under the rubric of network externalities or positive consumption externalities (Farrell and Saloner, 1985, 1986; Katz and Shapiro, 1985, 1986a, 1986b). In the presence of installed base benefits, the competition among firms becomes the competition to build an installed base through market penetration.

The third phase is characterized as the *competition for profits* and takes place *within a defined industry structure* that has emerged from the second phase after the development of standards and with the growth in the market. The competition in this phase has been studied and described in detail by traditional research in economics and strategy. In this phase, the market is maturing and an industry structure that is stable (relative to the state of flux characterizing the previous two phases) has already emerged.

The strategic imperatives, i.e. what the strategic choices of a firm in the industry need to address, vary from one phase to the other. The strategic choices that will lead to success in each phase are different. In addition, since the phases are linked in terms of the evolution of the industry, the choices of firms are important for their long-run competitive positions. In the following sections, we discuss the strategic imperatives in each phase.

## STRATEGIC IMPERATIVES IN PHASE I

In Phase I, the uncertainty regarding the product concept that will be preferred by customers makes it difficult for firms to commit to a particular course of action through the allocation of resources to a specific product concept or standard. There is immense value in maintaining *flexibility* in this phase of industry evolution since little is known or easily predicted about the future evolution of the industry. In particular, there is considerable value in learning from the market about the preferences of customers and about the technologies needed to develop product concepts that will address the needs of customers. The sources of these learning experiments are trials by the firm or the outcomes of trials by other firms. For example, in the VCR industry, the product concepts introduced by firms over Phase I reflect this learning. Similarly, manufacturers of prototypes in HDTV often used feedback from leading edge users (to whom they had donated the equipment) to refine their product concepts. Firms, such as RCA, which failed to learn fell behind in the race to develop a viable product concept in the VCR industry.

The second strategic imperative in Phase I is to accumulate technological learning which is broad and transferrable to a variety of specific product standards. For example, in the absence of a clear vision of which particular product concept will emerge as victorious, firms can only (i) *build broad competencies in the family of technologies that are likely to be of importance in the industry*, and (ii) *build the strategic infrastructure with which to commercialize their products*. The concept of an appropriate family of technologies is straightforward. Technologies that are likely to be used to deliver the desired functionalities need to be identified initially, developed, and refined over time. For example, in the VCR industry, a number of technologies were in contention in the early stages, such as magnetic tape recording, optical/laser technology, and so on. Of these, only magnetic tape was capable of providing the functionality of recording. Within magnetic tape media, the techniques to improve recording quality such as helical scanning, compactness, and so on were developed not by a single firm but by a variety of firms, and subsequently incorporated in the products of almost all firms. Similarly, the improvements in HDTV on encoding and compression to reduce bandwidth requirements were incremental, cumulative and across firms. In the proposed display systems for HDTV, some firms were building up the capability for large flat panel systems through product introductions in other business, such as laptop computers, which used similar display technologies.

The strategic infrastructure is the configuration of assets needed to deliver products to the market. This would include brand name capital and reputation, an established set of relationships in a firm's distribution system, and a network of outlets for auxiliary services such as after-sales maintenance and service. These assets are useful precisely because they take time to build. A firm having such a strategic infrastructure has the advantage of being able to deliver its products to the customer faster than a firm that has to build such an infrastructure from scratch. For example, firms such as Sony, Matsushita, and Philips all had established brand names, and distribution networks for consumer electronics over the globe, while a firm such as Ampex, which had been a pioneer in developing many of the technologies for the VCR, had always been focused on the professional market and did not have the strategic infrastructure for the consumer electronics market;

neither did Ampex succeed in developing this strategic infrastructure.

## STRATEGIC IMPERATIVES IN PHASE II

In Phase II, the primary strategic imperative is to establish industry standards or the dominant design, as characterized by Utterback and Abernathy (1975). By the time we enter this phase, we have already arrived at a product concept that is desired by customers. But also needed are the investments required for performing the activities that create value for customers. The imperatives in this phase are related to achieving an installed base for the firm's standard, i.e. increasing the number of users for a firm's compatible products. Since compatibility standards lead to an installed base effect, the attractiveness for future customers of one particular standard over another depends, in part, on the sizes of the installed bases of each of the compatibility standards. Since the relative sizes of installed bases are an important consideration for users/customers in their adoption of one standard over the other, the competition among firms revolves around the sizes of the installed bases of each compatibility standard.

The possession of a strong strategic infrastructure provides a competitive advantage in building an installed base for one's standard. A strong distribution network, well-regarded brand name reputations, and service networks are all valuable assets in achieving market penetration and building an installed base. The lack of a strategic infrastructure and the time needed to build one, while facing competitors who may be stronger in this regard, provides a strategic incentive to build coalitions with other firms to achieve market penetration for one's standard and to build an installed base larger than the installed bases for competing standards.

'Winning' Phase I does not translate into 'winning' Phase II. The ability to win Phase I depends on how well the product concept provides the functionalities desired by customers. But winning in Phase II depends on the ability of the firm to achieve market penetration and to build an installed base. The ability of a firm to translate a winning position in Phase I to one in Phase II depends on a number of factors, including the imitability of the winning product concept by competitors, and the ability of the firm with the winning product concept to achieve market penetration which, in turn, may depend on assets other than the product concept alone, such as brand names, distribution networks, and the strength of one's coalition partners.

## STRATEGIC IMPERATIVES IN PHASE III

In Phase III, the primary strategic imperative facing a firm is to be competitive within the established industry structure. The competitive position of a firm depends on the ability of the firm to (i) reduce its costs, (ii) provide value to its customers, and (iii) develop innovations within the particular standards established in Phase II. This phase of competition has been studied extensively in traditional research. The emergent structure is long-lived but not permanent. Progress in technology and changes in customer tastes may lead to a future restructuring of the industry.

A firm's ability to be competitive in Phase III depends on three factors. The firm must deliver value to the customer, which it does by building quality and reliability in its products. It must have a competitive cost position so that it is not at a disadvantage relative to its competitors. Finally, it should be able to design new features and innovations into its products, which again are valued by customers.

As in the transition from Phase I to Phase II, 'winning' Phase II does not automatically give one a 'win' in Phase III. Competition in Phase III depends on the ability of the firm to reduce its costs, to provide value to customers and to innovate with new products and features within the established standards. Any actions taken in Phase II that provide a firm with an advantage on the three dimensions mentioned above will translate into a better competitive position in Phase III, such as OEM strategies which reduce costs through scale economies from higher volumes.

## STRATEGIC WINDOWS OF OPPORTUNITY

The conceptualization of the evolution in terms of the three phases has profound implications for firms in an industry. The relative length of time for each phase of the process shows a striking pattern. Phase I, in which the firm engages in a process of experimentation and learning, and building competences, can be relatively long. Phase II, in which the industry structure is defined, can be relatively short, as in the VCR industry, or long, as in the case of HDTV. Phase III, in which the opportunities for profits arise for firms, can be long or short, depending on the pace of technological progress.

There is a strategic window of opportunity in which the industry structure emerges. This window of opportunity is the period of time between the arrival of a 'winning' product concept and the time after which the firm will be unable to change the structure of the industry since specific investments tied to a particular standard have already been made by competitors and customers. The window of opportunity in the case of the VCR industry is estimated by us to be very short: around 3 years. The case of HDTV reflects the other extreme: the difficulty of arriving at a set of standards. The standards for HDTV have to be chosen before the service can be delivered because no unilateral choice of standards is possible. A purely market-determined set of *de facto* standards is virtually impossible given the nature of the standards required, the difficulty of coordination across the set of players in the industry, the relatively large investments needed to initiate HDTV service, and asymmetric benefits in switching to HDTV across the various stages of production, transmission, emission and reception.

Strategic windows of opportunity may open and close quite rapidly. In the VCR case, the process of competition for a product concept (Phase I) was played out over 20 years, but the window in which the industry was structured (Phase II) was relatively short. Why did the window of opportunity open and close so rapidly? In our estimation, it was the relatively quick diffusion of the product in the market and the establishment of an infrastructure for the industry through the investments made by the major players that represented a commitment on their part to a particular standard. In industries in which there are installed base benefits, there are positive feedback effects—a particular product standard is preferred over others because it has a larger installed base. This results in an outcome in which one standard starts to dominate the market as the market grows. An early but small lead in the installed base can, through positive feedback, result in the domination of the industry by one standard (Arthur, 1983; David, 1985). In the case of HDTV, the product could not be delivered to customers until a set of standards had been chosen.

The establishment of *de facto* standards was not a viable option. The absence of a viable option to penetrate the market in order to force the choice of a set of standards in the case of HDTV makes it possible for firms to delay the ultimate choice of a particular set of standards.

The conceptualization also emphasizes the links between the three phases. Leadership for a firm in Phase III, which provides it with the opportunity to reap profits, depends also on the firm's actions in Phases I and II. A firm must be sensitive to the market learning needed in Phase I, and the need to act quickly in Phase II to capitalize on an emerging consensus in the market on the dominant product concept. Firms may fall behind and fail to catch up in Phase III, if they do not address properly the strategic imperatives in Phases I and II.

## WHAT IS THE CONCEPT OF STRATEGY?

The very concept of strategy demands re-evaluation in the context of our findings and our discussion. TABLE 13.2 summarizes the changing role of strategy in the three phases of industry evolution. By extending our focus to the competition before the emergence of a well-defined industry, we highlight two key dimensions in the concept of strategy that are ignored when attention is focused solely on the competition within a well-defined industry structure: market learning and competence building.

Market learning and competence building are key requirements in the early phases of industry evolution. In the absence of a clear vision of how the industry will evolve, the strategy of a firm is concerned with building broad competences necessary for it to be a major player in the industry. In Phase I, each product introduction, by any player, is the beginning of a learning cycle which becomes the basis for (i) identifying the technologies that need to be developed by the firm and (ii) incorporating refinements to the product concept based on learning from the market.

In Phase II, the key strategic requirements in the industry are directed at market penetration. This often entails making strong commitments in plant capacities and other choices directed at increasing one's volumes, especially in the presence of economies of scale.

TABLE 13.2   Strategy in the phases of industry evolution

| Key issue | Phase I | Phase II | Phase III |
|---|---|---|---|
| Point of transition | Creation of a viable product concept | Stability in industry standards and value-added structure | Next revolution |
| Basis of competition | Functionalities in product concept; developing technologies to to deliver functionalities | Creating an industry structure for competitive advantage | Profits Market share |
| Strategic imperatives | Building a strategic infrastructure Building broad competences | Market penetration Installed base Building coalitions | Cost control Differentiation Innovation within standards |
| | 'Learning' | 'Committing' | 'Competing' |

In the final phase, the key strategic requirements are related to achieving competitive cost positions, providing value to customers, and developing innovations within the established standard. Learning can be directed at each of these strategic requirements.

The learning objectives vary from phase to phase. In the first phase, the firm attempts to learn about the product concept that customers desire, and the technologies that should be developed to deliver the product concept. In the second phase, the learning by the firm is concerned with information regarding the features desired by customers, and the price–performance trade-offs made by customers; all of which are concerned with increasing the installed base of the product. In the third phase, learning from the market is focused on how the firm's costs can be reduced, and on how the firm can increase the value it delivers to its customers (e.g. what new features need to be incorporated to make its products more attractive to its customers).

## APPENDIX A

### RESEARCH DESIGN

The results presented in this chapter are part of a major project on the competitive consequences of standards. The conceptualization presented in this paper draws only on the study of two industries: the VCR and the HDTV industries. Data were collected from a variety of secondary and primary sources through detailed interviews with senior managers responsible for the strategy of the firm in the particular product class. The interviews were semistructured and each lasted around 2 hours. Based on the secondary materials and interview notes, research cases describing in detail the evolution of the industry were then written on each of the two industries. The data from the research cases are used as illustrative examples in the conceptualization discussed in the chapter.

### REFERENCES

Arthur, W.B. (1983). Competing technologies and lock-in by historical small events: The dynamics of allocation under increasing returns. Center for Economic Policy Research, Stanford University, Technological Innovation Project Working Paper No. 4, Publication No. 43.

David, P. (1985). Clio and the economics of QWERTY. *American Economic Review*, **75**, 332–336.

Farrell, J. and Saloner, G. (1985). Standardization, compatibility and innovation. *Rand Journal of Economics*, **16**(1), 70–83.

Farrell, J. and Saloner, G. (1986). Installed base and compatibility: Innovation, product preannouncement, and predation. *American Economic Review*, **76**, 940–955.

Hariharan, S. (1990). Technological compatibility, standards and global competition: The dynamics of industry evolution and competitive strategies. University of Michigan, unpublished doctoral dissertation.

Katz, M. and Shapiro, C. (1985). Network externalities, competition, and compatibility. *American Economic Review*, **75**(3), 424–440.

Katz, M. and Shapiro, C. (1986a). Technology adoption in the presence of network externalities. *Journal of Political Economy*, **94**(4), 822–841.

Katz, M. and Shapiro, C. (1986b). Product compatibility choice in a market with technological progress. *Oxford Economic Papers*, **38**, Supplement, 146–165.

Porter, M.E. (1980). *Competitive Strategy: Techniques for Analyzing Industries and Competitors*. New York: Free Press.

Spence, A.M. (1979). Investment strategy and growth in a new market. *Bell Journal of Economics*, **10**(1), 1–19.

Utterback, J.M. and Abernathy, A. (1975). A dynamic model of process and product innovation. *Omega*, **3**(6), 639–656.

# 14

# Entry into Threatening Young Industries: Challenges and Pitfalls[1]

CLAYTON G. SMITH, ARNOLD C. COOPER

## INTRODUCTION

The emergence of a new industry based on a major product innovation (such as the electronic calculator industry during the 1960s)
often poses a threat of substitution to companies with a base in a
more established industry (e.g. the producers of electromechanical
calculators). During the early stages of industry development, the
extent to which a substitution effect will occur is rarely clear.
Nevertheless, the managers of firms in the established, threatened
industry must decide how to respond to an innovation that may
have the potential to destroy their companies' existing business
(Cooper and Schendel, 1976; Foster, 1986).

This chapter considers the decisions confronting managers of
firms in threatened industries and, in particular, the alternative of
entering the emerging young industry. Such a response would
seem to represent a natural extension of a company's existing
business, one that, at a minimum, would allow the firm to build
upon its established marketing capabilities (including brand
names, customer relationships, and channels of distribution).
Furthermore, a strategy of participation in the young industry

*Building the Strategically-Responsive Organization.*
Edited by H. Thomas, D. O'Neal, R. White and D. Hurst.

provides a hedge, an opportunity to replace lost sales if the traditional product is displaced.

Our focus is on the challenges and pitfalls that are associated with this strategic response to a technological threat. The analysis is based upon a study of eight young industries and twenty-seven 'threatened firms,' with the companies being chosen based upon the strong competitive positions that they enjoyed in their home industries. TABLE 14.1 lists the industries, the firms, and the time periods over which the young industries were examined. (The young industries and firms were studied during the period that roughly corresponded to the 'introduction' and 'rapid growth' stages of development.) Nearly 250 sources of information from the secondary literature were considered in the analysis.

Each young industry involved the commercialization of a major product innovation. The nature of each innovation was such that, while firms from the threatened industry were sometimes able to build upon their existing technical capabilities, important new capabilities were required that were not associated with the traditional product. For example, the CT scanner harnessed both X-ray and data processing technology. Thus, while entrants from the X-ray equipment industry were able to build upon existing technical capabilities, they also had to develop important new resources and skills pertaining to computer technology and overall product design. Several innovations were what has been termed 'competence-destroying'—so fundamentally different that the technical capabilities for the traditional product were largely irrelevant for the new (Tushman and Anderson, 1986). Finally, these new industries attracted not only firms from the threatened industries, but also start-up firms and companies from other industries as well.

Prior work has suggested that, where established firms enter threatening industries, they do not pursue the new product aggressively because they are constrained by sunk costs and internal political difficulties (Foster, 1986). Other studies have considered how innovations can affect the value of existing competences, and suggest that unrelated new technologies can be especially challenging (Smith, 1990; Tushman and Anderson, 1986). However, little consideration has been given to the pitfalls that can be encountered by entrants from a threatened industry; in particular, the ways in which their experience in the threatened industry may affect their perceptions of how to compete effectively in the new field have received little attention.

TABLE 14.1  Summary of industries and firms considered

| Young industry (time period)* | Established industry and firms considered |
|---|---|
| Ball-point pens (1945–1962) | Fountain pens Eversharp Inc. Parker Pen Co. Sheaffer Pen Co. |
| CT scanners (1973–1979) | X-ray/nuclear medical equipment General Electric Co. G.D. Searle & Co. Technicare Corp. |
| Diesel–electric locomotives (1924–1953) | Steam locomotives American Locomotive Co. Baldwin Locomotive Works |
| Electric typewriters (1925–1965) | Mechanical typewriters Remington Rand Royal Typewriter Co. Smith–Corona, Inc. Underwood Company |
| Electronic calculators (1962–1976) | Electromechanical calculators Litton Industries (Monroe) SCM Corp. Singer Co. (Friden) Victor Comptometer Corp. |
| Electronic watches (1969–1980) | Mechanical watches Bulova Watch Co. K. Hattori & Co. (Seiko) Timex Corp. |
| Microwave ovens (1955–1983) | Gas/electric ovens General Electric Co. Magic Chef, Inc. Roper Corp. Tappan Co. |
| Transistors (1948–1968) | Vacuum tubes General Electric Co. RCA Raytheon Manufacturing Co. Sylvania Electric Products, Inc. |

*Using decision rules which were based upon yearly changes in unit sales volume and industry development histories, the young industries and the firms were studied during the time period that roughly corresponded to the 'introduction' and 'rapid growth' stages of development.

We begin by considering the characteristics of young industries that typically develop around major product innovations, characteristics that have important implications for companies that enter an emerging field. The participation strategies of the threatened firms that entered these new industries and the challenges and pitfalls that were often encountered are then considered. The implications of the analysis for decisions concerning a strategy of participation in a threatening young industry are examined in the final section. While there are no assured success formulas, our intention is to highlight some of the problems that can be encountered and suggest possibilities for avoiding them.

## YOUNG INDUSTRIES AND TECHNOLOGICAL THREATS

Any assessment of a technological threat obviously involves an appraisal of the new technology and the extent to which it will have advantages in meeting user needs. What may be less obvious, however, is the need to appraise the nature of the industry that is likely to develop around the innovation, and how competition in the new field may differ from competition in the threatened industry. Our study of these eight young industries highlights common patterns of industry development—patterns that managers of threatened firms should be sensitive to if they consider entering an emerging field that poses a threat of substitution.

In the eight industries, early versions of the new product were always crude and expensive, and there was great uncertainty about how rapidly the market would develop. For example, the first electronic watches were unreliable, and so bulky and unattractive that they were sometimes referred to as 'quarter-pounders.' Consumers were also deterred from purchasing early microwave ovens by the high price—roughly $1500, in 1950 dollars—and by the fact that microwave cooking left cold spots and changed food colors. In some instances, the initial lack of complementary products (e.g. cookbooks and cookware for microwave cooking) also retarded the market's development.

In this context, early entrants invariably had to overcome substantial technical difficulties, and they often had to remain patient when the market developed slowly. Indeed, in some instances, the new product may never gain widespread acceptance. But in all of the cases studied here, an industry did begin to emerge, and a time of rapid growth followed that promised substantial opportunities to participating firms. Beyond the prospect of significant increases in revenues, the environment created by burgeoning demand often limited competitive pressures and permitted lucrative profit margins. In addition to later entrants from the established, threatened industry, the growing promise of the new product encouraged start-up firms and established companies from other industries to enter the field as well.

Even in the 'growth stage,' however, these industries were characterized by high levels of uncertainty and risk. During this period, there was usually no clear success formula, and firms often followed different strategies; only time proved—or disproved—the validity of the assumptions on which these strategies were based. Thus, the producers of steam locomotives found that their new competitor in diesel–electrics, General Motors, disdained their traditional custom manufacturing methods and produced standard products for inventory instead. In fact, firms from the threatened industry and entrants from outside that industry often had different ideas about how to compete. In such cases, the traditional firms had to appraise and respond to the novel strategies that their new competitors chose to pursue.

During the time before 'dominant designs' became established, there was much experimentation with different technical approaches and product designs (Abernathy and Utterback, 1978). In the transistor industry's early years, for example, it was not clear whether germanium or silicon transistors would prevail. Similarly, in the electronic watch industry, models with light emitting diode (LED) and liquid crystal displays (LCDs) dueled for market acceptance. Industry participants had to decide which approaches 'to bet on,' and some companies committed to what later proved to be blind alleys.

Rapid rates of change characterized the industries as well. To stay in the game, participants often had to field successive generations of the product as the state-of-the-art advanced; in CT scanners, four generations followed one another in almost as many years. Companies also had to cope with constant changes in manufacturing methods. In transistors, one vacuum tube firm built the most automated plant for germanium transistors shortly before silicon transistors and newer manufacturing processes came to dominate. And while the competitive environment was usually not intense initially, cut-throat competition often emerged quickly when the period of rapid growth began to wane. In this context, participating firms needed strong R&D and financial capabilities to remain competitive, and to absorb the inevitable setbacks and risks.

For firms from the threatened industry, long-standing competitive strengths did not necessarily provide an advantage in the new field. All of the new industries required technical capabilities that were not associated with the traditional product; in several cases, the traditional technical capabilities were largely irrelevant. For example, the ability of electromechanical calculator firms to produce precise mechanical parts was of little value for electronic calculators. Even established marketing capabilities for the traditional product did not always provide a long-term advantage, as several vacuum tube firms discovered. While their distribution networks were important in the tube business as a means of quickly delivering replacement components, the value of this capability for transistors waned as the new product became more and more reliable.

TABLE 14.2   Characteristics of young industries

| Attribute | Managerial implications |
| --- | --- |
| New product crude and expensive at first; sometimes, an initial lack of complementary products | Difficult to judge rate at which market will develop; often must overcome substantial technical difficulties, and remain patient if market develops slowly |
| Entrants often start-up firms and established firms from other industries | Difficult to predict competitors' actions; must appraise and respond to 'different' strategies |
| Alternative and unproven technical approaches and product designs | Risks associated with 'betting on' particular approaches/designs |
| Rapid rates of change, especially in product and manufacturing methods | Strong R&D and financial capabilities needed to remain competitive over time |
| New technical resources and skills required. Existing technical/ marketing capabilities sometimes of limited or little value | Established competitive strengths may not provide a long-term advantage |

In summary, these industries were characterized by high levels of uncertainty, by new competitors that had different ideas about how to compete, by competing technical approaches and product designs, by rapid rates of change and, in some cases, by the obsolescence of technical/marketing capabilities for the traditional product. The characteristics of the young industries and the corresponding managerial implications are displayed in TABLE 14.2. Because of their dynamic nature, competitive positions were often unstable; success was often transient. Commitment to these new technologies was like entering a poker game in which the stakes kept increasing and the rules were not at all clear. These industries differed markedly from the mature, relatively stable industries that were threatened.

---

## THE STRATEGY OF PARTICIPATION: CHALLENGES AND PITFALLS

We now consider the strategic issues confronting a firm that responds to a technological threat by entering the new field. A strategy of participation involves determinations concerning: (i) the timing of entry; (ii) the magnitude of commitments, (iii) the degree of organizational separation between new and traditional product activities; and (iv) the competitive strategy for the new business. In the following subsections, the participation strategies of the 27 threatened firms are examined along these dimensions. Particular attention is given to the problems that many of the companies encountered, and to possible reasons for their occurrence.

---

### TIMING OF ENTRY

Prior research indicates that early entry by established firms into a young industry is associated with higher levels of long-term performance (Smith and Cooper, 1988). Balanced against this, however, are the risks of early entry, including the risk that the new product may never achieve commercial success. When faced with a major product innovation, a firm must often contend with the challenges of assessing the potential of an unproven technology and the speed with which market acceptance will occur. Furthermore, it must appraise the resources and skills needed to compete at a time when the requirements for success are not clear. Overall, a firm must decide whether and when to enter under rather uncertain circumstances.

It is often thought that established firms, when threatened by major product innovations, lack the vision and will to commit to the new technology (see, for example, Levitt, 1960). In reviewing these 27 companies, however, it was found that all entered the young industries. Indeed, 21 entered relatively early, before sales of the new product began to grow rapidly. Far from ignoring the new technology, these firms seemed to recognize its possibilities at an early date. But, surprisingly, 8 of the 21 early entrants made abortive commitments, in which they entered but then withdrew before achieving much success.

For example, Eversharp and Sheaffer, leading producers of fountain pens, were two of the earliest companies to introduce ball-point pens in 1946. Unfortunately, their new pens—and those of many new entrants as well—tended to skip, blot, and even leak into pockets. After an initial fad phase, public disenchantment set in and the ball-point pen industry virtually disappeared. Eversharp and Sheaffer both withdrew from the market and many of the new entrants went bankrupt. (In 1950, improved ball-point pens were introduced by a new firm, Papermate, and the young industry developed rapidly.)

Similar patterns were observed with producers of mechanical typewriters. Remington and Royal produced electric typewriters as early as 1925. However, their initial offerings were bulky, noisy, and prone to break down; the two firms discontinued their efforts after three or four years.' (IBM, which never made mechanical models, introduced the first successful electric typewriter in 1934.) American Locomotive introduced a number of experimental diesel–electric engines beginning in 1924. However, because of their high weight-to-power ratio and other difficulties, American subsequently ceased its development efforts. (In 1934, General Motors, which never produced steam locomotives, made the first successful introduction of a diesel–electric engine based upon improved diesel engine technology developed in its laboratories.)

In several cases, it appeared that the firm had little in the way of an R&D orientation that might have provided experience in managing the process of introducing *and improving* major product innovations. While they recognized the new product's potential, they seemed unable to make the further advancements that later led to commercial success. Furthermore, in industries such as diesel–electric locomotives and electronic calculators, the new technology was so different from the traditional one that the technical capabilities for the old product were largely irrelevant. At the outset, the firms may not have fully recognized the fact that their existing technical capabilities would be of little value in the new field. But this undoubtedly made it more difficult for them to overcome the technical obstacles that all of the early entrants faced.

Of the eight firms whose initial entry was abortive, two companies resumed their commercial efforts within a year. However, on average, the other six did not do so for more than nine years. For example, American Locomotive did not renew its efforts with diesel–electrics until 1936, two years after General Motors made the first successful introduction of the new product. Having been 'burned' once, these firms seemed content to leave the pioneering to others. With one exception (General Electric in microwave ovens), the six firms did not resume their commercial efforts until after the new product's viability had been demonstrated by other firms from outside the established industry.

## MAGNITUDE OF COMMITMENTS

Where corporate management chooses to enter the new field, important decisions must be made over time concerning the magnitude of commitments. The firm's initial involvement could vary widely, ranging from a token effort with only a few prototypes, to major and immediate investments. The magnitude of commitments may also change over time as the young industry evolves. Prior research has argued that major early investments should lead to greater long-term success, as the firm reaps the benefits of a stronger competitive position (Biggadike, 1979). However, such investments may also lead to substantial commitments to the 'wrong' technical approach, or to a market that develops very slowly.

Of the 27 companies examined, 24 made substantial investments over time. But while 4 of the 24 firms took an aggressive stance from the start, the investments made over time by most of the remaining 20 were uneven. It was quite common for these latter firms to make a limited initial commitment (relative to their capabilities), and permit other companies—usually from outside the established industry—to lead in improving the new product and in gaining market acceptance for it. Typically, they would then mount a more vigorous effort as the industry developed. This approach had the virtue of delaying major investments until after many of the technical and market uncertainties had faded. However, as it turned out, the net result in most cases was to fall behind, making it much more difficult to establish a viable competitive position.

For example, while Timex entered electronic watches early, the company continued to concentrate on mechanical watches in its marketing efforts. The firm was also slow to develop R&D/manufacturing capabilities for semiconductor components (which were critical to the new product's performance, quality, and cost), preferring instead to rely on outside suppliers for its requirements. Only after prices for electronic watches began to tumble into the firm's low-price niche did Timex begin to make a strong commitment. However, the combination of increasing competition and a late start in mastering the technology proved to be a severe handicap; each time the firm introduced a new watch line, other producers had already fielded superior models at lower prices. In 1980, after 4 years of heavy investments, Timex was still struggling to build and market electronic watches profitably.

Similarly, while Litton/Monroe and SCM entered the electronic calculator industry at an early date, their initial efforts largely took the form of marketing desktop models that were produced by Canon and Toshiba (firms that had never been active in electromechanical calculators). To a considerable degree, this was due to their belief that electronic calculators would be mainly used by scientists and engineers who had previously relied on computers to fulfill their computational needs. Subsequently, the broader applicability of the new product in the office equipment and other segments became apparent, and Monroe and SCM began a serious effort to develop their own technical skills for electronic calculators. But by this time, Canon, Toshiba, and other new entrants had gained a formidable lead in the requisite R&D and manufacturing capabilities, and were rapidly becoming established in the market under their own brand names.

In summary, the firms examined typically made substantial commitments, but only after the potential of the new product became clear. Such firms seemed to harbor the expectation (initially) that the new product would not penetrate the core markets of the traditional business. In several cases, there were also concerns that the new product's early imperfections could tarnish the firm's reputation; as such, there was a reluctance to make a full commitment until the product was 'proven.' In virtually every case, however, these companies appeared to underestimate the ability of entrants from outside the threatened industry to overcome important technological obstacles, to gain market acceptance for the new product, and to establish a defensible competitive position. Only after the miscalculation became apparent did these firms begin to mount a more vigorous effort.

---

## DEGREE OF ORGANIZATIONAL SEPARATION

The third area to be considered concerns the degree of organizational separation between new and traditional product activities. In choosing to enter the young industry, it would be natural to consider utilizing the established organization for the new product. Potentially, this arrangement could provide significant cost savings, facilitate the coordination of efforts with the traditional product, and permit the new business to benefit from the skills of executives from the traditional business. At the same time, however, it is important to have decision makers who are enthusiastically committed to the new product, even though it may cannibalize sales of the traditional product (Foster, 1986). Furthermore, it may also be necessary to violate the conventional wisdom that has developed over time in the established organization.

Specific information on parent–business organizational decisions was available for 17 of the 27 firms; 11 of the 17 appeared to have established close organizational linkages between new and traditional product activities. For example, based upon information obtained from annual reports, business articles, industry studies and other sources, it appeared that Remington, Royal, Smith–Corona, and Underwood handled the production, sales, and distribution of electric typewriters through the departments that had been utilized for mechanical models.

However, in a number of cases where the new and traditional technologies were fundamentally different, decisions to utilize the established organization proved to be ill-advised. Thus, while other firms were lowering costs by building new manufacturing facilities, Victor Comptometer decided to use its existing organization and build electronic calculators at an old three-story plant in Chicago, where electromechanical machines were being made. Victor eventually made nearly everything for its electronic calculators except the semiconductor chips at this facility. Unfortunately, the net result was a line of high-priced, high-cost machines that brought little or no return. As an executive from a rival firm said later, 'Victor failed to realize that its mechanical and technical expertise meant nothing in the electronics age.'

More generally, when the new product was closely tied to the established organization, business strategy decisions were often constrained by concerns about the obsolescence of existing investments. This appears to have been true for RCA, where transistor activities were initially placed within the vacuum tube division. In 1960, 8 years after entering the new field, RCA recognized the problem and separated its tube and semiconductor operations. However, the two divisions were recombined 3 years later when the transistor unit began to experience losses. The latter decision, in addition to reintroducing the original problem, apparently undermined the morale of the semiconductor people, as their unit's strategic direction kept changing with each reorganization (Soukup, 1979; Tilton, 1971).

Even when an independent unit was created for the new product, other problems sometimes emerged. At Timex, the decision to establish a separate organization for electronic watches in 1976 led to fierce rivalry between the mechanical and electronic groups. One old-guard manager acknowledged that his people had stood by while new managers in the electronic unit made mistakes that the company had made years earlier. Indeed, the rivalry became so intense that the electronic people accused the mechanical group of withholding essential information, and senior management had to enter the fray to lay the charge to rest (Anonymous, 1983). Needless to say, these difficulties compounded the firm's competitive problems in electronic watches.

These examples illustrate the fact that there were no easy answers to the question of how to organize the new business. There were trade-offs between the synergies to be gained from having close linkages with the established organization, and the benefits of having the flexibility and drive of an independent unit. However, the tendency among these companies was to forge close organizational linkages between activities for the new and traditional products. This decision may also have influenced the strategy that was developed for competing in the young industry, which we will now consider.

## COMPETITIVE STRATEGY FOR THE NEW BUSINESS

In making decisions concerning competitive strategy for the new business, companies from the established, threatened industry have a substantial base of experience to draw upon. Particularly when the firm's strategy in the established industry has historically been successful, it would be natural to consider employing the same basic approach in the new field (essentially to fold the new product into the existing strategy). However, if the new technology requires, or makes possible, different product concepts or ways of competing, strategies that are based on 'the conventional wisdom' may be less likely to succeed.

In cases where novel product concepts emerged, the traditional firms rarely pioneered the new design. For example, when Tappan and General Electric entered the infant microwave oven industry in the mid-1950s, they utilized product designs (built-in models and free-standing double ovens) that were quite similar to conventional models. However, because such designs implied the replacement of a household's existing range, and also since microwave ovens proved to be ill-suited for cooking (as opposed to heating) meats and other foods, sales were very limited. Indeed, rapid market growth did not begin until after Raytheon/Amana entered the field with its countertop design in 1967—a design that was intended to *supplement* a household's existing range. Furthermore, while other new entrants quickly followed Raytheon's lead, conventional oven producers were slow to respond to the promising countertop innovation (Smith, 1985). Tappan and GE did not begin self-manufacture of countertop ovens until 1973 and 1974, respectively, more than half a decade after Raytheon/Amana pioneered the countertop design.

Similarly, where new ways of competing emerged, traditional firms were usually slow to recognize the implications. In electromechanical calculators, for example, direct-sales and service organizations had historically been important requirements for success. In fact, the leading producers of such machines each had approximately 1500 sales and service personnel in several hundred company-owned branches. As a senior executive at Friden said at the time, 'You don't have a chance in this business without this capability.' However, firms from outside the established industry chose to sell their electronic desktop calculators through office equipment dealers. Because this permitted them to deal with a few hundred dealers rather than with thousands of end users, a sales force of fewer than 50 people was sufficient.

Office equipment dealers did not have the facilities for servicing electronic calculators. However, as the reliability of the new product (which had few moving parts) improved relative to electromechanical models (which had an average downtime of 10%), the need for a strong service network waned. The new competitors also engaged in aggressive price competition, a practice that was uncommon in electromechanical calculators. As the new technology improved over time, market prices for most desktop models fell to levels that made it difficult to cover the costs of direct-selling efforts. As a result, several firms from the threatened industry, such as SCM Corp., were eventually forced to develop a network of office equipment dealers for their electronic calculators (Creative Strategies International, 1978; Majumdar, 1977).

Analogous patterns were found in other industries. In ball-point pens, the concept of a throwaway pen was pioneered not by a fountain pen producer, but by BIC. In diesel–electric locomotives, it was General Motors that pioneered the concept of a standardized locomotive produced for inventory. As in transistors, firms from the vacuum tube industry emphasized process innovation in their business strategies, as they had in vacuum tubes. In contrast, new competitors such as Texas Instruments focused on product innovation—and sometimes obsoleted the designs of transistors that the vacuum tube companies were trying to produce in volume (Tilton, 1971).

In summary, these patterns suggest that the historic experience of the threatened firms in the established industry often 'colored' their perceptions of how to compete effectively in the emerging young industry. These companies were often among the earliest entrants in the young industries, but they rarely took the lead in developing new product concepts or ways of competing that might have allowed them to better capitalize upon the new technology's potential. Rather, they tended to pursue the same basic approaches that had been successful in the established industry.

## PATTERNS OF PERFORMANCE

Given the difficulties that have been described, an obvious question is, 'What were the overall patterns of performance for these 27 firms?' To explore this issue, the firms were classified as 'successful' or 'unsuccessful' based upon their survival or non-survival in the given industry, market share data, and descriptive information concerning business performance obtained from secondary sources (e.g. annual reports, business articles, and industry surveys). As noted earlier, these 27 companies were all leading firms in the established industries that were threatened. However, despite their presumed advantages, 20 of the 27 firms were unable to develop and sustain a strong competitive position in the young industries.

The remaining 7 firms were classified as having been successful, through the end of the study period. These firms were:

- Parker Pen (ball-point pens)
- General Electric (CT scanners)
- Technicare (CT scanners)
- Smith–Corona (electric typewriters)
- Litton/Monroe (electronic calculators)
- K. Hattori/Seiko (electronic watches)
- General Electric (microwave ovens)

For these companies, there was no single path to a strong competitive position, and they, too, encountered the problems that have been described (see TABLE 14.3). The entry of 5 of the 7 firms either preceded or coincided with the 'take-off' in market sales. Of the 5 firms, GE discontinued its microwave oven effort for several years when the slow rate of market development became apparent; K. Hattori/Seiko withdrew from electronic watches for nearly a year because of technical problems with its original offering. The two remaining firms, Parker Pen and Smith–Corona, were late entrants. Both had limited R&D and financial capabilities, but their late entry allowed them to avoid some of the technical challenges that earlier entrants faced. They also focused on niche markets (high-priced ball-point pens and portable electrics) and largely avoided the more competitive mainstream segments.

Relative to their capabilities, five of the firms made significant

TABLE 14.3  The successful firms

| Company* (young industry) | Time of entry | Magnitude of commitments | Degree of organizational separation | Competitive strategy for new business |
|---|---|---|---|---|
| Parker Pen Co. (ball-point pens) | Late entrant | Strong commitment | | Traditional strategic approach employed (ignored throw-away pen segment) |
| General Electric Co. (CT scanners) | Entered at outset of growth stage | Strong commitment | High | Traditional strategic approach employed |
| Technicare Corp. (CT scanners) | Entered at outset of growth stage | Strong commitment | High | Traditional strategic approach employed |
| Smith–Corona, Inc. (electric typewriters) | Late entrant | Significant commitment | Low | Traditional strategic approach employed |
| Litton/Monroe (electronic calculators) | Early entrant | Limited to strong commitment | | Traditional strategic approach employed (slow response to emergence of new distribution methods) |
| K. Hattori/Seiko (electronic watches) | Early entrant Initial entry abortive | Strong commitment | | Traditional strategic approach employed |
| General Electric Co. (microwave ovens) | Early entrant Initial entry abortive | Limited to strong commitment | High | Traditional strategic approach employed (slow response to countertop innovation) |

*These companies were all relatively successful as of the end of the study period. However, it should be noted that the fortunes of several firms subsequently waned when they later faced severe competitive pressures from overseas manufacturers or from still newer technologies.

or strong commitments from the outset. While Litton/Monroe and General Electric in microwave ovens made only limited initial investments, their considerable R&D and financial capabilities enabled them to establish a strong position in the new field after they began to make a whole-hearted effort. Regarding organizational decisions, three of the four firms for which data were available appeared to maintain a high degree of separation between new and traditional product activities. Finally, with respect to competitive strategy decisions, these firms rarely pioneered new product concepts or ways of competing. As it turned out, however, Parker Pen was able to ignore the throw-away pen because it never threatened its high-priced niche. And while GE and Litton were eventually compelled to respond to new product concepts and methods of distribution, they did so before their position was severely undermined.

## AVOIDING THE PITFALLS

The decision to enter an emerging young industry from a base in an established, threatened industry is clearly fraught with challenges and pitfalls. The limited number of successful firms makes any discussion of assured success formulas problematic. Much may depend upon how a young industry develops, including the extent to which there prove to be sizable market segments that are not attacked by new competitors. But based upon the experiences of these 27 firms, it is possible to highlight some of the potential problems that are associated with a strategy of participation, and to suggest possibilities for avoiding them.

Regarding the time-of-entry decision, most of the firms examined recognized the possibilities of the new technology at an early date, and entered the field before the market began to grow rapidly. There was little evidence that management 'buried its head in the sand' and refused to recognize the new product's potential. However, some of the companies may not have appreciated the ramifications of an early commitment. These firms often lacked the resources and skills required to overcome the initial technical obstacles, and they sometimes became disenchanted when the market did not develop quickly.

The implication is that, in considering an early entry, management should carefully appraise the firm's technical capabilities relative to the challenges involved. The challenge is not simply to introduce the new product; it is to make the follow-on advances in performance, quality, and cost that will be required for commercial success. Where the firm's competences are lacking, it should be understood that the inevitable technical obstacles will be especially formidable; developing the necessary capabilities will be a critical task. Furthermore, management should consider the extent to which the firm has the patience and the will to overcome substantial technical difficulties and to make continuing investments even if the market develops slowly. If these qualities are lacking, a decision to enter early is likely to be regretted.

In terms of the magnitude of commitments, these firms often made limited early commitments, but mounted a more vigorous effort as the industry developed. Perhaps this was due to the high initial levels of technical/market uncertainty, or to organizational resistance to more substantial investments. However, the result in most cases was to fall behind more aggressive entrants from outside the threatened industry. Thus, where a limited early commitment is being considered, management should weigh the impact of this on the company's ability to compete later in the industry's development, possibly when other firms have established a commanding technical lead. Deferring heavy investments may be possible if the firm has very strong R&D and financial capabilities that it can bring to bear (e.g. GE in microwave ovens), or if it can find markets where competition is not established (e.g. portable electrics for Smith–Corona). But, in general, limited early commitments seem likely to impair the firm's ability to establish a viable long-term competitive position.

Concerning the degree of organizational separation, close linkages between new and traditional product activities appeared to be fairly common among these firms. Indeed, there will often be synergies to be gained from utilizing the existing organization for the new product. But in considering this approach management should recognize that decisions concerning the new product will take place within an administrative system and culture that is attuned to competition in the established industry, and the needs of the traditional business. Management should be especially sensitive to the problem of divided loyalties that can result if the existing organization is utilized, and of the constraining effect that this may have upon the firm's actions in the young industry. In addition, if the decision is made to create an independent unit for the new product, senior managers should recognize that a high level of sponsorship and protection on their part may be required for this arrangement to succeed.

Finally, with respect to the competitive strategy that is developed for the new business, there was a tendency for firms to use the basic approaches that had been successful in the established industry—to fold the new product into the traditional strategy. It may be that they viewed the new product simply as a new way of meeting needs that they had previously served (for example, cooking food with a microwave oven rather than a conventional oven). Nevertheless, these firms seemed to be slow in recognizing possibilities for employing new product concepts and ways of competing that might have allowed them to better capitalize upon the new technology's potential.

The implication is that management should be willing to allow new or experimental strategies, and should carefully monitor the approaches that are pursued by other entrants. Appraising the strategies of new competitors may be especially important, since they will often possess different resources and skills, different ideas about how to compete, and little regard for the status quo. Overall, the conventional wisdom may no longer apply. Those who view an emerging young industry through the lens of their experience in an established, threatened industry may see what is familiar more clearly than what is different. A sensitivity to the problems encountered by the firms studied here may increase the chances of success.

## NOTE

1. Following the presentation of this paper at the Strategic Management Society Conference in Toronto in 1991 it was published as: Cooper, A.C. and Smith, C.G. (1992). How established firms respond to threatening technologies. *The Academy of Management Executive*, 6(2), 55–70. We are grateful to the Academy of Management for permission to publish this revised version of our paper.

## REFERENCES

Abernathy, W.J. and Utterback, J.M. (1978). Patterns of industrial innovation. *Technology Review*, 80(7), 41–47.

Anonymous (1983). Timex takes the torture test. *Fortune*, 27 June, 112.

Biggadike, R.E. (1979). *Corporate Diversification: Entry, Strategy and Performance*. Cambridge, MA: Harvard University Press.

Cooper, A.C. and Schendel, D. (1976). Strategic responses to technological threats. *Business Horizons*, **19**, 61–69.

Creative Strategies International (1978). Electronic calculators. San Jose, CA: Creative Strategies Inc.

Foster, R.N. (1986). *Innovation: The Attacker's Advantage*. New York: Summit Books.

Levitt, T. (1960). Marketing myopia. *Harvard Business Review*, **38**(4), 26–37.

Majumdar, B.A. (1977). Innovations, product developments and technology transfers: An empirical study of dynamic competitive advantage, the case of electronic calculators. Case Western Reserve University, unpublished doctoral dissertation.

Smith, C.G. (1985). Established companies diversifying into young industries: A comparison of firms with different levels of performance. Purdue University, unpublished doctoral dissertation.

Smith, C.G. (1990). Responding to substitution threats: A framework for assessment. *Journal of Engineering and Technology Management*, **7**(1), 17–36.

Smith, C.G. and Cooper, A.C. (1988). Established companies diversifying into young industries: a comparison of firms with different levels of performance. *Strategic Management Journal*, **9**, 111–121.

Soukup, W.R. (1979). Strategic response to technological threat in the electronics components industry. Purdue University, unpublished doctoral dissertation.

Tilton, J.E. (1971). *International Diffusion of Technology: The Case of Semiconductors*. Washington, DC: Brookings Institute.

Tushman, M.L. and Anderson, P. (1986). Technological discontinuities and organizational environments. *Administrative Science Quarterly*, **31**, 439–465.

# 15

# From Barriers to Entry to Barriers to Survival

PAUL J. VERDIN, PETER J. WILLIAMSON

## COMPETITIVE ANALYSIS AND THE THREAT OF ENTRY

No competitive analysis is now complete without an examination of entry conditions. Since the 'threat of entry' was allocated a slot as one of Porter's (1980) familiar 'five forces'—his key drivers of industry profitability—it has featured in countless industry analyses and business strategy documents. The relationship hypothesized by theory suggests that the stronger the threat of new entry, the lower the average profitability of an industry, other things being equal. This relationship should be even more significant if we look at actual entry, rather than only the threat of new competitors. Yet, despite widespread acceptance of these effects, empirical studies have found little or no correlation between the gross rate of entry and profitability across different industries (Baldwin and Gorecki, 1983, 1987). Instead, we find large numbers of new entrants as the norm in most markets, be they highly profitable or not. Entry rates (expressed as a percentage of the initial stock) of 40.8% were recorded in a cross-industry sample for the US between 1978 and 1982 (Dunne, Roberts and Samuelson, 1989), for example, while the corresponding figure over a 10-year period in Canada was 37.2% (Baldwin and Gorecki, 1987).

At the same time, we also observe large numbers of firms exiting most industries, even those that are growing strongly. Our

*Building the Strategically-Responsive Organization.*
Edited by H. Thomas, D. O'Neal, R. White and D. Hurst.
Copyright © 1994 the Strategic Management Society. Published 1994 by John Wiley & Sons Ltd.

own sample of 134 industries, based on Dun and Bradstreet data for the US between 1978 and 1984, exhibits average exit rates equivalent to 39% of the initial stock (measured by number of firms) over the period. The fact that in reality firms are entering and exiting most industries with high frequency must lead us to question the traditional interpretation of barriers to entry and their practical relevance as a determinant of competition and industry profitability. The industry membrane appears to be permeable, as illustrated in FIGURE 15.1.

Linking entry and exit, however, reveals that a high percentage of those leaving the industry are relatively young firms. Dunne, Roberts and Samuelson (1988), for example, found that 64% of their sample of new US firms had exited within 5 years of entry, while a full 79% had ceased trading 10 years after commencing operations. Survival, rather than entry, then, appears to be the real challenge.

Based on these observations, this chapter reassesses the role of entry barriers as a critical feature of industry structure. Within a sample of 160 000 independent firms that entered one of 134 US three-digit SIC industries between 1978 and 1984, we find that traditional proxies of barriers to entry are able to explain only 16% of

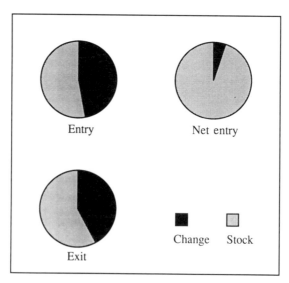

FIGURE 15.1   A large number of firms entering and exiting is the norm (computed from Dun & Bradstreet data covering 134 industries which was provided to the US Small Business Administration)

the cross-industry variance in entry rates. Rather than barriers to entry alone, the practical effect of entry appears to depend on the *barriers to survival* that new firms face post-entry. Successful entrants generally bring to the industry assets that are in short supply relative to current demand for the customer benefits these assets can deliver. These assets may embody new technology or systems for providing differentiation, which some segments of customers value. But they lack other, industry-specific assets like brand reputation on a reliable service network, which, in some industries, can only be accumulated through experience (Dierickx and Cool, 1989). Without these assets, they face a handicap relative to well-established incumbents. As a result, young firms are forced to run an uncertain, middle distance race for survival. They must attempt to accumulate the necessary industry-specific assets to reinforce their position before the incumbents destroy their differentiation, and hence their rationale for existence.

We conclude that in assessing the profit potential of an industry it is insufficient to look at barriers to entry alone. It is equally important for strategic analyses to take into account the barriers to survival that we find are faced by new entrants for up to 10 years after they are first established in an industry. This means looking beyond traditional scale, differentiation and absolute cost barriers in assessing the potential effect of new entrants on competition and profitability. More attention must be given to those product and buying characteristics that determine the importance of past experience in the market as a source of competitive advantage. Where industry-specific experience is critical, and slow and costly to accumulate, barriers to survival rise and the competitive pressures associated with entry are substantially reduced.

---

## BARRIERS TO ENTRY: THE WALLED CITY

In his seminal book, Bain (1956, p. 3) argued that the condition of entry was primarily a structural phenomenon, roughly akin to a wall, the height of which could be evaluated by:

*the advantages of established sellers in an industry over potential entrant sellers, these advantages being reflected in the extent to which established sellers can persistently raise their prices above the competitive level without attracting new firms to enter the industry.*

For those industries where barriers to entry were 'great' or 'substantial' Bain went on to predict: 'Relatively stable industry structures with very little entry occurring over time (unless occasionally through major innovations in product)' (Bain, 1956, p. 176).

The group of firms that were the first to take advantage of the preferred sources of inputs in terms of absolute costs, first reaped the advantages of large-scale operations, established the dominant brands and built a business infrastructure that would require large lump sums of capital for entrants to replicate quickly would have effectively constructed for themselves a walled city. Within its shelter a concentrated group of sellers who recognized the dangers of ruinous competition could jointly enjoy the benefits of monopoly rents.

Potential entrants would compute the likely profits to be had by sharing in this cosy enclave and the costs of putting in place the infrastructure rapidly enough to allow them to be competitive with the incumbents, who may have spent years building their positions when the industry was emerging. In 'blockaded' industries (Bain, 1956, p. 22), they would conclude that the game was not worth the candle before even starting down the fruitless path of actual entry. In industries where the barriers were moderate, judicious management of the incentives to enter at prevailing prices in the form of entry limit pricing could dissuade potential entrants from attempting to scale the wall while still maintaining a degree of super-normal profit (Modigliani, 1958; Sylos-Labini, 1962). In low entry barrier industries either opportunities to enjoy monopoly rents would be competed away as actual entry occurred or the threat of entry would result in such a low limit price that profits would be kept down to the level of 'normal returns'.

Various proxies for the height of entry barriers have been deployed in tests of their impact on industry performance in a large number of studies (see, for example, the review by Gilbert, 1989). These tests generally use 'reduced form' equations, which link entry barrier proxies to industry profitability. However this approach sidesteps a fundamental precondition: that the threat of entry is actually lower among those industries with structural characteristics that are supposed to imply higher barriers to entry. As we have seen above, the data on actual entry must cause us to question this proposition. Specifically, if the threat of entry is actually low in industries with characteristics like scale, advertising and capital intensity, why then do we observe high levels of actual entry into these industries?

## BARRIERS TO ENTRY AND THE RATE OF ENTRY

In this section we examine the existing evidence regarding the relationship between the height of barriers to entry and that observed rate of entry, and present a re-estimation of the traditional entry barrier equation which makes a clear distinction between new firm entry and the addition of plants or establishments by incumbents and diversifiers where there are strong reasons to believe the implications of entry barriers will be markedly different.

## EXISTING EVIDENCE

The first group of studies examining the relationship between entry barriers and observed entry focused on the *net* number of firms entering the industry based on the change in counts of firms at two points in time. Using Canadian data, and excluding industries where the net number of firms had declined, Orr (1974) found a significant negative impact for the capital required for a minimum efficient scale plant, advertising intensity and concentration. R&D intensity proved to be less clear an indicator of barriers. On the incentive to enter, industry growth and past profitability had a positive impact, albeit rather weak, and a measure of risk based on the variance of industry profit over time tended to act as a disincentive. Using a similar design with US data but examining industries with net increases or decreases in their populations, Duetsch (1974), however, failed to find a significant result for the traditional proxies for entry barriers used by Orr. Only the absolute capital cost barrier appeared to act as a barrier to a net expansion of the number of firms.

Both previous studies found that the larger the industry, in terms of the total number of firms, the more firms entering net. Hirschey (1981) therefore standardized by the total number of incumbent firms to compute the percentage rate of net entry. When this correction was applied, none of the traditional proxies for entry barriers appeared to explain this measure of the magnitude of entry relative to the existing stock of firms. On the contrary, he discovered a significant, positive 'entry promoting' effect for advertising intensity.

During the first half of the 1980s improved data on entry began to become available to researchers, allowing net entry to be separated into its underlying components: gross entry and gross exit. It rapidly became apparent that the net figure used in previous work had concealed much larger shifts of firms into and out of industries. As noted above, when the number of firms in an industry is tracked across a decade entry equivalent to almost 40% of the initial stock of firms is common. Meanwhile, studies like Baldwin and Gorecki (1987) also found that 43% of their initial population had disappeared 10 years later. Even more problematic, the gross entry figures were found to be unrelated to either traditional barriers to entry proxies or past industry profitability in a systematic way.

Further exploring the behaviour of gross entry, Khemani and Shapiro (1986) found a negative effect for advertising intensity, minimum efficient scale relative to market size, and capital requirements using Canadian data from the period 1972–1976. Kessides (1986), on the other hand, confirmed Hirschey's earlier finding of an 'entry promoting' impact of advertising intensity in US data. MacDonald (1986), using a sample of all establishments of over 20 employees in four-digit food industries, found only a systematic impact of capital cost barriers. Highfield and Smiley (1987), using the Small Business Data Base of the US Small Business Administration (SBA), found the predicted negative signs on each of the traditional barrier proxies as well as a measure of pre-emptive capacity expansion by incumbents, but none was significant at accepted confidence levels. In other variations of their base model, R&D intensity appears as a factor significantly encouraging gross entry. Among these studies higher industry growth was the sole consistent explanator of higher gross entry.

---

## A FURTHER EMPIRICAL TEST

One dimension of gross entry that has been less than fully explored in the literature is the question of its source (Hamilton (1985) and Baldwin and Gorecki (1987) are notable exceptions). In particular, a good deal of theoretical weight suggests the need to distinguish carefully between entry by new, independent firms, establishment of new operating entities by firms already in the industry, and diversification into the business by firms with bases in other industries.

Firstly, because of their ability to take advantage of multiplant economies (see, for example, Scherer *et al.*, 1975), incumbents establishing new plants or operating units will be able to avoid most of the impact of the kinds of barriers to entry that the original literature postulated that new entrants would face. In fact, the decision by an incumbent to construct new plants or establishments is more appropriately viewed as an alternative to expanding the capacity of existing sites as a way of meeting expected growth. It is likely to be impacted by the efficient plant scale for the relevant technology rather than by barriers to entry. The inclusion of plant investments by incumbents as 'entry' within the gross figure used as a dependent variable would therefore bias the results, understating the importance of the deterrent effect of barriers on new entrants.

Secondly, diversifying firms may have a similar ability to bypass at least some of the traditional entry barriers. It has been argued and empirically supported that diversification entry by firms already established in other industries is a possible means of overcoming barriers to entry by drawing on firm-specific assets and will thus more frequently occur in high-barrier industries (e.g. Gorecki, 1975; Hines, 1957; Montgomery and Harihoran, 1988; Yip, 1982). Again, therefore, if this diversification is included in the figures there is likely to be more observed gross entry than the traditional barriers to entry model based on newly established firms would suggest.

These considerations imply that the traditional barriers to entry model is most properly viewed as a hypothesis about the relationship between gross entry by single plant firms and the height of entry barriers.* This proposition can be tested by means of the following specification:

---

*We also tested the corollary that the number of new plants established by incumbent firms will depend on efficient plant scale and expected growth in demand, while the creation of establishments by diversifying firms will vary with the size of the benefits offered by access to firm specific assets. We found that *SCALE* tended to reduce the creation of new dependent establishments while *GRO* increased it. *KCOST* and *ADV* became insignificant for plant expansion by existing firms. In fact, the best predictor of how many new plants will be constructed by those already in business was a straightforward regression of plant expansion by existing firms on industry growth and the average size of existing plants.

$$eni_i = a_0 + \sum_{k=1}^{m} b_k BTE_{ik} + g_0 GRO_i + e \qquad (15.1)$$

where $eni_i$ is the number of new, single plant firms entering industry $i$ during the period relative to the total number of establishments in the industry at the start of the period. $BTE_{ik}$ are $k$ indicators of barriers to entry for each industry $i$. $GRO_i$ is the total growth in the industry during the period.

Data for entry were secured by extraction from the plant-based USEEM file of the US Small Business Administration (MacDonald, 1985; Phillips, 1985), on the composition of 134 three-digit manufacturing industries in terms of single-plant firms (i.e. 'independent establishments'), separating plants belonging to multi-plant or diversified firms ('dependent establishments'). Since this information was available over the years 1978–1984 and establishments could be tracked over time from one point of observation to another, we were also able to derive establishment-based entry measures for each industry by identifying those firms and dependent establishments that were in existence in 1984 but not in 1978.

Following Bain's (1956) original hypotheses, three proxies for barriers to entry $BTE_{ik}$ were tested:

- *SCALE*: scale economies, relative to the size of the market. These are measured on the basis of the minimum efficient scale, estimated by the average shipments of plants accounting for the top 50% of industry value-added, divided by the total industry shipments. This is then multiplied by the ratio of average value-added per employee for the largest 50% of plants in the industry over value-added per employee of the smallest 50% of plants (US Department of Commerce, 1982).
- *KCOST*: a measure of the capital cost as a potential barrier to entry, equal to the minimum efficient scale (measured as above) multiplied by the ratio of total investment in plant and equipment (US Department of Commerce, 1982) to total employment in the industry (US Small Business Administration, 1988).
- *ADV*: the advertising (traceable media advertising expense) to sales ratio (US Federal Trade Commission, 1976).

Industry growth (*GRO*) was measured by the growth in total employment in the industry between 1978 and 1984 (US Small Business Administration, 1988).

TABLE 15.1 Single plant firm entry ($eni_i$) versus barriers to entry

| Variable | Coefficient | $t$-Statistic |
|---|---|---|
| Intercept | 0.010 | |
| SCALE | −0.042 | 1.640 |
| KCOST | −0.0001 | 1.496 |
| ADV | 0.001 | 2.848 |
| GRO | 0.009 | 2.095 |
| $R^2 = 0.163$ | Adjusted $R^2 = 0.131$ | |

The results for Equation 15.1, gross entry by new firms, are shown in TABLE 15.1. *SCALE* and *KCOST* have the expected negative signs, suggesting that they do act as barriers to entry, but their significance is relatively weak. Industry growth, *GRO*, exhibits the predicted positive sign. As in a number of the previous studies reviewed above, however, *ADV* (our proxy for differentiation), as a barrier to entry, shows a positive and significant sign, suggesting that prevalent use of advertising actually encourages new firms to enter.

The data therefore provide some support for the predictions of the traditional barriers to entry model in the case of new firms once these are distinguished from plant expansion by incumbents. On the other hand the low overall explanatory power of the equation (explaining 16% of the total variation) and the relatively high variances associated with the estimated coefficients suggest that there is a good deal more to the story than traditional barriers to entry models suggest, even when we are examining actual, rather than potential entry.

One important refinement to the basic model has come in the form of dynamic limit pricing (e.g. Gaskins, 1971; Judd and Peterson, 1986). While this literature has little directly to say about inter-industry variation, it has the significant implication that it is the rate at which new entrants take market share from incumbents that is critical, rather than the 'in or out' effect of entry itself. In what follows, we take this logic a step further to examine the potential impact of how many entrants survive and prosper for what length of time on both the number of new firms that decide to enter and the performance of long-term survivors.

## BARRIERS TO SURVIVAL: THE MINEFIELD

A central assumption of traditional entry theory and classical limit pricing is that the entrants expect that incumbents will not reduce their output following new entry. The 'Sylos postulate' (Sylos-Labini, 1962), for example, is that established firms maintain their pre-entry output volumes, set at a level to make entry unprofitable. Exactly what happens if a new firm does enter contrary to rational expectation is not explicit. Presumably, however, it discovers that it has insufficient sales to cover its average costs and promptly exits. In other words, the classic analysis makes no distinction between barriers to entry and barriers to survival (after entry) since there is a zero probability of survival for an entrant in an industry subject to limit pricing.

The survival assumption adopted by dynamic limit pricing models generally lies at the opposite pole. Once a firm enters it stays. The incumbents' decisions revolve around how rapidly to cede share by holding prices up and the feedback that this will have on the rate of entry in the future.

In reality, of course, even among those firms who successfully enter the industry for a finite period, only some proportion of new entrants will remain in the industry for an extended period. This proportion would not be a relevant measure of involuntary exit if the market was to be perfectly contestable, making 'hit and run' entry viable (Baumol, 1982). Market contestability theory therefore alerts us to the fact that low survival rates do not necessarily imply a disadvantage on the part of new entrants relative to incumbents. Indeed, it may be that a low tenure rate among entrants is matched by a high rate of exit among older, established firms, reflecting the fact of easy entry and exit, allowing firms to opportunistically take advantage of the relative attractiveness of temporary potential in that particular industry versus elsewhere (Mills and Schumann, 1985).

Actual experience, however, suggests that successful 'hit and run' entry is not a widespread phenomenon, even in supposedly contestable markets such as air transport (Scherer and Ross, 1990). Instead, we generally observe a substantially higher probability of new firms leaving the industry during some significant period after entry compared with the probability that a long-established incumbent will exit during the same period. Rather than simply suggesting high firm turnover associated with hit and run strategies, this would lead an entrant to suspect that new firms faced disadvantages that might force them to exit the industry due to lack of profitability, instead of by choice. Such a recognition of the risk of involuntary exit after some period of operation, in turn, can be expected to influence entry decisions so long as there are any net costs associated with entry and forced exit.

The phenomenon of successful entry followed by risk of involuntary exit, possibly after a period of operation extending into years, may be explained by the concurrent existence of four basic conditions: (i) temporary scarcity of certain firm-specific assets among incumbents relative to uncertain demand from a segment of customers for the product of these assets; (ii) a significant role in the long-run production function for industry-specific assets; (iii) that a significant proportion of both firm- and industry-specific assets can only be accumulated through experience; and (iv) uncertainty as to the rate at which both types of assets can be accumulated, as well as the demand for them.

Disequilibrium in the market between the array of types and quantities of output supplied by incumbents and that demanded by customers offers scope for new entrants to attempt to fill this gap by bringing asset bundles new to the industry. This disequilibrium may arise from development of new and potentially relevant technology outside the industry which would better satisfy some segment of customers' needs, or from a change in customer tastes. The Body Shop chain, for example, entered on the basis of growing market demand for 'environmentally friendly' cosmetics which was undersupplied by incumbents. It brought into the industry various recipes for creating cosmetics from natural ingredients. The asset bundles that the entrants bring with them may have been accumulated by operation in another industry or by the experience of the individual entrepreneurs behind the entrant. The start-up of Next computer is a case in point.

New entrants who bring assets that are temporarily scarce in the industry, however, will have little direct experience of operating in the market. Their asset bundles, while containing some attractive jewels, will be incomplete because they lack assets that can only be accumulated through experience and that are subject to 'diseconomies of time compression' (Dierickx and Cool, 1989). Customer loyalty or the capabilities and infrastructure required to manage a product-specific distribution and service network would be examples.

Potential customers are then faced with a choice between alternatives that incompletely satisfy their needs. If they buy from the new entrant, they enjoy the advantage of the differentiated attributes offered by entrants, based on the new assets they have brought into the industry. However, this means forgoing the benefits that accumulated, experience assets would provide, since entrants' stock of these is negligible. If they buy from incumbents, who have a rich stock of experience-based assets and hence can provide the attributes that these underpin, they forgo the innovative benefits offered by the entrants' new assets.

## THE RACE FOR SURVIVAL

Over time, the choice set available to the customer will change. Successful entrants will improve their stock of industry-specific assets as they accumulate experience. Simultaneously, incumbents will seek to extend their asset bases by incorporating the new types of assets deployed by successful entrants into their own asset bases. Incumbents' effectiveness in deploying these new types of assets and integrating them with their existing asset stocks will also improve with time and experience.

If incumbents were rapidly able to obtain and effectively integrate the new types of assets with their formidable stock of industry experience, the customer would no longer have to forgo the benefits of buying from a supplier with a large stock of accumulated assets. The new entrants' offerings would be dominated and their *raison d'être* eliminated. Alternatively, if the new entrants rapidly accumulated industry-specific assets they could become strong, long-term competitors.

Uncertainty as to the speed with which both firm- and industry-specific assets can be accumulated over an extended period would mean that the entrants were engaged in a risky race for survival against incumbents that were seeking to eliminate these entrants' initial differentiation. This competitive race between incumbents and new entrants is illustrated in FIGURE 15.2.

Incumbents face an 'innovation gap' between what their existing assets and capabilities can deliver and what a changed market is beginning to demand—a gap being filled, albeit imperfectly, by new entrants. Closing this innovation gap involves incumbents in a potentially costly and slow process of internal

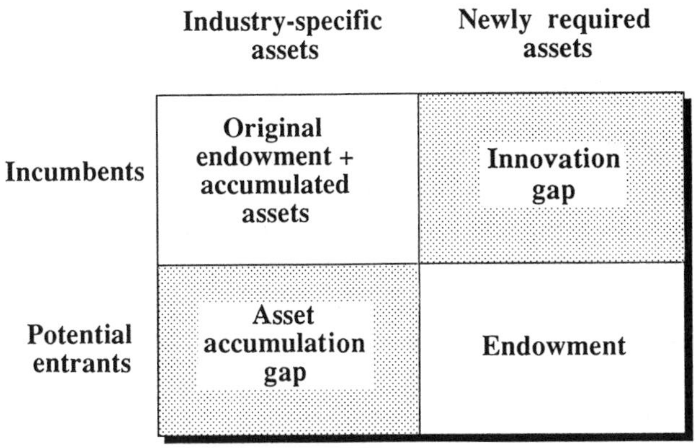

|  | Industry-specific<br>assets | Newly required<br>assets |
|---|---|---|
| Incumbents | Original<br>endowment +<br>accumulated<br>assets | Innovation<br>gap |
| Potential<br>entrants | Asset<br>accumulation<br>gap | Endowment |

FIGURE 15.2   The race for survival

change. New entrants, meanwhile, are faced with an 'asset accumulation gap' between what their initial endowments can deliver and other product features, information and service support that incumbents have been able to offer based on assets like process experience, established brands, and distribution and service infrastructure built up in the course of their history of supplying the market. Not all of these assets will be relevant to changed market conditions, but many will underpin attributes that are still demanded by consumers. The product may be new, for example, but many of the same supporting attributes such as convenience or reliable after-sales service will still be required. To close this gap entrants will generally need to replicate some of the asset stocks held by the established firms. Where these assets are not specific to the industry, they may be acquired elsewhere or transferred as part of the entrants' initial endowment, reducing the asset accumulation gap. The more of these assets that are highly specific to the particular industry, by contrast, the wider will be the asset accumulation gap.

The relative handicaps in the race to fill these gaps will depend on two sets of factors, firstly the size of the gaps opened up by a change in the market, and specifically, how much of the historic, industry-specific asset stocks continues to be relevant (determining the size of the asset accumulation gap) and how significant the innovations introduced by entrants (determining the size of the innovation gap).

The second important set of factors is the difficulty of replicating the assets required to close these respective gaps. For incumbents the magnitude of the problem will generally depend on the amount of change required and the degree to which change is unfamiliar to incumbents rather than routine. For entrants the difficulty of the task depends on the process by which industry-specific assets must be replicated. Theoretical work has suggested that this process is subject to a number of important frictions: diseconomies associated with attempts to speed up the rate of accumulation; delays caused by interconnectedness of assets limiting the rate of accumulation to the slowest 'critical path', causal ambiguity as to how to go about replicating intangibles, and so on (Dierickx and Cool, 1989).

In some industries, therefore, industry-specific, experience-based assets will be both important, and slow and costly for entrants to accumulate. In this case, more of the new entrants are likely to lose the race against incumbents. By the time they overcome the constraints and costs of replicating the necessary industry-specific assets, incumbents will already have closed the innovation gap and undermined the differentiation that entrants enjoyed initially. We define these industries as having high *barriers to survival*.

In what follows, we propose to measure the barriers to survival faced by new entrants in terms of the increased probability of exit during an extended period after entry, compared with the exit probability of incumbent firms. Our indicator is the ratio of the probability of exit of a new entrant relative to the probability of exit by an incumbent during a given period. The definition of when a firm moves from being a young 'entrant' to an established 'incumbent' is by necessity a grey area. Our data suggest, however, that the decline in probability of exit in most industries tends to flatten out about 6 years after entry, so firms that pass this age are indistinguishable from substantially older firms in terms of their probability of survival. We therefore choose this age as the cut-off point.

Barriers to survival are likely to be an important factor in determining how many new firms are willing to enter. The higher the barriers to survival, the greater the importance of sunk costs in deterring entry because of the lower probability of staying in business long enough and profitably enough to recoup these sunk investments. The observed success of past entrants, meanwhile, will feed back through expectations about the barriers to survival and hence to the rate at which entry occurs in the future.

To the extent that the height of barriers to survival differs across industries, they should therefore help to explain inter-industry variation in entry rates. Moreover, barriers to survival may be influenced by a different, or wider, set of features of structure and conduct that those included in the traditional entry barrier theory. In this case the distinction between barriers to entry and barriers to survival would lead to new hypotheses about the relationships between industry structure, the threat of new and effective competition and the relative attractiveness of different strategies.

## AN EMPIRICAL TEST OF BARRIERS TO SURVIVAL

Drawing on the same USEEM data file described above, but restricting the analysis to single plant firms, we computed a measure of the barrier to survival associated with each three-digit industry by taking the ratio of the probability of exit between 1978 and 1984 for firms who were 0–2 years old in 1978, divided by the corresponding probability of exit for firms who were between 6 and 9 years old in 1978 (BTS). We thus have a statistic capturing the relative survival disadvantage faced by new entrants early in their lives compared with the turnover rate of well-established incumbents, which is assumed to be voluntary.

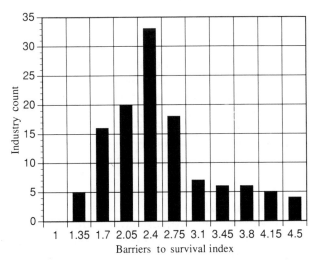

FIGURE 15.3   Cross-industry distribution of barriers to survival

The distribution of this barrier to survival statistic across our sample of industries is illustrated in FIGURE 15.3, which indicates a variation from industries where firms who have newly entered have almost no higher probability of exit than established incumbents (BTS close to 1.0) through to those where newly entered firms are more than four times as likely as established incumbents to exit the industry.

The next step is to test the impact of the BTS measure in our equation seeking to explain the rate of entry. Recall, however, that the deterrent effect of barriers to survival is expected to be greater the higher are the sunk costs associated with entering the industry. If sunk costs are insignificant then the losses associated with involuntary exit are likely to be small. In this case, there is probably little to be lost by entry even if forced exit is the result. We therefore test two specifications in which the standard entry barriers equation has been augmented by the inclusion of barriers to survival variables:

$$eni_i = a_3 + \sum_{k=1}^{m} b_k BTE_{ik} + g_3 GRO_i + h_0 BTS_i + \xi \qquad (15.2)$$

$$eni_i = a_3 + \sum_{k=1}^{m} b_k BTE_{ik} + g_3 GRO_i + h_0 BTS\ RD_i$$

$$+ h_1 BTS\ UN_i + h_2 BTS\ ADV_i + h_3 BTS\ KE_i + v \qquad (15.3)$$

Equation 15.2 simply adds the barriers to survival variable (BTS) to the traditional barriers to entry equation (Equation 15.1). In Equation 15.3 we seek to capture the joint effects of barriers to survival operating in conjunction with various proxies for sunk costs associated with entry and exit through a series of variables, in which BTS is multiplied by proxies representing research and development expenditure, redundancy costs, advertising investment, and expenditure on capital equipment which may have to be resold at a discount. These sunk/exit cost measures are as follows:

- *RD:* the ratio of total R&D expenditures to net sales (National Science Foundation, 1978)
- *UN:* the percentage of workers who are union members (Kokkelenberg and Sockell, 1985) on the expectation that redundancy costs are likely to be less avoidable when labour is unionized.

- *ADV:* the ratio of traceable media advertising expenses to net sales (US Federal Trade Commission, 1976).
- *KE:* the total investment in plant and equipment (US Department of Labor, 1979) divided by the total employment in the industry (US Department of Commerce, 1982).

We expect all of the BTS-related variables to discourage entry and hence to exhibit negative signs. The results of ordinary least squares (OLS) estimation of Equations 15.2 and 15.3 are presented in TABLE 15.2.

Our BTS statistic enters Equation 15.2 with a negative and strongly significant sign. Moreover, the traditional barriers to entry measures maintain their earlier signs and improve their statistical significance, while the proportion of inter-industry variation in entry rates of new firms explained by the regression improves substantially. These results suggest that the flow of entry is influenced both by the scale and capital cost barriers associated with initially establishing the capacity to supply (entering the industry by climbing a wall) and surviving after entry (crossing the minefield), and that these two influences are significantly independent.

The results of Equation 15.3, meanwhile, suggest that the deterrent effect of these barriers to survival are magnified by the level

TABLE 15.2 Single plant firm entry (*eni$_i$*) versus BTE and BTS

| Variable | Equation 15.2 Coefficient | *t*-Statistic | Equation 15.3 Coefficient | *t*-Statistic |
|---|---|---|---|---|
| Intercept | 0.028 | 2.750 | 0.020 | 2.100 |
| SCALE | −0.066 | 2.477 | −0.037 | 1.368 |
| KCOST | −0.00006 | 2.143 | −0.00002 | 0.629 |
| ADV | 0.001 | 2.507 | 0.002 | 1.442 |
| GRO | 0.006 | 1.416 | 0.013 | 2.569 |
| BTS | −0.006 | 3.911 | | |
| BTS × RD | | | −0.001 | 3.060 |
| BTS × UN | | | −0.007 | 2.228 |
| BTS × ADV | | | −0.0005 | 1.234 |
| BTS × KE | | | −0.0004 | 0.176 |
| $R^2$ | 0.293 | | 0.351 | |
| Adj. $R^2$ | 0.253 | | 0.286 | |

of sunk investments which would have to be abandoned in the event of involuntary exit, as well as by the redundancy costs involved. Barriers to survival appear to reduce the flow of entry most systematically when the industry is characterized by the need for investment in R&D to compete with incumbents and labour is unionized, a probable signal of redundancy costs (negative and significant coefficients on BTS × RD and BTS × UN).

Barriers to survival in combination with the need to invest in advertising (BTS × ADV) also appear to have a negative impact on the number of entrants for any given industry population. Although this effect is of lower statistical significance, it is of particular interest in the light of the frequent finding of a positive impact of advertising intensity on entry. While our results confirm the overall entry-attracting effect of advertising intensity, they also point to advertising acting as a sunk cost which deters entry when barriers to survival are high.

Capital intensity, although with a negative sign, exhibits a variance that is far too high for a statistically significant result. This may suggest that capital intensity does little to increase the deterrent effect of barriers to survival, a finding that is consistent with the contention that the resale value of many capital goods allows a high proportion of initial investment to be recouped if a new entrant is forced to exit involuntarily during the first few years. On the other hand, its lack of significance may reflect the weakness of our proxy in ignoring cross-industry variations in discount associated with disposal of the particular capital goods involved (Kessides, 1990).

When these sunk cost effects are added in combination with the barriers to survival in Equation 15.3, the significance of the traditional barriers to entry variables is substantially reduced.

---

## IMPLICATIONS FOR INDUSTRY AND COMPETITIVE ANALYSIS

A key conclusion of our results is that the 'threat of entry' faced by competitors in an industry is determined by two, at least partially independent, factors: barriers to entry and barriers to survival post-entry. Barriers to entry relate to an entrant's ability to establish the capacity to profitably supply the market immediately after entry, possibly in the face of instantaneous price attack by incumbents. Barriers to survival relate to the entrant's ability to maintain competitiveness over an extended period of time in the face of pressure for involuntary exit.

In relatively few industries, high barriers to entry mean that actual entry rates are low and likewise the threat of entry is muted. In the majority of industries, however, barriers to entry are insufficient to deter significant numbers of entrants. In some markets this flow of entry results in established firms facing new and powerful, long-term competition. In other industries, however, entry has little or no sustained impact on rivalry because new entrants face high barriers to survival. Here, entrants lose the race for survival against incumbents who are intent on eliminating any attractive differentiation that entrants initially enjoy. Handicapped by a lack of industry-specific assets, the new firms are unable to accumulate these fast enough to maintain a competitive edge against established firms who are able to exploit the benefits of assets such as consumer franchises, distribution and service infrastructure, and process experience built up through operating in the market.

These findings have important implications for analyses of industry structure, market attractiveness and business strategies where the 'threat of entry' plays a role. They suggest that we need to look well beyond traditional indicators like scale economies, capital intensity and advertising intensity in assessing the likely practical impact of entry and threat of entry on a market. Competitive analyses need to closely examine new features of market structure, particularly those that determine the barriers to survival faced by entrants. These include market characteristics that indicate the need for industry-specific assets which are slow and costly to accumulate, such as customer loyalty, intimate knowledge of customer needs, specialized process experience, and marketing and distribution infrastructure, but that are vital in order for a firm to compete effectively. Further work has shown various general indicators such as purchase frequency, customer fragmentation, channel dependence and employee skill requirements to predict the level of barriers to survival (Williamson and Verdin, 1992). Perhaps even more importantly, however, the concept of barriers to survival can improve understanding of the real threat of entry on a case-by-case basis. Rather than simply measuring the height of the industry wall, it directs analysts to consider the nature of the critical minefield beyond.

# REFERENCES

Baldwin, J.R. and Gorecki, P.K. (1983). Entry and exit to the Canadian manufacturing sector: 1970–79. Economic Council of Canada, discussion paper no. 225, February.

Baldwin, J.R. and Gorecki, P.K. (1987). Plant creation versus plant acquisition: The entry process in Canadian manufacturing. *International Journal of Industrial Organization*, March, 27–42.

Bain, J. (1956). *Barriers to New Competition*. Cambridge, MA: Harvard University Press.

Baumol, W.J. (1982). Contestable markets: An uprising in the theory of industry structure. *American Economic Review*, **72**, 1–15.

Dierickx, I. and Cool, K. (1989). Asset stock accumulation and sustainability of competitive advantage. *Management Science*, December, 1504–1514.

Duetsch, L. (1974). Entry and the extent of multiplant operations. *Journal of Industrial Economics*, June, 477–487.

Dunne, T., Roberts, M.J. and Samuelson, L. (1988). Patterns of firm entry and exit in US manufacturing industries, *Rand Journal of Economics*, Winter, 671–698.

Dunne, T., Roberts, M.J. and Samuelson, L. (1989). The growth and failure of U.S. manufacturing plants. *Quarterly Journal of Economics*, **104**, 671–698.

Gaskins, D. (1971). Dynamic limit pricing: Optimal pricing under threat of entry. *Journal of Economic Theory*, **2**, 306–322.

Gilbert, R. (1989). The role of potential competition in industrial organisation. *Journal of Economic Perspectives*, **3**, 107–127.

Gorecki, P.K. (1975). The determinants of entry by new and diversifying enterprises in the U.K. manufacturing sector 1958–1963: Some tentative results. *Applied Economics*, **718**, 139–147.

Hamilton, R.T. (1985). Interindustry variation in gross entry rates of 'independent' and 'dependent' businesses. *Applied Economics*, **17**, 271–280.

Highfield, R. and Smiley, R. (1987). New business starts and economic activity: An empirical investigation. *International Journal of Industrial Organisation*, March, 51–66.

Hines, H.H. (1957). Effectiveness of 'entry' by already established firms. *Quarterly Journal of Economics*, **71**, 132–150.

Hirschey, M. (1981). The effect of advertising on industrial mobility, 1947–72. *Journal of Business*, December, 329–339.

Judd, K. and Petersen, B. (1986). Dynamic limit pricing and internal finance. *Journal of Economic Theory*, **39**, 368–399.

Kessides, I.N. (1986). Advertising, sunk costs, and barriers to entry. *Review of Economics and Statistics*, **68**, 84–95.

Kessides, I.N. (1990). Market concentration, contestability and sunk costs. *Review of Economics and Statistics*, **72**, 614–622.

Khemani, R.S. and Shapiro, D.M. (1986). The determinants of new plant entry in Canada. *Applied Economics*, November, 1243–1257.

Kokkelenberg, E.C. and Sockell, D.R. (1985). Union membership in the U.S. 1973–1981. *Industrial and Labor Relations Review*, July, 497–543.

MacDonald, J.M. 1985. Dun & Bradstreet business microdata. *Journal of Economic and Social Measurement*, September, 173–185.

MacDonald, J.M. (1986). Entry and exit on the competitive fringe. *Southern Economic Journal*, **53**, 640–652.

Mills, D.E. and Schumann, L. (1985). Industry structure with fluctuating demand. *American Economic Review*, September, 758–767.

Modigliani, F. (1958). New developments on the oligopoly front. *Journal of Political Economy*, **66**, 215–232.

Montgomery, C.A. and Hariharan, S. (1988). Diversified entry by established firms. Northwestern University, J.L. Kellogg Graduate School of Management/University of Michigan, Graduate School of Business Administration, unpublished manuscript.

National Science Foundation (1978). *Research and Development in Industry, Technical Notes and Detailed Statistical Tables*. Washington, DC: NSF.

Orr, D. (1974). The determinants of entry: A study of the Canadian manufacturing industries. *Review of Economics and Statistics*, **56**, 58–66.

Phillips, B.D. (1985). *The Development of the Small Business Data Base of the U.S. Small Business Administration: A Working Biography*, November. Washington, DC: US Small Business Administration.

Porter, M.E. (1980). *Competitive Strategy: Techniques for Analyzing Industries and Competitors*. New York: Free Press.

Scherer, F.M., Beckenstein, A., Kaufer, E. and Murphy, R. (1975). *The Economics of Multi-plant Operation: An International Comparisons Study*. Cambridge, MA: Harvard University Press.

Scherer, F.M. and Ross, D. (1990). *Industrial Market Structure and Economic Performance*, 3rd edn. Boston, MA: Houghton Mifflin.

Sylos-Labini, P. (1962). *Oligopoly and Technical Progress*. Cambridge, MA: Harvard University Press.

US Department of Commerce, Bureau of Industry Economics (1982). *Census of Manufactures*. Washington, DC: US Government Printing Office.

US Department of Labor, Bureau of Labor Statistics (1979). *Capital Stock Estimates for Input–Output Industries: Methods and Data*. Bulletin 2034. Washington, DC: US Government Printing Office.

US Federal Trade Commission (1976). *Annual Line of Business Report 1976, Report of the Bureau of Economics*. Washington, DC: US Government Printing Office.

US Small Business Administration (1988). *Small Business Data Base*. Washington, DC: US Small Business Administration.

Williamson, P.J. and Verdin, P.J. (1992). Age, experience and corporate synergy: When are they sources of business unit advantage? *British Journal of Management*, **3** (No. 3; December), 221–236.

Yip, G.S. (1982). Gateways to entry. *Harvard Business Review*, September/October, 85–92.

# 16

# The Greening of Strategic Alliances: The Institutionalization of Environmental Compliance

SUSANNE ÖSTLUND, RIKARD LARSSON

## INTRODUCTION

Protection of the natural environment regained interest during the mid-1980s. Reports on oil spills, emissions of harmful gases, discharges of heavy metals and harmful chemicals into rivers, lakes, and seas, seal deaths, and reduction of natural resources, are seen more often all over the world. As a result, industry is faced with increased national and international pressures from consumers, environmental organizations, legislative bodies, and actors within the industrial system to take responsibility for environmental protection. These pressures will instigate new challenges and opportunities for industrial development, where it will be important to integrate environmental considerations into everyday business as well as into the strategic planning stage.

Corporations can address environmental issues in many ways:

*Building the Strategically-Responsive Organization.*
Edited by H. Thomas, D. O'Neal, R. White and D. Hurst.
Copyright © 1994 the Strategic Management Society. Published 1994 by John Wiley & Sons Ltd.

one prominent method is through alliances. They constitute collective strategies for coordinating the resources of two or more organizations in order to solve common problems. Organizations faced with industry-wide threats can be expected to utilize alliances defensively in order to minimize the costs of environmental compliance.

One important research problem in relation to the influence of environmental demands on industrial behavior and structure concerns the process and outcome of these collective attempts to solve environmental problems. Assuming that uncertainty exists on how to respond to environmental changes, how can the resulting patterns of environmental behavior in industrial networks be explained? Can we identify forces shaping solutions to environmental problems? The purpose of this chapter is to explore a process of collective problem solving in an industrial network in response to environmental demands. We will study a set of organizations facing uncertainty on what solutions to adopt for replacing chlorofluorocarbons (CFCs) as coolants and insulating materials in refrigerators and freezers.

## COLLECTIVE DEFENSE IN INDUSTRIAL NETWORKS

Alliances can be seen as interorganizational means for collaboratively achieving strategic objectives (Harrigan, 1988; Kanter, 1989). They include, for instance, joint ventures, federations, trade associations, franchising, licensing and other agreements, and have become a dominating organizational theme of the post-industrial era (Astley and Brahm, 1989). Traditionally, their strategic objectives are viewed in terms of collective opportunities to gain economies of scale and experience, resource access, and risk reduction, as well as to shape competition (Porter and Fuller, 1986). Alliances constitute cooperative expansions that can pursue these benefits cheaper and faster than acquired or own growth (Kanter, 1989), especially in the case of internationalization (Ohmae, 1989).

While alliances are typically viewed according to these collaborative expansion opportunities, they can also be used for defense against collective threats. In her study of a major change in the US coal industry, Rogers (1986, pp. 23–24) found that coalitions generally developed around uncertain areas in which firms felt vulnerable: '*Supraorganizations* emerge generally in response to an adversarial view of the environment. Firms seek safety in numbers. They consolidate their efforts and band together to withstand threats they perceive from the outside.' Accordingly, the Coal Exporters Association was enlarged and another group formed to ward off foreign government regulators.

In particular, trade associations seem to be activated by threats of government intervention. They 'follow political developments closely to influence the passage of legislation and, once enacted, to shape the implementation of the new legislation. Our survey . . . showed that most of the associations founded since the 1950s have arisen in response to what is seen by business as over-regulation by government' (Staber and Aldrich, 1983, p. 174). Besides governmental lobbying, trade associations can also attempt to enhance their members' image when the industry is facing public criticism (Oliver, 1990). 'Managing social issues such as consumerism and environmentalism requires a formal collective problem-solving process to match the organized activist collectives' (Dollinger, 1990, p. 278).

Alliances can also have low degrees of formalization, such as collusion and industry leadership (Bresser, 1988). Cartels are different from the formal and often political trade association, in that they are informal, 'purely economic organizations, aiming at the elimination or regulation of competitors. Often, trade associations act like cartels and it is precisely then that they come under the close scrutiny of antitrust enforcement agencies' (Staber, 1985, p. 214).

While cartels are normally viewed as existing for the collective pursuit of price enhancing opportunities, similar collusive behavior can be expected in industry responses to environmentalism, but in this case pursuing reduced environmental costs. Anecdotal indications point towards firms tending to view environmental issues as representing a threat of costly legislative compliance to be avoided rather than as opportunities to be exploited. The formal trade associations of industries facing environmental regulation are likely to more or less overtly lobby to minimize the extent and compliance costs of legislation along the same lines as indicated by the research mentioned above.

A more subtle form of environmentally collusive behavior may be found in the *informal industrial network*. According to the Swedish network school of thought on industrial marketing, informal cooperation evolves from a growing awareness of mutual interests (Håkansson and Johanson, 1988). Actors in the network form more or less stable, visible, and overlapping alliances to strengthen their position in the network, thus enhancing the ability to mobilize needed resources (Johanson, 1991). Besides lobbying for reduced and delayed environmental regulation, the involved firms can reap great savings from sharing the costs of complying with the regulation. The joint development of more environmentally apt production processes and product features can benefit costwise from the scale economies of pooled resources. This cost saving ability of strategic alliances is well known through the prevalent use of, for instance, research and development consortiums (e.g. Kanter, 1989; Ohmae, 1989; Porter and Fuller, 1986).

Strategic allying in an industrial network aimed at more cost-efficient use of resources is not in itself environmentally collusive behavior. On the contrary, economizing of resources needed for environmental improvement ought to be commended. The subtlety of the informal industrial networks' potential collusion lies not in using the cost-efficiency to produce better solutions for the same amount of input, but instead in using less input to achieve minimum requirements. As long as the industrial network views the environmental issues as threats, the involved firms are mutually motivated to minimize compliance costs by developing only one minimally acceptable joint solution to be implemented by everybody. Besides the cost savings from economies of scale, the needed compliance can be kept at the minimum of the sole solution. The government has no 'hard evidence' that there exists any better solution that they could enforce instead. Thus, the cost saving collaborative development of uniform solutions can also guarantee that the solution in question will be sufficient by providing no competing solutions.

The sole environmental solution is legitimized by being jointly developed by all or most of the leading firms in the industrial network. If there are no or very few competing solutions, however, the acceptability of the sole solution is won largely by default instead of inherent qualities of environmental aptitude. One must ask oneself whether such uniform collaborative compliance can stifle innovativeness towards more apt solutions. There may be a paradox in collaboration being viewed as a main approach to the greening of strategy, while the defensive side of strategic alliances suggests instead more competition to stimulate the innovation of better solutions.

## ENVIRONMENTAL COMPLIANCE IN INDUSTRIAL NETWORKS

There need not be any collusive intentions for this minimizing effect of environmental compliance to occur. The industrial network approach emphasizes that interests often coincide since actors are dependent on one another to gain access to resources (Axelsson, 1991; Johanson and Mattsson, 1991). This implies the importance of analyzing the interests of the constellations of firms involved to enable understanding of the constraints and opportunities in environmental problem solving. The industrial network is a specific structure coordinated through exchange relationships linking actors, activities, and resources in a certain pattern. The existence of this structure 'is in many ways a serious limitation of the space cf action of the firm' (Håkansson and Johanson, 1988, p. 375).

The institutional as well as the network approaches in organizational studies examine restraining processes in organizational action. The institutionalization is the process that constrains the perceived options for organizational change. Through a particular change process, the structure and behavior of organizations becomes institutionalized through isomorphic pressures. DiMaggio and Powell (1983, p. 149) address the constraining process of isomorphism 'that forces one unit in a population to resemble other units that face the same set of environmental conditions.'

They identify three mechanisms of isomorphic change: (i) mimetic/imitative, where isomorphism refers to organizations adopting elements utilized by others that they perceive to be more legitimate or successful; (ii) coercive pressures emanating from the legal, political, cultural, and organizational environments upon which an organization depends; and (iii) normative influence from the professionalization of occupations through the educational system, and from professional networks that span and influence organizational decisions.

Imitation can be expected to be prevalent in industrial networks since 'actors are aware that particular actors' changes also create changes for the others. Therefore, the actors watch each other closely' (Håkansson and Johanson, 1988). Thus, mimetic behavior tends to create homogeneity in organizational solutions to specific problems.

Industrial networks facing environmentalism may be highly susceptible to isomorphism, given the lack of understanding of

environmental impacts and their handling, as well as the sometimes contradictory goals involved in pursuing profit maximiza-
tion and/or environmental sustainability. The organizational
impact on the environment has just begun to be seriously
observed, and very few organizations have the competence and
motivation to understand and handle pressures to change. Thus,
there tends to be great uncertainty regarding what solutions to
adopt when faced with environmental problems. The seemingly
common view among businessmen that costs for improved environmental solutions are at best loosely coupled to corporate
revenues further adds to the uncertainty and reluctance in
handling these problems.

This may add up to the possibility that firms suffer from first-
mover *dis*advantages in developing and choosing environmental
solutions. Being the first to adopt a specific solution exposes the
firm in question to the risk of other firms adopting another
solution that becomes the standard. In that case, the firm not only
stands to lose their original investment, but will also have the
costs of changing and catching up with the adopted solution.
Besides the difficulty of predicting which solution will become the
standard, the pay-off of actually being the first to adopt such a
solution is also uncertain. The combination of uncertain rewards
and likely punishments for wrong choices provides strong incentives for not making the first move.

The 'wait and see' strategy can thus be more rewarding because
of lower levels of risk-taking and development costs as compared
with own innovation. Faced with threats of legislation or market
pressures to reduce its polluting behavior, the individual firm has
to find a new approach to the problem. Forming a strategic
alliance becomes the next logical approach because alliances both
increase the likelihood of the joint solution becoming standard
and decrease the cost of developing and implementing it. The
initial formation of strategic alliances is likely to be informal
because of the greater costs and time consumption involved in the
formalization of cooperation. Informal alliances can also be
expected to occur in publicly or legally sensitive issues, such as
lobbying activities to forestall environmental legislation.

Even though individual firms may not participate directly in
the collaborative development, those who imitate joint solutions
in industrial networks still indirectly contribute to the minimum
environmental compliance. Their imitation legitimizes the sole
solution instead of attempting to develop even better solutions.

Thus, isomorphic pressures can influence the whole industrial network to adopt a homogeneous solution through both collaborating developers and following imitators. In this way, minimum environmental compliance becomes institutionalized throughout the network. The process of compliant behavior should not be viewed as an environmental conspiracy, though. Rather, it is a systemic effect of individually rational firms attempting to reduce uncertainty and maximize profits in a network facing environmental problems with first-mover disadvantages.

In this chapter we examine the isomorphic process resulting from a pressure to find a replacement for CFCs in refrigeration. We use the theoretical framework to analyze the collective problem solving in the network, and its outcome, the chosen replacement for CFCs.

## CASE STUDY

This case describes some of the key international actors in the chemical and major appliances industries involved in finding alternatives to CFCs.* In 1988 the Swedish parliament voted in favor of a proposition regulating the use of CFCs. The focal firm in this study, Electrolux, the single largest user of CFCs in Sweden, had no solution to the problem. In order to find a replacement for CFCs in its products—refrigerators and freezers—it had to take immediate action to solve the problem.

## ENVIRONMENTAL PROBLEMS CAUSED BY CFCS

CFCs are a group of widely used chemicals that, when released into the stratosphere, are considered to be one of the single most

---

*A case study approach is taken, where historical, political, and social contexts are considered as the environment in which the actors make their decisions. The studied network builds around one focal actor, Electrolux, and the perceptions of its surrounding network as described by, primarily, six interviewees at Electrolux through multiple interviews during six months. The interviews were supplemented with over 3000 pages of various documents on Electrolux. Also, semi-structured interviews were made with representatives from six other international key actors in the network, including Philips–Whirlpool, Siemens–Bosch and Dannfoss. Over 1000 additional pages of product and firm information were collected at the Domotechnica Fair in Cologne (the world's leading annual fair for home appliances, etc.).

important causes of depleting the ozone layer. Ozone is, at ground level, a pollutant from smokestacks and tailpipes, contributing to smog. At the stratosphere, 14–44 km above the Earth's surface, a layer of naturally occurring ozone prevents the sun's dangerous radiation from reaching ground level. Without protection from the ozone layer, this ultraviolet radiation can cause an increase in the number of skin cancers, and eye cataracts, and crop damage.

CFCs were developed in 1930 by Thomas Midgley Jr, a chemist with the Frigidaire division of General Motors. They were originally developed for the home refrigerator industry as alternatives for potentially dangerous and hazardous refrigerants, such as methyl chloride and sulphur dioxide, but have since found a variety of applications. CFCs occur in both liquid and gas forms and are colorless, almost odorless, noncombustible, and have a low boiling point, factors that have contributed to their widespread use. CFCs have been sold under a number of trade names such as Freon, Frigen, Arcton, and Isotron. A small number of large chemical producers (10–15) accounted for the major part of the world production of CFCs (1.2 million tons in 1986). Sweden had no production of CFCs, but many users. The two largest usage areas of CFCs, as a refrigerant and as an active ingredient in the production of insulation foams, accounted for approximately 50% of the total consumption in Sweden.

The first *regulation* on the use of CFCs came into effect in 1979. Based on the scientific discovery of the hazards caused by CFCs and pressure from the general public, Canada, the US, Norway, and Sweden banned the use of CFC as a propellant in aerosol spray. In the mid-1980s, new data on the depletion of the ozone layer instigated new regulations aimed at controlling emissions of CFCs. As a result a UN treaty was signed by 24 countries in Montreal in 1987, restricting the emissions of CFCs (UNEP, 1987). Under the agreement, production of the most commonly used CFCs would be capped to the 1986 production level, beginning in 1989, and would gradually drop to 50% of that level by 1999. Sweden went one step further, regulating the use of CFCs with a gradually lowered usage level through 1994, when a complete ban will be imposed. The Montreal Protocol was subsequently revised at the June 1990 UNEP meeting in London, where 60 signing parties agreed to a total phase-out of the five CFCs and the three halons identified in the Montreal Protocol by the year 2000.

## HISTORICAL BACKGROUND TO CFCs IN REFRIGERATION

The first commercial machines for household refrigeration were developed during the early 1900s. With expanding cities came the need to preserve food for longer periods of time, thus creating the need for mechanical refrigeration. Although commercial refrigeration was widely available at the beginning of the century, it took almost another three decades before the industrial production of refrigerators for the domestic market began. Two methods emerged for household refrigeration: absorption and compressor technologies. The absorption refrigerator, industrially developed by Electrolux, was very successful during the 1930s and 1940s. With increased demand for larger sizes and the growing electrification of households, the absorption machine soon experienced competition from the compressor machine. Frigidaire, founded in 1916, was one of the larger companies involved in the compressor refrigerator business. In 1919 General Motors acquired Frigidaire in order to expand into the household refrigeration business, which further spurred the development and production of compressor machines.

In 1930, the General Motor chemists Midgley, Henne, and McNary developed a series of artificial refrigerants, CFCs, as cooling agents for compressor driven refrigerators. The objective was to find a stable, odorless, noncorrosive, and nontoxic replacement to the coolant gases used in refrigerators. The Du Pont Corporation and General Motors soon made an agreement that involved the technical development, production, and marketing of the newly developed CFCs (Hounshell and Smith, 1988). By the late 1940s, CFCs had become the dominant refrigerant. Later, in the 1960s, CFCs were introduced as a very effective ingredient in the insulation foam used between the inner and outer mantles of the refrigerator, as well as serving an important stabilizing function for the construction of the refrigerator.

Another milestone in the development of the compressor refrigerator was the start of large-scale production of the hermetical Tecumseh compressor in the US in 1946. Compressor technology became more reliable, quieter, more efficient, and the components smaller, which helped to increase the popularity of the compressor refrigerator. By the end of the 1950s, the compressor machine was the dominating technology used in refrigerators, leaving the absorption machine to niche markets like recreational vehicles and hotel mini-bars.

---

## MAIN ACTORS INVOLVED IN FINDING ALTERNATIVES TO CFCs

At the time of the study, the refrigerator industry was characterized by increased concentration in the three major market regions, Japan, Europe, and the US. A few large multinational firms dominated the manufacturing, although the products were sold under many brand names. The world's largest manufacturer in the major appliance industry was Philips–Whirlpool. Some of the other large manufacturers included Electrolux, AEG, Bosch–Siemens, Mitsubishi, Matsushita, Hitachi, and General Electric. As markets matured, low-cost production and product differentiation (mainly by adding features to basic models) became key strategies. Refrigerators were manufactured in plants with highly specialized and automated assembly lines, with most components and materials sourced externally.

Only a handful of firms controlled the worldwide supply of compressors: General Electric in the US; Matsushita, Sharp, Mitsubishi, and Sanyo in Japan; and Dannfoss, Necci, Aspera (Whirlpool), Zanussi and Unidad Hermetica (Electrolux), in Europe. The compressor may be considered a strategic component in the refrigerator, with manufacturing controlled to a large extent by the refrigerator and freezer manufacturers. One exception to the vertical integration in this area is the Danish firm Dannfoss. It is a critical developer of compressors for home refrigerators, and supplies most of the European manufacturers. Originally, Dannfoss manufactured the Tecumseh compressor under license, but due to the large size of the American compressors, Dannfoss developed a smaller size for European needs, starting in 1956. Since then, it has been among the leading firms in technological development of hermetic compressors for domestic refrigerators and freezers. The compressor and the refrigerant are closely related. Consequently, Dannfoss developed new compressors in close collaboration with some of their important customers (the refrigerator manufacturers) and a few chemical firms.

The chemical firms involved in the production of CFCs were a small number of large multinational corporations. The world leader in the production of CFCs was Du Pont, with 25% of the world's total output. Some of the other firms included Allied-Signal, ICI, Bayer, and Hoechst. The largest of the CFC producers were collaborating on research projects aimed at developing and testing substitutes (Moore, 1990). The chemical firms also cooperated closely with the user industries to find and modify suitable compounds that could replace CFCs in various applications. Chemical companies manufacturing plastics for the inner mantle of the refrigerator, lubricants for the compressor, and compounds for the insulation were also involved in the industrial network aiming to find a solution to the replacement of CFCs in refrigerators.

## MAIN EVENTS IN THE SEARCH FOR ALTERNATIVES TO CFCS

The manufacturers of CFCs were the first to experience pressures to find substitutes for CFCs. Prior to the first regulation in 1979, the chemical industry was opposed to a ban on the use of CFCs. In a 1975 advertisement in *The New York Times* (Moore, 1990), Du Pont urged a delay of the ban, arguing that research would develop 'definite information' about the CFC–ozone relationship.

After the regulation was introduced in 1979, the industry instigated the search for non-chlorinated substitutes. During the period following the first regulation, uncertainties existed regarding the exact relationship between emissions of CFCs and depletion of the ozone layer. The industry organized to prevent further regulation, arguing that the scientific evidence was too uncertain to justify further regulation, and called for additional research. The search for alternatives and the ongoing research on substitutes were dropped for two main reasons: (i) the uncertainties of the CFC–ozone relationships made it clear that no immediate new regulation was imminent; and (ii) the investigated substitutes were abandoned because of their relative costliness, and therefore perceived lack of business potential.

Until 1985, when the issue regained interest as a result of the discovery of the Antarctic ozone hole, the markets for CFCs expanded into new applications. The discovery increased public demands on controlling emissions of CFCs, and negotiations between political institutions and industry to reduce the use of CFCs intensified. As a result, the Montreal Protocol and Swedish national regulations were introduced in 1987 and 1988. As a response to the new bans on selected CFCs, the chemical industry in 1987 decided to select hydrochlorofluorocarbons (HCFCs) and hydrofluorocarbons (HFCs) as the most likely substitutes to develop. They were selected because of their lower ozone-depleting potential, while retaining the benefits of CFC compounds. They were also perceived as the options 'most likely to succeed' according to a statement by Mr Heckert, chairman of the board at Du Pont, in a letter to the US EPA administrator, March 1988 (Hoffman, 1990). The debate regarding the future of the HCFC alternatives, has been ongoing. Reservations about introducing HCFC, with its high level of chlorine and relatively strong greenhouse warming potential, have been expressed. HCFCs also have been mentioned as compounds that will potentially be banned in the near future.

Collaborative activities in the chemical industry to test and further develop the substitutes started. Because of the long development cycles, including toxicity testing, end use application tests, and large investments in production facilities, the chemical industry estimated that it would take 5 years to commercialize substitute compounds. Governmental and supranational organizations also engaged in encouraging industrial collaborations and research activities. For example, the US Environmental Protection Agency (EPA) supported industry cooperation by helping industries to obtain exemption from anti-trust laws for joint research, as well as being active in the search for substitutes. In 1988, leading US, European, and Japanese chemical firms jointly announced a collaboration project intending to avoid duplication of research effort as well as shortening the completion of toxicity tests. Once the strategic decision was made to concentrate the efforts to the selected substitutes, projects started with end users to test the new compounds.

During 1987, the Swedish government investigated the possibilities of regulating a faster phase-out for the use of CFCs than that proposed in the Montreal Protocol. Evaluations for all applications of CFCs were made, in an attempt to establish available substitutes and the time needed for change. Industrial trade organizations from the different application areas, together with some of the larger industrial users of CFCs, were involved in the evaluation through a submission system normally used in policy making processes in Sweden. Some of the firms were also called to hearings at the Department for Environmental Affairs, where they could give their views on the impact that the proposed regulations might have on their business.

The most commonly used CFCs in refrigerators were CFC-11 and CFC-12. They were commodity chemicals, marketed by most of the chemical companies involved in the production of CFCs, i.e. sold in large volumes at low prices. At the time, the substitutes had undergone practically no testing in end use applications, but since then tests of HFC-134a as a replacement for CFC-12 as a refrigerant, and HCFC-123 as a replacement for CFC-11 in insulation foam have been conducted.

Electrolux, being the single largest user of CFCs in Sweden, was involved both indirectly, through its trade organization, and directly through submitting its views to the legislative body, before the proposal was adopted. Top management from Electrolux also met with representatives from the legislative authorities during the process. Electrolux and its trade organization were against a specific national regulation that did not harmonize with European Community or UNEP regulations. Instead, Electrolux agreed with the line proposed by the Swedish Industrial Board, arguing for a voluntary program for the reduction of CFCs (Swedish Government Proposition 1987/88:85).

The proposition to gradually reduce the use of CFCs, with a total ban from January 1995, was adopted by the Swedish parliament in May 1988. The refrigerator industry was given until 1994 to find a substitute for CFCs. Electrolux called a meeting, where it was decided to start a CFC project aimed at testing, evaluating, and implementing different substitutes. Tests with various compounds for insulation, including water-based ones, were done by Research & Innovation at the Electrolux headquarters in Stockholm. At the same time, Dannfoss in Denmark tested different compressor refrigerants in cooperation with a few chemical firms. After a few initial tests, the Product Area Board (PAB) at Electrolux decided to work along the two main lines of reduction and replacement of CFCs by HCFC-123 and HFC-134a. PAB made strategic decisions regarding the products and production, setting the framework for the work at the different divisions. Beside staff members from Electrolux Major Appliances, division managers and representatives were members of PAB. Attending the meeting at which the decisions on the CFC project were taken, were the Major Appliance subsidiary, Product Division Refrigeration (including its marketing department, Marketing Europe), and Research & Innovation.

During phase one, Electrolux's aim was to reduce the amount of CFC-11 used in insulation by 50% by spring 1989. By the end of 1989, most of the large refrigerator firms had reduced the amount of CFCs used in insulation by half. Parallel to the reduction project, several alternative substitutes were tested and evaluated at the Electrolux R&I department in Stockholm. R&I was working together with Hoechst and ICI on a few HCFCs as an alternative to CFC-11 in insulation foam. A decision was made internally during the fall of 1989, and publicly announced in February 1990, to concentrate further efforts on HCFC-123. Among the reasons that were given for this choice, its insulation properties and price were considered the most important.

While testing HCFC-123, problems were discovered regarding the fit to the material used in the inner mantle of the refrigerator. To solve these problems, R&I worked with the chemical companies ICI, Dow, and Bayer. Several of the chemical firms also joined forces to find solutions to this problem, for example, ICI and Montedison. New polyol materials were tested in Stockholm, together with foaming tests at the Mariestad plant. The insulation foam was evaluated for (i) how well it filled the space between the inner and outer mantles; (ii) its ability to attach to the materials; and (iii) its insulation capacity.

The problem was not solved within the group of relations with the chemical firms that Electrolux had already established. In 1986 Electrolux acquired Zanussi, the leading Italian major appliance firm. Through Zanussi's network of relationships, Electrolux came in contact with Montedip, a subsidiary to the industrial conglomerate Montedison. Montedip found a solution to the problem by inventing a technique to 'nap' the surface of the plastic, as well as using materials that could be recycled.

Regarding the replacement of CFC-12 as a refrigerant, the initial screening and tests were mainly done by the compressor firms. Electrolux did not have any compressor manufacturing facilities until the acquisition of Zanussi, which owned the ZEM plant. Electrolux was working with ZEM and Dannfoss to find alternatives to CFC-12. Dannfoss was Electrolux's strategically most important supplier of compressors, but ZEM and Matsushita also delivered compressors to the Mariestad plant. Around one-third of the compressors were sourced internally from ZEM. Electrolux was initially working on two alternatives as a refrigerant: HCFC-22 and HFC-134a. The major problem was the compounds' compatibility with the lubricant used in the compressor. ZEM was testing different lubricants during 1989, and eventually found an ester oil that seemed to be functional with HFC-134a. Cooperative research projects between universities and the refrigerator industry were also done to find alternative refrigerants. In Germany, for example, Bosch–Siemens, Electrolux, AEG, and a few other refrigerator manufacturers, jointly funded a research project at a technical university aimed at finding CFC substitutes.

In May 1990, the first refrigerator was manufactured using both HFC-134a as a refrigerant and HCFC-123 as an ingredient in the insulation foam. The preceding product development of the 'CFC-free' refrigerator involved several phases, of which some were intimately connected to other industrial actors and their perceptions of suitable solutions to CFC replacement. Electrolux's first 400 CFC-free refrigerators were delivered in November 1990 to a newly constructed apartment complex in Stockholm. During 1991, deliveries of the refrigerators started on a small basis. The main restriction to a complete switch to the manufacturing of CFC-free refrigerators was the limited supply of HCFCs and HFCs. All major competitors also started production of refrigerators with the same type of solution.

On 21 August 1991, the Du Pont Corporation announced its decision to construct the world's largest plant for production of CFC substitutes in Corpus Christi, Texas. The production capacity will be 32 000 metric tons per year of the compounds HFC-134a and HCFC-124 (Svenska Dagbladet, 1991).

## ANALYSIS

The actors in the industrial network in this case have coordinated their resources to solve the problem of replacing CFCs in refrigerators. Personnel from R&D departments, product and production engineers, and managers from refrigerator, chemical, and supplying companies joined forces in the process. Individual actors in the involved industries also built relationships with legislative bodies in negotiating different solutions to the CFC problem.

The coordination of resources can be viewed as the formation of an informal, loosely coupled strategic alliance, with the purpose of pursuing an acceptable solution to the CFC replacement issue. Reasons for using the collaborative form were: (i) reduction of lengthy development and testing procedures, thus increasing the speed of the process as well as reducing costs; (ii) gaining access to other actors resources, both knowledge- and capital-based; (iii) reduction of overlapping activities; and (iv) legitimizing the chosen solution.

The collaboration or informal strategic alliance formed in this case was an extension of earlier exchange relationships between the actors in the network. A tighter cooperation on research projects was implemented in order to test and modify the new compounds for use in refrigerators as well as on the production line. The chemical manufacturers, being pressured to find CFCs substitutes, had to test quickly their suggested replacements for various applications. Engaging in collaborative network projects enhanced the diffusion and support of the chosen solution in the industrial network of users. The support in the industrial system also strengthened the negotiation power towards legislators, reducing the risk of regulatory action against the new compounds.

A number of observed isomorphic pressures were propelling this process of uncertainty reduction. Coercive pressures stemmed from the international and national regulation of CFCs. The previously discussed alternatives to CFCs were included as suggested substitutes in the Governmental and UNEP documents. These suggested substitutes could be understood as standards for what solutions to adopt. Coercive forces could also be identified in terms of pressures felt from within the network to adopt a certain solution. The process of finding substitutes to CFCs was mainly performed within already established relations. The probable greater relative power of the chemical corporations enabled them to steer the refrigerator and compressor firms towards HCFCs and HFCs as substitutes. The chemical firms had the knowledge and resources to engage in developing and evaluating different compounds that the other actors lacked or had no interest in pursuing. These established relations could be viewed as a force of persuasion towards a homogeneous solution, thus hindering the refrigerator firms from finding solutions outside the established relationships.

Once a solution became perceived as successful by leading firms, other refrigerator manufacturers applied the same solution. Thus, mimetic behavior was observed when the solution applied in one firm was adopted by others through imitation in the network. The mimetic pressure could be observed in both the chemical and refrigerator industries. The CFC manufacturers quickly adopted the solution proposed by some of the leading firms, such as Du Pont and ICI. Collaborative research forces were soon organized, thus reinforcing the institutional processes towards a homogeneous solution. Collaboration to find alternatives to CFCs quickly was also supported by environmental policy makers and other legislative bodies. No evidence was found of significant attempts to develop competing solutions with better environmental qualities than the HCFCs and HFCs.

## CONCLUSIONS

One possible explanation for the widespread and rapid adoption of this homogeneous solution of choosing HCFCs and HFCs as substitutes for CFCs is that all of the actors in the study belonged to large, international, and mature industries, with long, well-established exchange relations to one another. The established network of relationships enabled the chemical firms to rapidly test the suggested substitutes for different applications in close cooperation with the refrigerator and compressor firms. More fragmented industries would probably have had a slower process. In this case, the network relationships can be said to have been both a blessing and a curse: a blessing because they facilitated the organization of resources and activities to solve common problems, but a curse in that they probably hindered the adoption of innovative solutions originating outside the established structure.

It would have been very expensive and risky for Electrolux to develop the chemical competence needed to find a better solution on its own. It was also viewed as quite uncertain whether customers would be willing to pay significant premiums for 'greener' refrigerators. Thus, Electrolux had negative incentives to compete in developing its own solution. While they were faced with these first-mover disadvantages, Electrolux could not simply 'wait-and-see' due to the mandated substitution. Instead, they participated in the collaborative development of the limited environmental compliance replacing CFCs with HCFCs/HFCs throughout the industrial network. The institutionalization of this homogeneous solution was thus driven, at the firm level, by strategic choices to collaborate when faced with first-mover disadvantages and, at the network level, by the isomorphic pressures of coercion and imitation. The defensive side of strategic alliances has several implications, especially in terms of the concept of first-mover disadvantages. Beside the research opportunity of cross-fertilizing strategic and institutional theories, first-mover disadvantages may be a conceptual cut at the Gordian knot of minimum environmental compliance by organizations, policywise. These disadvantages need to be turned into environmental first-mover advantages to spur competition towards better solutions. Governments can encourage greener demand through educating customers on product differences in environmental impact. Independent research is required to develop sufficient environmental competence for the governments to effectively educate consumers. The creation of a green market pull will provide incentives for individual firms as well as strategic networks to pursue minimization of environmental harm instead of colluding towards minimum compliance in tight industrial networks. Firms with innovative rather than defensive environmental stances will also be better able to create and utilize the green market opportunities arising from increased consumer awareness.

## ACKNOWLEDGEMENTS

This research was funded in part by the Technology Science Foundation of J. Gust Richert, the Swedish Institute of Management (IFL) and the Bank of Sweden Tercentenary Foundation. The conference participation was made possible by a grant from Wallander and Hedelius Research Foundation. We wish to express our appreciation to Professor Lars-Gunnar Matsson at Stockholm School of Economics for helpful comments on an earlier draft.

## REFERENCES

Astley, W.G. and Brahm, R.A. (1989). Organizational designs for post-industrial strategies: The role of interorganizational collaboration. In C.C. Snow (Ed.) *Strategy, Organization Design, and Human Resource Management* (pp. 233–270). Greenwich, CT: JAI Press.

Axelsson, B. (1991). Corporate strategy models and networks. In B. Axelsson and G. Easton (Eds.) *Industrial Networks—A New View of Reality*. London: Routledge.

Bresser, R.K.F. (1988). Matching collective and competitive strategies. *Strategic Management Journal*, **9**, 375–385.

DiMaggio, P.J. and Powell, W.W. (1983). The iron cage revisited: Institutional isomorphism and collective rationality in organizational fields. *American Sociological Review*, **48**, 147–160.

Dollinger, M.J. (1990). The evolution of collective strategies in fragmented industries. *Academy of Management Review*, **15**, 266–285.

Håkansson, H. and Johanson, J. (1988). Formal and informal cooperation strategies in international industrial networks. In F.J. Contractor and P. Lorange (Eds) *Cooperative Strategies in International Business* (pp. 369–379). Lexington, MA: Lexington Books.

Harrigan, K.R. (1988). Strategic alliances and partner asymmetries. In F.J. Contractor and P. Lorange (Eds) *Cooperative Strategies in International Business* (pp. 205–226). Lexington, MA: Lexington Books.

Hoffman, J.S. (1990). Replacing CFCs: The search for alternatives. *AMBIO*, **XIX**(6/7), 329–333.

Hounshell, H. and Smith Jr, J.K. (1988). *Science and Corporate Strategy—Du Pont R&D, 1902–1980*. Cambridge: Cambridge University Press.

Johanson, J. (1991). Exchange networks in business. Paper presented at the IAREP/SASE Conference at Stockholm School of Economics, 16–19 June.

Johanson, J. and Mattsson, L.G. (1991). Network positions and strategic action—An analytical framework. In B. Axelsson and G. Easton (Eds) *Industrial Networks—A New View of Reality*. London: Routledge.

Kanter, R.M. (1989). Becoming PALs: Pooling, Allying, and Linking across companies. *Academy of Management Executive*, **3**(3), 183–193.

Moore, C.A. (1990). Industry responses to the Montreal Protocol. *AMBIO*, **XIX**(6/7), 320–323.

Ohmae, K. (1989). The global logic of strategic alliances. *Harvard Business Review*, **65**(2), 143–154.

Oliver, C. (1990). Determinants of interorganizational relationships: Integration and future directions. *Academy of Management Review*, **15**, 241–265.

Porter, M.E. and Fuller, M.B. (1986). Coalitions and global strategy. In M.E. Porter (Ed.) *Competition in Global Industries* (pp. 315–343). Boston, MA: Harvard Business School Press.

Rogers, K.S. (1986). *U.S. Coal Goes Abroad: A Social Action Perspective on Interorganizational Networks*. New York: Praeger.

Staber, U. (1985). A population perspective on collective action as an organizational form: The case of trade associations. In S.B. Bacharach (Ed.) *Research in the Sociology of Organizations* (pp. 188–219). Greenwich, CT: JAI Press.

Staber, U. and Aldrich, H. (1983). Trade association stability and public policy. In R. Hall and R. Quinn (Eds) *Organizational Theory and Public Policy* (pp. 163–178). Beverly Hills, CA: Sage.

Svenska Dagbladet (1991). Du Pont bygger jättefabrik, 21 August.

Swedish Government Proposition 1987/88:85 (1987). Enclosure 6.2: List of submitting bodies and compilation of their considerations in regard to the Swedish EPA's report 3353 CFC/Freon—propositions to protection of the ozone layer. Sections 3.13 and 4.30: Electrolux AB.

UNEP (1987). Montreal Protocol on Substances that Deplete the Ozone Layer, Final Act.

# Section IV

# Managing in and Around the Global Value Chain

Of all the issues facing managers in today's business environment, globalization is one of the most discussed and least understood, by researchers and practitioners alike. To the already complex task of strategic management, particularly in large companies, globalization adds as many as four new levels of complication: host-country politics, culture, currency exchange, and language.

To help clarify these important management issues, the chapters in this section view globalization from the perspective of firms' value chains.

Gupta and Govindarajan set the tone with an empirical study of how the heterogeneity of the value chain from one country to another influences a global corporation's methods of coordination and control. They look at four value chain configurations: pure manufacturing, pure marketing, manufacturing and marketing, and full value chain subsidiaries.

A panel discussion then offers the perspectives of business executives from two North American firms on the changing environment in which foreign subsidiaries operate.

Discussions 'Whither the Country Manager' and 'Global Localization of Japanese MNCs', focus on the issue of the changing environment in which the foreign manufacturing subsidiaries of MNCs must operate. In this section we utilize the presentations of two of those discussants to illustrate some of the primary forces that have influenced these changes, and changes in the operation of foreign subsidiaries that have resulted.

R. Ian Lennox, President and CEO of Monsanto Canada, Inc., describes the ways in which such forces as new technologies, information access, local governments, and the environment have changed the way in which managers of Monsanto's foreign subsidiaries must operate to achieve globally-competitive success.

Toshikazu Mitsuda, Chairman of the Board, Sharp Electronics Corporation, North American Operations, briefly describes the history of Sharp Electronics, and its presence in North America, and how and why the involvement of Americans in North American operations has continued to increase while Japanese involvement has continued to decrease.

---

Chapter 18    Whither the Country Manager?
*R. Ian Lennox*

Chapter 19    Global Localization of Japanese MNCs
*Toshikazu Mitsuda*

---

This section sheds important light on some of the strategic issues facing firms intending to operate foreign manufacturing subsidiaries in today's increasingly sociopolitical environment. The management style required to be successful in this situation has changed dramatically in recent years, from rigid bottom-line focused authoritarian command/control management, to flexible, competence-building leadership, featuring empowerment of employees and community awareness.

It also illustrates the importance of increased involvement of host-country nationals as a condition of acceptance.

Recommended readings:

Michael Porter (1980). *Competitive Strategy: Techniques for Analyzing Industries and Competitors*, and (1990) *The Competitive Advantage of Nations*.

Erin Anderson and Hubert Gatignon (1986). Modes of foreign entry: A transaction cost analysis and propositions. *Journal of International Business Studies*, Fall. Addresses the question, 'Under what circumstances is a particular mode of *foreign entry* the most efficient long-run choice?'

Sumantra Ghoshal (1987). Global strategy: An organizing framework. *Strategic Management Journal*, **8**. A comprehensive overview and synthesis of literature on *global strategies*, primarily directed at managers of multinational corporations.

Stephen Hymer (1976). *The International Operations of National Firms*. Develops theories to explain *foreign direct investment*, and the distinction between portfolio investment and direct investment.

David Teece (1981). The multinational enterprise: Market failure and market power considerations. *Sloan Management Review*, Spring. Suggests that foreign direct investment should be based on a firm's ability to *transfer* its *technology* successfully, rather than on market power considerations.

Alfred Chandler (1986). The evolution of modern global competition. In Michael Porter (Ed.) *Competition in Global Industries*. Describes the rise of large multinational firms in the United States, United Kingdom, Germany and Japan, and their different approaches to *managing international activities*.

Christopher Bartlett and Sumantra Ghoshal (1988). Organizing for worldwide effectiveness: The transnational solution. *California Management Review*, Fall. Firms that are unable to gain firm strategic control over their worldwide operations and manage them in a *globally-coordinated* manner will probably not succeed in the emerging international economy.

C.K. Prahalad and Yves Doz (1981). An approach to strategic control in MNCs. *Sloan Management Review*, **22**. Examines the problem of how the head office of an MNC can *control* the strategies of its *subsidiaries*.

Christopher Bartlett (1986). Building and managing the transnational: The new organizational challenge. In Michael Porter (Ed.) *Competition in Global Industries*. Stresses the role of management processes and culture in *implementing global strategies*.

Bruce Kogut and Harbar Singh (1988). The effect of national culture on the choice of entry mode. *Journal of International Business Studies*, **19**. Empirically tests the role played by *culture* in determining the mode of entry into foreign arenas.

Bruce Kogut (1989). The stability of joint ventures: Reciprocity and competitive rivalry. *Journal of Industrial Economics*, **38**. Investigates the conditions leading to cooperation, given the potential competitiveness between *joint venture* partners.

Pankaj Ghemawat and Michael Spence (1986). Modeling global competition. In Michael Porter (Ed.) *Competition in Global Industries*. Focuses on the *trade-offs* between responding to local conditions, and standardizing to gain global economies of scale.

# 17

# Alternative Value Chain Configurations for Foreign Subsidiaries: Implications for Coordination and Control within MNCs

ANIL K. GUPTA, VIJAY GOVINDARAJAN

## INTRODUCTION

The historical approach to the study of coordination and control processes within multinational corporations (MNCs) has been to treat the entire MNC as the unit of analysis (e.g. Fouraker and Stopford, 1968; Franko, 1976; Perlmutter, 1969; Prahalad and Doz, 1981). It is only recently that scholars have begun to pursue explicitly the question of how heterogeneity across countries might result in intra-MNC differentiation in coordination and control (Bartlett and Ghoshal, 1989; Doz, 1978; Eghelhoff, 1988; Gupta

*Building the Strategically-Responsive Organization.*
Edited by H. Thomas, D. O'Neal, R. White and D. Hurst.
Copyright © 1994 the Strategic Management Society. Published 1994 by John Wiley & Sons Ltd.

and Govindarajan, 1991; Hedlund, 1986; Poynter and Rugman, 1982). The primary aim of this chapter is to add impetus to this emerging trend by developing and testing hypotheses regarding variations in corporate control mechanisms across subsidiaries that differ from each other in one key strategic respect, namely that they have substantially different value chain configurations (Porter, 1986) in terms of the inclusion or exclusion of research and development (R&D), manufacturing, and marketing activities in the subsidiary's charter. Data for this study were collected directly from the presidents of 330 foreign subsidiaries of 75 major MNCs headquartered in the US, Japan, and Europe.

## THEORY

### VALUE CHAIN CONFIGURATIONS FOR FOREIGN SUBSIDIARIES

While the term 'value chain configuration' is most closely associated with Porter (1986), the main premise that different foreign subsidiaries may have a different mix of functional responsibilities has been accepted for a long time. For instance, Root's (1987) conceptualization of different entry modes (e.g. 'export' versus 'investment' modes) implies quite directly that some subsidiaries may have only a marketing function, whereas others may have both manufacturing and marketing functions. Similarly, Vernon's (1971) product life cycle theory regarding the evolution of US multinationals is explicit about how foreign subsidiaries will typically start out as marketing units but will gradually come to assume first manufacturing and then R&D responsibilities. Whereas both Root (1987) and Vernon (1971) focused on downstream ('market seeking') motives behind the evolution of MNCs, more recently, upstream ('efficiency seeking') motives have also become important, giving rise to purely manufacturing subsidiaries often located in lower-cost regions such as Latin America or Asia (Crookell, 1990).

Unlike Root (1987) and Vernon (1971), Porter (1986) does not take an evolutionary perspective on the functional charters of foreign subsidiaries. Instead, he argues that, even in an established multinational, achieving competitive advantage will often require the MNC to adopt different geographical configurations for different value chain activities, so as to best exploit the differential comparative advantages of different countries:

> International strategy has often been characterized as a choice between worldwide standardization and local tailoring. . . . It should be clear from the discussion so far that neither character- ization captures the complexity of a firm's international strategy choices. A firm's choice of international strategy involves the search for competitive advantage from global configuration/ coordination throughout the value chain. A firm may . . . con- centrate some activities and . . . disperse others. (p. 35)

Thus, following Porter (1986), Root (1987), Vernon (1971) and others, it can be concluded that industry structural characteristics coupled with the differential comparative advantages of different countries will generally result in a situation where different foreign subsidiaries have different strategic characters in terms of the scope of the value chain embedded in the subsidiary. In fact, as Porter (1986) has argued, the design of these configurational differences constitutes the essence of a firm's global, as opposed to domestic, strategy. From a coordination and control perspec- tive, the critical question now becomes: would subsidiaries with different value chain configurations be managed differently and, if so, how? Take, for example, Sony's operations in Italy. Sony has two subsidiaries in Italy, which are managed quite independently of each other. One is a purely *manufacturing* subsidiary whose charter is to produce a single product line for the entire European market; the other is a purely *marketing* subsidiary whose charter is to sell all of Sony's product lines—but within Italy. It would seem that some of the critical organizational issues facing Sony must pertain to whether and, if so, how coordination and control mechanisms for these two subsidiaries should differ from each other and from those for subsidiaries with yet other patterns of value chain configurations.

Despite the criticality of the configurational differences descri- bed above, no research has so far been conducted on their organi- zational implications. Driven by the primary goal of redressing this deficiency, this chapter focuses on differences in coordination and control mechanisms across the following four patterns of value chain configurations: (i) purely manufacturing subsidiaries (MFG), (ii) purely marketing subsidiaries (MKT), (iii) manufactur- ing-cum-marketing subsidiaries (MFGMKT), and (iv) full chain subsidiaries (FULL-CHAIN) defined as those having responsibility for marketing and manufacturing, as well as R&D. In our sample, foreign subsidiaries with other configurations (i.e. with just R&D, R&D-cum-manufacturing, or R&D-cum-marketing responsibilities) were too few in number and were not incorporated into the analysis.

---

## IMPLICATIONS FOR COORDINATION AND CONTROL

Our hypotheses linking value chain configurations to coordination and control mechanisms derive from the differential impact of alternative value chain configurations on (i) the extent of transactional interdependence between a focal subsidiary and the rest of the corporation, and (ii) the need for local orientation on the part of executives managing the subsidiary. In order to map adequately the richness and complexity of the task facing managers in MNCs, we interpret the term 'coordination and control mechanisms' broadly and use it to represent not just the formal control system but also other powerful formal and informal organizational mechanisms and processes generally available to corporate headquarters for shaping the decisions and actions of subsidiaries (Martinez and Jarillo, 1989).

---

### Transactional Interdependence

It is obvious that the less complete the value chain embedded in a subsidiary, the greater would be the subsidiary's dependence on the parent and sister subsidiaries for complementary activities. An MFG subsidiary must depend on the corporation at both the upstream (i.e. technology) as well as downstream (i.e. marketing) ends. An MKT subsidiary would do its own marketing but must depend on the corporation at the upstream end (i.e. design and manufacture of goods). Similarly, an MFGMKT subsidiary's dependence on the corporation is likely to be only at the upstream end for some technology-intensive components, whereas a FULL-CHAIN subsidiary can be expected to have the least amount of interdependence with the rest of the corporation.

Consistent with Thompson's broader arguments (1967), the greater the degree of a subsidiary's transactional interdependence with the rest of the corporation, the greater would be the need for global coordination of the subsidiary's activities. As organization theory informs us, coordination can be effected through a variety of both formal and informal mechanisms (Tushman, 1977; Van de Ven, 1986). In this study, we focus on four such mechanisms: (i) centralization versus decentralization (Ford and Slocum, 1977; Vancil, 1980), (ii) incentive mechanisms (Lawler, 1990; Salter, 1973), (iii) communication patterns (Allen and Cohen, 1969; Jablin, 1979; Tushman, 1977), and (iv) organizational socialization (Edstrom and Galbraith, 1977; Ouchi, 1979; Van Maanen and Schein, 1979). Consistent with organization theory, our predictions are that strategic contexts that require greater coordination will be associated with higher centralization, greater reliance on group-based incentives, more intense communication patterns, and greater organizational socialization. In the specific case of foreign subsidiaries with different value chain configurations, these predictions can be translated into the following specific hypotheses:

1. Hypothesis 1: The extent of parent–subsidiary decentralization will vary across different patterns of value chain configurations; specifically, it will be lowest for MFG subsidiaries, low for MKT subsidiaries, medium for MFGMKT subsidiaries, and highest for FULL-CHAIN subsidiaries.
2. Hypothesis 2: The dependence of the subsidiary president's bonus on the performance of a cluster of subsidiaries will vary across different patterns of value chain configurations; specifically, it will be highest for MFG subsidiaries, high for MKT subsidiaries, medium for MFGMKT subsidiaries, and lowest for FULL-CHAIN subsidiaries.
3. Hypothesis 3: The intensity of parent–subsidiary communication will vary across different patterns of value chain configurations; specifically, it will be highest for MFG subsidiaries, high for MKT subsidiaries, medium for MFGMKT subsidiaries, and lowest for FULL-CHAIN subsidiaries.
4. Hypothesis 4: The global corporate socialization of the subsidiary president will vary across different patterns of value chain configurations; specifically, it will be highest for MFG subsidiaries, high for MKT subsidiaries, medium for MFGMKT subsidiaries, and lowest for FULL-CHAIN subsidiaries.

It is well recognized that 'intensity of communication' is a multidimensional construct (Gupta and Govindarajan, 1991; Jablin,

1979). Thus, in testing Hypothesis 3, we will focus on the following two dimensions: *frequency* of communication and *density* of communication. In the MNC context, the need to look at density of communication was first suggested by Bartlett and Ghoshal (1989) who observed that, in Matsushita, parent–subsidiary communication occurs not just through the subsidiary president but also through linkages along multiple layers of the subsidiary's hierarchy.

## Need for Local Orientation

Many scholars of MNCs have discussed the need for foreign subsidiaries to choose between a global versus a local orientation (e.g. Perlmutter, 1969). However, as Bartlett and Ghoshal (1989) and Porter (1986) have suggested, global coordination and local orientation may be independent dimensions, thereby raising the possibility that some subsidiaries may have to pursue both simultaneously, and not have the luxury of choosing one or the other. In this section, we posit that the need for local orientation would be high for FULL-CHAIN, MFGMKT, and MKT subsidiaries but low for MFG subsidiaries. Our arguments reflect the expectation that, if a subsidiary's primary charter is to serve the local market (whether through imports from the corporation or through local production), then the local orientation of the subsidiary must be high. Note that it is only in the case of MFG subsidiaries that the subsidiary's primary charter is to serve global rather than local markets.

In this study, we focus on two organizational mechanisms that are expected to have a positive effect on the local orientation of subsidiary managers: (i) the proportion of local nationals in the subsidiary's top management team, and (ii) the length of the subsidiary president's tenure within the local subsidiary. Several studies have indicated that national background accounts for significant differences in managerial perspectives. Specifically, relative to expatriates, host country nationals have been reported as being more familiar with the local environment, as developing a stronger rapport with local managers, and as developing a stronger identification with and commitment to the local subsidiary than to the parent (Tung, 1982; Zeira, 1976). The explanation for these findings appears to lie in the cognitive and motivational contexts of subsidiary managers. Cognitively, relative to expatriates, host country nationals are likely to have a more comprehensive understanding of the local sociocultural, political, and economic environments. Motivationally, the local commitment of host country nationals results from the fact that, in most cases, their career progression outside of the local subsidiary and into the hierarchy of the parent corporation tends to be rare. We anticipate that, irrespective of nationality, subsidiary managers' understanding of local markets would also be a positive function of their length of tenure within the subsidiary. In the context of subsidiaries with different value chain configurations, these expectations can now be translated into the following specific hypotheses:

5. Hypothesis 5: The proportion of local nationals in the subsidiary's top management team will vary across different patterns of value chain configurations; specifically, it will be low for MFG subsidiaries and high for MKT, MFGMKT, and FULL-CHAIN subsidiaries.
6. Hypothesis 6: The subsidiary president's tenure with the local subsidiary will vary across different patterns of value chain configurations; specifically, it will be low for MFG subsidiaries and high for MKT, MFGMKT, and FULL-CHAIN subsidiaries.

## METHOD

### SAMPLE

Data were collected through a pilot-tested questionnaire survey of the heads (variously titled presidents, managing directors, or general managers) of 374 foreign subsidiaries of major MNCs headquartered in the US (19 MNCs), Japan (41 MNCs), and Europe (15 British and Scandinavian MNCs). The number of subsidiaries from each of these three regional groups of MNCs in the total sample is 117, 112, and 145, respectively. Every MNC in the sample had sales exceeding $US 1 billion and the number of employees per subsidiary averaged 985. In overall terms, participation in this study was sought from the presidents of 997 subsidiaries. Thus, the final sample of 374 represents a response rate of 38%. By geographical region, the response rates were 28% for subsidiaries of US headquartered MNCs, 41% for Japanese MNCs, and 46% for European MNCs. The higher response rates in the case of Japanese and European MNCs appear to reflect the fact that, in most of these companies, subsidiary presidents also received supporting letters from either the head of an industry-sponsored research institute or the corporate CEO. Subsidiary presidents within Japanese MNCs received both an English and a Japanese language questionnaire; initial interviews with the European companies indicated that the English-language questionnaire alone would suffice.

## MEASURES

A summary of how all of the coordination and control variables were measured is contained in Appendix A. As discussed earlier, intensity of communication was measured along two different dimensions: frequency of communication and density of communication, i.e. multiplicity of communication linkages between the parent and the subsidiary. In virtually all cases, we used standard well-established research instruments with minor changes in wording to adapt the instrument to the multi-national context. Given below are details pertaining to the classification of subsidiaries in terms of alternative value chain configurations.

Each subsidiary president was requested to answer three quite straightforward questions: (i) 'Does your subsidiary have one or more research and development facilities?' (ii) 'Does your subsidiary have one or more manufacturing facilities?' and (iii) 'Does your subsidiary have one or more marketing and sales facilities?' Of the 374 subsidiaries in the total sample, complete responses to these questions were obtained from 350 subsidiaries. This group of 350 did not include any subsidiary with just the R&D but neither manufacturing nor marketing functions. In addition, there were 8 subsidiaries with R&D-cum-manufacturing (but not marketing) activities and 12 with R&D-cum-marketing (but not manufacturing) activities. Because of the small numbers, these two types of subsidiaries were dropped from the analysis. This left a sample of 330 subsidiaries where each subsidiary could be classified into one of the four dominant patterns of value chain configurations. TABLE 17.1 presents details of the resulting sample structure.

TABLE 17.1  Sample structure

| Type of subsidiary | Total number of subsidiaries in the sample | Breakdown of sample by location of corporate HQ | | | Average number of years since establishment or acquisition | Selected descriptive statistics | |
|---|---|---|---|---|---|---|---|
| | | US | Japan | Europe | | Ratio of purchases from parent or sister subsidiaries to cost of goods sold (%) | Ratio of sales to parent or sister subsidiaries to total sales (%) |
| MFG | 22 | 4 | 14 | 4 | 11 | 8 | 37 |
| MKT | 65 | 25 | 27 | 12 | 19 | 29 | 4 |
| MFGMKT | 83 | 38 | 21 | 24 | 22 | 20 | 10 |
| FULL-CHAIN | 161 | 44 | 25 | 92 | 25 | 13 | 7 |
| Total sample | 330 | 112 | 98 | 140 | 22 | 18 | 9 |
| F-statistic | | | | | 3.70 | 6.91 | 23.64 |
| Degrees of freedom | | | | | (3294) | (3326) | (3326) |
| Significance | | | | | $p < 0.0122$ | $p < 0.0002$ | $p < 0.0000$ |

Out of the total sample of 374 subsidiaries, data on value chain configurations were missing for 24 subsidiaries. The remaining sample ($n = 350$) included 8 subsidiaries with R&D and manufacturing (but not marketing) activities and 12 with R&D and marketing (but not manufacturing) activities. Because of the small numbers, these two types of subsidiaries were dropped from the analysis.

## RESULTS

All variables were standardized prior to testing the hypotheses. TABLE 17.2 gives zero order correlations among the seven coordination and control variables of interest. As can be seen, over and beyond the conceptual distinctness of these variables, none of the correlations is so high as to suggest empirical redundancy among them.

TABLE 17.3 contains the results of ANOVA tests conducted to check for hypothesized differences in the mean values of the organizational variables across the four subgroups of subsidiaries, each subgroup representing a different value chain configuration.

As an overall observation, it should be noted that, for five of the seven organizational variables, there are significant intergroup differences; intergroup differences were not found only in the case of the subsidiary president's corporate socialization as well as his/her tenure with the focal subsidiary. These results provide

TABLE 17.2  Zero-order correlations among the coordination and control mechanisms

|  | V1 | V2 | V3 | V4 | V5 | V6 | V7 |
|---|---|---|---|---|---|---|---|
| V1: Parent–subsidiary decentralization |  |  |  |  |  |  |  |
| V2: Bonus dependence on a cluster of subsidiaries | ***−0.24 |  |  |  |  |  |  |
| V3: Frequency of parent–subsidiary communication | **0.15 | −0.00 |  |  |  |  |  |
| V4: Density of parent–subsidiary communication | *−0.10 | **0.16 | 0.08 |  |  |  |  |
| V5: Subsidiary president's corporate socialization | −0.05 | ***0.25 | −0.08 | ***0.34 |  |  |  |
| V6: Local nationals as proportion of top management team | **0.13 | −0.07 | ***0.36 | ***−0.33 | ***−0.43 |  |  |
| V7: Subsidiary president's tenure with current subsidiary | 0.04 | *−0.13 | 0.03 | −0.08 | ***−0.21 | ***0.30 |  |

*one-tail $p < 0.05$; **one-tail $p < 0.01$; ***one-tail $p < 0.001$.

TABLE 17.3  Alternative value chain configurations for foreign subsidiaries: implications for coordination and control

| Coordination and control mechanisms* | Alternative Value Chain Configurations | | | | F-statistic | Significance† | Significant cell differences‡ |
|---|---|---|---|---|---|---|---|
| | Cell 1 MFG ($n = 22$) | Cell 2 MKT ($n = 65$) | Cell 3 MFGMKT ($n = 83$) | Cell 4 FULL-CHAIN ($n = 161$) | | | |
| V1: Parent–subsidiary decentralization | 0.14 | −0.48 | −0.08 | 0.24 | 9.31 (3325) | *** | (1–2)(2–3)(2–4)(3–4) |
| V2: Bonus dependence on a cluster of subsidiaries | 0.35 | 0.21 | 0.25 | −0.21 | 4.92 (3256) | ** | (2–4)(3–4) |
| V3: Frequency of parent–subsidiary communication | −0.32 | −0.11 | −0.05 | 0.20 | 3.07 (3326) | * | (1–4)(2–4) |
| V4: Density of parent–subsidiary communication | 0.21 | 0.27 | −0.06 | −0.11 | 2.75 (3326) | * | (2–4) |
| V5: Subsidiary president's corporate socialization | 0.05 | 0.11 | 0.03 | −0.08 | 0.68 (3326) | n.s. | |
| V6: Local nationals as proportion of top management team | −0.62 | −0.34 | 0.04 | 0.31 | 11.52 (3326) | *** | (1–3)(1–4)(2–3)(2–4)(3–4) |
| V7: Subsidiary president's tenure with current subsidiary | −0.30 | −0.12 | −0.01 | 0.13 | 1.80 (3325) | n.s. | |

*All variables were standardized prior to these tests.
†$*p < 0.05$; $**p < 0.01$; $***p < 0.001$.
‡Duncan's multiple range test.

strong reinforcement of the emerging notion of MNCs as networks of differentiated subsidiaries (Bartlett and Ghoshal, 1989; Ghoshal and Nohria, 1989) and of the corollary implication that strategic control within the MNC varies widely and systematically across subsidiaries. The next question is whether or not the differences in coordination and control variables are linked to those in value chain configurations in the theoretically predicted manner.

Hypothesis 1 predicted that parent–subsidiary decentralization will be lowest for MFG, low for MKT, medium for MFGMKT, and high for FULL-CHAIN subsidiaries. While the results are supportive of predictions regarding the steady increase in decentralization from MKT to MFGMKT to FULL-CHAIN subsidiaries, they do not support our expectation of very low decentralization (i.e. high centralization) for MFG subsidiaries. In fact, the decentralization given to MFG subsidiaries is not significantly different from that for FULL-CHAIN subsidiaries. Perhaps the explanation for this unexpected finding lies in the possibility that the strategic charter of MFG subsidiaries is likely to be the most clearly defined; hence, there is little parental interference in the operations of these subsidiaries on an ongoing basis.

Hypothesis 2 predicted that the dependence of the subsidiary president's bonus on the performance of a cluster of multiple subsidiaries will be highest for MFG, high for MKT, medium for MFGMKT, and low for FULL-CHAIN subsidiaries. The results are supportive of predictions for MFG, MKT, and FULL-CHAIN subsidiaries; however, they indicate that the dependence of a typical MFGMKT subsidiary president's bonus on a cluster of subsidiaries is not any less than that in the case of MFG or MKT subsidiaries. In other words, what seems to matter here is whether, in an either/or sense, the value chain is complete or not and not the *extent* of value chain incompleteness.

Hypothesis 3 predicted that the intensity of parent–subsidiary communication will be highest for MFG, high for MKT, medium for MFGMKT, and low for FULL-CHAIN subsidiaries. While the results support these directional expectations in the case of *density* of communication, they are exactly the opposite of predictions in the case of *frequency* of communication. More directly stated, we find that MFG and MKT subsidiaries are managed through a high density *but* low frequency of communication; in contrast, FULL-CHAIN subsidiaries are managed through a low density *but* high frequency of communication. The supportive findings for density of communication appear to reflect the fact that MFG and MKT subsidiaries would need greater 'operational' coordination than that needed in the case of MFGMKT or FULL-CHAIN subsidiaries.

Perhaps the explanation for the interesting but counter-intuitive results pertaining to frequency of communication lies in the fact that parent executives perceive considerable risks of agency loss (Jensen and Meckling, 1976; Pratt and Zeckhauser, 1984) in the case of FULL-CHAIN subsidiaries. As can be seen from other results in TABLE 17.3, FULL-CHAIN subsidiaries are given very high decentralization and managed largely by local nationals who are compensated almost exclusively on the basis of the local subsidiary's performance. In such contexts, there is every likelihood that parent executives would perceive a very high degree of information asymmetry *vis-a-vis* subsidiary executives. Given the completeness of the value chain inside such subsidiaries, reduction of information asymmetries through centralization might not be a feasible solution; thus, parent executives appear to be attempting to reduce the risks of agency loss through very frequent interaction with and monitoring of the presidents of such subsidiaries. By the same logic, the risks of agency loss might be viewed by parent executives as considerably less in the case of MFG and MKT subsidiaries because of management through expatriates and bonus dependence on a cluster of subsidiaries; accordingly, the perceived need for more frequent interaction with the presidents of such subsidiaries might be considerably less.

Hypothesis 4 predicted that the subsidiary president's corporate socialization would be highest for MFG subsidiaries, high for MKT subsidiaries, medium for MFGMKT subsidiaries, and low for FULL-CHAIN subsidiaries. There was no support for this prediction.

Hypothesis 5 predicted that the proportion of local nationals in the top management team will be low for MFG but high for MKT, MFGMKT, and FULL-CHAIN subsidiaries. In large part, this hypothesis was supported. However, in a partial departure from predictions, the results also indicate that the top management teams of MKT subsidiaries consist of expatriates to a significantly greater degree than is true for MFGMKT subsidiaries; similarly, the proportion of expatriates in the case of MFGMKT subsidiaries is greater than in the case of FULL-CHAIN subsidiaries. It would appear that parent executives make their decisions to rely on expatriates as opposed to local nationals primarily on the basis of the degree of incompleteness in the value chain and not on the basis of whether the subsidiary is responsible for selling to local markets.

Hypothesis 6 predicted that the subsidiary president's tenure with the local subsidiary will be low in the case of MFG subsidiaries but high in the case of the other three configurations. Paralleling the non-findings with respect to corporate socialization, this hypothesis also was not supported.

## DISCUSSION

Departing from the macro-focus of virtually all research on strategic control within MNCs, in this chapter, we have argued that the strategic contexts of subsidiaries within the same MNC can differ in important respects and that there is a need for strategy–organization coalignment research using individual subsidiaries as the unit of analysis. More concretely, we operationalized inter-subsidiary differences in terms of alternative value chain configurations. In this context, it might be noted that Porter (1986) has argued rather persuasively that differences in value chain configurations constitute the essence of global strategy.

Taking into account both downstream ('market seeking') as well as upstream ('efficiency seeking') motives for going abroad, the study focused on the four dominant patterns of value chain configurations: (i) purely manufacturing subsidiaries, (ii) purely marketing subsidiaries, (iii) manufacturing-cum-marketing subsidiaries, and (iv) full value chain subsidiaries defined as those that have control over not just marketing and manufacturing but R&D activities as well. While most of the hypotheses were supported, we also discovered some interesting surprises. The results indicated that, across the four configurations, there exist systematic differences in (i) extent of parent–subsidiary decentralization, (ii) dependence of the subsidiary president's bonus on the performance of a cluster of subsidiaries, (iii) frequency and density of parent–subsidiary communication, and (iv) proportion of local nationals in the subsidiary's top management team. Perhaps, the most interesting surprise was the finding that, totally contrary to predictions, the frequency of parent–subsidiary communication was highest in the case of FULL-CHAIN subsidiaries and lowest in the case of MFG subsidiaries. We explained this finding by speculating that parent executives must perceive the risks of agency loss (Pratt and Zeckhauser, 1984) as particularly severe in the case of FULL-CHAIN subsidiaries; as is obvious from TABLE 17.3, these subsidiaries are given very high decentralization and are managed mostly by local nationals whose bonus compensation is tied almost exclusively to the performance of the local subsidiary. If our speculation is correct, then it is likely that parent executives in MNCs must face their greatest control challenges in the case of FULL-CHAIN subsidiaries. It would seem that a more focused examination of these challenges would constitute an important avenue for future research.

---

## APPENDIX A

## MEASUREMENT OF COORDINATION AND CONTROL VARIABLES

### Parent–Subsidiary Decentralization

This variable was measured through a nine-item instrument patterned after Vancil (1980) and Tannenbaum (1968). Responses across the nine items were averaged to yield a composite measure of parent–subsidiary decentralization (Cronbach alpha = 0.86). Higher values on this measure indicate higher decentralization (range = 1.2 to 5.0; mean = 4.0).

---

### Basis for Bonus Determination

Based on Salter (1973) and Gupta and Govindarajan (1986), subsidiary presidents were asked to indicate the percentage of their incentive bonus that was based on (i) their own subsidiary's performance versus (ii) the performance of a cluster of subsidiaries. Responses to the second item were used as a measure of bonus dependence on the performance of a cluster of subsidiaries (range = 0 to 100%; mean = 24%).

---

### Intensity of Communication

The measure for *frequency of communication* was adapted from Van de Ven and Ferry (1979). For each of four modes of communication (face-to-face, over the telephone, routine and periodic formal reports, and electronic or paper-based letters or memos), the respondents were asked to indicate the frequency of communication between themselves and executives from the parent corporation on a seven-point scale (ranging from '1 = daily' to '7 = less often than once a year'). The responses were reverse scored and averaged across the four items to yield a composite measure of frequency of communication (Cronbach alpha = 0.80; range = 1.0 to 7.0; mean = 4.7). *Density of communication* was measured by asking the respondents the extent to which (i) 'yourself,' (ii) 'senior managers just below you,' (iii) 'middle managers,' and (iv) 'other employees' interacted with their counterparts from the parent corporation. A three-point response scale was used: 'rarely,' 'sometimes,' and 'frequently.' For the aggregate of four levels, the total count of 'sometimes' or 'frequently' responses was used as a measure of the multiplicity of communication linkages between the local subsidiary and the parent (range = 0 to 4; mean = 3.0).

## Corporate Socialization

This measure was adapted from Bartlett and Ghoshal (1989). For each respondent, the total count of 'yes' responses to the following four questions was treated as a measure of corporate socialization: (1) 'Have you worked for one or more years at corporate headquarters in this corporation?' (2) 'Have you worked for one or more years in other subsidiaries of this corporation?' (3) 'Have you participated in executive development programs involving participants from several subsidiaries?' and (4) 'Do you have a mentor at corporate headquarters?' (range = 0 to 4; mean = 2.1).

## Proportion of Local Nationals in the Top Management Team

For managers heading each of seven positions, the subsidiary presidents were asked to indicate the nationality of each person on a four-point scale: 'local national,' 'home country expatriate,' 'third country expatriate,' and 'not applicable,' implying that there was nobody heading such a position. The instrument also explained the precise meanings of these terms. The percentage of applicable positions that were headed by local nationals was regarded as a measure of the extent to which the subsidiary's top management team was localized (range = 0 to 100%; mean = 64%).

## Subsidiary President's Tenure with the Subsidiary

This variable was measured through a straightforward question that asked the subsidiary president to indicate the number of years that he/she had spent working for the current subsidiary (range = 1 to 43 years; mean = 7.8 years).

# REFERENCES

Allen, T.J. and Cohen, S. (1969). Information flow in R&D laboratories. *Administrative Science Quarterly*, **14**, 12–19.

Bartlett, C.A. and Ghoshal, S. (1989). *Managing across Borders: The Transnational Solution*. Boston, MA: Harvard Business School Press.

Crookell, H. (1990). Organization structure for global operations. In P.W. Beamish, J.P. Killing, D.J. LeCraw and H. Crookell (Eds) *International Management: Text and Cases* (pp. 91–102). Homewood, IL: Richard D. Irwin.

Doz, Y.L. (1978). Managing manufacturing rationalization within multinational companies. *Columbia Journal of World Business*, Fall, 82–94.

Edstrom, A. and Galbraith, J.R. (1977). Transfer of managers as a coordination and control strategy in multinational organizations. *Administrative Science Quarterly*, **22**, 248–263.

Egelhoff, W.G. (1988). *Organizing the Multinational Enterprise: An Information-Processing Perspective*. Cambridge, MA: Ballinger.

Ford, J.D. and Slocum, J.W. (1977). Size, technology, environment, and the structure of organizations. *Academy of Management Review*, **2**, 561–575.

Fouraker, L.E. and Stopford, J.M. (1968). Organizational structure and multinational strategy. *Administrative Science Quarterly*, **13**, 47–64.

Franko, L.G. (1976). *The European Multinationals: A Renewed Challenge to American and British Big Business*. Stamford, CT: Greylock.

Ghoshal, S. and Nohria, N. (1989). Internal differentiation within multinational corporations. *Strategic Management Journal*, **10**, 323–337.

Gupta, A.K. and Govindarajan, V. (1986). Resource sharing among SBUs: Strategic antecedents and administrative implications. *Academy of Management Journal*, **29**, 695–714.

Gupta, A.K. and Govindarajan, V. (1991). Knowledge flows and the structure of control within multinational corporations. *Academy of Management Review*, **16**, 768–792.

Hedlund, G. (1986). The modern MNC: A heterarchy. *Human Resource Management*, **25**(1), 9–35.

Jablin, F.M. (1979). Superior–subordinate communication: The state of the art. *Psychological Bulletin*, **6**, 1201–1222.

Jensen, M.C. and Meckling, W.H. (1976). Theory of the firm. *Journal of Financial Economics*, **3**, 305–360.

Lawler, E.E. III (1990). *Strategic Pay*. San Francisco, CA: Jossey-Bass.

Martinez, J.I. and Jarillo, J.C. (1989). The evolution of research on coordination mechanisms in multinational corporations. *Journal of International Business Studies*, **20**, 489–514.

Ouchi, W.G. (1979). A conceptual framework for the design of organizational control mechanisms. *Management Science*, **25**, 833–848.

Perlmutter, H.V. (1969). The tortuous evolution of the multinational corporation. *Columbia Journal of World Business*, January/February, 9–18.

Porter, M.E. (1986). Competition in global industries: A conceptual framework. In M.E. Porter (Ed.) *Competition in Global Industries* (pp. 15–60). Boston, MA: Harvard Business School Press.

Poynter, T.A. and Rugman, A.M. (1982). World product mandates: How will multinationals respond? *Business Quarterly*, Autumn, 54–61.

Prahalad, C.K. and Doz, Y.L. (1981). An approach to strategic control in MNCs. *Sloan Management Review*, Summer, 5–13.

Pratt, J.W. and Zeckhauser, R.J. (1984). *Principals and Agents: The Structure of Business*. Boston, MA: Harvard Business School Press.

Root, F.R. (1987). *Entry Strategies for International Markets*. Lexington, MA: Lexington Books.

Salter, M.S. (1973). Tailor incentive compensation to strategy. *Harvard Business Review*, **49**(2), 94–102.

Tannenbaum, A.S. (1968). Control in organizations: Individual adjustments and organizational performance. *Administrative Science Quarterly*, **7**, 236–257.

Thompson, J.D. (1967). *Organization in Action*. New York: McGraw-Hill.

Tung, R.L. (1982). Selection and training procedures of U.S., European, and Japanese multinationals. *California Management Review*, **25**(1), 57–71.

Tushman, M.L. (1977). Communications across organizational boundaries: Special boundary roles in the innovative process. *Administrative Science Quarterly*, **22**, 587–605.

Vancil, R.F. (1980). *Decentralization: Managerial Ambiguity by Design*. New York: Financial Executives Research Foundation.

Van de Ven, A.H. (1986). Central problems in the management of innovation. *Management Science*, **32**, 590–607.

Van de Ven, A.H. and Ferry, D.L. (1979). *Measuring and Assessing Organizations*. New York: John Wiley.

Van Maanen, J. and Schein, E.H. (1979). Toward a theory of organizational socialization. In B.M. Staw (Ed.) *Research in Organizational Behavior*, Vol. 1 (pp. 209–264). Greenwich, CT: JAI Press.

Vernon, R. (1971). *Sovereignty at Bay*. New York: Basic Books.

Zeira, Y. (1976). Management development in ethnocentric multinational corporations. *California Management Review*, **18**(4), 34–42.

# 18

# Whither the Country Manager?[1]

## R. Ian Lennox

## Introduction

The globalization of production and investment, the challenges of new technologies, the proliferation of access to information, trends toward greater economic integration, and the pervasiveness of government, the environment and community in decision making are breaking all the rules and challenging the structure and responsibilities of the 'traditional' organization. Nowhere is the responsibility to change to the new environment more evident than in the new role of the country manager.

## Tradition

The basic strategy that has served multinational subsidiaries well in the past—producing a wide range of 'parent' products for the subsidiary market—was dependent for its success on tariff protection. Recent trends toward greater economic integration are threatening the existence of the 'traditional' subsidiary organization, and, in some instances, the very existence of the country manager.

*Building the Strategically-Responsive Organization.*
Edited by H. Thomas, D. O'Neal, R. White and D. Hurst.
Copyright © 1994 the Strategic Management Society. Published 1994 by John Wiley & Sons Ltd.

In the environment of the past the country manager was king. The style of management was control; the manager exercised considerable autonomy from the parent company, human resources were plentiful and government contact was directed at ensuring that an industry's 'oligopoly' was insulated from 'unfair' competition (defined as anything entering the country that conflicted with the subsidiary's prosperity). High value-added meant higher price—not higher quality, service or customer acceptance.

The country manager of yesterday was the chief operating officer (COO) of the parent's subsidiary. Most multinational companies were industry-focused (automotive, insurance, banking, chemicals) and centralized. The country manager was directly accountable for the financial performance of the subsidiary. He reported to an executive vice-president, or to the president of international operations—but not to both—who was always located at 'headquarters'. The organization chart was neat and clean. Matrix organizations—introduced during the 1970s and 1980s—were, in most cases, quickly dissolved because of the dilution effect on control.

The drive for the subsidiary to be competitive was highlighted to government when tax or labour legislation was proposed (another time to contact government), but, more often, higher costs were accepted—and immediately passed on to customers or consumers, since the competition was local and always under a similar cost structure. Cost, by the way, really meant manufacturing cost, or unit cost. Accountants, financial analysts and engineers rich with data from the surge of information availability, worked at head office trying to decide how to increase yields, reduce waste and remove labour content. In fact, during the late 1970s, IBM had software for 'fill-in the blank' organizational charts and slightly more complex models for 'managing price for margin'. As we will see, these truly were 'the golden days' for country managers.

---

## THE RULES CHANGED

The trend toward greater economic integration and the competitive need to operate with only the most productive capital has resulted in multinational corporations transcending national boundaries.

Multinationals, in fact all businesses, have begun 'right-sizing' their operations. Challenges associated with new technologies are resulting in companies focusing on their 'core competencies' again. Decentralized organizations—sometimes into separate companies—are seeking alliances with complementary organizations in order to gain faster access to the market, with an expectation of recovering research and development costs more rapidly. Examples are numerous, and include automotive alliances between US and Japanese firms (Chrysler/Mitsubishi) and merger/acquisition activities in the high development cost pharmaceutical industry (Merck/DuPont). Even 'Big Blue' (IBM) has solicited joint venture relationships (with Apple) to accelerate successful market introduction.

Sometime during the mid-1980s, cost was redefined to mean 'total cost'; quality was defined as 'total quality' and the customer—regardless of his geographic location—was determined to be important to the financial success of the business.

Sometime during the mid-1980s, the rules changed.

## THE DEVELOPING CHANGES

The result of the changing environment leaves leaner operating structures. Layers of middle management (not labour) have disappeared; companies have decentralized; decision-making has moved down in the organization—to where the best information to implement tactical decisions is available. Furthermore, companies—and even divisions of operating companies—began to develop their own 'cultures' and 'reward systems' with a heavy emphasis on the theme of 'teams'. Employee empowerment and workforce diversity were taken out of the textbooks and put into action.

Manufacturing facilities, depending on their progress of culture development, began to be viewed very differently. Uncompetitive production facilities—regardless of whether they were in the 'parent's' homeland or subsidiary location—'surfaced'. The meaning of 'competitive' has grown in definition. The historic meaning—lowest unit cost—changed depending on the industry. The pervasiveness of government, the environment, and communities' 'right to know' changed the rules more than any other factors. Once 'perceived' low-cost plants have become liabilities to the corporation. Lack of community understanding, and unacceptable practices as viewed by environmental groups and government (local, provincial, federal) regulations have become a crucial factor in a business' competitiveness and 'right to operate'.

## FACTORS THAT DETERMINE SUBSIDIARY RESPONSIBILITIES

The role of the country manager of a multinational subsidiary has changed because of the altered business environment. Three principal factors have influenced how the responsibilities have changed, for different country managers.

1. Competitive environment
2. Corporate culture
3. Competencies of the subsidiary

## COMPETITIVE ENVIRONMENT

What determines the business' competitive advantage? If the answer is 'unit cost' the company will have all the characteristics of a commodity business. Strategy, marketing, regulatory affairs, and legal and public policy play an insignificant role in the successful operation of the business. In this extreme case, the role of the country executive is suspect—if he or she does not have strong 'technical' skills (sales, engineering, distribution), then he or she is probably redundant.

## CORPORATE CULTURE

This is a complex factor. Companies even in the same industries—with the same products—behave differently.

Globalization is intimidating from a subsidiary perspective. If the local market is small (and it is almost always smaller than the parent's home market), and if the parent company management has limited international understanding, then the trend will always be toward 'integrating' the local market (production, distribution, legal, marketing) into the parent's decentralized organization. Combined with an unregulated competitive environment, this is probably the best organization to control costs. In combination with the regulated or highly differentiated market, the results vary. Most often, 'management from abroad' will yield ill-devised strategies, products and policies on an increasingly dependent— and ultimately leaner and weaker—local management organization.

## COMPETENCIES OF THE SUBSIDIARY

In an unregulated, undifferentiated market, the competencies of the subsidiary will perhaps be limited to sales and distribution. In more complex markets, which are more often the case, a subsidiary must be positioned to become a natural leader in selected products (product mandate); research initiatives (select R&D focus); development (pilot plant/market acceptance trials) and/or functional areas (safety, environment, human resources, legal, technology). Initiatives such as these must be agreed upon with the parent company in order to be successful in reinforcing, *to the parent*, the subsidiary's competence. Failure to develop a set of competencies will result in subsidiary dependence, and a failure to attract and retain 'the best and the brightest'—an untenable situation.

## THE CHANGING ROLE OF THE COUNTRY MANAGER

As we progress through the last decade of this century we are witnessing unprecedented change. The 'management style' of the country manager is changing from 'command and control' to an 'empowerment' philosophy. The once centralized organization is now *decentralized*, with a multitude of divisions or business units, each with their own *specialists*. Organizations are flat—layers of middle management between the customer and the country manager have been removed. Reporting relationships are almost meaningless—'straight' and 'dotted' lines have been replaced by 'teams' whose membership is likely to be spread over three or four continents.

The most successful organizations will have local executives focused on:

- Providing a clear, concise vision for the subsidiary which can be translated into results by a diverse management team.
- Ensuring the subsidiary's 'right to operate'.
- Supplying, preparing and testing high potential talent within the subsidiary for local and global opportunities.
- Developing the unique competencies of the subsidiary.

---

## VISION

The new country manager must have the capabilities to assemble, interpret and articulate a 'vision' for the subsidiary's activities in the local country. Since the management structure is lean, the country manager may be the only person who sees the 'big picture' (most operating company directors in the subsidiary will be fighting fires and will be focused on short-term results). In Monsanto Canada, the 'vision' provides meaning to our people in transforming the company to a highly respected and profitable technology-driven life sciences organization.

---

## PRIVILEGE-TO-OPERATE

The new country manager must take a proactive leadership role in providing his/her company's privilege-to-operate. The mechanism may vary by industry; however, the company must be accepted within its community (involvement in education, charitable activities, social inputs), respected by government (local, provincial, federal) and admired by employees.

At Monsanto, this is a complex task. Initiatives including Responsible Care, Junior Achievement, United Way and Pride focus on our communities. Participation with government and academic institutions reinforces our thrust to responsibly develop new technologies (plant sciences/biotechnology) in a well-balanced regulatory environment. Employee involvement and communication foster an empowered culture motivated to outperform.

---

## HIGH POTENTIAL TALENT

In the changing business environment, perhaps the single most important responsibility of the country manager is to attract and develop high potential talent from a diverse population, which will ensure the subsidiary's future success *and* contribute to the corporation's 'global talent pool'.

Monsanto takes succession planning and implementation seriously. It consumes—and should dictate—20% of the country manager's efforts. This job is no longer a human resource function in today's competitive environment. If you're not receiving dividends from a diverse and talented employee pool, you don't own the right stock!

---

## SUBSIDIARY COMPETENCIES

Multinational corporations must gain value from their country subsidiaries. In the past, we saw the role of making and/or selling the 'parent' products or services as the prime value. Today and tomorrow, country subsidiaries must contribute in ways that deliver unique competencies to the global enterprise, ranging from designing, developing, producing, and/or marketing products and/or services to seeking unique opportunities that can be offered to the total organization.

In Monsanto, we have a host of newly developing competencies, ranging from the development of a research base subsidiary in Japan for new pharmaceutical science to managing a $500 million performance products division in Europe. NutraSweet's new fat substitute Simplesse—recently approved for use in a variety of foods—was developed in Canada and licensed to NutraSweet for worldwide development. These are visible examples, and each subsidiary country manager should be 'charged' with the assignment to contribute one or more to the global corporation.

## CONCLUSION

In conclusion, the traditional role of the country manager has changed. In some instances, depending on the competitive environment, corporate culture and competencies of the subsidiary, the position may even be redundant. In global organizations determined to be successful, the new country manager must work in an environment of ill-defined organizational structures, change from the traditional command-and-control style and take a leadership position in providing clear direction, ensuring the subsidiaries' privilege-to-operate, cultivating talent and developing unique competencies within the subsidiary.

## NOTE

1. Following the presentation of this paper at the Strategic Management Society Conference in Toronto in 1991 it was published as: Lennox, R.I. (1992). Whither the Country Manager? *Business Quarterly*, Spring 1992. I am grateful to the publisher, Western Business School, The University of Western Ontario, for permission to publish this revised version of my paper.

# 19
# Global Localization of Japanese MNCs

TOSHIKAZU MITSUDA

---

I am honored to have the opportunity to tell the Sharp story in North America and briefly explain our efforts in localizing the company's operation.

Although the name of our company—Sharp—is English, we are still a Japanese company. Our brand was registered by Mr Tokuji Hayakawa, our founder, in 1912. Mr Hayakawa invented the 'Ever-Sharp' pencil in 1915, which is why we use the brand name 'Sharp'. The company started by manufacturing the 'Ever-Sharp' pencil and progressed into electronics. Today, we manufacture such electronic products as the Wizard, a pencil-less product.

I would like to give you a brief account of our profile. Overall, consolidated sales as of March 1993 were $US 14.6 billion. We currently have 63 900 employees worldwide, with 29 500 of these overseas. In our headquarters offices in Osaka we have a total of 8100 engineers. We manufacture over 3000 products in total. As you probably know, our major consumer products include color TVs, camcorders, VCRs, MD players, microwave ovens, refrigerators, washing machines, and air conditioners. Our office products include copiers, PDAs, calculators, facsimiles, personal computers, cash registers, printers and many other products. Components include semiconductors, LCDs and optical components. Our latest product, of which we are very proud, is our

*Building the Strategically-Responsive Organization.*
Edited by H. Thomas, D. O'Neal, R. White and D. Hurst.
Copyright © 1994 the Strategic Management Society. Published 1994 by John Wiley & Sons Ltd.

LCD ViewCam camcorder with an LCD monitor in place of a viewfinder.

In our overseas activities we currently have 59 operations in 32 countries. Our sales subsidiaries total 20 in 18 countries: the US, Canada, Germany, the UK, France, Switzerland, Italy, the Netherlands, Austria, Spain, Sweden, Taiwan, Hong Kong, Thailand, Malaysia, Singapore, Australia, and New Zealand. Our manufacturing bases total 19 in 26 countries including 2 in the US, 2 in the UK, France, Spain, Korea, 2 in Taiwan, 4 in Malaysia, Thailand, 2 in China, the Philippines, Australia, India, and Brazil. In addition, we have 5 technical collaborators in 5 countries. This gives a brief overall picture of our operations.

Under my area of responsibility, which is Sharp North American Operations, we have a headquarters in New Jersey and one in Toronto, Canada. We also have factories located in Memphis, Tennessee and Camas, Washington. Our Tennessee factory manufactures color TVs, microwave ovens and LCD video projectors. Our Camas factory designs semiconductors and manufactures, beginning in December 1991, LCD panels. Twenty percent of sales comes from these factories, and in the near future we plan to increase this to 30%. Our total sales in North America for fiscal year 1993 were $2.9 billion. Our North American operations employ over 2900 people, of whom 2800 are American or Canadian and 130 Japanese. We started our operations in the United States in 1962, and celebrated our 30th anniversary in 1992. This is a brief overview of our operations in North America.

Regarding the localization issue, as I have explained, Sharp has made rapid progress in the United States over the past 30 years. With this progress, we have localized as we have grown. A few Japanese companies were doing business overseas prior to World War II. Following the war, almost all Japanese companies began doing very well in overseas operations. During more than 30 years that we have been doing business overseas we have made several mistakes, but we have also learned several things from these mistakes.

As you know, the UK and other European countries have a much longer history in foreign countries, and they have an advantage over Japanese companies in that the language and accounting systems are similar. Therefore, I assume that localization would be easier for these companies. In Japanese companies, however, the language and accounting systems are totally different: it is like the difference between chopsticks and a knife and

fork. These differences have made it difficult in areas of localization. But, despite these handicaps, after only 30 years in the
United States, Sharp has a total of 28 vice presidents, of whom 21
are American with only the remaining 7 being Japanese. In fact, at
our Camas factory the president is American. Our Camas factory
also has a design center, so the design activities are being carried
out in Washington rather than in Japan. Our Memphis operations
recently began designing products in Tennessee, so some of the
products are basically of American design.

In the 30 years we have been in operation in the US the number
of Japanese staff versus American staff has decreased every year,
from 100% Japanese in 1962, to almost 95% American in 1990. In
the future we plan to *decrease* the number of Japanese even
further. We also have plans to *increase* the number of senior
American staff in top management in the near future.

I know of some German and French companies that still have
their own people in their senior management positions, either
because of the language barrier or due to management policy.
Many of these companies have a much longer history than Sharp
and they, too, are finding that localization is not an easy process.
In fact, I recently heard of a British company that tried to recruit
an American CEO, but, because of the expense of hiring an
American, have given up their attempt.

Of course, we know that total localization is very important to
continued progress and we are always striving toward that goal.
But, as I said, even British, French and German companies, which
are an example for newer overseas ventures, cannot achieve
perfect localization. I hope that you can understand that we are
working hard in the direction of localization, but this is not an
overnight process: it is continuing and ongoing.

(Translations into US dollars are based on Y102 = US$1, the
approximate exchange rate on March 31, 1994.)

# Section V

# Environmental Implications for Global Marketing

This section is based on a panel discussion entitled 'Marketing "Green" Products in the Triad'. Although in its original context it represented three individual perspectives, each primarily addressing one leg of the triad, considering the firms represented by the presenters—three of the most significant global consumer product firms—elements appear to be generalizable to a more global perspective. In that context, it is offered here as a thought-provoking discussion of some of the more challenging environmental implications of marketing across national boundaries—any national boundaries, not just Japan, Europe, or the United States.

Professor Simon's chapter provides a solid overview of government policy, consumer attitudes, and company strategies in the Triad, and serves as a conceptual basis for integration of the other three presentations.

Jane Barnett, of Jergens/Kao, compares how Japanese and American governments and firms approach the environmental issue of solid waste, and its effect on packaging and consumer products.

T.C. Woods, of Nestlé-Canada, describes how his firm has taken the initiative, in Canada and Europe, in reduction of packaging, energy conservation, reduction of solid waste, and treatment of air and water emissions.

John Alvord, of Procter & Gamble, addresses the issue of providing environmental information to consumers in an accurate, reliable, and timely manner, through product labeling.

The types of environmental issues illustrated in this section imply significant strategic challenges for firms attempting or intending to market products across national boundaries (or even across state boundaries). Particularly important considerations include:

- Solid waste: disposal concerns are a top priority in many countries
- Product packaging: a major contributor to solid waste
- Regulation inconsistency: different compliance requirements from one jurisdiction to another
- Company initiatives: require integration/communication between R&D, production, and marketing functions
- Environmental seals: favored by consumers, but considered by manufacturers to be too ambiguous to be useful
- Consumers: have environmentally-conscious attitudes, but 'convenience'-driven behavior.

Failure to address any of these issues can result in unsuccessful, if not disastrous, attempts at global marketing.

# 20

# Environmental Strategies in the Triad

## FRANÇOISE L. SIMON

In the same way as the quality movement and process re-engineering are systemic endeavors transcending functional boundaries, environmental performance has become an all-encompassing corporate goal, key to long-term competitiveness and even survival.

Companies such as Procter & Gamble have already entered what has been called the 'age of eco-strategy'; with its Total Quality Environmental Management (TQEM), Procter & Gamble uses the same tools that gave the Japanese automobile and electronics industries world-class status, and adapts them to assess and improve its environmental results, from its production lines to its finance departments.

Implementing a global environmental strategy, however, continues to be a massive challenge, given wide variations in government policies and consumer attitudes within the Triad. The very structure of international trade is now directly affected by environmentalism, since progress on the North American Free Trade Agreement (NAFTA) was slowed in part by US opposition to weaker regulation in Mexico, perceived as giving an unfair advantage to local producers.

Similarly, green issues have fostered attacks on the General Agreement on Tariffs and Trade (GATT) by groups as diverse as

*Building the Strategically-Responsive Organization.*
Edited by H. Thomas, D. O'Neal, R. White and D. Hurst.
Copyright © 1994 the Strategic Management Society. Published 1994 by John Wiley & Sons Ltd.

Ralph Nader's Public Citizen, the United Methodist Church and the Sierra Club. For environmentalists, the GATT objective of removing trade barriers prevents countries from applying appropriate environmental policies. In 1991, for instance, the US was found to be in breach of GATT rules when it blocked imports from Mexico of tuna caught in ways that also killed dolphins.

That environmentalism is key to corporate survival is demonstrated by the costs of not doing it (Exxon's expenditures for the Valdez oil spill are over $1 billion and still climbing), but also by the rewards it may entail; from the quick spread of Henkel's phosphate-free detergents in Germany to the rapid growth of specialty retailers such as the Body Shop, new products and concepts are reshaping consumer markets worldwide.

Before analyzing the interplay between consumer power, public policy and industry initiative, it may be useful to review briefly the 'baseline situation' across the Triad.

## REALITY VERSUS PERCEPTION: THE STATE OF THE ENVIRONMENT IN THE TRIAD

While a majority of consumers in OECD countries believe that their environment is continuing to deteriorate, reality is considerably more nuanced. Although 20 years of environmental policies have brought significant results, the OECD countries are still the world's major polluters. Although their combined population of 849 million represents only 16% of the world's total, they generate 68% of its industrial waste and account for 38% of global greenhouse emissions (World Resources Institute, 1992, pp. 17, 18). Key improvements, however, relate to air quality, especially in Japan, where, after heavy investment, sulfur and nitrogen oxide emissions as a share of GDP are less than one-quarter of the OECD average. Lead emissions have also fallen by 85% in North America and by 50% in most European cities since 1970. Since OECD economies grew by 80% over the same period, the World Bank concluded that economic growth can be effectively 'delinked' from pollution. Results are notably poorer in areas dependent on individual behavior, such as nitrogen oxides (largely emitted by cars), which rose by 12% since 1970 in the OECD except Japan, and solid waste, which grew by 26% between 1975 and 1990 (World Bank, 1992, p. 40).

## GREENHOUSE EMISSIONS INDEX

On a per capita basis, the US is by far the largest polluter; with a world median of 1, the US reaches 8.8, as opposed to 4.6 for Japan. Europe varies widely, from 5.3 for Germany (which would be much higher if the former GDR were included) to 3.3 for France (World Resources Institute, 1992, p. 210) (FIGURE 20.1).

## ENERGY CONSUMPTION

Between 1975 and the late 1980s, the amount of energy used in the OECD countries to produce a unit of output fell by a fifth. Here again, the US is still one of the least energy-efficient Triad members. Cars, appliances, and commercial buildings in the US still use 20–33% more energy per unit of activity than in most other OECD countries (FIGURE 20.2). Consumer behavior clearly impacts not only energy measures, but also other practices such as pesticide use. Thanks to periodic panics such as Alar in apples, average annual pesticide use in the US fell by 19% from the 1970s to the 1980s; by contrast, it actually *rose* in France and Germany by the same amount, and decreased in Japan, but only by 6% (World Resources Institute, 1992, pp. 21, 275).

## WASTE GENERATION

Solid waste, the most consumer- and media-sensitive of all pollution indicators, is the area where rich countries are showing the worst performance. By the late 1980s, annual per capita waste generation in G-7 countries was topped by the US at 864 kg, followed by Canada, then Japan at 394 kg, while Europe varied from 357 kg in the UK to 303 kg in France (World Resources Institute, 1992, p. 319). However, classification variance may understate Japan's problem, since its definition of municipal solid waste does not include recyclables such as glass, newsprint, and office paper. Waste disposal is also an ambiguous picture. At first

410

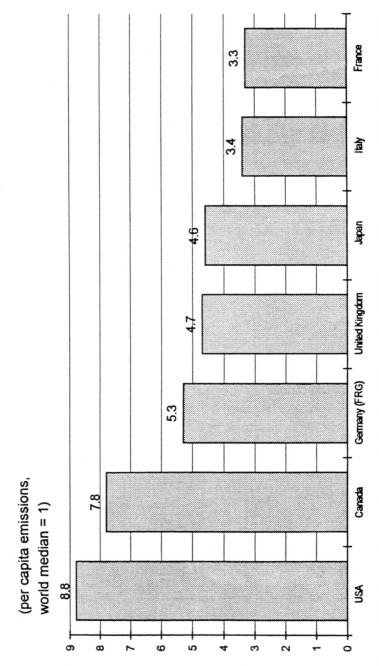

(per capita emissions, world median = 1)

FIGURE 20.1  Per capita greenhouse emissions for G-7 countries, 1989. Sources: Intergovernmental Panel on Climate Change (1990). *Climate Change: The IPCC Scientific Assessment.* Cambridge, 1990; World Resources Institute (1992), p. 210

**Energy (gigajoules) (total fossil fuels)**

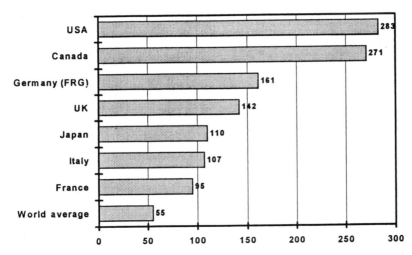

FIGURE 20.2    Average annual energy consumption per capita, 1989. Sources: UN Statistical Office (1991). UN Energy Tape; World Resources Institute (1992), p. 18

glance, the US is again the main culprit with massive landfill use; however, landfill expansion is now politically quasi-impossible in the US and Japan's dependence on incineration is itself unsustainable (FIGURE 20.3).

Recycling practices cannot point to a clear winner either, since they vary by material. Whereas Japan has the highest paper recycling rate in the world, its facilities for plastics recycling are virtually nonexistent (see TABLE 20.1). While the US has an overall 32% aluminum recycling level, some companies such as Anheuser–Busch have achieved a 100% rate for their cans.

## GOVERNMENT POLICIES IN THE TRIAD

While global brands continue to be a goal for many companies, their 'green quotient' is far from being uniformly marketable worldwide. Across the Triad, regulation varies as much as actual environmental performance.

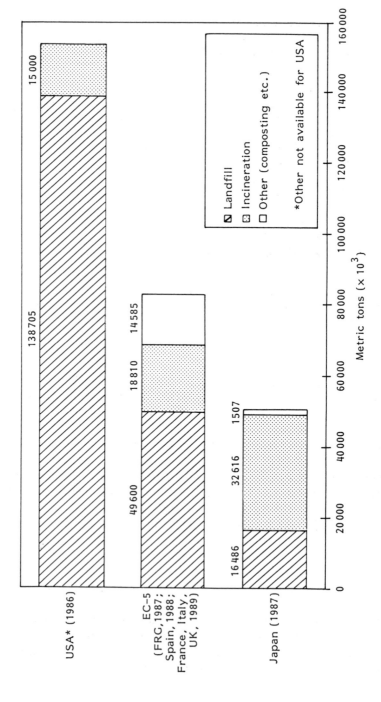

FIGURE 20.3 Waste disposal in the Triad. Sources: OECD; UN Statistical Commission and Economic Commission for Europe; World Resources Institute (1992), p. 319

TABLE 20.1    Recycling levels in the Triad

| Commodity | Total waste (kg/head/ year) | Recycled* (%) | Trends in recycling |
|---|---|---|---|
| **Paper** | | | |
| Western Europe | 170–180 | 40–45 | Up in 1970s–1980s, leveling |
| Japan | 170 | 50 | now 39% in 1975, 49% in 1985, level since |
| United States | 270 | 25 | Up from 19% in 1975 |
| | | | |
| **Aluminum** | | | |
| Western Europe | 18–20 | 30 | Level since 1984 |
| Japan | 22 | 40 | Level since 1986 |
| United States | 10 | 32 | Up from 9% in 1975 |
| | | | |
| **Glass** | | | |
| Western Europe | 25 | 30 | Up in 1980s, leveling off |
| Japan | 7 | 55 | Up since 1980 |
| United States | 50 | 12 | Up from 3% in 1975 |
| | | | |
| **Plastic** | | | |
| Western Europe | 17 | 5 | Consumption and recycling |
| Japan | 25 | 0 | rising |
| United States | 55 | 1 | |

*Sources*: OECD, US EPA; *The Economist*, 13 April 1991, p. 18.
*Does not include incineration.

## TYPES OF CONTROLS: RELATIVE SUCCESS

Most policies adopted over the past decades have been 'end-of-pipe' controls, although Europe has stressed source reduction. In the US, under the 1980 Superfund Act, 99% of federal and state environmental spending has gone so far to 'end-of-pipe' controls. Enacted to handle 1300 hazardous waste sites, Superfund has cleaned fewer than 200 and spent over $15 billion—roughly 75% of which has gone to legal fees (Anonymous, 1993a). Under the new administration, however, the Environmental Protection Agency's (EPA) central priority is clearly prevention. New approaches include building a network of prevention programs and developing innovative partnerships with the private sector. For example, the voluntary 33/50 Program initiative to reduce emissions of 17 chemicals (including benzene, cyanide, lead, and mercury) by 33% at the end of 1992 and by 50% at the end of 1995 has been adopted by over 1100 US companies. Similarly, the DfE Program (Design for Environment) aims to support the use of 'green design' such as Intel's development of its computers to maximize chip recovery (Carra, 1993).

Given that *economic instruments* often entail lower compliance costs, many governments are now introducing these or hybrid approaches. World CFC production, for instance, has dropped by 40% since 1986 through a combination of a mandated phase-out by 2000 (now brought forward to 1995) and a 'green tax' on products containing CFCs in countries such as the US and Norway (Anonymous, 1992a).

Within economic policies, the US has taken the lead with the most market-based approach, i.e. the use of tradable pollution credits. For about $3 million, Mobil's refinery in Torrance, California, acquired credits from the city of Southgate, which had bought them from General Motors when it closed a plant and sold the property. Similar trades last year involved Northrop, Allied–Signal and Shell Oil. Although credits were accused of allowing companies to 'buy the right to pollute,' they are now combined with caps on emissions. TABLE 20.2 summarizes these policies across the Triad.

## REGIONAL POLICY DYSFUNCTIONS

Besides these variations, each region still exhibits inconsistencies which make it difficult for companies to standardize their environmental marketing.

### US Dysfunctions: State versus Federal Law

In the absence of federal legislation, several states have begun to fill the void with their own measures. Rhode Island recently ruled that no product sold in the state can include a recyclability claim if a local infrastructure does not exist, which forces manufacturers to modify labels or remove claims nationwide. Two states (New York and Massachusetts) have adopted and 10 others are considering the 1990 California guidelines, mandating the phasing-in of alternative fuels, and dictating that 10% of all cars will have to

TABLE 20.2  Environmental policies in the Triad

| Type of policy | Variables affected | | |
| --- | --- | --- | --- |
| | Price | Quantity | Technology |
| Regulation: command-and-control | | Emissions standards (USA, federal/California) Quotas and bans (USA, CFCs) | Mandated technical standards (USA, Europe, Japan, catalytic converters) Efficiency standards (USA, fuel efficiency) |
| Economic incentives | Effluent charges (Netherlands) Deposit plans (bottles, Germany; cars, Norway) Green taxes (fuel taxes, Netherlands Sweden) | Tradable emissions permits (USA, sulfur dioxide) Tradable production permits (USA, lead trading program) | Research & development subsidies (Japan, MITI electric battery program) |
| Industry self-regulation | | Individual corporate targets (USA, Pollution Prevention Pays, 3M) Industry collection systems (Germany, DSD; France, Eco-emballage) | Guidelines on cleaner technologies (Japan, Keidanren, Environmental Charter) |

Source: Adapted from World Bank (1992).

be emission-free by 2003. It is likely that here again, manufacturers will have to align themselves with the toughest state rules in the absence of a federal standard.

---

### Europe: Free Trade versus Green Protectionism

Even though Europe adopted as early as 1972 the 'polluter pays principle' and has since issued over 150 environmental directives, there are now increasing tensions between the Community's open market mandate and national laws that amount to restraint of trade. The most aggressive is Germany's 'Töpfer Law,' named after its environment minister. Effective since December 1991, it sets an 80% waste collection target by 1995. Manufacturers must take back their own packaging or join DSD (Duales System Deutschland), a collection system set up by 400 German companies. Faced with navigating the DSD bureaucracy or repackaging specially for the German market, the British, French and Belgians have complained, so far with no results.

Other governments have also set up schemes, ranging from France's Eco-Emballage, aiming to raise packaging recycling by 50% over 3 years, to the voluntary but drastic Dutch 'Covenant' binding companies to reduce packaging weight to below 1986 levels, to end all landfilling and incineration, and to take back at least 90% of non-reusable packaging by 2000 (Anonymous, 1993b). The DSD scheme, however, has created additional problems by succumbing to its own success. It announced recently that it was operating at an annual loss of $300 million, partly due to storage fees for waste in excess of what markets could absorb. While it expected 105 000 tons of plastic packaging in 1992, it took in 409 000 tons and was faced with massive exports—which were met by threatened bans from countries such as France. While the German Industry Federation is calling for more incineration, the government is moving toward a 'closed-loop economy,' with a proposed bill requiring manufacturers to take back and recycle not only their packaging, but also their products themselves, at the end of their useful life (Anonymous, 1993c).

At the other extreme, the UK has recently been accused of 'eco-backtracking.' A bill to create a new, integrated environmental protection agency has been dropped, and a licensing scheme for waste disposal has been postponed indefinitely. The public, plagued by economic worries, is indifferent. A MORI poll showed that only 3% of respondents placed the environment among their top concerns, compared to a peak of 35% in 1988 (Anonymous, 1993a).

Meanwhile, the EC continues its struggle to harmonize legislation. Its environment ministers have agreed on a voluntary EC-wide eco-audit by 1994 for the manufacturing and power sectors, including a performance self-assessment, full disclosure of results to the public and verification by external auditors, to be repeated every three years. Initiating a new drive to establish an EC code of civil liability, the Commission has also released a 'Green Paper' on repairing damage to the environment. While reinforcing the polluter pays principle, the code would ensure that costs to industry would be manageable, unlike the US Superfund Act (Anonymous, 1993e). Given this chaotic context, the most proactive companies are starting to follow the 'highest common denominator' approach, i.e. produce everything to the world's toughest standards. In this spirit, Hewlett-Packard redesigned and reduced its office machine packaging worldwide to meet German requirements.

---

## Japan: Policy Fragmentation

While less conflictual than Europe or the US, Japan still offers a confusing picture. The Health Ministry did devote its 1990 *White Paper on the Environment* to a solid waste problem severe enough to have caused the construction of artificial garbage islands in Tokyo Bay, but the Japanese Environmental Agency has far less enforcement power than the US EPA. The initial pollution control framework, set in the late 1960s by the Diet, decentralized environmental management by dividing responsibilities among various levels of government and the private sector. The latter has now taken the lead by issuing in April 1991 the Keidanren Global Environmental Charter. Keidanren guidelines include company audits, individual corporate targets, new procurement policies and the development of cleaner technologies.

As in Europe but for different reasons, the Japanese situation may act as a trade barrier. There are now some 28 000 locally-tailored and negotiated environmental agreements in force between Japanese industry and local communities, and this very decentralization may be difficult to handle for foreign companies operating in Japan.

While massive investment during the 1970s, when over 14 environmental laws were passed, gave Japanese firms a competitive edge in world markets for cars and air pollution equipment, industry performance now varies by sector. In electronics, companies such as NEC are furthering innovation by engraving chips with lasers to eliminate the use of CFCs. In automobiles, consumer tastes for larger cars have affected performance; by 1988, new Japanese cars averaged 27.3 miles to the US gallon, less than the 28 miles per gallon achieved by the average American car.

While the government is considering a new law making it easier to introduce new green taxes such as a carbon tax, the Japanese Ministry of International Trade and Industry (MITI) prefers a mix of subsidies for energy conservation and penalties for energy waste. Here again, however, subsidizing some of Japan's most powerful export industries is likely to meet with international opposition on the basis of fair trade (Anonymous, 1992b).

---

### Environmental Labeling Initiatives

One final regulatory issue that directly impacts the marketing of global brands, i.e. eco-labeling, is still without a consensus. Here again, Europe leads, albeit in a fragmented way. Its prototype eco-seal is Germany's Blue Angel label, based on a partial life cycle assessment and in operation since 1977. It has appeared on over 3200 products and is recognized by 80% of German consumers. However, only about 10% of Blue Angel labels are held by foreign firms (Cairncross, 1992). Although the European Commission is attempting to finalize a pan-European system, participation will be voluntary, and national logos will be allowed to coexist with the EC-wide labeling. In Japan, a quasi-governmental program has awarded over 850 Ecomark labels in 31 categories since 1989. The assessment is less complex than the German system, relying on more limited criteria such as energy efficiency and environmental impact during production.

The situation is murkier in the US, where two private initiatives are competing in the absence of federal standards. Announced in 1990, the Green Seal program initially planned a full life cycle approach, but retreated due to costs and settled for a simplified version. The rival Green Cross system, now appearing on about 400 products, merely verifies a company's claim, such as percentage of recycled material. Life cycle analyses presently have the most credibility, even though methodologies are still in development.

At the US federal level, no legislation has yet been passed, but the Federal Trade Commission (FTC), with support from the EPA and the US Office of Consumer Affairs, issued a set of guidelines in July 1992. Although voluntary and not legally enforceable, they are designed to help companies to avoid prosecution under a federal law prohibiting deceptive advertising. The types of claims addressed by the FTC guidelines include 'recyclable,' 'degradable,' 'compostable,' 'recycled content,' 'source reduction,' 'refillable,' and 'ozone-safe'; for all of these, any objective environmental claim must be substantiated by scientific evidence (Federal Trade Commission, 1992a,b). A complaint is that these rules do not override state laws. Since 1989, 18 states have proposed or enacted regulation of green claims. From 1990 to 1993, almost 50 cases were brought against marketers by the FTC and local authorities. Since the guides are not due for review until 1995, the EPA is now researching a uniform labeling approach.

---

## ENVIRONMENTAL CONSUMER TRENDS IN THE TRIAD

In keeping with disparities in baseline situation and public policies, consumers in the Triad vary widely between and within regions. Information levels, priorities, purchase and post-purchase behavior as well as willingness to pay do not show any great convergence. Although environmentalism has now reached the stage of a mass movement in industrialized countries, a new set of questions arises:

- How do environmental concerns vary by region? How do consumers rate their own country, and what problems do they prioritize?
- What role is business expected to play, relative to government and individuals?
- How do consumer attitudes translate into actual behavior?

- What is the gap between 'political correctness' (i.e. self-definition as an environmentalist) and actual change?
- How do levels and types of commitment vary by region?
- What is the consumer's 'green IQ'?
- How do green consumers segment across the Triad?
- What is the relative impact of 'green advertising'?
- How does willingness to pay differ between regions?
- How large and homogeneous are the Triad markets for green products?

Several multicountry studies by Louis Harris, Gallup and others have recently tracked some of these variations.

## LEVELS AND TYPES OF ENVIRONMENTAL CONCERNS

In the most recent multicountry study, Gallup's *Health of the Planet* survey, conducted in 1992 in 22 countries, Germans (only West Germans were polled) showed the most concern: 67% rated their national environmental problems as 'very serious', versus 51% in the US and 42% in Japan (Gallup, 1992). Perceptions of dangers at home were remarkably uniform, with air/water pollution and waste disposal topping the list. Sharper distinctions emerged in regard to global threats; Germans were much more concerned than others about global warming, ozone loss and the rainforest, which may be due to greater activism as well as to local factors such as deforestation through acid rain (FIGURE 21.4).

## EXPECTED ROLE OF BUSINESS

Across the Triad, business is perceived as the chief cause of environmental problems. It was named first in Japan, West Germany and Britain, and came second in the US, after individual waste. When presented with a list of remedial actions, consumers also placed the onus on business; 'regulating business' or 'banning product sales' came first or second everywhere in the Triad (Gallup, 1992).

This unanimity strongly suggests that companies' efforts to self-regulate and publicize their achievements may be a case of 'too

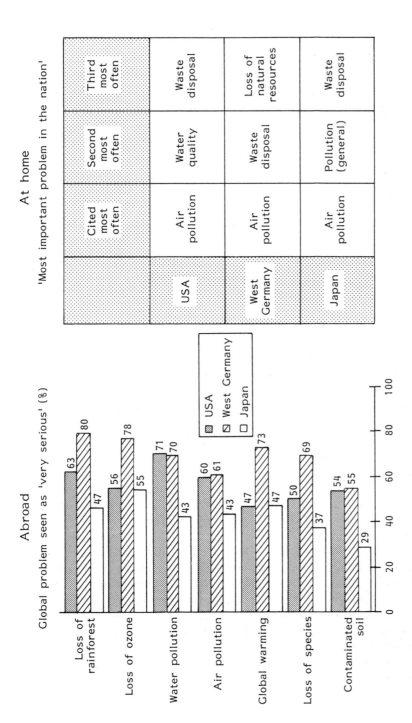

FIGURE 20.4  The fear factor, 1992. Source: Gallup (1992)

TABLE 20.3  Personal environmental commitment in Triad countries

Percentage engaging in 'green' behaviors in past year

| Countries | Avoided environmentally harmful products | Active in environment group | Voted/worked for pro-environment candidate |
|---|---|---|---|
| USA | 57 | 11 | 19 |
| Canada | 77 | 12 | 15 |
| Japan | 40 | 4 | 14 |
| Germany (West) | 81 | 10 | 18 |
| United Kingdom | 75 | 10 | 10 |
| Netherlands | 68 | 7 | 21 |
| Denmark | 65 | 10 | 18 |

*Source*: Gallup (1992).

little, too late.' Negative perceptions of business and the public's wish for punitive actions such as bans appear well-entrenched at this time.

## CONSUMER INVOLVEMENT LEVELS

*Activism*, as measured by Gallup through membership of an environmental group, remains limited in the US and Europe (7–11%) and quasi-nonexistent in Japan (4%) (see TABLE 20.3).

In keeping with consumer skepticism, *purchase behavior* is more clearly defined in terms of avoidance than through positive choice. As many as 81% of Germans, 57% of Americans and 40% of Japanese have so far actively avoided products perceived as harmful. Consumer surveys tracking positive choices tend to find them occurring at lower levels; the 1990 Roper survey on the US environment, for instance, found that only 14% of Americans regularly bought products with recycled content or in refillable packaging (Roper Organizations, 1990). This is linked to the current lack of eco-labeling standards, but it may also suggest that the 'greenness' of a product is not in itself a purchase trigger, but rather one component among others of perceived overall quality.

*Post-purchase behavior* would appear at first to show clearer patterns, but it is in fact more difficult to interpret. Recycling was found to be practiced by 71% of Americans in 1990, according to Roper, and by 40–65% (depending on product category) in the 1991 Simmons study. However, recycling ranges from mandatory in some areas (particularly metropolitan suburbs and the Northeast) to near-impossible in others. Recycling rates may therefore reflect compliance with the law rather than individual commitment. Other behaviors which may have a greater impact were resisted, if they conflicted with personal freedom: only 8% of Americans polled by Roper cut down car use, for instance.

## SEGMENTATION PATTERNS

Wide variations in green attitudes and behaviors suggest the existence of distinct segments in the Triad. Some surveys, such as the Harris 1988 multi-country poll, have found relatively few demographic variations, particularly among age groups. Other studies have attempted to profile distinct segments. In the US, Roper in 1990 and Simmons in 1991 both identified five main clusters based on their commitment level. Both segmentation bases show a positive linkage between green commitment and higher-than-average income and education, as would be expected.

## VARIANCE IN INFORMATION LEVELS

For global marketers, between-region variances in 'green IQ' may be more challenging than within-country distinctions. The perception, by Americans themselves, that they are inadequately educated about the environment is well confirmed by several measures. As a follow-up to their 1990 study, Roper released in late 1991 'America's Environmental GPA,' a survey testing a nationwide cross-section of nearly 2000 adults on their 'green point average.' Faced with 10 questions ranging from global warming to CFCs and biodegradable plastic, Americans scored on average only 33 out of a possible 100 points—'a low score by any standard,' concluded Roper. Education and income did not help, since college graduates as well as upscale Americans (with income over $55 000) earned average scores of only 40 points.

While the best scores dealt with wilderness issues, some of the worst dealt with products—which suggests that the Sierra Club and other groups may have been more successful than corporations in their communication strategies.

Particularly striking is the case of CFCs; even though they were banned as early as 1978 by the EPA and the FDA for nearly all consumer products, only 14% of Americans knew it 14 years later. Misperceptions also apply to the main sources of waste. While paper is by far the largest waste component across the Triad, ranging from 46% in Japan to 35% in the US and 29% in Britain, many Americans underestimate its importance and focus on plastics instead; whereas plastic amounts to less than 9% of waste in G-7 countries, it was ranked almost equal to paper by Americans (Roper Organization, 1991). These inadequacies in basic 'green knowledge' have had dramatic impact on products such as fast food and disposable diapers, leading companies such as McDonald's and Procter & Gamble to face intense consumer pressures that might have been avoided with preventive information.

By contrast, several factors have helped to increase consumer awareness in Northern Europe. A milestone was the publication of *The Green Consumer Guide*, which shot to the top of the British bestseller list in 1988, and which (unlike its American edition) offered specific ratings for companies and products; a similar success was reached by the guide's German equivalent, *Okologie im Haushalt*. Retail chains also play a powerful information role in Europe; Tengelmann began a campaign to win early green customers in 1984 in Germany, and in Switzerland, Migros has developed a computer program to assess the life cycle impact of its packaging (Cairncross, 1992).

## IMPACT OF 'GREEN' ADVERTISING

In the US, even though corporate and product-specific 'green' advertising has steadily expanded, it has had relatively little impact so far. Strikingly, in the 1991 Advertising Age survey rating specific brands and companies, 66% of the 1500 respondents could not name a single 'environmentally-conscious' company. Of the firms named, Procter & Gamble was first, but with only 6% of the votes. For accuracy of information, advertising was ranked last, after product labeling (63%) and self-education (75%).

| Product category | Attribute traded | Risk of eco-alternative |
|---|---|---|
| Packaging | Time (for sorting and recycling) | None (in non-food products) |
| CFC-containing aerosols | Performance (pumps) None (other aerosols) | Risk with early aerosol alternatives (HCFCs) |
| Laundry whiteners, detergents | Performance | Subject to debate |
| Disposable diapers | Time, convenience | Subject to debate |
| Plastic drink containers | Convenience | Lower risk with some alternatives (glass) |
| Fuel | Cost, convenience | Lower risk with alternative fuels |
| Automobiles | Comfort, safety | Less accident protection in smaller cars |
| Tamper-proof drug packaging | Safety | Risk of drug poisoning |
| Hospital disposables (syringes, dressings) | Safety | Risk of HIV and other infections |

*Low* — *Level of direct health impact* — *High* (left-margin scale)

FIGURE 20.5  Environmental trade-off assessment. Source: Simon Associates (1992)

## WILLINGNESS TO PAY

The ultimate measure of environmental commitment is clearly the consumer's willingness to pay green taxes or a green premium on an eco-safe product. Several studies show a consistent pattern over time. In 1988, when respondents in the Harris survey were asked whether they would accept 'a less good standard of living but with much less health risk', 84% agreed in the US, followed by Germany at 69% and Japan at 64% (Harris, 1988). Four years later, the Gallup respondents, when tested on their willingness to pay, showed a similar pattern, with 65% of Americans in favor, compared to 59% of Germans but only 31% of the Japanese (Gallup, 1992).

While environmental activism has been affected by a recessionary context in the Triad, growth appears to be sustained in the US. From 1990 to 1992, the total of green segments identified by Roper grew by 8% (Rehak, 1993).

It is worth noting that categories where acceptance has spread fastest have involved no perceived risk (CFC-free aerosols) and little attribute loss (recycling packaging takes little time and costs nothing); products representing a larger trade-off, and where alternatives are debatable, such as diapers, have shown mixed reactions. Finally, in categories where an eco-alternative would mean a direct health risk, consumer acceptance would become nil (FIGURE 20.5).

## ECOLOGY-DRIVEN STRATEGIES

While industry strategies have so far varied widely across the Triad in their linkage of technology and marketing, initiatives have been taken in most sectors, and a number of competitive trends and success factors are now emerging.

The scope of the environment's impact on industry is exceptionally broad, ranging from product displacement and creation to an expanded product life cycle, new process development, shifts in the value chain and even the restructuring of some industries; in addition, environmentalism has led to a rethinking of communication strategies.

## PRODUCT DISPLACEMENT AND CREATION

In sectors ranging from cosmetics to automobiles, green products are rapidly displacing conventional ones. In a largely stagnating industry, the Body Shop experienced exceptional growth, expanding in 15 years to over 700 shops worldwide with anti-animal-testing, largely natural line recycling/refilling policies. Larger players have had to follow, with Lauder's launch of its New Origins line and Revlon's New Age Naturals, both with similar ingredients, testing and packaging claims.

A market creation process of much larger scope is expected in automobiles, with the possible commercialization of 'zero-emission vehicles' (as noted above, mandated to account for 10% of all vehicles in California by 2003). Across the Triad, new models are in development, and all are supported at least partly through a government/business alliance. Although prototype electric cars have been introduced by General Motors, Nissan and others, they all have a small range and long recharging time, and depend on a technical breakthrough for commercialization. Accordingly, GM, Ford and Chrysler have formed a joint venture, with Washington contributing half of the $262 million annual budget, to develop better batteries. Although the current leaders in the ultimate clean technology, i.e. hydrogen power, are Mercedes–Benz and BMW (the latter spending one-third of its $845 million annual research budget on cleaner processes), Mazda has announced a possible limited-production launch by the late 1990s of a hydrogen model aiming to match or surpass the German targets (Anonymous, 1992c). This goal is facilitated by heavy government support. MITI, as part of its biotechnology program, is funding research applications to hydrogen production, using gene-splicing methods to boost the productivity of hydrogen-producing organisms instead of using the massive amount of electricity now required to separate the gas from water. Once developed, this technology could render obsolete not only current cars but also solar cells and other energy sources (Anonymous, 1992d).

## Expanded Product Life Cycle

Besides creating an entirely new product class, the automobile industry is also engineering a radical expansion of the life cycle concept, beyond sales and service and toward total re-manufacturing. Volkswagen leads in this area with its '3V' policy (*Vermeiden, Verringen*, and *Verworten*, or prevention, reduction, and recycling). Prevention includes reducing solvent emissions at source by switching to water-based paints, and recycling has a 100% target—despite the complexity of car materials, which entails establishing several different resource loops. Based on its experience at a pilot dismantling plant, VW announced that it would take back its new Golf model free of charge—a factor that helped the Golf to win the 1992 European Car of the Year award (Schmidheiny, 1992). The attribute hierarchy for cars is

| Success Factors | Relative Importance | | | Changes |
|---|---|---|---|---|
| | Low | Moderate | High | |
| Performance/power<br>Performance/mileage | | ● ◄——— △<br>△ ———► ● | | Environmental criteria become part of performance |
| Reliability/safety | | | △● | Add—environmental safety |
| Price | | ● ◄——— △ | | Higher price acceptance for 'greener' cars |
| Image | | | △● | Add —green image |
| Service | | △ ———► ● | | Compliance with regulations as part of maintenance |
| Alternative fuel capability | △ ————————► ● | | | New factor |
| Recycled content | △ ————————► ● | | | New factor |
| Reverse assembly capability | △ ————————► ● | | | New factor |

△ Traditional importance; ● 'Green' importance

FIGURE 20.6  Changes in key success factors: automobiles. Source: Simon Associates (1992)

now being gradually remodeled, with some attributes changing their meaning, others shifting in importance, and entirely new attributes emerging. 'Performance' now relates as much to mileage as to power, 'safety' ranges from airbags to emissions, and 'service' will soon include post-use collection. In addition, new features such as alternative fuel capability and recycled content are likely to be key competitive factors in the future (FIGURE 20.6).

Design for disassembly has also been developed in other sectors. As part of its commitment to sustainable development, Eastman Kodak is moving its 35 mm single use cameras, branded as Fun Saver, toward an ultimate closed-loop goal. This product concept, where the consumer returns the entire camera to the photofinisher for processing, is the fastest-growing segment of the photography business. Total sales are expected at 30 million units in 1993, representing a 36% increase over 1992 (which was 64% up from 1991). Each camera returned to Kodak is 85% recycled, with a total of 15 million cameras recovered to date from the US, Canada, Europe and Japan. In order to encourage independent photofinishers to participate in the program, Kodak reversed the bottle deposit concept by paying the photofinishers 5 cents per returned camera, in addition to shipping costs.

The Kodak Envirowatch system includes continuous improvement in other categories, such as a 22% reduction of plastic in 35 mm film canisters, an elimination of instruction sheets (now printed on packages) which saves 3500 pounds of paper per million rolls of film, and a switch to 100% recycled paperboard, with at least 35% post-consumer content (Bartlett, 1993).

## VALUE CHAIN SHIFTS

Beyond impacting products throughout their life cycle, environmentalism is triggering fundamental changes in the value chain. From a linear pattern starting with design and ending with service, the value chain is being remodeled into a circular remanufacturing/reconsumption process (FIGURE 20.7). Industry leaders are striving to close this loop entirely in order to minimize

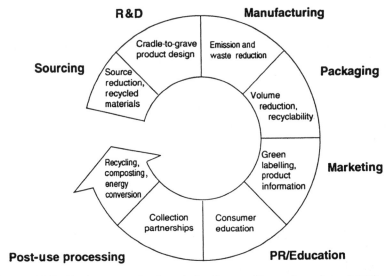

FIGURE 20.7   Environmental value chain. Source: Simon Associates (1992)

waste and emissions, but also to maintain the value of the waste-stream.

In the beverages industry, the global leadership in achieving a closed-loop process belongs to Anheuser–Busch, the world's largest brewer, with $12.6 billion in 1991 sales, but also the world's largest recycler of aluminum cans. In 1991, the company reached a milestone by recycling one used can for every one of the 17 billion cans it produced. It is also a lucrative process, since production from recycled materials saves 95% of the energy needed to make aluminum from raw ore. Set up in 1978, the Anheuser–Busch Recycling Corporation (ABRC) reached its goal by building an *extensive network*, bringing together over 1000 wholesalers, scrap dealers and charitable groups, and *incentivizing* this partnership at all stages. Besides providing many industry partners with capital equipment, ABRC built five processing plants and developed a grassroots infrastructure made up of schools, hospitals and other nonprofit organizations, paying consumers a total of $150 million in 1991 for their recycling efforts (Anonymous, 1992e).

In Japan, a survey by the Japan Economic Bureau found that consumers named Kao as the most environmentally-conscious company in the country. It is the largest manufacturer of household and personal care products in Japan, and has adopted for over 15 years an integrated approach linking source and energy reduction to product development. Kao is aggressively source-reducing products, first with the introduction of its compact detergent, Attack, then with other concentrated soaps and fabric softeners. Their reduced packaging has so far increased transportation efficiency by 20%. Overall energy use was reduced by 40% in the last 17 years, and another 40% is planned by 2000, based on co-generation, packaging reduction and recycling. New detergents are phosphate-free, and even gift pack configurations have been redesigned to allow a 30% source reduction (Jane A. Barnett, vice president, The Jergens Company (a Kao subsidiary), personal communication).

---

## INDUSTRY RESTRUCTURING THROUGH NEW ALLIANCES

Beyond integration, environmentalism is restructuring industries around new types of alliances, some of which have evolved into actual 'industrial ecosystems.' Focused alliances have centered on collection and recycling logistics, leading plastics manufacturers to team up with waste management companies: Du Pont and Waste Management in the US, as well as BASF, Bayer and Hoechst with a number of German collectors. Beyond these partial alliances, complex waste exchange systems leading to quasi-symbiotic networks are being set up. A pioneering system in Denmark links the town of Kalundborg, a power plant, an enzyme plant, a refinery and a wallboard factory, which use one another's by-products as source materials. The Asnaes coal-fired power station sells its process steam to the Novo-Nordisk biotechnology plant and to the Statoil refinery, and its surplus heat to the town and to a fishery. In turn, Statoil sells Asnaes treated wastewater for cooling, as well as desulfurized gas to burn. Asnaes sells lime-stone products to Gyproc, the wallboard maker, and nitrogen wastes from Novo-Nordisk are distributed to local farmers as fer-tilizer (Anonymous, 1992f). Industrial ecology on this scale requires a longer than average planning horizon, and also depends on advanced environmental impact assessment techni-ques and on government/business cooperation.

## GREEN COMMUNICATION STRATEGIES

Besides inventing new supply-side relationships ranging from alli-ances to planned interdependence, winning companies will need to invent new ways to relate to their markets. Although most companies have by now launched some type of environmental marketing program, many are superficial and some are downright dangerous, given consumers' universal skepticism of 'green hype.'

Most frequent so far, and by now rapidly becoming illegal, are *unsupported and unspecific green appeals.* These opportunistic claims have been found on everything from pet food to shampoo, usually labeling a product as 'environmentally-friendly' when this may in fact apply only to a small component. As noted earlier, the FTC is ruling against this approach in the US.

The corporate equivalent of these vague appeals is the rapidly spreading practice of *cause marketing,* whereby companies attempt to 'buy green points' through contributions to environmental groups, even though these are often peripheral to the companies' core business. General Motors has thus been charged with 'greenwashing.' While its fuel-efficient Chevrolet Geo line sponsors an environmental tree program, planting more than 150 000 trees over the past few years, GM has also been a leader in the lobby against enforced fuel efficiency standards in cars (Anonymous, 1993f).

Representing a higher level of company commitment, but even riskier, are what could be called 'premature green claims.' The best-known of these relates to Mobil's 1989 launch of its 'biodegradable' Hefty trash bag line. A leader in the $1.1 billion US trash bag market, with a 23% share, Mobil initially favored the EPA hierarchy prioritizing source reduction over recycling. However, pressured by retailers, themselves sensitive to the public cry that 'plastics are forever,' Mobil had to follow its competitors and launch a degradable line. The new line was reformulated with an additive speeding degradation by 25–40%, if exposed to the elements. The launch was low-key, with consumer information only through product labeling. The new package design featured the term 'degradable' prominently but included an explanation concerning the required conditions. Six months after the launch, public thinking on degradability reversed itself; the Environmental Defense Fund called for a consumer boycott, including the Hefty and Glad lines, and the FTC requested claim substantiation. By June 1990, Mobil was facing lawsuits from seven US states for deceptive advertising and consumer fraud, even though it had voluntarily removed its degradable claim three months earlier. This illustrates clearly the danger of a specific 'green' claim—however modest—prior to the establishment of national standards and in the absence of an integrated communications strategy conveying to the public the entire scope of a company's environmental programs (Anonymous, 1991).

For several companies, the ability to build appropriate partnerships has proved crucial in minimizing the communication risks of environmental claims or programs. McDonald's, for instance, was able to avert disaster with its four-year experiment in recycling polystyrene packaging, partly thanks to a *working* partnership with the Environmental Defense Fund, going beyond cause marketing to encompass actual joint strategy development. McDonald's recycling activities have been analyzed by several researchers, including Lodge and Rayport (1991) and Anonymous (1992g).

Similarly, Coca-Cola joined Hoechst Celanese to develop a breakthrough technology for a two-liter PET bottle made with 25%

recycled plastic—the first package using recycled plastic for a food container to be favorably reviewed by the FDA. Coca-Cola's environmental strategies range from source reduction to recycling rates, cleaner manufacturing and life cycle assessment of packaging options. For instance, glass bottles, aluminum cans and plastic soft drink bottles have been reduced by 43%, 35% and 21%, respectively, since their introductions (Coca-Cola Company, 1992).

An integrated strategy and a *performance-based approach* were also success factors for Procter & Gamble. As one of the largest consumer goods companies, marketing over 160 brands in 140 countries, Procter & Gamble is a highly visible target, especially with its environmentally-sensitive detergent and disposable diaper lines. In recent years, it faced two vastly different communication challenges in these two product groups. Survey data showed that a large proportion of US consumers (70%) wanted refillable containers for household cleaners and soap, a trend also noted in Europe. The opposite applied to disposable diapers, negatively perceived by 65% of consumers (Simmons, 1992).

In the laundry category, an approach favoring source reduction, using life cycle analysis to assess options, stressing product performance and supporting cautious environmental claims with consumer education has yielded positive results.

For a standardized softener marketed as Downy in the US and Lenor in Europe, Procter & Gamble used *dual source reduction* for the product itself and its package. Although a triple concentrated version had been available years earlier in the US, it was ahead of its market and met with weak response. A relaunch was now appropriate, for which different options were systematically evaluated using life cycle analysis. Recycling was found to be inferior to the refillable option, which led to 95% waste reduction and was offered in a paperboard carton in the US and a flexible pouch in Europe. Within a year, the refill had reached nearly 40% of US Downy sales, with similar results in Europe for Lenor.

The situation was quite different with the diaper category. Seen as a breakthrough when they were launched in the 1960s, Pampers had by the late 1980s become a lightning rod of public fears about garbage. Publicity peaked in 1989 when the National Association of Cloth Diapers and Environmental Action, an activist group, launched a $100 million campaign stressing the category's environmental costs. Since 1985, Procter & Gamble had been studying source reduction, launching in 1986 superabsorbent diapers and in 1989 compressed packaging, which reduced source materials by 80%. At stake, then, was the company's leadership in the $3.5 billion US disposable diaper market, where it had a commanding 49.5% share, accounting for 18% of sales by 1990. Procter & Gamble again used life cycle analysis, but only as part of an integrated research program. The analysis and a later audit found that neither disposables nor cloth diapers was clearly superior; while the former created more solid waste, the latter generated more air and water pollution.

The company initially opted out of advertising and focused on public relations, mailing a 1990 pamphlet to 30 million households and updating other literature to reflect scientific studies. More importantly, it engaged in long-term research on composting, which could apply not only to disposables but also to about 60% of total municipal waste. After a successful regional test, the company is now investigating compostable substitutes for the 20% of disposables that is made of plastic and not paper (Anonymous, 1991). Recent advertising citing this research as it relates to Pampers has been extremely cautious, including several disclaimers about the limited scope and availability of the program nationwide.

## CONCLUSION

While environmental legislation in the Triad is still fairly chaotic, it clearly is converging upward, with more and more stringent requirements from industry. On the demand side, consumer activism has been affected by recessionary factors but continues to grow and drive product categories or entire businesses. The Western Europe 'environmental market' will exceed $200 billion annually by the year 2000; in North America, it doubled in size from 1970 to 1990 (to $115 billion per year) and is expected to double again to over $200 billion annually as early as 1995 (Kiernan, 1992).

Taking advantage of these opportunities for sustainable growth will depend on several key success factors:

- Integrated strategy linking all business functions and supported by long-term investment
- Restructured value chain striving toward a closed-loop reconsumption system

- Systematic benchmarking and auditing of the environmental impact of each activity in major product lines
- Continuous assessment of consumer demand, its evolution and variations across regions
- Strategic networking for purposes ranging from technology transfer to communications, between producers, retailers, environmental groups and government agencies
- Communications strategy based on actual performance improvement and stressing consumer education.

Despite policy uncertainties and consumer fluctuations, companies with the vision, structure, market understanding and capacity to innovate will be able to adopt environmental performance as a central component of quality, and will use it as a key factor of sustainable competitive advantage, as many have already demonstrated across the Triad.

## REFERENCES

Anonymous (1991). The green marketing revolution. *Advertising Age*, 29 January, 12.
Anonymous (1992a). CRCs: Hole-stoppers. *The Economist*, 17 March, 76.
Anonymous (1992b). Muck into money again. *The Economist*, 19 September, 44.
Anonymous (1992c). The greening of Detroit. *Business Week*, 24 February, 54–55.
Anonymous (1992d). One green giant? It may be Japan. *Business Week*, 24 February, 74.
Anonymous (1992e). Anheuser–Busch Recycling Corporation. *St Louis Commerce*, June, 32–33.
Anonymous (1992f). Corporate steps toward sustainable development. *Business Week*, 11 May, 75.
Anonymous (1992g). Food for thought. *The Economist*, 29 August, 64–66.
Anonymous (1993a). The hurricane called Superfund. *Business Week*, 2 August, 74.
Anonymous (1993b). Survey on 'Waste and the Environment'. *The Economist*, 29 May, 3–18.
Anonymous (1993c). Germany's push to expand the scope of recycling. *New York Times*, 4 July.
Anonymous (1993d). Turning brown. *The Economist*, 3 July, 55.
Anonymous (1993e). EC adopts Eco-Audit plan. *EURECOM*, April, 1–2.
Anonymous (1993f). Survey on 'Environmental Marketing'. *Advertising Age*, 28 June, S1–S6.

Bartlett, R. (1993). Recycling at Kodak. Presented at the UNEP/EMAC Conference on Business and the Environment, New York, 30 June.

Cairncross, F. (1992). *Costing the Earth: The Challenge for Governments, the Opportunities for Business*. Boston, MA: Harvard Business School Press.

Carra, J. (1993). EPA's pollution prevention program under the new administration. Presented at the UNEP/EMAC Conference on Business and the Environment, New York, 30 June.

Coca-Cola Company (1992). Recycling planning and programs, corporate information.

Federal Trade Commission (1992a). *FTC News*, 28 July. Washington, DC: Federal Trade Commission.

Federal Trade Commission (1992b). *Guides for the Use of Environmental Marketing Claims*. Washington, DC: Federal Trade Commission.

Gallup (1992). *The Health of the Planet Survey*. Princeton, NJ: George H. Gallup International Institute.

Harris (1988). *Public and Leadership Attitudes to the Environment in Four Continents* (conducted for UNEP). Louis Harris & Associates.

Kiernan, M.J. (1992). The age of eco-strategy. *International Executive*, May/June, 197–214.

Lodge, G. and Rayport, J. (1991). Knee deep and rising: America's recycling crisis. *Harvard Business Review*, September/October, 128–139.

Rehak, R. (1993). *Greener Marketing and Advertising* (p. 12). Emmaus, PA: Rodale.

Roper Organization (1990). *The Environment: Public Attitudes and Individual Behavior* (commissioned by S.C. Johnson & Son), July.

Roper Organization (1991). *America's Environmental GPA* (commissioned by S.C. Johnson & Son), November.

Schmidheiny, S. (1992). *Changing Course: A Global Business Perspective on Development and the Environment* (pp. 102–103, 305–308). Cambridge, MA: MIT Press.

Simmons (1992). *Earth Calling: Is America Listening?* New York: Simmons Market Research Bureau.

World Bank (1992). *World Development Report 1992: Development and the Environment*. New York: Oxford University Press.

World Resources Institute (1992). *World Resources: A Guide to the Global Environment, 1991–93*. A report in collaboration with UNEP and the UNDP. New York: Oxford University Press.

# 21

# Green Marketing: A US–Japan Perspective

## JANE A. BARNETT

Today in the US, it is difficult to find agreement to the question: 'What is the most pressing environmental problem facing our nation?' We are in a state of environmental angst for industry, government and general citizens. Our state and federal governments are fighting to decide who should set the standards and whose money will be used to pay for the programs. Consumers know that they should be doing something different, but many are unwilling to accept the inconvenience. Industry is sure it can handle the situation, as long as only voluntary guidelines are set, not regulations. Even between environmentalists, the debate on which environmental issues have the longer term pay-off is still open.

With this confused backdrop, we find ozone layer depletion, toxic dump pollution and our landfills bulging with waste. The questions that each of us should be striving to answer are: 'How can our corporations, or clients, better accept the moral responsibility of global citizenship?' and 'How can each country best make its environmental contribution?'

The answer is not a universal, single truth. Using the environmental slogan of 'Think globally, act locally,' the environmental response is situationally determined and must be coordinated on a national or regional level. Each country must evaluate its

*Building the Strategically-Responsive Organization.*
Edited by H. Thomas, D. O'Neal, R. White and D. Hurst.
Copyright © 1994 the Strategic Management Society. Published 1994 by John Wiley & Sons Ltd.

principal environmental problems from both a local and a global viewpoint. Then, the resources can be allocated toward environmental projects. The concept of sustainable development relies on the fact that environmental solutions must be developed hand-in-hand with business growth. And environmental solutions must make sense within the country of application. The days of American Imperialism, thrusting its view of environmental political correctness, are over. The future belongs to international cooperation and acceptance of locally determined environmental solutions that sustain economic growth.

When comparing environmental philosophies between nations, we must first address the question: whose criteria do we use? In the US, with 80% of its waste landfilled, the solid waste dilemma response is determined by its theoretical assumptions: divert waste from landfills.

In the US, we are centering on the area of solid waste as a primary concern. Of course, we have legislation such as the Clean Air Act, EPA rules for chemical disposal, RCRA debates, and a host of legislative actions to monitor industry environmental concerns. But the solid waste issue, and its effect on packaging and product offerings to consumers, is of prime interest today.

The EPA has established a hierarchy for the solid waste issue, calling for source reduction and recycling with incineration and landfilling only as a last alternative. Source reduction, making less waste in the first place, is the logical environmental first step. However, the majority of the state laws for consumer packaging issues center on recycling, use of recycled content and marketing claims. In the US, we have a wide disparity between the first logical goal, reducing waste, and the multitude of state regulations governing consumer package goods companies in the market-place. However, the legislative thrust is still to reduce landfilled waste.

Yet, Americans cannot expect all other countries to respond to the solid waste crisis in the same manner. Variations between environmental responses will come from the country's theoretical assumptions of environmental needs. In Japan, with 70% of its waste incinerated, an appropriate environmental response to solid waste will not center on reducing landfilled waste. It will contain a balance of landfill reduction and uses for incinerated energy recovery.

In the US, we view the debates between state and federal

governments, environmentalists and industry as a signal that we are accomplishing something great. We are addressing the problem. In Japan, drawn out public debates on the issue are not necessarily a sign of action. The action may be accomplished through the government and industries working together for a common solution.

And finally we come to the consumer. In the US, some view the 70–80% of consumers who call themselves environmentalists as 'untapped markets.' But we are dismayed when we find that they don't want to spend 15% more for an environmentally sensitive product. In Japan, consumer environmental interest is growing, but the market research numbers are not as alarming. But does anyone really think Japanese industry will wait until they have dissatisfaction at the 80% level before this consumer issue is addressed?

There is no doubt that Japanese industry has lagged behind the quick-fix mentality displayed by some American companies. And both nations are behind Europe's initiatives in solid waste and packaging regulation. However, the environmental business paradigm is unfolding in new ways, with many problems yet unsolved.

When examining the Japanese environmental response, we must not make the mistake of viewing Japan as a small island cut off from the mainstream of the rest of the world, unconcerned with environmental issues. However, many Americans have viewed Japan as behind the US, simply because plastic recycling is not a primary industry initiative. Japan is a global competitor composed of multinational corporations and well aware of the environmental concerns of the global community.

How could Japanese businessmen not take notice of the rising environmental concerns of Germany and Europe while they are doing business in those countries? Or not be aware of the emerging trends in Canada and the US?

The Japanese passion for listening to consumers, cooperating with competitors and solidifying government and academic support to direct change is targeting the environmental area.

Already, Japan has very strict pollution control regulations and chemical handling procedures. However, before delving into the Japanese approach to environmental areas, let us examine the similarities and differences between Japan and the US.

## Similarities between US and Japanese Environmental Initiatives

As outlined in Arthur D. Little's book *Packaging for the Environment*, Japanese and American consumers share many environmental concerns, including:

- use of agricultural chemicals
- elimination of dioxin
- automobile exhausts
- CFCs
- noise pollution
- deforestation
- phosphates in soaps
- nuclear plant sites.

Consumers are looking to emerging seal programs as a way of guiding them in their purchases.

The US has a few fledgling private seal programs, and individual states are interested in providing state seals for marketing claims. Japan's Environmental Association has awarded approximately 1300 products with the ECO MARK seals.

Both countries have a history of returnable glass bottles that are giving way to convenience packaging. The Japanese standardized ISSHOBIN sake bottle and soy sauce bottles cover more product categories and are interchangeable between suppliers. The US returnable bottle system has been manufacturer-specific. However, both countries have seen a movement away from glass bottles to plastic packaging for higher consumer convenience.

Both actively recycle aluminum cans, with the US having a better infrastructure and a recycling rate between 60 and 70%. Japan's recycling rate for aluminum cans is at 45%. Global awareness of polystyrene issues and McDonald's switch from polystyrene has had an impact on some US and Japanese food outlets. CFCs are being replaced in both countries, and were banned in aerosol products earlier in the US.

Finally, industries in both countries are aware of the importance of managing their companies in an environmentally responsible manner.

## DIFFERENCES BETWEEN US AND JAPANESE ENVIRONMENTAL INITIATIVES

However, it is easier to understand the differences between the Japanese and American businesses on environmental issues.

In the US, consumers are more vocal in their displeasure with industry's handling of environmental issues, and attitudinally more concerned about potential environmental damage. As mentioned earlier, the handling of solid waste is different, with the US relying on landfills and Japan using incineration as the primary method.

Plastic recycling is virtually non-existent in Japan, with no standardized collection system. Since this type of waste is incinerated, plastic recycling has not been a high priority. However, investigation into biodegradable plastics is being pursued in Japan. In the US, with our philosophy of preserving our waste underground, biodegradability is perceived as a strong negative.

Japan is very concerned about air pollution and sulfur oxide emissions. Annually, worldwide emissions of sulfur oxide total 100 million tons. Total emissions are shared by the former USSR and Eastern Europe (43%), North America (26%), Asia (19%) and Western Europe (11%). Japan's share is only 1%. In the late 1960s Japan began a program to reduce sulfur oxide emissions, and leads the world in legal regulation to prevent air pollution. Today, 80% of the equipment for flue gas desulfurization is concentrated in Japan.

One major cultural difference is the importance placed on elaborate gift packaging in Japan. Although there are examples of change, the aesthetic beauty of packaging is a strong cultural norm. Even small gifts may have elaborate wrapping, similar to that reserved for high end products in the US. Therefore, source reduction in packaging is more unevenly practiced in Japan. And, often, the luxuriousness of the packaging remains even when source reduced.

However, when we highlight conservation methods and environmental actions of consumers, Japan ranks as having the highest paper recycling rate in the world. Historically, this was done at the consumer level, with office paper recycling coming on stream later. Japan's collection rate (volume collected) is 48% compared to 33% in the US. However, the volume of paper consumed (the recycling rate) is 50%, compared to 27% in the US.

TABLE 21.1   Japan versus the US: policies and market trends

| Issues | Similarities | Differences |
|---|---|---|
| Disposal systems | | Primary in Japan: incineration (80%), versus only 10% in US, with 80% in landfill |
| Collection systems | | US curbside (separate plastics, glass, paper, aluminum) and compost (food, yard waste) Japan curbside (separate combustibles, non-combustibles, and large size waste) |
| Regulation | | Tighter regulation on packaging and advertising claims in US (FTC guidelines) |
| Labeling | Emerging green seal programs | |
| Consumer activism | | US consumer movement more developed |
| Recycling practices | Glass is manufacturer-specific in US, more cooperative in Japan | |
| | Plastic: PET is widely used in Japan and the US | Recycling rate higher in US (PET recycled at 28% and HDPE at 10%) |
| | | Paper recycling rate in Japan is the highest worldwide |
| | Aluminum: Better infrastructure and recycling rate in US | |
| Cultural practices | | Japan has a strong tradition of elaborate gift wrapping |

Because of the difference in disposal options, Japanese con-sumers sort their garbage in a different way, separating it into combustibles, non-combustibles and large size waste. In the US, the consumer would separate into recyclable plastics, glass, paper, aluminum and waste.

These are the obvious sociocultural differences (for a summary of these differences, see TABLE 21.1). But where is Japanese business headed in the future?

In April 1991, the Federation of Economic Associations, an influential business organization in Japan, presented its findings on environmental issues in the Keidanren Global Environmental Charter. Traditionally, once a Keidanren has been published, Japanese companies are to incorporate these initiatives into their business organizations to insure nationwide accomplishment of the goals.

The Keidanren calls for a pooling of resources of Japanese business, academic and government bodies to address the global environmental issues. General guidelines include:

1. All company activities shall be scientifically evaluated for their impact on the environment, and any necessary counter-measures shall be implemented.
2. Care shall be taken in the R&D stages of product development to lessen the possible burden on the environment at each level of its production, distribution, appropriate use and disposal.
3. Companies shall strictly observe all national and local laws for environmental protection and they shall set additional stan-dards of their own.
4. When procuring materials, including materials for production, companies shall endeavor to purchase those that are superior from such viewpoints as conserving resources, preserving the environment and enhancing recycling.
5. Companies shall employ technologies that allow efficient use of energy and preservation for the environment in their product and other activities.

With the Keidanren as a philosophy for Japan's future, increased environmental performance can be expected from Japan.

In the last section of this chapter, I review Kao Corporation's actions as an example of Japanese business environmental philo-sophy. Kao is the largest manufacturer of household and personal care products in Japan. Worldwide, it is also an integrated

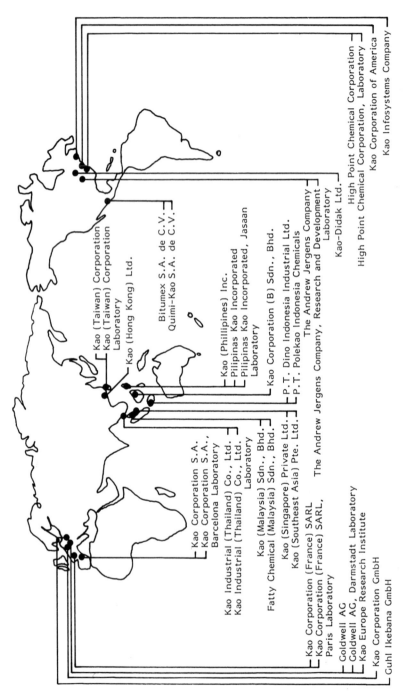

FIGURE 21.1  Global positioning of Kao

manufacturer producing personal care and household products, floppy disks, professional salon products and cosmetics (see FIGURE 21.1).

As we examine the areas of Kao's involvement, similarities and differences between the Japanese and American environmental initiatives will begin to emerge.

Kao has an Environmental Steering Committee of which the Chairman of the Board, Dr Maruta, is a fundamental working member. Their corporate environmental philosophy includes the standard environmental areas linked with worker safety standards.

Kao has historically employed strict pollution control standards in terms of air and water emissions. As proof, they have tropical fish living in the waste water from the plant operations in all production facilities in Japan. We have long believed in energy and national resource conservation, and introduced the concept of compact detergents to the world with Attack detergent. Kao's environmental philosophy may be summarized as follows:

- Environmental Steering Committee
- Corporate environmental philosophy
- Strict pollution control standards
- Energy and national resource conservation
- Source reduction in products and packaging
- Efficient distribution systems
- Long-term planning for sustainable development.

Kao is actively involved long-term planning for sustainable development, living in harmony with the environment. Kao strives to include natural ingredients in their products. For over 15 years Kao has promoted increased production of coconut oil as a renewable resource and primary ingredient in many of their household products. The ingredients in the bar soap and facial cleaners are 100% derived from natural plant and animal ingredients, 95% natural ingredients are used in shampoos and conditioners, and 40% in detergents, with the average for all household products being 60%.

Kao has achieved a 40% reduction in energy usage per production volume in the last 17 years and plans another 40% reduction by the year 2000. This reduction has been based on recycling materials, co-generation within the facilities and packaging changes. The switch to concentrated packaging in Attack accounted for a 6% reduction in energy usage (FIGURE 21.2).

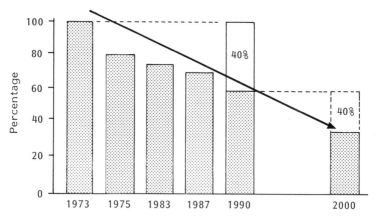

FIGURE 21.2  Kao energy reduction (per production volume): recycling, co-generation and packaging changes

Concern for the environment and a desire to use natural materials were prime factors in Kao's development of de-inking agents used to produce quality recycled materials. Kao accounts for 70% of all de-inking agents used to recycle paper in Japan.

Kao is also a primary user of recycled paper, with all corrugates and paper packaging for detergents, soap and bath additives currently using between 60 and 90% recycled paper. The goal is 100% usage of recycled paper in all paper and corrugated packaging (FIGURE 21.3).

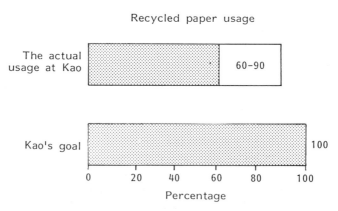

FIGURE 21.3  Kao's usage of recycled paper products

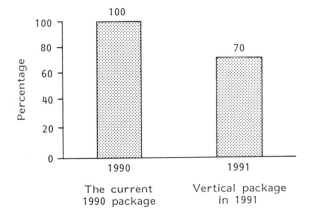

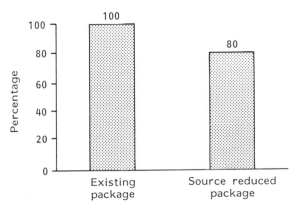

FIGURE 21.4   Comparisons between (a) existing package and vertical packaging, and (b) existing package and source reduced package

Kao uses a totally recyclable drum which has a unique rinsing system built into its sides. Kao also uses collapsible shipping containers as a source reduction method.

We are aggressively source reducing both powders and liquids by the use of concentrated products for brands such as Zabu detergent/bleach combination product and Hemming fabric softener. The concentrated packaging contributed to an overall 6% energy source reduction and efficiency of transportation increased by 20%.

The collapsible carton used in the Hemming fabric softener has achieved a 70% source reduction in plastic usage over the original all-plastic bottle. The Hemming carton is also made from recycled paper.

By compressing the packages in products such as our Merries Diapers, we have achieved a 20% source reduction in packaging. Also, by changing design configurations of gift packs, a 30% source reduction has been achieved (FIGURE 21.4).

Along with concentrating the detergents, the new detergents and dishwashing formulas are phosphate-free. The measuring systems in these new products assure accurate consumer use and help to eliminate over-sudsing and excessive water use. This technology is found in the Just detergent, Family Fresh dishwashing products and Attack detergents.

In addition, all sales materials, point of purchase materials, office paper and consumer literature are printed on recycled paper. Recycling activities within the Kao plants range from office recycling to conservation of materials throughout all phases of production.

Kao has been awarded many prestigious Japanese honors for its environmental awareness and contributions. The Japan Economic Bureau (similar to the *Wall Street Journal*) survey has found that Japanese consumers name Kao as the most environmentally sensitive company in Japan.

After this brief description of a Japanese company, the question remains: 'What differences really exist between Japanese and American companies in the environmental arena?' We propose the answer, 'All superior global corporations are seriously involved in achieving high environmental standards. Any other differences are superficial.'

# 22

# Environmental Management in North America and Europe

## TIMOTHY C. WOODS

Nestlé began manufacturing products in Canada in 1928, with a small milk plant in the village of Chesterville, Ontario. Today, Nestlé employs more than 5000 people and operates 12 factories, and a multitude of sales offices and retail outlets across Canada. Our headquarters are in Toronto.

We manufacture soluble and R&G coffees, confectionery, frozen entrees, canned beans and pastas, instant beverages, non-dairy creamers, bottled waters, frozen french fried potatoes, hamburger buns and, until recently, pet foods. Last year, the sales of these products came to more than $1 billion. A significant portion of these sales, close to 10%, came from exports to the US and Europe. Nestlé is the largest food company in the world, and a leading food processor in Canada (FIGURE 22.1).

While Nestlé was growing to its present size, concern about environmental consequences relating to industrial development was growing faster. Angus Reid polls have shown how seriously Canadian consumers regard protection of the environment. It has become a *permanent* concern, and will remain a high priority to Canadians as a whole, despite the current recession (TABLE 22.1).

*Building the Strategically-Responsive Organization.*
Edited by H. Thomas, D. O'Neal, R. White and D. Hurst.
Copyright © 1994 the Strategic Management Society. Published 1994 by John Wiley & Sons Ltd.

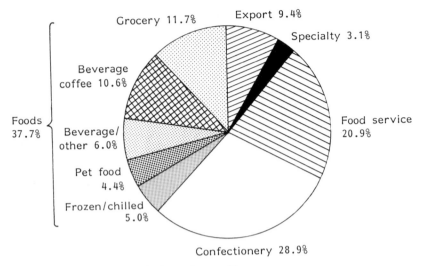

FIGURE 22.1   Nestlé Canada Inc. sales profile

On the issue of Canada's environment, Nestlé is determined to make a specific and meaningful contribution. Our commitment is to limit the impact of the company's manufacturing processes, packaging materials, and products on Canada's air, soil, lakes and rivers. This policy represents a bit of a tightrope act for us. We are constantly faced with a challenge: we must balance the environmental concerns of today's society with our own need to maintain the highest standards of quality, value and product safety.

## INTERNAL 'GREEN' STRUCTURE

To help achieve this balance, Ian Murray (then chairman and CEO) formed a special task force in June 1989. We called it the 'Green Team'. The role of this team was to come to grips with issues such as packaging reduction, solid waste disposal and recycling. This team was made up of senior people representing all sectors of our company (FIGURE 22.2). It reported directly to Nestlé's CEO and received counsel from a special board of external Canadian advisers. Members on this board include:

TABLE 22.1 Canadians' public policy issues agenda (February 1988 to May 1993). Respondents were asked: 'Thinking of the issues presently confronting Canada, I'd like to know which one you feel requires the greatest attention from the country's leaders? What other issues do you think are important for Canada right now?'

| | Feb. 1988 (1523)* (%) | Nov. 1988 (1508) (%) | Jan. 1989 (1509) (%) | July 1989 (1521) (%) | Feb. 1990 (1505) (%) | July 1990 (1501) (%) | Jan. 1991 (1507) (%) | July 1991 (1508) (%) | Jan. 1992 (1519) (%) | July 1992 (1500) (%) | Sept. 1992 (1522) (%) | Dec. 1992 (1500) (%) | Jan. 1993 (1507) (%) | Feb. 1993 (1501) (%) | Mar. 1993 (1501) (%) | Apr. 1993 (1500) (%) | May 1993 (1501) (%) |
|---|---|---|---|---|---|---|---|---|---|---|---|---|---|---|---|---|---|
| Unemployment/jobs | 18 | 11 | 14 | 14 | 11 | 8 | 8 | 14 | 24 | 24 | 28 | 39 | 42 | 45 | 42 | 44 | 44 |
| The economy: general | 10 | 6 | 7 | 10 | 14 | 22 | 30 | 31 | 62 | 44 | 48 | 56 | 53 | 47 | 43 | 37 | 34 |
| Deficit, government spending | 5 | 5 | 10 | 13 | 11 | 7 | 6 | 12 | 8 | 4 | 4 | 10 | 11 | 18 | 21 | 33 | 31 |
| Environment | 6 | 10 | 23 | 31 | 24 | 24 | 6 | 17 | 8 | 9 | 5 | 9 | 7 | 6 | 7 | 8 | 7 |
| Taxes, tax reform, GST | 4 | 6 | 4 | 6 | 25 | 14 | 15 | 17 | 7 | 5 | 4 | 4 | 5 | 5 | 5 | 5 | 7 |
| Free trade | 37 | 6 | 33 | 15 | 9 | 4 | 1 | 7 | 3 | 8 | 4 | 6 | 7 | 6 | 6 | 3 | 5 |
| National unity | – | – | – | – | – | 12 | 8 | 29 | 17 | 21 | 12 | 6 | 6 | 6 | 4 | 4 | 3 |
| Constitution, Meech Lake | 2 | 1 | 6 | 4 | 20 | 40 | 5 | 9 | 30 | 34 | 44 | 7 | 5 | 3 | 3 | 3 | 2 |
| Abortion | 20 | 9 | 6 | 16 | 5 | 2 | 1 | 1 | 1 | 1 | – | – | – | – | 1 | – | – |

*Number of respondents given in parentheses.
Source: Wright, W.J. (1993). Canadians and the Environment. A Syndicated National Study of 1500 Canadians. Copyright 1993 The Angus Reid Group. Reproduced by permission.

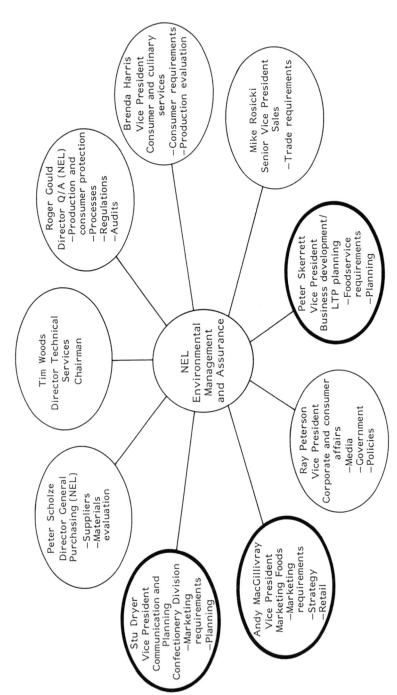

FIGURE 22.2 The 'Green Team': task force on the environment, formed September 1989

- Allan Gotlieb (former ambassador to the US)
- Angus Reid (top pollster in Canada)
- Pat Delbridge (environmental advocate)

This advisory board assists our management to chart the future strategic direction of our Canadian company in today's fast-changing global environment. Its members also advise our company on appropriate responses to important business and social issues.

The 'Green Team' has now been disbanded, having achieved its objective of establishing awareness and action plans. The environmental leadership torch has been passed on to the Executive Committee, consisting of presidents of operating divisions, and facilitated by a senior vice president of consumer and corporate affairs. All employees understand that they have a mandate to assist the company in its efforts to become more responsible in its activities that bear environmental consequences.

We decided to involve our product marketing people in a series of environmental subcommittees, along divisional lines. Each committee is chaired by a director of operations, reporting to the divisional president. Simply stated, their task is to make things happen within our action plan. Another important organizational move was the appointment of a well-qualified manager, responsible for environment and safety engineering.

---

## CANADIAN CONTEXT: 'GREEN TRENDS'

Moving to the political arena in Canada, Angus Reid polls clearly tells us that many industrial sectors have a poor public image for environmental consciousness (FIGURE 22.3). Also, their findings show that government and industry continue to have little credibility on environmental issues, whereas environmentalists and scientists enjoy the greatest belief (FIGURE 22.4). It is no small wonder that federal and provincial governments have been consulting directly with environmental organizations (and not industry) prior to releasing their various environmental action plans and regulations.

A national task force was created to look into packaging and solid waste. Much of the attention of the task force and, later, public meetings, focused on the role that packaging played in the

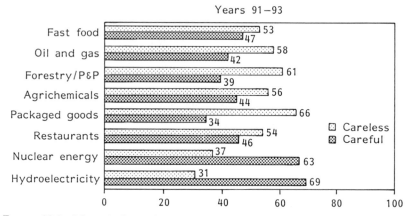

FIGURE 22.3    Many industrial sectors have a poor public image for environmental consciousness. Source: Wright, W.J. (1993). *Canadians and the Environment. A Syndicated National Study of 1500 Canadians.* Copyright 1993 The Angus Reid Group. Reproduced by permission.

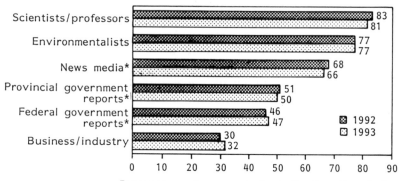

Percentage of respondents indicating they believe 'most' of what that information source says about the environment

*Wording differed in the 1989 and 1990 surveys

FIGURE 22.4    Government and industry continue to have little credibility on environmental issues. Source: Wright, W.J. (1993). *Canadians and the Environment. A Syndicated National Study of 1500 Canadians.* Copyright 1993 The Angus Reid Group. Reproduced by permission.

landfill problem. The aim of this task force was to issue a national packaging protocol (TABLE 22.2). Representatives of our Green Team attended more than one public meeting of the task force, to provide food industry input. However, suggested definitions for terms, and the role of energy usage, advice to use a 'cradle to

TABLE 22.2   National packaging protocol

| Year | Milestone diversion targets |
| --- | --- |
| 1992 | 90% of packaging sent for disposal in 1988: to be achieved through source reduction and recycling |
| 1994 | 80% of packaging sent for disposal in 1988 |
| 1996 | 70% of packaging sent for disposal in 1988 |
| 1998 | 60% of packaging sent for disposal in 1988 |
| 2000 | 50% of packaging sent for disposal in 1988 |

grave' approach, to plan for energy recovery from safe incineration, and urgings to take an international perspective fell on deaf ears at that time.

The reaction of business to the release of the protocol was quite predictable. A 50% equivalent source weight reduction of packaging by the year 2000, versus base year 1988, is drastic for the food industry, to say the least!

## NESTLÉ'S RESPONSE: QUANTITATIVE TARGETS

At Nestlé, we have set ourselves a target of 10% reduction, per year (by weight) of our total product packaging for the years 1991, 1992, and 1993, using 1988 as the base year. For a company in our line of business, this is a very tough target indeed. It is slightly ahead of the protocol. We achieved 10.1% overall source reduction for 1991, but 1992 preliminary figures showed very little further source reduction progress. One reason was a major skew in production mix toward glass, with the launch of Nestea Iced Tea in partnership with Coca Cola. We need to aggressively pursue more drastic packaging changes if we are to arrive at our three-year objective. There is no commitment to further weight reduction beyond 1993: we have to rely upon a level of diversion from landfill by means of component-specific recycling.

In almost all of our factories we are now using the best available technology for packaging our products. For years we have been striving to reduce the costs of packaging. Reducing the content and weight have been pursued as a matter of good business sense (FIGURE 22.5). We have been using double-reduced

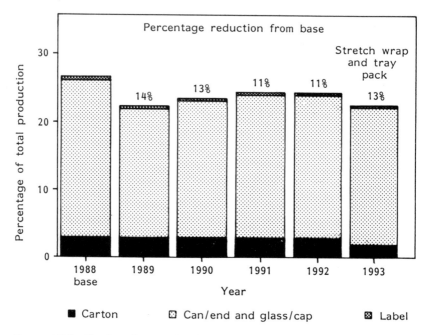

FIGURE 22.5   Total packaging, Wallaceburg 1988–1993

tin-plated steel cans since the late 1970s. Technology is not in place to achieve similar source reduction of retorted canned products.

At the provincial and municipal level, we are facing a patchwork quilt of different measures, many aimed at relieving the solid waste pressures on rapidly diminishing landfill sites, and the corresponding public perceptions (TABLE 22.3).

Recycling, still regarded by the public as being environmentally responsible, is becoming less popular with those authorities fiscally responsible for carrying it out. The fiscal deficits being experienced at all levels of government across Canada are leading to some very arbitrary positions, many aimed at using the environmental umbrella to raise revenues for other priorities. Deposits on beverage containers are spreading, not only geographically, but to *other* product categories.

Various levels of government are looking at measures that will influence the material content, weight, size and availability of packaging. Very few of these regulators have a clear under-

TABLE 22.3   Canadians' community environmental priority list, 1992–1993

| Issue | 1992<br>(n = 1503)<br>(%) | 1993<br>(n = 1654)<br>(%) |
|---|---|---|
| Water pollution | 33 | 31 |
| Garbage/landfill waste | 27 | 23 |
| Air pollution | 18 | 21 |
| Acid rain | 3 | 3 |
| Chemicals | 5 | 5 |
| Industry/factories | 10 | 10 |
| Auto exhaust | 12 | 9 |
| Pollution, general | 2 | 4 |
| Forestry/deforestation | 6 | 5 |
| Nuclear pollutants/toxic waste | 2 | 2 |
| Sewage problems | 3 | 2 |
| Oil spills | 1 | 1 |
| Other | 1 | 1 |
| (Unsure) | 6 | 8 |

Source: Wright, W.J. (1993). *Canadians and the Environment. A Syndicated National Study of 1500 Canadians.* Copyright 1993 The Angus Reid Group. Reproduced by permission.

standing of the total role played by packaging. When we add food to the equation, the situation is even more volatile.

Matters become more complicated in the food industry, when despite the fact that consumers continue to express strong willingness to make financial sacrifices for the environment, they are not demonstrating willingness to give up *convenience* (FIGURE 22.6).

Food products packaged to provide convenience continue to grow, despite the presence of alternatives with less packaging. Microwaveability has its place! Single servings suit households where both partners are working.

In Canada, we suffer from distorted statistics, changing interpretations of data and confusing public statements.

Early on in the controversy all paper was regarded as packaging in landfill data (FIGURE 22.7). Newspapers were not identified as a separate category. Yet close to 85% of the capacity of trucks collecting packaging materials for recycling is occupied by newsprint. Is a paper bag (from a renewable resource) better for the environment in the long run than a plastic bag? Anyone following the styrofoam cups and clamshells versus paper saga must be confused. One point emerged very clearly from McDonald's

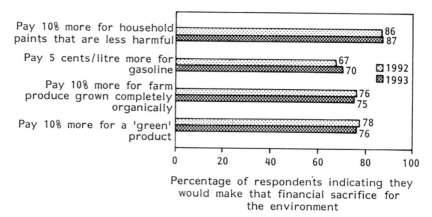

FIGURE 22.6   Consumers continue to express strong willingness to make financial sacrifices for the environment. Source: Wright, W.J. (1993). *Canadians and the Environment. A Syndicated National Study of 1500 Canadians.* Copyright 1993 The Angus Reid Group. Reproduced by permission.

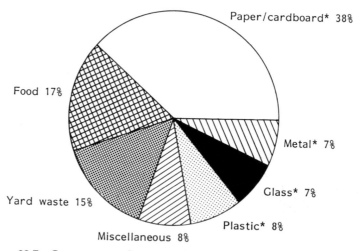

FIGURE 22.7   Components of municipal landfill waste. *While NEL products packaging is a miniscule amount of the total—they are within 60% of the portions measured

decision: customers/consumers carry very powerful influences on directions followed by food industry, even if their perceptions are misguided.

At Nestlé, we believe that environmental problems call for an informed and integrated response. This response should come from industry, government agencies, the general public and distribution chains. If the solutions for packaging materials and their disposal are to be realistic, we believe they must combine source reduction, waste-to-energy incineration, reuse, recycling, composting, and landfill.

Our environment and safety engineer has conducted environmental assessments of all 12 factories in Canada. The data he demanded, and in many cases developed himself from factory records, has formed the foundation for 1988 base year data being used to measure progress against committed Nestlé objectives on solid waste and packaging source reduction. Establishing credible 1988 base year and 1990/1991 actual performances on solid waste and packaging usages is a major undertaking. These figures will be subject to audit and verification by government authorities in future years. The data, obtained by every product label, will be available for measuring source reduction progress, against time, by product groups under the control of brand managers. Lack of progress against commitment will require explanation to senior management.

---

## NESTLÉ'S COMMUNICATIONS

All senior managers in marketing and production have environmental targets as part of their 1993 personal objectives, including the presidents of each division.

If we are Nestlé do not widely publicize our 'green' strategies, it is because we regard minimizing the environmental impact of our business as a very serious matter. We are *not* given to making frivolous comments, using cliches or adopting slogans for something this fundamental (the use of the title 'Green Team' to describe our task force was reluctantly adopted—only because we couldn't stop our employees using this name):

- We will *not* market any of our products under a 'green' label.
- We will *not* position a product to take advantage of apparent environmental attributes of 'our package versus theirs'.
- We will *not* use the media to pat ourselves on the back for all the good things we have done. We have not done enough. We do not have all the answers. We are concerned; but we will continue to move forward in our attempts to improve.

TABLE 22.4   Nestlé environmental checklist

---

*A. General Marketing*
- Does your marketing plan include specific, environmental objectives and programmes?
- Have you devised clear and workable strategies for achieving those objectives?
- Have you established structures and/or systems capable of pursuing those strategies to their successful conclusions?
- Have you determined what long-term changes, if any, you will want to make in your product line and set targets for accomplishing those changes?

*B. Communication*
- Have you developed a programme to draw attention to product features which are environmentally positive?
- Can you, through better consumer instruction or some innovative service programme or both, convince customers to use products in ways that reduce their negative environmental impacts?
- Have you developed a reality check for all environmental claims to make sure they are not only true and capable of substantiation, but that they are stated in a way that is believable?
- Do all your advertising people understand that, on this issue especially, actions speak louder than words? And, that it is better to put money into good performance than into good reports on mediocre performance?

---

This may be conservative, but it is not self-serving. The public will very quickly see through positions that are taken using quasi-environmental claims as a means to a marketing end.

In order to implement our functionally-integrated approach, we have developed an environmental checklist for marketing and distribution, which has been sent to all Nestlé markets from our global headquarters in Vevey, Switzerland. The checklist emphasizes performance improvement through benchmarking before setting up communications goals (TABLE 22.4). Our communications programme itself is both internal and external, using an environmental newsletter and videos to reach all employees, customers and various public forums.

How do we expect consumers to become aware of Nestlé's commitment to environmental responsibility? We think the answer is in our actions, not in our words. When all of our employees are involved in trying to protect the environment—as part of their normal daily activities—doing small things, as second nature; making changes to their own and the company's way of life, they will be our best ambassadors to the trade, consumers, schools, communities, associations, environmental groups and churches.

In Nestlé, we have a common global approach when striving for reduction in packaging and solid wastes, plus treatment of air and water emissions around the world.

However, in Europe we have also been instrumental in other initiatives. Bimonthly meetings of a multi-representative committee are held in Brussels, moderated by an outside consultant. The purpose of this committee is to exchange information, facts, methods, and reasons for each type of packaging used in the food industry. Typical participants are:

- Food industry: Nestlé, Unilever, BSN
- Resin producers: ICI, Dow
- Converters: Bishof & Klein (Germany)
- Environmentalists: Sustainability UK (John Eckelton)
- Waste management: Otto (Germany)
- Trade: Sainsbury (UK), Albert Heign (Holland)

The discussions are well balanced, with the moderator ensuring that everyone gets ample opportunity for comment. Minutes are issued. This has had the important result of establishing good communications between all interested parties and is leading to a common perspective and to a definition of terms and priorities.

Nestlé is also a founding member of the European Reduction and Recycling Association (ERRA). This group supports the capital costs of equipment, and expenses of advertisements and promotion of residential recycling organizations in selected communities such as Leeds, Barcelona, and so on. Operating costs are not included, but ERRA assures a guaranteed price for recycled materials for three years. The emphasis is on establishing a viable demand for recycled materials before setting up the recycling system. Many communities are now coming to the end of the three-year guaranteed period, and ERRA are now folding back into those communities to ensure that their recycling efforts will continue to be effective. ERRA is now the principal advisor to most European governments with respect to community recycling.

In Europe, a joint industry and EC government pact was announced with the objective of funding research by major municipalities into waste generation, collection, sorting, handling and disposition. Nestlé is a founding member of this venture.

In closing, a few words about willingness to change in perspective are warranted. Nestlé's objectives in Canada have been in concert with policies and direction from our headquarters in Switzerland, in terms of environmental strategies and activities. However, we are part of a North American commercial zone, linked directly with the US, and, with growing closeness, to Mexico. The erosion and ultimate removal of tariffs, under FTA and NAFTA, has shifted our perspective. We are now taking more than an academic interest in environmental matters evolving in US and Mexico. If we are to continue to maintain highly effective manufacturing operations in Canada, we have to honour current, and future, environmental obligations concerning the US and Mexico with all the products we make in Canada and ship into those markets.

In short, a good environmental record can become a strategic advantage, not only at the national level, but also within the context of emerging regional blocs and also within the global competitive context of our industry.

# 23

# Environmental Labeling and Industry Regulation

## JOHN B. ALVORD

Whether we are labeled as consumers or customers or constituents or the public, we are realizing that solid waste is not someone else's problem; it is ours. Recent industry studies bear this out.

Firstly, we agree that solid waste is a big problem. In a June 1991 Environmental Opinion study, 79% of Americans said that solid waste was an extreme or very serious problem. The majority also said that it is ours to solve. When respondents were asked to identify which two of five choices will be most important in solving environmental problems, 54% chose individual action, compared to 46% for business action, 42% for federal regulation, 23% for technology and 22% for federal spending.

The most fascinating insight from this study, though, was that 60% of respondents now think of themselves as environmentalist, and an additional 30% say that they lean that way. There is no question that 'political correctness' is a factor in some of these responses. But to get 90% of Americans to lump themselves together on any subject of this substance is quite remarkable.

Now let us get beyond what we are *thinking* to what we are actually *doing*. A Gallup study in January 1991 suggested that in a

*Building the Strategically-Responsive Organization.*
Edited by H. Thomas, D. O'Neal, R. White and D. Hurst.
Copyright © 1994 the Strategic Management Society. Published 1994 by John Wiley & Sons Ltd.

number of areas our actions are matching our words. For example, 87% of us have recycled newspapers, glass, aluminum, motor oil or some other items; 82% of us have bought products made from or packaged in recycled materials; 23% reported using cloth diapers rather than disposable ones; and 22% reported boycotting a company's products because of its record on the environment.

Where are we getting the information for these choices? From a number of sources—books, magazines, brochures and conferences, editorials and exposés, and many others. All of these will stimulate our thinking; all of these have their proper place. But I want to make the argument for a source of information that is often underrated or even overlooked in its ability to influence positively our behavior—the product label. To do so, I would like to explore three questions:

1. Why should we have environmental information on our packages in the first place?
2. If we are going to have environmental information on our packages, what criteria should it meet?
3. In the current uncertain regulatory environment, what will be needed to keep the most useful information flowing to us on our packages?

Let's take these questions one at a time. Why should we have environmental information on packages in the first place? Let me suggest three reasons. The first is that consumers look for environmental information on packages and want more. In the Gallup poll, 75% of respondents recalled seeing environmental information on packaging; 62% said they read for environmental information; 41% reported making a purchase decision because of environmental information they had seen in advertising on labels. In an environmental tracking study run every six months at Procter & Gamble, 59% of consumers said they wanted more environmental information about products and 46% said they wanted more about packages; and these numbers are growing.

The second reason is that we need product and package facts to make environmentally responsible choices. We have choices to make on several different fronts, and facts will be key to each of them. At the most basic level, we need to make choices at home. Some of these are habit changes. Am I willing to sort garbage in the kitchen? Am I willing to carry out recyclables on a rainy night before garbage day—and am I willing to pay $2 more per month for the privilege?

Then there are product choices. Am I willing to buy and mix concentrates rather than throw away containers? Will I choose products with minimal packaging, or recycled content, or the ability to be recycled in my community? Finally, am I willing to stand up for the development of responsible, integrated solid waste systems in my community? Recycling, composting and incineration can reduce solid waste going into landfills by up to 80%, but there are siting issues and capital involved in developing these systems, and we are the ones that are going to have to insist that the issues get resolved and the capital gets appropriated.

A third reason for putting this information on packages is that point-of-purchase is where the rubber meets the road for environmental decisions. What other source but the label is there at the exact moment we pick up a product? What other source can describe the precise attributes of a particular product and enable us to compare them with our other product choices at that time? What other medium is flexible enough to keep pace with the rapid product improvements and changes in technology currently occurring in this area? What other medium can guarantee to reach 100% of a given product's users?

If I have made the case that environmental information should be on our packages, let us move on to our second key question: what criteria should these environmental messages meet?

The first is that the information should help consumers to gain a basic understanding of environmental problems and solutions. Let me give you an example, 'A Downy refill is better for the environment because it has less packaging to throw away.' What is the problem? The volume of solid waste. What is one solution? Refill packaging.

Secondly, claims should be specific. General claims like 'environmentally friendly' are not enough. Compare them with another example, 'Bottle made from 100% recycled plastic.' What does the consumer take away? This package has kept garbage out of a landfill.

Thirdly, it goes without saying that environmental information should be true, accurate and non-misleading. Environmental information should stand up to the same level of scrutiny as any product claim, with support such as tests, analyses, research, and so on.

Finally, claims should not place an environmental halo over all aspects of the product. This is our basic concern with seal programs such as Green Cross or Green Seal. Seals do nothing to educate consumers, but simply train them to look for logos. Several recent focus groups shown in support of Green Cross confirmed our worst fears about how consumers will respond to these programs, as the following quotations show:

- 'I look at the Green Cross and I relate it to the Red Cross, and the word "help" comes to mind.'
- 'If I saw a product that had the Green Cross on it, it would make me think that this is an environmental type product.'
- 'It would mean the product meets government standards.'
- 'It would just be, you know, you walk into the grocery store and you can see the Green Cross, and you'll know.'

How we wish that this issue were that simple! Beyond consumer misperceptions, there are questions of objectivity, validity and workability of such programs being raised by scientists, environmental groups and manufacturers alike. Suffice to say, we are concerned that it is not possible to validly reduce all the complex elements involved in environmental evaluation into a simple symbol.

Now let us turn to our last major question: what will be needed to keep the right kind of environmental information flowing to the consumer? Our answer, and the answer of many others, is national, uniform guidelines coupled with industry self-regulation.

In the absence of a federal voice in this area, states and municipalities have begun to fill the vacuum with their own legislation and herein lies the problem: the states and municipalities do not agree either, and that is a major problem for those of us who sell our products across state lines.

Let us take a case in point, where what may be right in one area is wrong in another. Rhode Island enacted legislation saying that any product manufactured for sale in Rhode Island cannot include recyclability information for any material for which a recycling infrastructure does not now exist in Rhode Island. Given the national distribution of our products, what this means is that we are removing statements such as 'recyclable where facilities exist' from our packages nationwide, regardless of the status of infrastructure capability outside of Rhode Island. Now how does this affect the consumer in Baltimore, for example, who can recycle detergent bottles under a 'closing the loop' partnership that provides both collection and a market for recycled plastics? Unfortunately, our friends in Baltimore simply will not have this assurance on their packages.

Even in areas where plastics recycling is not currently available, we believe package information of this type can stimulate community support. If a consumer's community is still 100% landfill, consumers should be asking, 'Why can't we have recycling here?' 'Why can't we have composting here?' And governments will have to listen.

In any event, the uncertainty made manufacturers understandably reluctant to proceed with environmental claims. After all, what is broadly permitted on today's packages may be constrained by tomorrow's new legislation and the costs of misjudgment—dollar costs as well as negative publicity in the case of a challenge—may outweigh the benefit.

National uniform standards were needed to help manufacturers enrolled in this educational process and competing on the basis of improvement in the environmental attributes of their products and packages. The National Food Processors Association and 10 other industry associations, representing about 2500 companies, petitioned the FTC in February 1991 to issue industry guides for environmental labeling and advertising, and to enforce them under their truth-in-advertising charter. After 17 months of hearings and study, Guides were issued in July 1992.

FTC Industry Guides are not law and do not pre-empt the states from regulating in this area. What they do provide is a safe haven and a level playing field for all manufacturers who genuinely want to provide appropriate environmental information to consumers. And they do provide the FTC and other governmental agencies with authoritative benchmarks for judging truth and accuracy in this area. The effectiveness of the Guides approach is amply demonstrated by FTC Guides on advertising testimonials, which brought a much greater discipline to testimonial advertising.

Guides have also provided an important benchmark for industry self-regulation under the National Advertising Division (NAD) of the Council of Better Business Bureaus. In this process, competitors, government agencies, individuals and the NAD itself challenge false or misleading claims. The NAD then determines the issues, collects and evaluates data, and negotiates agreements with advertisers. Results are published in NAD proceedings, *Advertising Age* and other news media.

The NAD approach is faster than public sector enforcement—the process takes about 10 weeks—and less expensive than governmental case development and prosecution. The public nature of the process makes it very effective in ensuring compliance and reinforcing standards across the industry.

This process has been extraordinarily successful in policing the truth and accuracy of major print and broadcast media for the past 20 years. The NAD has resolved about 2900 cases since its inception in 1971. During that period no company that has completed the NAD/NARB process has rejected the final outcome. Only occasionally—perhaps two or three cases per year—are there companies that refuse to participate, and these are referred to the appropriate government agencies.

The NAD has stepped up their scrutiny of environmental advertising and packaging claims. They opened an increasing number of new environmental cases in each of the last two years. The FTC Guides are a primary resource in their deliberations.

So why is it important to have environmental information on packages? Consumers want it and look for it. We need it to make the right choices at home and in our communities. And there is no better place to provide it than at the point of purchase.

What criteria should messages meet? They should educate us concerning problems and solutions. They should be specific, accurate and non-misleading. They should not try to reduce complex environmental issues to a single symbol.

What is the best way to keep this information flowing? National uniform guidelines issued by the FTC and increased scrutiny by the NAD should create the level playing field that responsible manufacturers are looking for, in order to continue providing this information.

# Parting Shots

Presented at the final session of the Conference, Henry Mintzberg's 'Parting Shots' is a fitting summary of the challenges facing both the Society and its members.

| Chapter 24 | Parting Shots: Our Real Ridge |
| --- | --- |
| | *Henry Mintzberg* |

# 24

# Parting Shots: Our Real Ridge

## HENRY MINTZBERG

I used to have a poster in my office of 'l'Arrêt irréel'—the unreal ridge—so called because it is almost better than perfect. It forms part of the western edge of the Mont Blanc chain, one of five ridges known as 'Les dômes de miage.' Richard Rumelt, the Society's new President-elect, and I set out to climb it some years ago. The approach is very long, many hours of trudging to a refuge, to try to get some sleep before rising at 4 a.m. L'Arrêt irréel is the middle ridge of the five, the first two having a surface of mainly rock, the last three of snow. One has the choice of doing all five or of going up the middle, to begin with l'Arrêt irréel and then doing the other two snow ridges.

We set out to do all five. They are not difficult at all, but I am petrified on rock and Dick dragged me along like a dog on a leash. At the top of the second ridge, we stepped, literally, from rock to snow, and immediately reversed roles. Dick had never been on a snow ridge before, nor had he ever worn crampons. Some place to start! The right side dropped sheer into the valley, perhaps 3000 feet below (although after 100 feet or so it hardly matters), while the left sloped steeply down. There was not a lot of place to stand as we descended and Dick was not happy, to say the least, although he did not realize that one could walk on the upper edges of the slope. (Dick is a skier, used to edging on

*Building the Strategically-Responsive Organization.*
Edited by H. Thomas, D. O'Neal, R. White and D. Hurst.
Copyright © 1994 the Strategic Management Society. Published 1994 by John Wiley & Sons Ltd.

a slope, while with crampons the foot has to be placed flat, an unnerving posture for anyone not used to it.) We managed to make it down that ridge to the flat before the start of l'Arrêt irréel, and then took the center connection back to the refuge. Barely half an hour from the top of l'Arrêt irréel, after maybe fifteen hours of drudgery, and back down we went, so that I could return home to stare at that damn poster in my office.

Well, Dick may have been bad that first day on a snow ridge and I am always bad on rock ridges, but there is another type of ridge on which we are both comfortable. It does not have a great deal of space—barely enough to accommodate the membership of the Strategic Management Society—but it is quite a wonderful ridge, and an important one. On one side, which I call A, is the cliff of academic irrelevance (it is indicated by a transparency of tiny typed letters). If you look carefully over the edge, you can see the debris of research crushed by its disassociation with practice (game theory is on its way down). On the other side, which I call B and C, is the slippery slope of management practicality (it is indicated by a glossy colored slide). One can just about make out the various fall lines of the consultants' five easy steps (to total quality, and more faintly, strategic planning), not to mention all those business people's 'one best way down.'

Dick likes to shock his climbing partners by sitting with his feet dangling over the edge, looking into the abyss of economics. When he shows off like that, my inclination is to untie the cord. If he is going to fall down that cliff, I have no intention of being pulled along. But, of course, he doesn't fall and I don't untie the cord.

In fact, when one climber goes over the edge of a ridge, the only hope is for the other climber to throw him or herself down the other side. We can, of course, do that in the Strategic Management Society. We can balance those members who wish to be academically 'respectable' by others who have gone down the slippery slope of being ever so 'practical.' But a simple consideration of this predicament makes it quite clear that we are all better off up on the ridge together, however narrow it may be. True, some of our academic members may get close to the edge, while other of our practitioner members may walk along the slope a bit of the way down. But each remains rather close to the others and in fact, in this society, they even change places rather easily, our insightful academics delving thoughtfully into the consulting and practice of management, our thoughtful practitioners providing insightful articles and talks. We zigzag back and forth, especially at these conferences.

If I have had one obsession as President of this Society, it has been to keep our collective feet firmly planted on that ridge. It has not been easy, and we may sometimes do it badly, but I know that we are the only ones who really try. I used to be concerned that our meetings and our membership were not larger. Now I believe that not that many people are comfortable on that ridge. I only hope we can attract all of them. And one thing is sure: our own real ridge is not only an important, but also an exhilarating place to be, sometimes threatening perhaps, but always exhilarating.

And what of l'Arrêt irréel—the perfect ridge—just in front of us? Well, perhaps we shall never climb it. But it should always remain clearly in our vision—our ideal, if unattainable, goal, that perfect blending of theory and practice.

# Index

*Index compiled by Susan Ramsey*